Alan D. Gaff and Donald H. Gaff

Amid the RUINS

Damon Runyon

World War I Reports from the Trenches, October 1918–March 1919

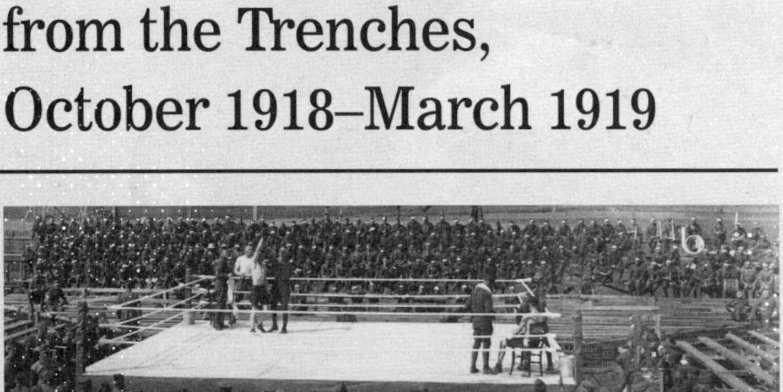

American literary icon in the fields of sports reporting, fiction, and Broadway

Collects Runyon's dramatic and entertaining dispatches from WWI along with his war-themed poetry

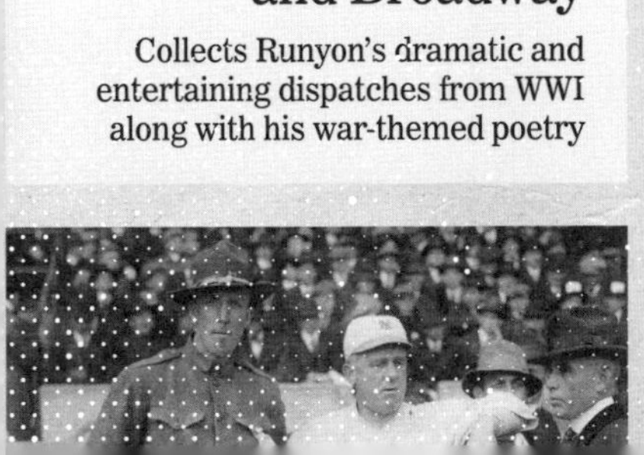

SCHIFFER PUBLISHING
4880 Lower Valley Road • Atglen, PA 19310

To Wayne Fauchier

Felix qui potuit rerum cognoscere causas

Library of Congress Control Number: 2019935795

Designed by Molly Shields
Cover design by Justin Watkinson

Type set in News706 BT/Cambria

ISBN: 978-0-7643-5785-5
Printed in China

Published by Schiffer Publishing, Ltd.
4880 Lower Valley Road
Atglen, PA 19310
Phone: (610) 593-1777; Fax: (610) 593-2002
E-mail: Info@schifferbooks.com
Web: www.schifferbooks.com

Contents

Preface

This collection contains all the World War I dispatches that could be tracked down and verified as having been authored by Damon Runyon, and, at this point in time, should be considered the definitive collection of his war journalism. He sent dispatches both to the *New York American* and the *Denver Post*; sometimes accounts of the same events differed significantly in these papers, and sometimes they were identical. In assembling these dispatches, priority was given to stories from the *American*, with material being added from the *Post* when the latter had additional or different information. Runyon's poetry was published in a wider set of venues and included a lot of verse not pertaining to the war. The poetry that is anthologized here was selected from this wider pool and was chosen for its direct portrayal of soldiers, or for its representation of broader topics that were war related, such as life on the home front.

In preparing the text, dispatches were transcribed and minimally edited for consistency in punctuation and style. Then they were assembled into chronological order as best as could be determined after focusing on missing dates and delays from censors. As the editors searched for dispatches, it became evident that there was a paucity of reports from February 1919. Illness was suspected, and subsequent research confirmed that idea. A paragraph from the *Fourth Estate*, a newspaper about the newspaper industry, is worth quoting in full: "Damon Runyon of the Hearst Organization, who has also been ill with influenza, suffered from a relapse and was in critical condition in Coblenz. He is much better now and back in Paris."[1] Presumably, the initial bout of the flu explains the absence of dispatches from early February, while his relapse accounts for the lack of stories from later in the month. The decision was made to keep the formatting of the original dispatches as close to the originals as possible. Editing of the poetry included fixing obvious typographic errors and formatting the poems to resemble the formatting in the original publications.

Great effort was made to identify individuals named in Runyon's dispatches. This was frequently challenging and not always successful since, as noted above, the multiple steps in wartime transatlantic communication resulted in the alteration of many names. For example, the "Fred Riley" of the dispatches was actually "Fred J. Riler." Similarly, "Jack Hanigan" in the newspaper was really "George Hannigan." Correctly identifying people mentioned in the text proved to be one of the greatest editorial challenges. Background information on these individuals varied, but every attempt has been made to identify persons for whom significant information could be uncovered. With Damon Runyon as a muse, footnoting individuals, places, and key events involved concentrating on lively and unique stories to further enhance Runyon's already colorful portrayals. In addition to the use of standard references to make identifications, interesting anecdotes were culled from a variety of sources, including newspapers and magazines. By focusing on the backstories of the people involved, the editors believe these embellishments give a certain flourish to the normally staid scholarly apparatus, and feel that Damon himself would value the attempt to make the notes "Runyonesque."

The editors would like to acknowledge the help we received in assembling the volume. The Allen County Public Library provided interlibrary loan services and research support, as did the indefatigable Rosemary Meany and the Rod Library at the University of Northern Iowa. Megan Schneider produced the maps that accompany the text. Our biggest debt of gratitude, as always, goes to Maureen Gaff. We appreciate that she set aside Mahjong in order to share her comments, to subject the manuscript to her impeccable proofreading, and to track down those little bits of knowledge that eluded us. Damon Runyon, like us, would never bet against her.

Introduction

> And now he's packed his type machine an' tooth brush in his grip
> And headed for the battle line, to make a pleasure trip—
> A pleasure trip for him, because his chief idee o' fun
> Is bein' there to see and hear when fightin's bein' done.
> A pleasure trip for you and me, because he sure knows how
> To make a lyric of a scrap—an epic of a row.
> Don't wait to buy your papers, friends—just order in advance—
> You'll never want to miss a line that Runyon sends from France.[1]

As a gambler and smoker and associate of fighters and gangsters, Damon Runyon lived the life he wrote. Hailing from the Plains and later the West, he took New York City by storm, making a name for himself by sensationalizing life in the Big Apple with his Broadway stories. Writing of goons and hoodlums and the women they loved, Runyon created an entire language, "Runyonese," to describe this fascinating underworld. More than a short-story writer, he originally came to notoriety through news and sports reporting, a profession he pursued throughout his adult life, even after short stories made him famous. While some of his reporting is well known, such as his profile of the fighter Jack Dempsey, Runyon's reporting from the front lines of the First World War remains virtually unknown.

This volume brings together all of Damon Runyon's dispatches about that war, along with a selection of his war-themed poetry. After filing the occasional story about preparations stateside, Runyon traveled to Europe in the late autumn of 1918 and immediately began sending back dispatches. He continued to do so until his return to New York in the early spring of 1919. This collection of his reporting includes every newspaper article with his byline, ranging from the first one from France to the last one he wrote describing the victory parade in New York City. For the first time, Runyon's World War I reporting is gathered in one place. While not his true calling, poetry provided Runyon with another outlet for his writing, and, importantly, especially early in his career, an additional revenue stream as newspapers and magazines clamored for popular poetry to fill their pages. In addition to his news stories, this volume also includes a generous sample of his poetry from the World War I years. The poetry is drawn from a period that begins before he heads overseas, starting with a poem from early June 1917 and ending with one from March 1919, penned on the transport bringing Runyon back to America.

By assembling these World War I writings together in a single collection, it provides a unique opportunity to read Damon Runyon in an early and influential phase of his career that has not been fully addressed in biographies or represented in anthologies. In these works, readers will get a glimpse into his developing writing style a decade before his Broadway stories brought him fame. Particularly, an emphasis in these works on everyday people, the use of dialect, and using geography to help set a scene will resonate as familiar with Runyon fans as elements easily recognizable in later works and partly form the language of "Runyonese." This collection also serves to bring attention to a war correspondent and a body of work that has been overlooked in favor of better-known reporters of the war such as Herbert Swope, Peggy Hull, and Floyd Gibbons, whose first major story was how the transport he was taking to Europe was sunk.[2] Also contained within the stories is an insight into what life was like for a war correspondent during World War I, which was remarkably different than news coverage of wars today. One aspect that is immediately apparent is that several of Runyon's reports were delayed due to military censors. Observant readers will feel the censor's hand throughout the dispatches.

Finally, this collection is noteworthy for the poetry. Runyon published his two main books of poetry long before America's entry into the war. Like his news reports, his poetry from this period had not been collected until the publication of *Poems for Men* in 1947. While not rising to the quality of the best World War I poets, such as Edmund Blunden, Robert Graves, and Siegfried Sassoon, Runyon's verse displays a folksy national pride designed to appeal to his readers. Similar to his news reporting of the war, many of his poems tend to focus on the daily life of the common soldier. As a whole, these dispatches and poems represent the first appearance of Damon Runyon's World War I writing in a single volume and constitute a valuable new resource for Runyon scholars and fans alike.

Damon Runyon, whose name is synonymous with New York City, was actually born a midwesterner. Manhattan for young Damon was not the one of bright Broadway lights and soaring towers but instead meant the rolling hills and prairie grasses of the much-smaller Manhattan, Kansas. October 3, 1880, found Alfred Lee Runyan and Libbie J. Runyan, née Libbie Damon, welcoming their only son into the world.[3] Born Alfred Damon Runyan, he would later become Damon Runyon when, over the course of his early career, different printing problems resulted in the dropping of Alfred and vowel replacement, both changes meeting with his approval. That typographic issues resulted in two name changes has a certain irony given that Runyon, himself a writer, was the son of a newspaperman, his father, Alfred, being the editor of Manhattan's *Enterprise* newspaper.

His father's experience in the newspaper business provided income for the young family after they moved to Pueblo, Colorado, in a failed attempt to improve the declining health of Damon's mother. In Pueblo, Alfred Runyan had to settle for a typesetting and printing job with the *Pueblo Chieftain*. This 1887 move altered the family, since a homesick Libbie returned to Kansas with little Damon's sisters. Upon her return, she succumbed to tuberculosis and died in 1889. With his sisters sent off to be cared for by relatives, Damon lived alone with his father and enjoyed the carefree life of a lightly supervised boy in a frontier town.

Perhaps a life in newspapers was unavoidable for Runyon, since he grew up around them and the lifestyle they facilitated, having spent many after school hours in the Arkansas Saloon.[4] In early 1892, Damon approached his father's newspaper with a proposal, and on February 6 his first work saw print, a small poem titled "Creede."[5] By the following year, Damon had stopped attending school and began regular work for the town's newspapers. Within a short time, Runyon was a teenage cigarette-smoking, whiskey-drinking, whorehouse-visiting newspaper reporter. It was here, too, that Runyon likely adopted his lifelong passion for gambling as well as his stoic approach to it:

> Long ago our old man told us what he said his old man had told him and what he had learned himself at bitter cost, that the Runyons came into the world with no card sense and with no flair for games of chance whatever, and that the only way they would ever get anything was by work.[6]

Like many Americans, Runyon's world changed on February 15, 1898, when the US battleship *Maine* went down from an explosion that initiated the Spanish-American War. With cries of "Remember the *Maine*" resonating through the country, Damon Runyon volunteered for service but was initially rejected for his youth and small stature.[7] Eventually, he talked his way into Company L of the 13th Minnesota Volunteers (transferring to Company A on June 26) and, after a brief delay, found himself in the Philippines shortly after the cessation of hostilities.[8] His time was spent like that of most young men who find themselves at war in a foreign land: "he spent much of his time avoiding work, and the rest of the time he spent in a 'house of ill repute,' which was conveniently located adjacent to Company L's headquarters. There he met and fell in love with the first love of his life, a young Filipina girl."[9] A soldier from the 1st California Volunteers suggested that he and Runyon had been under fire as part of the conflict, though that effort was likely modest: "We did our level, and you know that Damon and I are not athletes. Two laps around a billiard table would founder us."[10] While in this exotic locale, Runyon turned to the familiar (and perhaps the less strenuous) and began writing both for the *Manila Freedom* and *Soldier's Letter*.

Damon Runyon at the Denver Press Club with Jim Wong, night porter. *Courtesy of the Denver Public Library*

Upon his return to the states in 1900, Runyon kept up with his wild ways. As he later remembered of the victory parade in which his regiment marched in Minneapolis: "[Joe Mannix] introduced us to something called a sherry flip, as nice a dram as anybody ever slapped a lip over, and it was with eight or nine of these under the old cartridge belt that we paraded. We remember with pride that the whole regiment was plumb out of step but us."[11] After mustering out of the service with an honorable discharge, Runyon spent months learning the art of being a hobo on the way back to Colorado. At some point during these years, while continuing to smoke and gamble, he gave up drinking.[12]

Reasons for the abstemious behavior are unclear but include the possibility that he suffered from an undiagnosed medical attack, that he had gotten to the point where he shook so badly he needed the bartender to hold his drink, or that he lost a fight to eventual friend Charles Van Loan, who weighed seventy-five pounds more than Runyon.[13]

For the next several years, the newly minted Runyon, still called "Al" by his friends, took on an assortment of writing assignments for several western newspapers.

During this interregnum, in addition to reporting, Runyon worked at his poetry. Written for profit and a popular audience, this verse never aimed for literary acclaim but instead served as little amusements, evocative reminiscences, or heartwarming pieces to be used as filler in newspapers and magazines. Some of these poems had martial themes reflecting his time in the service, such as one of his early poems, "Song of the Bullet," published by *Collier's* in 1904. Runyon's early poems were brought together in two collections—*The Tents of Trouble, Ballads of the Wanderbund and Other Verse* (1911) and *Rhymes of the Firing Line* (1912)—both of which appeared shortly after his momentous move to New York City in 1910.

Damon Runyon, in the passenger seat, outside the *Denver Post* office. *Courtesy of* Denver Post *Historical Collection (#10027914), History Colorado*

Lured by the offer of staying with the aforementioned Van Loan, it was not long before Runyon accepted a sports-writing position with one of William Randolph Hearst's best-known newspapers, New York's *American*.

This same friend lent his house in May 1911 to Runyon in order for him to marry Ellen Egan, herself a newspaper writer from Colorado. Marriage was not the only big change for Runyon. That same year, famous sports editor Harry Cashman dropped the name Alfred from the byline to free up space, resulting in the now-famous name Damon Runyon.

The years leading up to America's participation in the First World War were busy and prosperous ones for Runyon. First, his daughter, Mary Elaine, was born on August 24, 1914. As for his writing, he rapidly adjusted to life in New York, receiving his first introduction to the criminal underworld when he covered the trial for the murder of Herman Rosenthal. While he was adapting to life in Manhattan, Runyon continued with his international and military reporting; notably, Hearst called upon Runyon to join Gen. John J. Pershing in the chase for Pancho Villa. He also went abroad in February 1914 to cover exhibition games by the Giants and White Sox[14] and in 1915 went to Havana to report on the Johnson-Willard heavyweight championship fight. The diversity of Runyon's reporting over this time span not only included his celebrated sportswriting but also encompassed politics, such as his coverage of the Republican convention and the appearance of a daily column.

As Runyon found himself meeting with success, war raged in Europe. In July 1914, the Austro-Hungarians attacked Serbia, igniting a conflict that would pull in many European countries, and eventually the United States. However, at the outset of the war, America maintained a neutral stance. It is in this way, that in the fall of 1916, Runyon found himself not once, but twice, covering the German submarine *Deutschland* as it broke a British blockade to bring trade goods to America. Sympathies in the country varied, but Runyon's employer, William Randolph Hearst, proved loyal to Germany. Jimmy Breslin,[15] a journalist and Runyon biographer, noted

> When America was on the verge of entering the war in Europe, Hearst, who had more Germans working for him than the Kaiser, became one of America's most hated men by lauding Germany in editorials. He filled newspapers with stories about the hideousness of the European war and the need to keep Americans out of it.[16]

Hearst tried to get Runyon to work his pro-German agenda by doing a story on the American Truth Society. However, Runyon demurred, concerned that his financial livelihood might be at stake.[17] As Hearst and his famed editor, Arthur Brisbane, continued to promote the German cause, Runyon's son, Damon Runyon Jr., was born on June 17, 1918. As the summer progressed, Hearst began to change his opinion about the war, a reversal that, no doubt, was influenced by accumulating German losses. Hearst called upon Runyon to cover the war, and though his reporter showed concern about who would report on the upcoming World Series, Hearst assured Runyon he could name his replacement if he went to Europe.[18] To reinforce his about-face and curry political favor, Hearst impressed upon his reporter the importance of covering Pershing, knowing well of his employee's acquaintance with the general from his time chasing Pancho Villa.

After putting his affairs in order—particularly the care of his family—Runyon shipped out for France in September 1918. Runyon biographer, Edwin Hoyt, states that his first dispatch for Hearst's Universal Service, a press service that supplied stories to over a hundred morning newspapers, was on October 12.[19] However, there are at least two earlier dispatches from the destruction of Rheims, dated October 7 and October 10. While these two earlier dispatches describe the general aftermath of battle, the October 12 dispatch is noteworthy for its description of Maj. Charles W. Whittlesey and the now-famed "Lost Battalion."[20] Whittlesey and his men had been surrounded by Germans and fought their way out, as part of the broader Meuse-Argonne Offensive, the last major Allied push of World War I. Runyon's dispatches from the Argonne front continue through mid-October, until his byline switches to the "With the American First Army." Several of his dispatches showed how far of a reach Runyon had as he documented encounters with friends and acquaintances, many from the world of sports. He was not in France long before he wrote of such famed persons as fellow writer Grantland Rice, who was serving as a lieutenant (first mentioned in a story dated October 16), or Boston Braves catcher Hank Gowdy (also first mentioned on October 16), one of the first major-league baseball players to volunteer to serve in the war. Some of these portrayals of the well known and famous were somber, as in his telling of the death of the New York Giants' Eddie Grant in a dispatch from October 23. Other individuals recur in his stories, such as his eventual friend, flying ace Eddie Rickenbacker. Runyon spent at least part of his time in the company of other writers, such as Junius Wood and Edwin "Jimmy" James, as part of the Raspberry Club. This club consisted of an informal gathering of correspondents who hosted a variety of guests in the lounge of the Riesenfurstenberg Hotel in Coblenz, where they enjoyed drinking, music, and gambling. Guests of the club included Charles M. Schwab, who beat Runyon, a manager of the club, in a game of poker.[21]

Runyon remained in Europe after the cessation of hostilities and the signing of the Armistice in November 1918 to cover the aftermath, which can be seen in the varying bylines placing him with the 1st Army in France, marching to the Rhine in Luxembourg, and in the Rhineland. He spent some of this time in Germany, covering the occupation, reporting on daily life, and giving a sense of how both soldiers and civilians were adapting at the end of the conflict. While having the opportunity to visit with and interview many senior officers, including Gen. Pershing, most of Runyon's dispatches from the occupation showed his deep interest in the common soldier and the everyday person on the street. Returning to France for the peace negotiations, Runyon fell ill with pneumonia and wrote little while under the care of Adm. Cary Grayson, President Wilson's personal doctor.[22] The decision was then made to return to America.

Damon Runyon left for New York City on the SS *Leviathan*. Onboard and in transit, Runyon apparently gave some thought to life after the war. He contemplated starting a business with an interesting group of people—himself, Rickenbacker, Gen. Pershing, and the singer Enrico Caruso. One envisioned plan was to build a car to be named the "Caruso-Rickenbacker-Pershing." The closest they got was eventually naming a horse after the popular tenor. The long-term goal of this scheming was to get Rickenbacker elected president, with Runyon working in a laid-back embassy position that would afford him time to write.[23] Eventually, the transport ship docked at Hoboken, and he quickly went to Manhattan to cover the triumphal return parade and file his story the same day.

Shortly after his return, Rickenbacker sought out Runyon. He needed the writer's assistance because he was going on a speaking tour and needed help. Runyon rescued him by, among other things, working with him to prepare a set of notecards. This aided Rickenbacker greatly, but little came of Runyon's plan to get him into the White House. Returning to sportswriting, Runyon achieved real acclaim with a series of articles about boxer Jack Dempsey in 1919. "A Tale of Two

A young Damon Runyon, a decade before he found himself overseas reporting on the Great War. *Courtesy of* Denver Post *Historical Collection (#10035923), Colorado Historical Society, History Colorado*

Fists" was a serialized, biographical look at one of the day's top fighters leading up to his world championship victory on July 4th, a fight in which Runyon bet heavily on his subject to win in the first round, but lost as the match lasted three.[24] Runyon repeated his success by bringing out another set of Dempsey stories in 1921. *Cosmopolitan* magazine published the first of what came to be called his Broadway stories in 1929. This fictional story "Romance in the Roaring Forties" was rumored to have been written to pay for an appendectomy.[25] However, it is just as likely he needed the money to pay for his children and wife, from whom he separated the same year. Coincidentally, Ellen Runyon died in 1931, the same year that the first collection of Broadway stories, *Guys and Dolls*, appeared in print. The next year, Runyon consoled himself by marrying a young Spanish dancer, Patrice Amati.

Though he kept up with his newspaper career, the Broadway stories made Damon Runyon famous. Not only were the stories themselves well received, but one of them was made into the movie *Lady for a Day*. Frank Capra directed this 1933 film, which was nominated for four Academy Awards. The movie, along with the popularity of early stories, prompted Runyon to keep writing, and anthologies of his writing began to appear regularly, including *Blue Plate Special* (1934), *Money from Home* (1935), and *Take It Easy* (1938), among others. Runyon also began to see his books published overseas, and his short stories were republished in a London newspaper to much fanfare.

After a great run of professional success, the end of the 1930s foreshadowed bad times when he experienced throat troubles in 1938 and was encouraged by his doctor to forgo tobacco. In 1944, throat cancer was diagnosed and Runyon had his larynx removed. Shortly thereafter, in 1946, Runyon separated from his second wife, giving her most everything, including a stake in his writing. Later that year, she divorced him and quickly remarried. With cancer spreading rapidly through his body, Damon Runyon succumbed, passing away on December 10, 1946. In what could only be considered the ultimate denouement, Runyon's ashes were taken aloft by Eddie Rickenbacker and spread throughout the air over his beloved Broadway.

Runyon's legacy persists well beyond his death. Walter Winchell, a fellow journalist and radio personality, made a call for his listeners to donate money to fight the disease. Enough money was raised that he started the Damon Runyon Cancer Memorial Fund. Today, known as the Damon Runyon Cancer Research Foundation, this institution has distributed almost $300,000,000 in funding.[26] Damon Runyon continues to haunt Broadway as well. Shortly after his passing, Frank Loesser took two of Runyon's Broadway stories and some of his other writing to create a musical for the theater. This show was a success and has witnessed many revivals on Broadway and was also turned into a movie featuring Marlon Brando and Frank Sinatra. The musical met with universal praise and received numerous awards. And every time tough guys and dames meet on stage on Broadway, Damon Runyon will live on with each new production of *Guys and Dolls*.

In this collection of Damon Runyon's World War I writing, it is clear to see that his experiences as a war correspondent did not differ remarkably from other journalists working in wartime. One of these similarities was the question of censorship and how to adequately report the news without revealing too much about military tactics and strategy. During this period in American history, the relationship between a free press and the government was unlike that of today. According to Michael Sweeney, as soon as the United States entered the war in the spring of 1917, it promptly began censoring—including military censorship. The War Department, as early as 1914, began preparing a censorship plan, with Douglas MacArthur in the role of censor. In due course the government came up with a plan that involved supplying the journalists with press releases through the newly formed Committee on Public Information. This, coupled with laws aimed at controlling journalists, formed the basic approach conducted by the United States for the duration of the war. The federal government even went so far as to publish its own newspaper. A major problem, of course, was that while the Committee on Public information did release factual information concerning the war, it was also largely responsible for distributing propaganda too, mainly in the form of pamphlets and public speaking, with over 750,000 speeches given in over 5,000 different places.[27]

Sweeney also presents an account of how military censorship worked in practice in the field. To begin with, reporters were subject to a system of accreditation that had them swear an oath of loyalty and post a bond. The bond was for $10,000 to be given to charity if the reporter violated the rules. Additionally, the reporter had to pay $1,000 for his costs.[28] After that, they had to adopt a special military armband that identified the wearer as press. Photographers in particular found themselves strongly censored because the military was concerned about the demoralizing effects of the citizens at home seeing images of trench warfare. Similarly, reporters were banned from mentioning specific losses, as described by Thomas Johnson, one of Runyon's colleagues: "The War Department wished relatives to hear from it officially before they read of casualties in the newspapers, which meant two or three weeks' delay. Dispatches mentioning killed or wounded by name were held until word was received that the relatives knew."[29]

For their print censor, the government selected a newspaper reporter, Frederick Palmer. Reporters fell into two general kinds—those assigned directly by the military (similar to today's embedded reporters, since most of them were assigned to a particular division) and visiting reporters. Those writers placed with divisions were important to the overall war effort since "the people at home felt they were in direct touch with their boys at the front."[30] Despite strict censorship rules, many reporters and photographers covered the war. Runyon, himself, seemed to think that correspondents were fairly numerous:

> Then, too, we thought that if all the war correspondents in the late unpleasantness tried to get together, they would be unable to find any one city large enough to accommodate them. The entire nation of France was scarcely big enough for them all during the war. Had General Pershing been able to mobolize [*sic*] the war correspondents under arms, he would have an extra division, though we are not prepared at this late date to estimate its probable value.
>
> One thing about that war, as far as the Americans were concerned, it was the best covered war in history. At one time there were so many war correspondents there, the truck drivers were complaining that they were continually running over correspondents on the roads, and gumming up the gears. . . .
>
> The big war became the war to end war correspondents, and it succeeded to some extent in its purpose. The wars since then have been rather lightly attended by war correspondents, and it is agreed by military authorities that, as a result, it is possible to move troops with greater speed and facility. There is not so much danger of a troop movement being impeded by the automobiles of war correspondents hastening to dinner.[31]

The quality of reporter varied, as noted by a Raymond G. Carroll, a reporter for the *El Paso Herald*: "Men of all sorts of capabilities came. There were finished writers and police reporters, who had never been abroad before, there were drafters of cable bulletins, and foreign correspondents requisitioned from their posts in Paris, London, and Rome, and sent to the press headquarters of the American Army."[32]

All the reporters worked vigorously around the censors. One, Heywood Broun, became particularly adept at tiptoeing up to the line with statements such as "The American army is doing as well as can be expected."[33] Sometimes soldiers blatantly crossed that line, as in the case of a young man who wrote a letter home saying his regiment was at the "corner of Third and Main Street," which was the location of the Metz Lumber Company, Metz also being the name of a city in northern France.[34] In this kind of atmosphere, it is no surprise that a gallows humor evolved around the censors. For example: "Who censors the censor's love letters? The censor has no love letters."[35] In another instance: "The censor cuts out all the interesting parts of his letters, but he's found a way to get even with him. What's that? He says he's going to quit writing."[36] The complex word games and general disdain lend a certain irony to official statements by the press division, such as

> I wish to thank the correspondents for the faithful performance of their duties. They have played the game fairly and so have the newspapers and magazines in the United States which you represent. Thanks to the joint work of the censors and correspondents the American public has been given a splendid portrayal of the American army.
>
> No event in history has been more faithfully, more accurately and more truthfully reported.[37]

Runyon indicated, while writing of censorship, that many of those involved were keenly aware of some of the more ridiculous aspects of this back and forth: "Army censorship is usually pretty dumb. Mind you, I say censorship, not censors. Censors do not make the rules of censorship but only carry them out, and most censors are smart fellows who realize the dumbness of the rules as much as the correspondents to whose copy the rules apply."[38]

Though Palmer left his position at the end of 1918, he presided over a large censorship program that went well beyond military matters. Sweeney writes that censors went so far as to eradicate references to the French sharing wine with American soldiers so as not to upset those who favored temperance back home.[39] So, this was the situation Runyon found himself in—one where he could not even mention a guy having a drink. In fact, in all of the dispatches written by Runyon, there is only one story of Americans drinking beer. All other mentions of beer and wine in these stories pertain to the Europeans or are utilized in descriptions of cafés. In spite of these limitations, Runyon seems to have excelled in being a war correspondent, as the following anecdote by fellow newspaperman Walter Winchell attests to:

> Another reason for Damon Runyon's reportorial genius was his ability to concentrate under the most difficult conditions. When he was a war correspondent during the initial global fracas a cannon exploded a few yards from where Damon was typing a yarn. But he continued working without batting an eyelash. Only after he had completed his story did he look up and nonchalantly enquire: "Did I hear something?"[40]

This story illustrates the danger that Runyon faced daily, as did the other correspondents and censors. According to Bert Ford,

> There was a mistaken notion among those unfamiliar with modern warfare that the front line trench was the most hazardous area. It was then the enemy attacked, or when the Allied forces went over the top, but with both sides resting on their arms, while the big guns played the back areas were the most dangerous. Experts estimated that upward of 60 per cent of the causalities occurred from three to eight kilometers back, due to shells and bombs.
>
> Now that we have a chance to calmly look back at it all, is it surprising that there were not more casualties among correspondents. A French correspondent was instantly killed by a machine gun bullet. An American photographer was killed by a shell ten days before the armistice. Another American correspondent was struck twice in the arm and one of his eyes was gouged out by machine gun bullets. Two other American newspapermen were nipped, one while serving on the Italian front. . . .
>
> Often correspondents wrote and censors read their copy during air raids. While buildings tumbled and people were crushed to death a block or two away. Reports were churned out in odd places and under the greatest difficulties at times.[41]

Loss of limb or life, then, was a daily hazard for Runyon and his contemporaries.

Increasing the complexity of understanding Runyon's role as a war correspondent is that the nature of journalism itself was different early in the twentieth century. Generally, reporters tended to be a bit looser with the truth. For example, respected newspaperman H. L. Mencken fabricated stories ranging from the history of the bathtub to the creation of a naval battle between Japan and Russia weeks before it actually happened. He even wrote of making up multiple news stories every day early in his career.[42] Furthermore, Runyon became a newspaper writer squarely in the middle of the era of Yellow Journalism. Notably, Joseph Pulitzer and Runyon's future employer, Hearst, involved themselves in a battle for readers and profit. Exaggerated storytelling, often unsupported by facts, let alone multiple sources, made for exciting reading that was not always accurate. Yellow Journalism reached its height of popularity as it flamed the passions of the Spanish-American War. As an aspiring reporter before and during the war, Runyon would have been exposed to and influenced by this trend.

Hints of these issues in Runyon's writing can be seen prior to the Great War. In an unsubstantiated story written by Jimmy Breslin, during the Pancho Villa insurrection Runyon came across a commotion involving some Japanese and a dead dog. He had stumbled across a practice attempt for a plot to poison Villa. Pershing personally asked Runyon not to report on what he had just witnessed. Runyon's reply was "Now that you ask, I won't do it. But even if I did, your people would have censored whatever it is." Upon the appearance of Pershing's chief surgeon, the Japanese indicated he provided the poison, at which point Pershing invited Runyon into his tent, where he implored him again to forget the potential news story. In the words of Breslin: "Runyon told Pershing that he was an American first and a reporter after that." Consequently, there are no Pancho Villa poisoning stories with Runyon's byline. Breslin notes that Pershing thanked Runyon more than a few times and in exchange offered to be of assistance to the writer in the future.[43]

This brief anecdote illustrates that some of the problems that plagued Runyon's reporting of the Villa insurrection were very much the same he faced during World War I. First, there is his awareness that the US Army would censor the poisoning story. Edwin Hoyt writes that while Pershing kept Washington informed, "the *American* did not hear from Runyon for a week, and when his first dispatch was filed it was heavily censored."[44] His World War I dispatches should also be considered similarly censored and read with that critical fact in mind. Second, Hoyt also points out that these stories, once Runyon began producing them, focused more on the daily lives of the soldiers and their personalities than on the "real news" of maneuvers and strategy. These stories are precisely the same kind he would write during the war.

Also described by Hoyt is the process by which news traveled during the Villa chase, and it is worth quoting in full:

> The news in Mexico was hard to come by, and even harder to get out of Mexico and into New York. Damon sent dispatches by airplane to Columbus, and by radio from there to New York. But the dispatches were almost always delayed three to four days, and by the time readers of the Hearst newspapers and other papers that subscribed to the INS service were reading Damon's articles, he was far afield from the scene of the action described.
>
> Sometimes the dispatches were mixed up, and stories written early were received after later articles. So, after Damon had described the fighting at San Gerónimo ranch, a story came in which told how the soldiers were "at last smelling powder as they go rolling along down the rich valleys of Chihuahua, but it is not gunpowder. It is face powder."[45]

Technology changed little between the hunt for Villa in 1916 and Runyon's coverage of the war in 1918–19. Arguably, the communication challenges were more extreme, because unlike trying to get a message to New York from Mexico, there was a rather large ocean between New

York and France. Keeping in mind that during the war, carrier pigeons were a viable option to carry information, it is not unlikely that Runyon's dispatches from Europe were equally as garbled as the Villa reporting. Though impossible to know the exact route for the dispatches, the transmission of a Runyon piece probably resembled this: Runyon's original passing through the censor, then telegraphed across the ocean, then likely telegraphed or otherwise decoded and provided to the newspaper, probably edited, and then finally sent to the printers. Without a doubt, the dispatches read by New Yorkers and others were not identical to the ones originally written by Runyon.

Another benefit of bringing together Runyon's World War I reports and poetry is to document the emerging style and themes that would come to be called "Runyonesque." Runyon helped shape American English, and no less an authority than Wilfred J. Funk felt Runyon was one of the top influences on the "jargon of Americana" in the 1930s, along with H. L. Mencken, Sime Silverman, T. A. Dorgan, Walter Winchell, Bugs Baer, Ring Lardner, Gelett Burgess, George Ade, and Gene Buck.[46] There is no doubt that Runyon's language was unique, and its impact was felt in the cross-fertilization of ideas that takes place during war, such as in this example about baseball:

> All England made new wrinkles trying to understand the slang of the game. And English editors, trying to be Americanese and slangful, put over some of the weirdest possible combinations of Oxford and Spaulding—mixtures, say, of the extremest Webster with Bugs Bear and Damon Runyon.[47]

One of the central features of Runyon's style is a focus on regular, everyday people. This might be easily interpreted as Runyon writing what he knew because he identified with people whose origins were similar to his own midwestern background. In a comparison with fellow writer Ring Lardner, Tom Clark highlights Runyon's affiliation with more-common people:

> Ring lived and played with the Great Neck set in his later years, while Damon strayed toward Broadway. Ring drank and Damon did not. Ring had great success as a fiction writer while Damon was still only a newspaperman, and by the early twenties he was socially conversant with a "literary" crowd that was never to accept Runyon—and vice versa. Ring distrusted the "criminal" element that Damon embraced (and was embraced by) and never did much more than dip a toe in the whirling night life of the Avenues. Edmund Wilson and Scott and Zelda Fitzgerald and Dorothy Parker—bright, exportable moderns all—were Lardner's friends, while Runyon moved with and among such indigenous figures of town and track as Jimmy Walker, Lou Clayton, and Abba Dabba Berman, and numbered Al Capone and Arnold Rothstein among those he could count on for a favor. The contrasting milieus were instinctive choices that reflected the opposing characters and *upbringings* [emphasis added] of the two men.[48]

This predisposition helps explain why, as Hoyt points out, when on the Villa expedition, Runyon wrote "a story about 'Dutch,' an army teamster and his mules, Rip, Nell, Paddy, and Mash," and his first dispatch about the Lost Battalion in the Argonne emphasized Whittlesey, a New York lawyer described elsewhere as a "regular guy."[49] So, with his rough-and-tumble heritage from the Midwest, and later West, Runyon more easily felt comradery with tough guys than literary ones. In his own words, "I have met no considerable number of the high muck-a-mucks of the world, and when I did I was always too self-conscious to hear what they said."[50] Walter Winchell also saw the importance of the Midwest to the shaping of Runyon: "He was never able to completely shake the dust of the Midwest from his heels—the earthiness of people was his weakness, just as it is so often theirs. . . . And so he remained to the end an Achilles in tight shoes."[51]

The Midwest influenced Runyon in other ways too. Parallels can be made with another author from the Midwest: Mark Twain. Beyond both being born west of the Mississippi River and getting their start in working for newspapers, they each found greater fame and wealth from their later fiction writing and in developing a distinctive, folksy style. Like Runyon, Twain's stories and novels frequently featured characters drawn from the lower classes and marginalized populations. It is easy to imagine a grown Tom Sawyer and Sky Masterson traveling in the same circles. In addition to depicting characters from similar social worlds, both writers employed regional dialect to add color to their narratives. For example, when Runyon attributes these words to an African American soldier: "Mistah Kaisah, count youah men!," a reader hears echoes of Mark Twain's Jim. Runyon relied heavily on dialogue, and two of the dispatches gathered here are made up almost exclusively of conversation: a January 1919 piece titled "Doughboy Dialogues: Voices of the Night," consisting of soldiers chattering with each other while their truck convoy is stalled, and a March 1919 story called "Nearing God's Country, a Doughboy Dialogue," with soldiers on the *Leviathan* talking about the voyage and anticipating their return home.

Runyon's flexibility with the truth in his reporting, as described earlier, can also be contextualized in terms of place. Like Twain, there is a feeling of exaggeration in their writing that owes something to the "tall tales" tradition of the Old West. One later example from Runyon that reads like Twain in exaggeration for humorous effect is a reminiscence of Army food:

> Our unit's cook was one of the few in that army era who was appreciated properly. It was due to his genius with such delicacies as pig bosom, salt horse and certain choice cuts of the cow that were sometimes known as embalmed beef. We never quite could understand that title. We always thought embalming was something that involved the use of formaldehyde. The so-called embalmed beef had no formaldehyde in it. We know because we once got some formaldehyde and sprinkled it on the beef, giving it much finer flavor than ordinary.[52]

As Daniel R. Schwarz succinctly describes the impact of place on Runyon's writing:

> Given his frontier heritage, it is not surprising that Runyon drew upon another area that captured the imagination of both the nation and the world, namely, the American West, with its possibility defined by images of immense space, uncultivated land, and unformed if not inchoate communities. His sportswriting—the field in which he first made his mark—drew upon a sense of hyperbole, derived from the western tall tale tradition, with a visceral and amazed enthusiasm for exceptional athletic prowess.[53]

This description of Runyon's sportswriting is easily transferred to his war writing as well. Soldiers thrown together in war are inchoate communities, and especially those in Europe during the First World War embody an open America. An appreciation for athletic ability was easily transmuted into an appreciation for the hard life of a soldier. This understanding goes even further since Runyon himself, while never having fought a boxing match or hit a home run in the majors, did serve in the military.

The frontier's effect on Runyon's life and writing cannot be underestimated. The West was deeply rooted in him, starting with the fact that his father served under Custer with the 19th Kansas Cavalry in 1868. Frontier life fixed itself in Runyon during his formative years. He grew up in taverns with his father and then went to war halfway around the world with other young men and returned to briefly live as a hobo. When he arrived in New York, there were few differences between the lawless West of his youth and the wild underworld of Prohibition with which he became closely associated. World War I stands as the bridge between those two worlds. Other than the hierarchy of military discipline, daily life on the front had the same feeling of barely constrained chaos and unexpected violence that were ever present in the Saturday night saloons of his youth and Jazz Age gin joints of his postwar years. The characters were always the same; only the uniforms differed. Runyon's cowboy is Runyon's doughboy is Runyon's gangster. So, these dispatches provide a critical link in his writing life, since it is a short trip from the man in the trench to the man on the street. Unlike the unique world of sports, with its singular stars performing in the rarefied air of stadiums and boxing rings, a strong case can be made that Runyon's military experiences informed the writing of the Broadway stories more than his familiarity with sports. On a daily basis, America's doughboys, like the Broadway criminals Runyon depicted, lived in a world of excitement with the threat of violence always looming. Both gambled, but whereas Hot Horse Herbie bet cash, soldiers staked their lives.

Damon Runyon, chronicler of Broadway's guys and dolls. *Courtesy of Damon Runyon Cancer Research Foundation*

Runyon's poetry, on the other hand, yields a different perspective on the war. Despite early aspirations to write poetry, Runyon eventually drifted away from it as a means of making a living. Perhaps this might be the result of having been rebuffed by a bartender who declined to exchange whiskey for a poem in imitation of poet Eugene Field.[54] Regardless, poetry never proved to be central to his career. One possible explanation for this is that, in a way, his poetry mirrored many elements common to Runyon's other writing. His poems are drafted in simple, ballad-like forms and often depict the low and working class or their outlook. As Patricia D'Itri described it: "Runyon drew graphic portraits that touch a humorous or sentimental vein among readers who like the vernacular and the common touch,"[55] which is a quintessential description of his overall style whether poetry or prose. Though some reviews of his early poetry were flattering—"They elbow along—these verses—with a devil-may-care stride and an oath like one of Kipling's now and then."[56]—most straightforward poetry such as this possesses little literary value beyond brief entertainment. As D'Itri explains, "Runyon offered little to feed the egos of the intellectual elite: no tension or complexity, few symbols or subtleties. His personal mythology is conventional, drawn primarily from universal human emotions."[57] D'Itri continues with this theme of straightforwardness and writes that "Runyon often called his poems ballads or songs, and in some ways they have the simplicity and untutored form of traditional ballads."[58] This particular characteristic of his poetry explains why his words were frequently put to song and why he can be found as the lyricist on sheet music such as 1917's "Hold 'em Yale! Marching Song for the Sammies" and 1921's "Left: A Soldier's Soliloquy."

Obviously, Runyon aimed to entertain his lower- and middle-class readers with his poetry in the same way he did with his journalism and short stories. Because of this particular audience, a reader can see that his verse was attractive to those in the military, since they too were drawn from the lower end of the social spectrum, and a majority of his poetry appealed directly to that audience:

> It is not surprising that some of Runyon's poems were widely published in military newspapers and magazines. He unabashedly praised officers, marines, the Corps of Engineers, and even the rear guard.

The uncritical appreciation in these poems starkly contrasts with individual soldiers' more biting reflections on the ongoing dilemmas of war.[59]

The things that made Runyon a great story writer are the same that prevented him from being an equally great poet. As an instance of this, in the poem "Pool-Shootin' Roy" he begins with the line "Son o' ol' Miz McAuliffe, the wider o Box-Car Jack," and the use both of folksy dialect and colorful characters is on display. By contrast, T. S. Eliot's "The Love Song of J. Alfred Prufrock" was written the year before "Pool-Shootin' Roy," and "The Waste Land" would appear a few years after.

The matter of quality aside, this collection of Runyon's war poetry is significant because he himself stopped anthologizing his poetry after his first two books and would not publish another collection of poetry until his posthumous *Poems for Men* in 1947. The collection provides an opportunity to compare Runyon with other poets of the era. Grantland Rice, also a popular sportswriter from New York, published a volume of war poetry, *Songs of the Stalwart*, in 1917. Runyon's verse makes a good companion piece to Rice's work. Last, the poetry gathered in this volume will be of use to those studying the role of nationalism and propaganda in World War I, since Runyon's rhymes, with their appeal to emotion and emphasis on the role of regular Americans in the global struggle, show evidence of both.

Together, Damon Runyon's war dispatches and his war poetry, as collected in this volume, offer rare insights into Runyon from a period of his career often overlooked by biographers and critics. This collection makes the case that World War I was not a minor diversion from sportswriting and Broadway but that it was a vital part of his development as a writer and provides a missing link between the early Runyon of Kansas and Colorado and the mature Runyon of Broadway. The significance of this book resides in its ability to show Runyon's deploying his emerging literary style of regular Joes turned into larger-than-life characters with crackling dialogue during America's participation in the Great War. Rarely do generals or grand strategies appear is these pages. Instead, it is the men, and in the words of Damon Runyon, "What men they are—God, what men!"

REPORTAGE

October 1918

October 7, 1918. Amid the Ruins of Rheims

I entered Rheims with the first party of staff officers to walk into the liberated cathedral city, immediately after we had received the news of the capture by the Americans of the Champ De Wagram, which forced General von Mudra's[1] army to withdraw from the forts of Brimont, Witry, and Nogent-La-Bassee, where the German batteries had dominated the city.

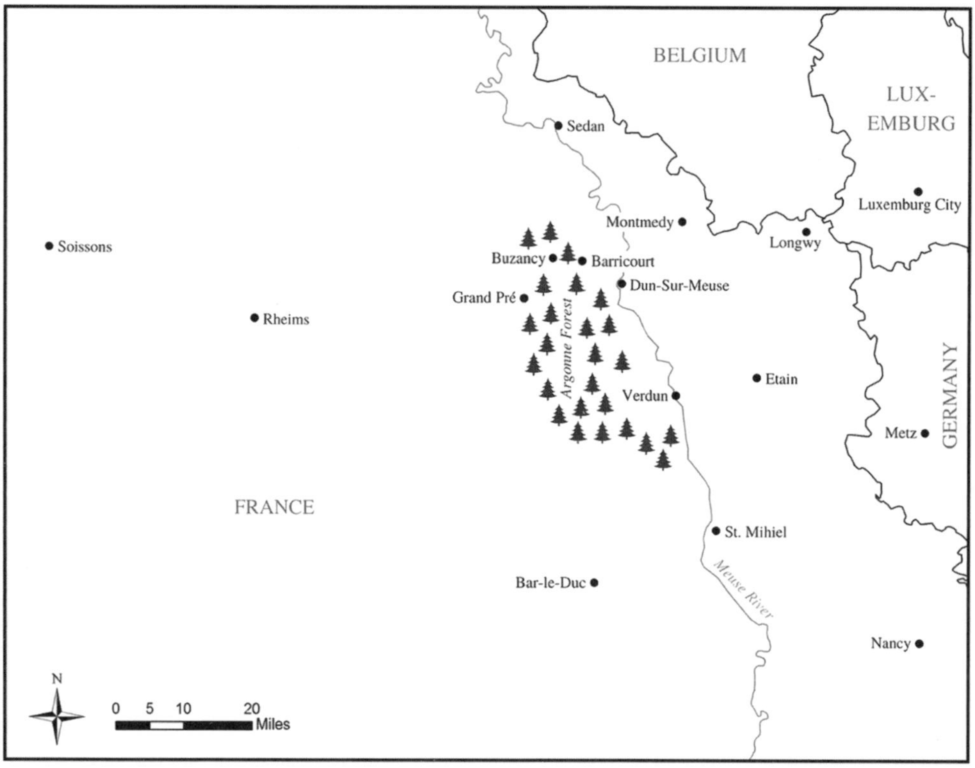

Eastern France

The roads leading into Rheims were still barricaded with barbed wire. Not a living human being was inside the town, which the Germans had been continually flooding with gas. The fumes still hung heavy in the half-wrecked buildings and other low-lying places.

Among the shelled ruins of a public school I found tiny gas masks. These had belonged to the pupils before the city was evacuated last May, when all civilians wore gas masks.

Corpses of the last soldiers and civilians killed while leaving the city were still lying in the streets. Dead horses lay everywhere.

Later I explored an eastern suburb of the cathedral city, Cernay-Les-Rheims, which the enemy had occupied for four years. I examined some German sharpshooters' nests, from which snipers had picked off the people walking in the streets of Rheims.

Everyone needed gas masks, even the mules. *Courtesy of United States Army Heritage and Education Center*

The former German trenches were littered with thousands of empty champagne bottles, looted from the vast vaults in the surrounding countryside.

Rheims was liberated Saturday after three-quarters of the city had been encircled since July. The seizure of the Blanc Mont heights by our troops threatened the Germans with being cut off from their rear communications.

The city had been entirely evacuated by civilians since May 27, when the incessant German bombardment began. Even the French kept no troops in the city after that.

The ancient cathedral is battered all around by shells.[2] Hundreds of statues have been knocked off at the north end and on the two sides. The edifice was exposed to the German artillery fire everywhere except in front.

A great hole has been torn through the roof, which also shows two smaller holes. Every bit of leaded glass in the windows has been shattered.

A shell struck the pedestal of the statue of Joan of Arc in front, but the statue itself was removed. The Hotel Grand, Hotel Lion D'Or, and the municipal theater, as well as all buildings in the vicinity of the cathedral, are battered to pieces by shells. The German retirement places Rheims outside the normal artillery range.

The Rheims Cathedral framed by ruins. *Courtesy of Library of Congress*

October 10, 1918. Amid the Ruins of Rheims

Inside the shrapnel-bitten walls of the historical old cathedral of Rheims Wednesday, several souvenir hunters were already plying around among the debris, seeking bits of sapphire-like blue glass from the famous north window.

Outside, the battered streets echoed to the clump of marching feet and the grind of wheels as French infantry and artillery rolled steadily forward in the wake of the retreating Germans.

Months ago, when Rheims still was occupied by civilians, some convivial soul apparently ordered up a round of drinks in a little corner barroom not far from the cathedral. A German shell came along and peeled off the front of the café, leaving the interior gaping wide open.

Five glasses of wine stood on the bar Wednesday morning, with the contents untouched. It was a windfall for a big French soldier riding by on a joggling wagon, munching a hunk of bread.

He hopped down from his perch, drank off two of the glasses of wine, and then hurriedly regained his seat.

There is scarcely a building in town, however big or however small, that hasn't been touched by the torrent of shells which fell over Rheims through long years.

The whole city is like a great heap of rubbish which has been shoved to one side of the road to let the soldiers through. Blocks of houses have been ripped open on one side, showing furniture and the pictures on the wall, like a stage setting. Big buildings that once housed magnificent stores are mere piles of debris, white with the dust from the stone from which Rheims was built centuries ago.

Up to a few months ago, the town was well occupied by civilians. It was here that little children went to school in gas masks. Their school now is a wreck.

Constantly throughout the war Rheims has been sprayed by gunfire. Finally the Germans moved so close the city was completely evacuated, and until we entered it after the deliverance of the ruins by the converging drive of the Americans and French, no civilian had been in the place since May. One of the richest and most beautiful cities of all France, Rheims was greatly coveted by the Germans but they were never able to take it. They were only able to ruin it. It is one of the most complete of their devilish jobs in France.

Baltimore or San Francisco, after their great fires, were only slightly damaged compared to Rheims. Here every roof and tree, every form of habitation has been flattened or punched through by giant shells until the whole thing amounts to total destruction.

Hovering not far beyond a long line of soldiers and guns streaming through the streets today are many civilians who formerly lived in Rheims. They are eagerly waiting for a chance to rush back to what is left in the homes and places of business. They will not find much.

Many left the town without waiting to pack up any belongings. Tables stand all set for meals that were never eaten. Big shells have popped through open bedrooms and scattered the clothes of men and women and children far and away. Rheims was badly damaged early in the war, but it managed to retain some semblance of what it used to be until lately. Now it is of a piece with the sad picture presented by Arras and other smashed towns in northern France.

The walls and towers of the cathedral are still standing, but the building is hardly more than a smoke-blackened skeleton. Many shells have fallen through the great vaulted roof. All glass has been smashed from the windows. Long ago the secret of making this glass was lost. That is why it is so eagerly sought by the relic hunters.

Many famous gargoyles have been chipped off and lie scattered around the building. Several paintings still hang on the walls uninjured. In view of what has been done to the rest of the town, it is remarkable that the Germans were unable to do even more damage in the form of shell marks showing that no effort was spared to level it.

The Grand hotel, just across the way, is smashed. So is nearly every other building for blocks around.

A few French soldiers were on guard at the cathedral Wednesday. A few others were quartered around the town. Throughout Wednesday the streets resounded with the tramp of columns marching through. Some soldiers had secured copies of Paris papers along the road and were reading as they marched. The men were laughing and shouting to each other.

Ruins of the Hotel de Ville, Rheims. *Courtesy of Library of Congress*

October 12, 1918. At the American Argonne Front

Out of the fog of fighting that hangs over the Forest of Argonne came limping today Whittlesey's[3] battered battalion, which made the epic defense in the dark glades beyond.

They are men of New York's own Seventy-Seventh Division—most of them from the big town itself.

A little over a year ago this writer reported the parade of these same men, when they marched in straggling columns down Fifth Avenue between walls of cheering people. Nearly all of them wore vintage straw hats that day. Some of them were in crumpled Palm Beach suits. Some of them were in overalls, having come direct from their jobs to appear in the first parade of drafted men on Manhattan Island.

Some of them were late of the Hudson Dusters.[4] Some of them once trained with the Gophers.[5] Some of them were from ornate houses on Park and Madison Avenues or the upper reaches of the Seventies and Eighties.

More were from the lower East Side. Broad and Harlem, Broadway and the Bronx shuffled down the avenue in that strange procession that day, while the bands bawled "Over There."

Later the writer saw them tumble off the trains at Yaphank,[6] carrying scarfed suitcases and big bundles, saw them form into irregular lines, and march to their new barracks.

Many of them had been celebrating their departure for camp the night before and looked it. Hester Street quarreled with Greenwich Village—not the Greenwich Village of long-haired fame, but the hardier, close-cropped region around the docks.

A couple of fist fights occurred at the landing place between querulous parties from the vicinity of Erie Basin, Brooklyn. Nervous young officers, fresh from Plattsburg,[7] fluttered about trying to get a semblance of order. Their commands brought small, alert replies from the new recruits.

There were Chinamen from Mott Street. Also, there were Japanese and Italians all jabbering in their own language at once.

Hopeless enough as military material they seemed then, but some of the same faces, faces I saw at Yaphank that day were under biscuit-shaped steel helmets in the muddy columns that tramped out of the Argonne Forest today.

The big town's polyglot population sent heroes of one of the Homeric fights of the war.

For four days and four nights the one-time counter jumpers, brokers, clerks, gangsters, newsboys, truck drivers, collegians, peddlers, and what not held the positions which they had been ordered to take and hold, while several times their number of Germans were busily engaged shoveling a variety of hell upon them.

They served as the anchor catch for the whole advance. Totally cut off from their main command, without food, and with very little water, the boys from the big town hung on.

They fought under a man who only a short time ago was a New York lawyer. Charles Whittlesey is a tall, lean-flanked fellow, around forty years old. He has a funny little smile.

He smiled this funny little smile when one of his men who had been taken prisoner was sent back to him by the Germans with a neatly typewritten note requesting his surrender. It would make this story more dramatic to say that Whittlesey sent back some stirring phrase in answer to the Germans. But as a matter of fact, he merely smiled his funny little smile after reading the note and tucked the paper away in his pocket.

The Germans got their real reply the next time a Boche poked his head up. It was in form of a bullet.

They are telling in some quarters that Whittlesey's reply to the demand for his surrender was "Go to hell!"

Whittlesey says he did not say it, but that it covered his thoughts at the time, anyway.

Not all men in his command are New Yorkers. Some time ago the Seventy-Seventh Division had to take on replacements. Many new recruits came from Oregon and other parts of the Northwest. One in the first bunch out of the forest, however, was a little chap who used to sell newspapers around Times Square.

He was covered with mud. His eyes were heavy with battle sleep, but he was grinning broadly.

The commander of the beleaguered force was a captain when he led his men into battle. He has since been recommended for lieutenant colonel. He had six companies with him, three from the First and three from the Second Battalion of his regiment.

One battalion was commanded by Captain George G. McMurtry,[8] a former New York broker. As hour after hour and day after day went by, there was no sign of a relieving column. The officers in command commenced to believe their case was hopeless.

On the fourth day a soldier told McMurtry that Captain Whittlesey was talking to some officers of another regiment of the division over in the woods.

McMurtry doubted the story, but investigated. He found Whittlesey conversing with officers of a relieving force which had just got up. Whittlesey was eating a sandwich as he talked.

McMurtry walked over to him. His first and only words were "For God's sake, give me a bite of that!"

The men greeted the members of the relieving column with requests for food and water. They had gone into the fight with the usual two days' rations. For two days they had absolutely no food.

There was a little spring near where they took up their position, but the Germans sniped them whenever they tried to go for water. First they went only at night. Finally they got so desperate from thirst they took chances in broad daylight. The officers posted a guard near the spring to keep the men from exposing themselves.

Whittlesey had been ordered to advance to a certain position. He advanced there. The Germans slipped in behind him through an old trench. Presently Whittlesey realized he was cut off and surrounded. A torrent of shell and machine gun fire and grenades came over.

The Americans were on sloping ground. Whittlesey ordered his men to dig in. They quickly burrowed into the ground like moles. They had machine guns and returned the German fire with these and with their rifles. Fortunately, they had plenty of ammunition.

They could constantly hear the Germans in the woods. The Germans were talking and shouting to each other as they tried to advance on the little band. Sometimes they got as near as thirty yards. The Americans let them come on as far as they would, then opened fire on them. At night Whittlesey kept out patrols who maintained contact with the enemy.

Just as soon as they were certain they were completely cut off, the officers made it plain to all men that they were expected to hold the position at all hazards.

Maj. Charles W. Whittlesey, commander of the "Lost Battalion." *Williams College in the World War*

The announcement was received with grim nods.

Time and again the best men in the command were picked and sent out as runners, in the hope they might get through the German lines.

Of nine men thus sent out, four were killed, four wounded, and the ninth was captured. It was this man[9] who was sent back by the Germans with the note demanding surrender. He was taken before the German commander and closely interrogated, but declined to give any information whatsoever. The German commander mentioned this fact in the note to Whittlesey. Then the American was blindfolded and given the message.

The Argonne Forest in which the Seventy-Seventh Division is fighting is a maze of trees. They are not big trees, but stand close together like stalks in a wheat field. Woven through them in the undergrowth are vines. It is impossible for a man to walk through the woods straight for any distance in any direction. It is impossible even to see through them to any great depth.[10]

It is said the French lost 60,000 men trying to take these woods since the outbreak of the war. The Germans must have lost many more in holding them.

It was in a particularly deep section of this modern wilderness that the little command of New Yorkers was trapped. Before the war Central Park probably was the largest forest ever seen by most of these men.

About forty men were killed as they lay there. The fellows buried their dead as best they could, usually under fire. Rarely did the Germans cease pounding them with bullets. Minenwerfers (mine throwers) came through the trees in bunches.

The wounded men were given the best attention possible. In his note demanding surrender, the German commander appealed to Whittlesey on the grounds of humanity, saying the Germans could hear the cries of the American wounded.

The soldiers say that as a matter of fact our men were particularly stoical and made little outcry, while on the other hand they could hear Germans squalling in the woods after every volley.

In a couple of days Whittlesey's men had exhausted every vestige of food. Cold rain came on and drenched them day and night. Only a few of them had their overcoats. It gets bitter cold in the Argonne woods at night, whatever the season of the year.

They could get little sleep on account of the terrific din of the gunfire. They say they never saw any sign of food. Other supplies were dropped into the woods by American airplanes. Neither did they ever find the box of carrier pigeons flung into the trees from aloft.

The rain soon made big walls out of their little trenches. They could not get warm and began to suffer intensely from the exposure and lack of food. Some of them were very weak when they reached the rear at last.

But the men came out of that hellish wood singing the praises of their officers, especially of Whittlesey.[11]

"You are certainly a great anchor man for the division," said the general commanding that front to the New Yorker.

"You held on where you were caught—"

Whittlesey merely smiled his funny little smile.

The battalions were sent back for rest. As soon as they have got warmed up and washed up they will be back in the line. They are less excited about their exciting exploit than anyone else in the army that speculated on nothing else for days but their probable fate.

October 16, 1918. With the Americans on the Argonne Front

It has been "old home week" these last seven days on the road through the Argonne Forest behind the advancing American lines. Sergeant Alexander Woollcott,[12] former New York dramatic critic, hurrying forward on a mission for *Stars and Stripes*, the soldiers' newspaper, says every new American attack reminds one of a big "first night" because you meet everyone you know.

Homer Rodeheaver,[13] Billy Sunday's[14] trombonist, was one of many familiar figures that passed along the muddy roads leading into the dark woods where New York's Seventy-Seventh Division chopped its name into history. Rodeheaver wears the Y.M.C.A. uniform. He was saying he would like to see the commanding general, as he had an idea which he thought might help the commander in his work. The nature of "Rody's" idea is unknown.

Bill Wellman,[15] former automobile racing promoter, was discovered swinging a pick with Colonel Reggie Foster's[16] pioneers, who were repairing the shell-torn highway within sound of the cannon.

Bill had just received a work appointment to an officers' school. Colonel Foster hated to lose him, as he says Bill swings a mean pick.

Elizabeth Brice,[17] actress, and Margaret Mayo,[18] playwright, with Tommy Gray,[19] also playwright, and Bill Morrissey,[20] vaudevillian, went splashing past Wellman in an army automobile. They went on up to an artillery position and put on a show with the guns serving iron hail to the Germans on the distant hills between acts.

The members of the quartet are Y.M.C.A. entertainers. They call their unit the "shock unit," because some of Gray's gags were a shock to the Association.[21]

Sergeant Hank Gowdy,[22] old Boston catcher, now with the Rainbow Division, who has been in all kinds of war, was chiefly interested in the announcement that his old teammate Christy Mathewson[23] is in France, an officer with the new gas service.

Harry Niemeyer,[24] former New York sporting editor, prowled along the road in Y.M.C.A. apparel.

John LeRoy Scott,[25] author, stood ankle deep in mud, watching the procession of trucks. He also is a Y.M.C.A. worker.

Herman Whitacker[26] and Maximilian Foster,[27] more authors, held a parley amid the ruins of Varennes, where Marie Antoinette and Louis XVI were arrested when they tried to escape to Germany and were brought back to Paris and executed.

It was almost "authors' day" on the road to the Argonne.

Out of the woods where the big guns were ripping away tramped a muddy officer. He was Grantland Rice,[28] lieutenant of artillery. He was complaining of "cooties,"[29] saying querulously they were a handicap to poetry. Rice has been serving with the guns pounding the forest. He was the only poet encountered on the road.

Luke Lea,[30] former United States Senator from Tennessee, was found commanding a regiment of artillery.

It will be seen a rather mixed aggregation cluttered the road to the Argonne. Celebrities could be picked out of the welter of traffic like flies out of a boarding house soup.

Will Irwin,[31] war correspondent, was found busy deciphering German signs along the forest thoroughfares. "Jerry," as the soldiers call the German, had laid out regular streets and named them all.

A famous American general has located a headquarters in a concrete house recently vacated by a German general. He was directing the battle by telephone. He took pride in exhibiting a dugout under the house as elaborate as mine workings. It had been a German bombproof shelter.

The general called it his "Annette exit," saying he did the Annette Kellerman[32] into it when "Jerry" came bombing of nights.

A stretcher bearer, who said he lives opposite Belmont Park when he is home, was found at the crossroads in a former Y.M.C.A. hut, now an American dressing station, watching a German plane hovering above the trees. American guns were breaking sooty little balls of smoke around it. The plane dropped close down so the observer could have a look at the transport. Finally the machine glided away, unharmed.

The ground was strewn with German canteens, ammunition, boxes, helmets, and articles of clothing all through the woods.

"Jerry" went away from there lickety-split when the New Yorkers got going. The Manhattan Islanders are ensconced in "fox holes," or little rifle pits, which were still warm from their German occupants when they arrived.

Deep trenches and great stretches of barbed wire run this way and that through the close-woven trees. American transport followed the fighting line so close it almost piled up on itself on the narrow road, which is the only road that goes anywhere in particular through the woods.

It has been said that the old army mule has been replaced by motor vehicles, but the mule did great service and was plentifully cussed at through Argonne.[33] Vocabularies acquired while driving trucks along West Street came mighty handy to New Yorkers in the forest campaign.

The mules hauled the guns and dragged the "grub." There were numerous motor lorries, too, but the road was muddy and mules' hoofs stuck better.

Artillery, mounted men, and infantry weaved their way through the woods, which echoed with "whoops" in Brooklyn accents. Not far ahead the guns were pounding steadily. Occasionally a shell squawked through the forest. It never caused half as much excitement as when a motor vehicle skidded off the road and became embedded in soft ooze.

From parts of the road going into the forest, the soldiers could look down into the little valleys where the Germans had built small villages with tiny houses of artistic design. They had electric lights, baths, and other conveniences.

"Jerry" had bedded himself down for the winter when rooted out by the men from the big town. Deep amid the trees of the forest were villages not so elaborate but quite permanent.

For many years to come, explorers probably will be coming upon whitened bones in those dark labyrinths.

Mixed in with the traffic were prisoners. Some of them said they were from the Elizabethan Guards, which is a crack German organization.[34] One fellow said he had been a waiter in the Knickerbocker Hotel,[35] New York. Any bunch of German prisoners which did not contain at least one former New York waiter would be a rarity.

The German army must have an amazing number of waiters in it.[36]

October 17, 1918. At the American Argonne Front

There was a hot fight in the trees ahead. It was an affair later summed up in the official corps report as a "satisfactory advance."

Corps reports can dispose of, in a few words, incidents which will remain in life-time memory for many men. This was such an affair.

A big colored soldier came hobbling painfully down the road. He had been wounded in the leg and was making his way unaided toward a dressing station. His progress was slow because he had to keep turning out of the road to avoid the processions of guns and infantry and ammunition trucks, as well as "wife-killers," which are lightning-fast little motorcycles, with side carriers.

The wounded colored gentleman was accosted by a war correspondent anxious to learn some details of what was going on up above.

"What happened there?" he asked the soldier, who at once assumed the air of a raconteur, cleared his throat, waved a hand in the direction of the battle line, and said:

"Well, s'pose an I'll tell you jest what happened. Ah was climin' ovah de babbed wire and dey shot me."

Then he hobbled on. He had left nothing untold as far as he was concerned.

There was a handsome little chap of about seventeen lying on the ground in a field hospital. He had been slightly wounded. He said he was from Ohio and had been a runner, or messenger, in his battalion.

"There were a couple of swell French officers with our outfit," he said. "I saw them running along in front of our dugout hollering "Boche fine," laughing like the dickens. Pretty soon I saw them again. They had been hit by a shell and were both dead. I felt bad about that, I tell you. Then I got hit myself."

At the same hospital was a young Frenchman, who greeted the doctor with a volley of questions. He wanted to know if he was going to be sent to a French or American hospital, saying he preferred an American. Being assured on that point, he ventured some offhand criticism of the American method of fighting.

"They go too fast," said he. "They are always in a big hurry."[37]

Bert Boyden[38] bobbed out of the woods, covered with mud, wearing a big reddish mustache, and smoking a villainous pipe. Boyden is a New York magazine editor. He has been on the front line and worked eight straight days with one division, which just came in. He says the news of the German peace move[39] was received by the men on the firing line with particular interest, especially when first received.

Interviewing soldiers on what they think of the peace talk was a popular pastime today. Any interviews secured near the front line were apt to be interrupted by disquieting chatter from the machine guns and by meowing shells. This morning they were giving "Jerry" blazes in the American front.

In such circumstances peace talk seemed rather "de trop," as they say in Noo Yolk.

The roads were crowded with American infantry moving forward. Tainted at intervals by mist, the day was cold, and a biting rain drizzled down. Most of the infantry was moving a short distance, so they made the journey by shanks' mares.

They scuffled along through the mud, bending under their dripping packs, toward the steady thump of guns ahead.

It was rather fatuous to interject questions as to opinions on peace into the march. Grover Cleveland Alexander,[40] former big league pitcher, was seen in one of the base towns along the road. His $6,000 arm is used chiefly for carrying a rifle nowadays.

Many German prisoners were streaming back from the American front, some looking particularly woebegone in their sodden uniforms.

The American advance in 1918 captured thousands of German soldiers. *Courtesy of Library of Congress*

A comic poking fun at doughboys for collecting war souvenirs. *Courtesy of Library of Congress*

Americans are finding much German baggage, indicating the enemy's retreat is becoming more and more precipitate. As a rule, the Germans, especially their meticulous officers, gather up all personal effects before fleeing, but now they are leaving everything. Some of the German officers travel with as much junk as a prima donna. The souvenir hunters in the wake of the American army are having their "field day."

One of the officers captured today said the German soldiers have the bad habit of carrying on them letters of instruction when going into battle. These documents provide information for the enemy. He said the American soldier didn't do this. The same officer said the Germans are suffering from a shortage of horses, declaring the American artillerymen and bombers seem to have an uncanny knowledge where the Germans hide their livestock.

Furthermore, he said, the Germans underestimated the value of the tanks.

October 17, 1918. [Delayed] At the American Argonne Front

Figuring that the advanced positions would be interested in the news of the day, the headquarters of a heavy artillery outfit telephoned such details of the peace negotiations as had trickled up to them Wednesday to the bunch with the light guns away up at the front.

The telephone service on the American front is very good. It is not quite as easy to give a man in a first-line dugout a ring as it is to call up "Spring 3100, New York,"[41] but, all things considered, the service is good.

The "heavies" got Captain Milt Brown, of Tennessee, on the wire. Brown was in charge of the "lights." He is a brother of Innis Brown,[42] of New York, the newspaperman.

Captain Milt listened intently to what the "heavies" had to say. When he had heard all the news he answered dryly:

"Hell, I reckon nobody's told these birds opposite us yet. They're shelling hell out of us."

The news was telephoned on to a French outfit still farther ahead. The commander was quite excited about it, but his answer was in line with Brown's remark:

"So the Boche, he don't know it?" he said. "He still fighting here."

From another light battery position, a voice that had a familiar sound to the listener in the "heavies" dugout came rasping along the wire:

"Hey, who is that?" demanded the listener.

"This is Frank Cavanaugh,"[43] said the voice. "Who are you?"

The old Dartmouth coach was well up amid the fighting with the light guns. He said Minot,[44] the Harvard back, was with his outfit.

For a few minutes football was the topic of the conversation, with the shell fire making more racket at each end of the wire than the rooting section at the Yale-Harvard game.

This day produced mighty dreary weather. It rained. It was cold. A gray haze hung over the world. Out of the grayness moved that everlasting parade of dripping infantrymen, trucks, wagons, and artillery sloshing to the front, as the echoes of the thundering guns came drifting back. If the men could choose the days for battle, no man would ever choose such a day as this. The horses gave off steam as they strained against the tugs.

The men went along kicking blobs of mud from their shoes with every step. The rain seeped through one's very soul.

Tanks were used in the fighting this morning. It was the first time in this particular attack. Mud makes no difference to the tanks. They lumber out of the haze like big mud turtles and move against the enemy lines.

The "heavies" and "lights" were pasting "Jerry's" line with dreary monotony. The heavy artilleryman has a prosaic job in these particular drives. He works on the Germans from a couple of miles away.

Often he is shooting from behind hills. Big shells come drifting his way out of the distant horizon without him being able to see any.

The "lights" sometimes go forward right on the heels of the infantry. They are occasionally used to "pot" machine guns. However, back with the big guns life is precarious even if it is largely routine. A whole flock of shells may fall into a battery without doing any damage, like a futile shot into a covey of quail. Then, along will come one loose chunk of metal and cause all kinds of trouble.

The other day two heavy artillerymen heard a shell wheezing in their direction. Both flung themselves on the ground, close together. Shells burst sixty yards from them. One man got up wholly unhurt, but the other man lay quite still. He was dead. A splinter from a shell had flipped along the ground and penetrated his neck.

Arthur Richardson, of Schroon, New York, came out of the fight today. He talks in a slow, drawling voice. He was in a dugout this morning with two other men when a shell landed among them. Richardson's companions were killed.

If any psychologist is interested in what the soldiers are going to do after the war, he might talk to Jars Metlock, a colored gentleman who proclaims himself an engineer.

Jars has been hanging around the fringes in much of the recent fighting, patching roads and what not.

"Ah come from Clarksville, Red Rivuh County, Texas, yas, sah," said he today. "Ah suttinly wish ah was back in ole Clarksville. Dere's no place like Clarksville, no sah. Ah got me one of these heah Boche guns to take back to Clarksville to show to the folks."

"Dey's goin' to be mighty s'prized when ah tell 'em all ah see. I suttinly wish ah was back in Clarksville right this minute."

October 18, 1918. At the American Argonne Front

"It reminds me of the last few minutes of the last quarter of a football game, when our side has only ten yards to gain and they blow the whistle for time." This is the way one American soldier commented Thursday on Germany's acceptance of President Wilson's[45] peace conditions.

The soldier is a former Harvard football player. He was standing in the muddy road reading a damp newspaper, with the raindrops trickling from his steel helmet. He spoke quite dispassionately.

"Yes, or in the last round when a guy is on the floor being counted out," said another, who didn't go to Harvard. He was just as dispassionate. All along the roads leading to the front, soldiers could be seen standing in the doorways of wet billets, looking at the papers fresh from Paris carrying the news. Some had papers printed in English and were reading aloud. Others were trying to read French papers.

Some of them were excited and cheering, but most of them seemed to take it as a matter of course. For days the American soldiers have apparently felt that peace was not far away. They considered the capitulation of Germany inevitable, so the materialization of the fact, if it is a fact, does not appear to surprise them much.

"Jerry's dogging it," is the way a big infantryman expressed it when news of the first German offer reached the front line, "Jerry" being the soldier name for the enemy. Much speculation has been indulged in by the soldiers as to whether Germany is up to some new treachery. Its proposal to evacuate this particular part of France is being commented on sarcastically by the doughboys,[46] in view of the enforced evacuation that has been going on during the last week or so.

Up on the front line the men read their papers huddled in dripping dugouts with German shells still breaking around them. Under such conditions a man has a better perspective of war than some of the men sitting at the fireside in their carpet slippers. Under such conditions a man is not apt to be as blood-thirsty as the "firesiders."[47]

It was probably difficult for the men in the trenches to reconcile the peace talk in the papers with their surroundings. It is still all war up there. Farther back behind the lines the soldiers are already speculating on how long it will take to get them home after peace really comes, and what they will do after they get there. Even while they engage in such speculation they are busy loading munitions and other supplies for the front or making ready to go there themselves.

There is no cessation of the long transports churning up the roads leading to the cannon, although the drivers gossip of their future plans as they go. The infantry still moves forward afoot and in motor lorries. The men may be commenting on the prospect of peace as they shuffle along. The roads are bending under the dripping packs, but they push on to the trenches. In the little French towns women laugh and chatter over the news, because it means that their menfolk will come back to them

They will resume the tilling of the fields and going about peaceful pursuits, fearless of shellfire and bombs. But they listen eagerly to the American soldiers' explanations of the situation. The wonderful French soldiers, who are also still shoving steadily along on their front, beam when "la paix" is mentioned.

They have seen war as no other soldiers in the history of the world have seen it, and they have remained steadfast throughout it for four years. They are pleased over the possibilities of peace, but chiefly it is peace with victory.

Probably the most delighted men in France are the German prisoners. Batches of them in the dull gray uniforms, which seemed unusually dull this somber, rainy day, could be seen here and there along the roads, herded by American and French guards. They had no hesitancy in saying they were glad that the end seems in sight.

One of them in a bunch taken by the Americans once tended bar in a saloon on Ninth Avenue, New York. He is going back there as soon as he gets his liberty. One thing is certain in the minds of all—that it is a complete triumph of the Allies and Americans over the Germans. The first thought that strikes the mind of the American here who has seen the ruined towns and the devastated countryside is that the Germans are getting off only too easy if their own land escapes retribution.

It is reported they are not now burning towns up at the front, as they retreat, but they already have done so much in that line that no last-minute sparing by their inhuman hand can ever repay. Civilians are re-entering the towns almost as fast as they are evacuated. They live in the ruins in their former homes until they can get something better.

October 19, 1918. At the American Argonne Front

In all the history of the American army there can be recorded no such exploits, no such fighting, as has been done by Pershing's First Army on the Argonne front during the past three weeks.

Beside it, Chateau Thierry and the St. Mihiel salient were mere incidents. It is a modern Battle of the Wilderness, enormously enlarged, spread out over more time and territory, and dotted here and there with an Antietam or a Gettysburg.

It has been three weeks of unremitting hell. In fact, the comparison is hardly fair to hell. Nobody really knows what hell is like except that it is probably warm. Many thousand Americans now know the Argonne only too well. They know it is never warm there.

God only knows where the sun has gone. It has been raining continuously since the drive started. That was on September 26. It is always cold. The rain is as finely woven and as clammy as a funeral garment. It has a way of soaking through the skin on into the body of a man until his very heart seems to be pumping the rainwater along the veins instead of blood. It wets all the world. Falling from the trees into the grass, raindrops gleam damply under a dripping sky. Overhead hangs a gray, cob-webby vapor.

It is most oppressive. It seems to clog the lungs and make breathing difficult. It is a smothering, chilling, depressing fog. A man gets a hungering for just one blast of clean, fresh, warming sunshine.[48]

Dawn comes about 5 o'clock these mornings. As soon as the first streaks of light begin splitting the thick mist, John Soldier lifts himself out of his "fox hole," which is hastily dug and into which he hastily plastered himself when he scooped it out in the wet ground with a shovel or bayonet, or even with a tin mess plate.

It affords some protection from the shells and machine gun bullets. Not much, but some. The soldier comes out of his hole matted with mud. The rain does not stop when the battle pauses. It goes on through the long, dreary night, trickling into the "fox holes," turning them into wallows.

The man pulls himself out of his shelter with a noise like yanking a rubber boot out of the mud. He has had no sleep. No man can sleep in a cold puddle, with gun fire for a lullaby.[49]

He has had little to eat except a snatch of his field rations, which he carries when he goes into battle. After the first day few men have much of that left. It is a tough enough job lugging extra ammunition and other equipment without bothering with extra rations. What he has is sure to be wet.

Sometimes they are able to get grub up to the men on the first line during battle, but not often. With dawn, the artillery and machine guns resume. Their fire has been only intermittent during the night. Now the shells fall splashing into the watery fields, raising geysers of mud. Machine gun bullets swish in layers through the fog.

The line goes forward. His clothes clinging to him like a cold, filmy epidermis, his feet slipping in the mud at every step, the American ace picks up additional ground. The American ace is the American infantryman. Foot by foot, yard by yard, the line moves. Always it moves forward. The ground yielded by Americans in this war so far can be counted in inches.

A typical US Army ration dump in France. *Courtesy of United States Army Heritage and Education Center*

The men take cover as best they can. They advance and dig in. Then they advance some more and dig in. It is slow work. It is deadly work. They are moving on against the fire from the German guns, which thicken the air like the very mist.

This campaign in the Argonne is the kitchen work of the war. It is sheer drudgery. There is nothing spectacular about it. It compares to the average great battle in point of glamor as ditch digging compares to portrait painting.

In the Argonne all glamor is pretty well dotted by mud. Yet, it is a very great battle. It is one of the most important of the war. The German view of it is indicated by the terrific resistance they are making. They pour in their crack divisions daily in an effort to stop the American infantry. They use their veteran soldiers against the lads who little over a year ago knew practically nothing of soldiering.

The veterans have orders to hang on at all costs. Day by day, however, the boys from the American cities and farms keep gaining. You can see big bunches of the Kaiser's seasoned soldiers coming down the roads from the front at most every hour of the day, minus their guns, with American soldiers herding them along toward the prison camps.

You can see the Germans lying dead in clusters on the ground over which the Americans advance. In three weeks the Americans have gained about ten miles on a front of twenty miles. Every mile was a mile of bitter resistance.

It is a rolling, hilly country over which they fight. There are frequent stretches of woods so thick it would be impossible to ride a bicycle through them without a road. The Argonne Forest, where Whittlesey's lost legion made its immortal battle, was part of the country covered by the operation.

New York's Seventy-Seventh Division took much of that forest. They had to dig out there by the very roots. Little towns occur at frequent intervals over most of the region. They are mere wide places in the road as a rule, but about them Americans and Germans build battles which will be historic.

There are spots which are bywords in the army at present as scenes of terrible scars—scenes which will be hard to locate after the war. This fighting is not a matter of every day or so. It is a daily affair. It has developed almost into routine business.

The soldier gets out of a "fox hole" in the morning, picks up his rifle, and goes to fighting methodically as a working man back home picks up his dinner pail and starts for his daily job. Both knock off at nightfall. Instead of a warm dinner, however, the soldier crawls into another reeking "fox hole."

That is, unless he is dead and buried on some damp hillside of France or wounded and on the way back to the hospital in a joggling truck.

A man may put in several days at the very front line. Then he goes back for a short rest. Fresh divisions are always moving in while worn divisions are coming out. The Americans have so perfected the machinery of war for this drive that everything moves automatically.

Long lines of ghostly helmeted men suddenly appear out of the mist on the roads which feed the battle front and as suddenly disappear again.

They march silently. Their heads are bent forward against the rain. Occasionally an officer mutters a low command, but there is little talking among the men. This is especially true when they are going in.

When they are coming out there is apt to be more conversation. The tension is relaxed. Besides, they are returning to something to eat, dry clothes, and warm beds.

The saddest part in the coming out is the reduced number of the marching men. So it goes on day after day. So it has gone on for twenty-one days.

Out of this scullery of war the American infantry is emerging as the greatest fighter the world has ever seen.

October 23, 1918. With the American First Army

Harvard's Eddie Grant,[50] the Old Giants' third baseman, sleeps in the Forest of Argonne, only a few yards from where he fell. His grave is marked by some stones and a rude little cross tenderly reared by his own men.[51]

Eddie died leading his battalion in a desperate fight to relieve Whittlesey's beleaguered men two weeks ago.

He was commanding a company of the Three Hundred and Seventh Infantry from Camp Upton when the battle began.

For four days and four nights his company was part of the command which was trying to get to Whittlesey. On the morning of the day that relief was effected, Eddie was so worn out he could scarcely move. Some of his brother officers noticed him sitting on a stump with a cup of coffee in front of him. Two or three times, they say, he tried to lift the cup, but he was so weak he couldn't do it. Finally, with a terrific effort, he gulped down the coffee when the command came to move. He stepped off at the head of his company as briskly as ever.

On the way through the forest, fighting at every step, Grant came upon stretcher bearers carrying back the major, commanding the battalion, who had been wounded. The major shouted to Grant:

"Take command of the battalion!"

Eddie Grant was then one of the few officers left.

The major had hardly spoken when a shell came through the trees, dropping two lieutenants in Grant's company.

Eddie shouted: "Everybody down!" to his men, but without hunting cover for himself. He called for more stretcher bearers for the two lieutenants. He was calling and waving his hands when a shell struck him. It was a direct hit.

Officers and men say Eddie's conduct during the fight was marvelous. He never slept while the drive for Whittlesey's position was on.[52] The writer yesterday saw Christy Mathewson, Grant's old teammate and roommate while Eddie was with the Giants. "Matty" was greatly saddened by the news. He is a captain in the gas corps.

One of the men who saw Eddie Grant killed was a former policeman at the Polo Grounds.

"Eddie Grant was dog tired," said this man Tuesday. "But he stepped off at the head of his outfit with no more concern than if he were walking to his old place at third base after his side had finished its turn at the bat. Like many others, he was worn down almost to a shadow. He staggered from weakness when he first started off, but pretty soon he was marching briskly with his head up."

Grant is the first big league ball player to be killed in the war. His chum, Harry McCormick,[53] was shell shocked some time ago and is back in the States. They went to Plattsburg together.

October 23, 1918. With the American First Army

"Gentlemen, it's my birthday and I am bringing some of my friends to take dinner with you," was the naïve announcement of a German officer in surrendering to Lieutenant Reardon of New York's Seventy-Seventh Division, up in the Argonne the other day.

He spoke perfect English. His face was wreathed in smiles. He waved his hands toward the woods behind him. Out popped thirty German soldiers. They also were smiling. They had been surrounded by a detachment of the Seventy-Seventh for some time. After making a brisk fight, they decided to give it up.

It seems it was really the German officer's birthday. He and his friends got their dinner with the Americans all right.

Joe Jenkins,[54] former White Sox catcher, was discovered Monday scraping the mud off himself in a wayside billet. He had just come out of the line with his outfit. He has seen quite a lot of service.

Some of the men from the Seventy-Seventh are now at a "de lousing" station. This is just what the name implies. There's no use making bones about it.

"C'est la guerre," as the Frenchman says and the "cootie" is part of it. The men are marched there direct from the lines. They strip themselves, and each man's clothing is tied up in a bundle with his name on it. The bundles then are passed through a steaming process, which destroys what the soldiers call "seam squirrels." This process takes about forty minutes. In the meantime the men wait around with nothing on but their raincoats, sometimes not even them. After being rid of their unwelcome roommates they get rest.

The Germans are great hands at building elaborate dugouts and other shelter in their trenches. Our men move in these habitations as fast as they can chase the Germans out.[55]

They always discover that "Jerry" has left many of his pet cooties behind. When a man gets the German breed mixed up with his good, old-fashioned, home-like Uncle Sam grayback, much unrest develops.

The fighting has passed beyond the Argonne, but every day scores of new stories come floating out of the forest of startling incidents of the great campaign. A whole book could be written about the battle in the woods. One division was under command of General Alexander,[56] bluff, a thick-set old warrior. He made the division pop like a new saddle from the moment he took hold. One of his brigades was under General Wittenmyer,[57] who started with the division at Upton. He helped form and develop the outfit, saw it through its baptism of blood on the Vesle as well as through its great trial by fire in the tangled grove of eastern France that will forever be hallowed to Americans.

Wittenmyer is a grizzled foot soldier who has followed the flag all over the world. He was with the Ninth Infantry in the Boxer campaign. Hand-to-hand scraps were frequent.

Monday night we had the first clear moonlight in this region, close to the front, in many months. "Jerry's" Fokkers[58] promptly took the air. They went out sightseeing. In one little town which was once the scene of much bombing during different periods of the war, a major or commandant walked into an officers' club where a big crowd was dining. He announced casually that "alert" had been sounded and that it might be a good idea for the folks to go to the abris (shelters).

Then he saluted calmly and began eating his own meal. No bombing was reported.

Lining up to kill the "cooties." *Courtesy of Library of Congress*

November 1918

November 1, 1918. [Delayed] With the American First Army

Five-thirty was the "H" hour this morning on the American front. They used to call it the "zero" hour. It is the hour appointed for the infantry to move into a big attack—for the "kick-off."

They employ a lot of football terms in the army. The "H" hour was scarcely a five-minute memory this morning before General Hunter Liggett's[59] veteran American troops were going through the German line like a bunch of seasoned Harvard backs going through a "prep" school eleven.

They were the lean and dusty foot soldiers of the American First Army. They hit on a twenty-mile front. Before the morning mist had fully lifted from the fields, gray lines of bedraggled German prisoners were plodding back down the roads with American bayonets at their hips.

Reports on the attack from various parts of the long front came sifting into headquarters in fragmentary fashion all day, like election returns, but by nightfall the tabulators triumphantly reported 3,000 prisoners, with several districts yet to be heard from.

In territory the Americans gathered in about four and a half miles, which includes a batch of important villages and other strong defensive points. The Germans fought back fiercely, keeping a curtain of machine gun, rifle, and artillery fire hung in front of the advancing Americans, but they could not stop the Yankee rush.

This attack was the continuation of the attack begun September 26. "Operation" is the army name for any fighting. In this particular connection it is a mild, off-hand characterization of the greatest and longest battle in the history of American arms. There have been phases in this affair. First was the beginning. Second was the advance which started October 5.

Today's smash was the third phase. They picked a gorgeous morning. It was so pretty it seemed a pity to mar it with bloodshed. The sun came out while our troops were slugging their way over the flatlands up the gentle slopes of the French countryside. The warm sun rays were feathering the world with silver.

In the little towns behind the lines within sound of the guns, the people were out early in their duds. They were observing the "Fete Des Morts," which is equivalent to our Memorial Day. A small procession of women and children moved through the streets bound for church. One town even mustered a drum corps of boys who will presently be soldiers of France.

French civilians and soldiers gathered in little knots at the corners and read newspapers bearing the latest news of the peace situation, while great trucks bearing supplies for the fighting forces, crammed with grimy American and French infantry, being shifted from one point to another, flowed past.

Soon in the afternoon, however, the success was fully darkened by a white fog cloud over the fields. The air grew cold enough to suggest snow. All this time Liggett's men were driving ahead. They attacked, in conjunction with the French Fourth Army on their left. The American line extended from the northeast of the shattered village of Grand Pré beyond the Argonne Forest eastward to the Meuse River.

General Gouraud's[60] French troops moved on a ten-kilometer (six and one-half miles) front. It was a sort of general Franco-American shove. It had been planned to start some days ago, but it was held up for one reason or another. That the Germans would make desperate resistance was expected. They must hold the Argonne front, because on that depends the retreat of the German army in the north.

To prevent their army from being annihilated, they threw nine of their crack divisions into the line, with several divisions held in reserve. All this sounds technical, but it means that the enemy fought today for mighty big stakes.

At 3:30 this morning the Germans got formal notice that the Americans were coming. It was in the form of a titanic artillery bombardment. For nearly two hours and a half the Yankee guns thumped in chorus, tossing enough metal into the German lines to make a good-sized smelter slag dump.

"Jerry" had dug himself in fairly well, but even Mother Earth herself can't afford much protection against that sort of thing. Then the machine guns began unfolding blankets of steel and lead under cover of which the foot soldiers moved out as the "H" hour arrived.

Overhead buzzed numerous Yankee airplanes serving as eyes of the army. Rumbling along with the infantry were some ungainly tanks.

The army report, evidently composed by a man who has an understanding of sports, says it was "perfect team play." And so it was. Among the first prisoners taken by the Americans was a woman, according to a report sent in from one outfit.

It appears to be authentic, although war correspondents have commenced to look askance at such reports. They have heard tales of German women serving in the army before, which failed to "pan out." In this instance there is much detail. The prisoner was dressed in man's clothes.

Throughout their advance the Yankees were facing relentless machine gun fire. The Germans have fairly draped themselves with machine guns as they fall back. Their machine gunners hang on pretty well, too, even when the German infantry is fading into the distance behind them.

Every objective was reached by the Americans today. They ran right on schedule. Tonight they bivouac on terrain that up to the "H" hour this morning was "Bocheville."

November 2, 1918. With the American Army West of the Meuse

Rival "snowstorms" of the stage variety are being put on around Verdun by fliers of the Allies and the Boche. Our planes scoot over the enemy's lines and drop huge batches of handbills.

"Jerry," as the Boche is called by our men, comes back and whitens the ground on the Allies' front with his own dodgers.

The air often is filled with fluttering bits of paper in the propaganda duels. One Boche document evidently was written by a chap who has some knowledge of American slang. He referred to the language of the diplomats as "high-falutin."

Another, printed both in English and German, keeps mentioning the "new German government." It is a direct appeal to the soldiers but suggests if the war goes on, more French and Belgian cities will be destroyed.

In a bunch of wounded Germans captured Thursday by Americans was a young officer who spoke excellent English. He had been shot through the wrist. He expressed surprise at the large number of Americans he saw upon arriving back of the lines.

"I always thought the submarine a mistake," declared this officer, "but I had believed they had been effective in keeping Americans from being landed in Europe in large numbers."

The return of cows on farms way back home is brought to memory of the soldiers in the trenches at night when German raiders try to pass our entanglements. The wire fences are hung with old tin cans, which make a terrific racket when anyone tries to get through the wire.

The first thing German prisoners are allowed to do is to build houses for themselves. The Americans provide the lumber and other material, and overnight their Boche guests throw up long one-story shelters and quickly transform them into comfortable quarters. They get the same rations as those served to American soldiers, which are better than they got in their own army.

Our government has to pay their wages the same as the German government has to pay the wages of any American soldiers they capture. The Germans get the worst of this arrangement, as the American wage scale for the soldier is several times that of the Boche.

"Jerry" agrees that otherwise our treatment of prisoners in the matter of food and quarters is much better than the German system.

Our prison camps are picked out with as much care as are sites for our own soldiers. The German officer mentioned above said that he could not have received more attention. He was in a hospital tent with a lot of others, both American and German wounded. The Germans had been dressed in clean pajamas and occupied comfortable cots the same as the Yankee boys beside them. They were being looked after by American hospital doctors.

The Boche officer, asked if German soldiers had been told they would be killed if captured by Americans, said he hadn't heard it and that anyway he doubted if the story would have had much effect because of too many Germans having lived in America and known our people. After being settled in prison camps, the prisoners are taken out every day with picks and shovels and set to repairing roads. American soldiers stand guard over them with fixed bayonets.

"They work pretty well," observed an American sentry, "especially privates. Non-commissioned officers are not so good, an' I don't believe I'd want no colonels or generals if I was trying to get something done. But the privates like work—it keeps them warm."

German prisoners always look cold. They may be warm enough, but they never look it. In nine cases out of ten they come in without overcoats. It seems to be a settled principle with the German to throw away his overcoat first in a retreat. The drab gray color of their uniforms is best of all for fighting, but it gives them a singularly forlorn appearance when they are stripped of accouterments and are wet and muddy.

Every German soldier carries a little clothes brush in his pocket. The first thing he does when he lands in a prison cage is to get out his brush and start cleaning his clothes. His second act is to take off his clothes and go through them for extraneous tenants. It's a remarkable fact, but mighty few attempts to escape from American camps have been made by German prisoners.[61]

November 3, 1918. With the American First Army

Out of the hills to the south of Liggett's fast-lengthening firing lines today came roaring another fleet of American airplanes carrying the fear of God into the German lines.

They emptied three tons of explosives into the town of Montmedy, which is the headquarters of the German Fifth Army Corps and one of the most important points still held by the Germans. They made a mess of part of the town.

There were forty of the planes. Many of them were the same planes, manned by the same men, which had bombed the town of Stenay yesterday, where it is now expected the Germans will try to make a stand.

They were daylight bombers from Colonel Thomas Bowen's[62] day bombing group. A little over two years ago, Bowen was one of the men who piloted a tiny flock of wobbly old planes into the mountains of Chihuahua, ahead of Pershing's punitive expedition. These planes then represented all of America's aerial strength.

Bowen wears a crooked nose as a memento of a fall at Colonia Dublán,[63] in Mexico, the result of a faulty plane. His bombers today were but an infinitesimal unit in our army of the sky. They were all Liberty planes.

High and fast they move past admiring infantry, turning in the sunlight like silver fish in a bowl. To their bellies were hung their bombs. They suggested suckling pigs. In each plane were two hooded men, a pilot and an observer. The observer unhooks the bombs. The same moment he takes photographs showing what the bombs do. The fleet found Montmedy a fair target.

The railroad yards were chocked with trains. One train had over 100 cars in it. Wagon roads leading into the town were clogged with trucks. The bombers were greeted with a terrific burst from the anti-aircraft as they hovered over the town. None of them were hit.

One youngster came back with a story of a strange gun that seemed to erupt five great balls of fire. The flyers had never seen anything like it before. None of the balls came anywhere near the machines.

From a considerable height the bombers cut loose their explosives. One set with a fearful roar right in the center of the town. The Germans were manifestly in panic while the raid lasted. They have never gone in for daylight bombing much themselves.

An expedition made an aerial prowl over Beaumont yesterday after liberally bombing the premises. American infantrymen got in there today.

It is at Montmedy that American prisoners taken by the German Fifth Corps are held. Yesterday these dispatches regarding deserters from the German line told of a number of American soldiers in a prison cage there.

The flyers say they did not see the cage. It was pretty difficult for them to distinguish the objects because the German guns were very active. No flyers came out to offer battle, however.

The bombers roved around back of the clouds as high as 14,000 feet, watching for opportunities to dodge out through the rift and let go a chunk of explosives.

Finally, when the work was done, they flew back into the south again, passing over Liggett's men, leaving Montmedy seething like an agitated beehive.

It is announced by our air service that since the beginning of the present drive, 129 enemy planes have been gathered in. America's first pursuit group, which includes Eddie Rickenbacker,[64] the American ace of aces, has brought down a total of 174 since its organization. Today the American flyers are among the greatest in the world. They had trouble at the beginning, but, like the rest of the army, they have "arrived."

Lieutenant L. C. Holden,[65] of the First Pursuit Group, went out and speared one of those fat observation balloons for himself this morning.

November 3, 1918. [Delayed] With the American First Army

The eyes of the American army peeked far behind the scenes of the German front Sunday. They saw a mighty disorder on the back of the stage. Flocks of speedy Spads that look like great wasps, with Uncle Sam's stars encircled by a ring painted on the sides, buzzed out ahead of Hunter Liggett's fast-moving infantrymen, poking their inquiring noses deep into districts recently held by the Germans.

They came back reporting that everywhere the enemy seems to be hastily gathering up his war props and legging it for the misty border of his home country. His retreat before the wild dash of Liggett's men is taking on the aspect of a stampede.

The American flyers said the roads below them were undulating with marching troops heading out the other way.

"He's moving his aerodromes back with the rest. We didn't see anything of 'Jerry,'" announced one young Yankee scout disappointedly as he un-hooded himself from his throbbing plane and stretched his six feet of fur-padded sinews. He meant they hadn't encountered any German airmen. Twenty-five American fighting planes floated out over the German-held town of Stenay and dumped four tons of explosives on it. Geysers of flame spurted below them as a huge ammunition dump in the town took fire. The bombers themselves felt the shock of the explosion as they careened aloft.

A lot of German troops were being concentrated in Stenay, so the pursuit planes drifted low and drenched the roads with machine gun fire. It was like kicking into an ant hill.

Great gray patches that represented German soldiers scattered in every direction. Quite a few more gray patches did not join and scatter. They remained on the roads. The war was over for them forever.

Long lines of trucks and wagons that had been moving without friction were suddenly all a-snarl. The bombers then emptied a few scuttlesful of explosives on the towns of Sommanthe, Vaux, Beauclere, and Beaufort, which were thickly peopled with German soldiers. Some of the pursuit planes stabbed a big pot-bellied observation balloon with their machine gun bullets, crumbling it up like empty sausage skins.

It was one of the most successful air raids conducted by Americans. In the meantime, in the marshy fields below, Liggett's men were slashing steadily ahead. They began the third day of the drive as usual, at dawn. After a day of rain, the sun came out as if to light a triumphant way for the Americans, but it was soggy underfoot.

Shells and bullets hitting into the wet ground tossed up little spurts of water and blobs of mud. There is a place called Barricourt, which was originally supposed to be the extreme objective in this particular shove. Here the Germans attempted to make a stand. They stuck there with their machine guns going at full blast, making a noise like hundreds of motorcycles in a close race until a bunch of American soldiers were on top of them.

The Americans came with fixed bayonets. In this place called Barricourt, which is not much of a place, a pitched battle was fought. The soldiers still talk about the woman prisoner who has been reported captured by the Americans. It is said she was fighting in the German front line, in soldier's clothes. Rumors keep floating around that she really exists, but no one has been found who will admit having seen her.

Every bunch of German prisoners that go tramping down the roads is closely scanned for feminine features. Among them are mere boys and bearded men, bespectacled fellows of scholarly aspects, but so far none that looks like a woman has appeared.

Late in the afternoon one lone German airman appeared high above the American back lines, taking a leisurely look at things. He sailed along placidly as if out for a pleasant afternoon stroll, up and down the air aisles.

Presently the whole countryside below him broke into staccato of coughing. Shells began popping about his ears. Acres of air around him were soon smudged with spots of smoke. None of our pursuit planes was around when he first showed up. Only a couple of observation planes were in sight.

One of them turned and tore for the region where our fighting planes were hanging out. Compared to the speed of the German scout it was like a fat man lumbering uphill against a jackrabbit, but the sluggish aerial Paul Revere carried his message of alarm home all right.

Soon our Spads began streaming out of the horizon like ducks in flight. From the little towns on the roadsides and the fields below, doughboys, truck drivers, pioneers, road builders, engineers, French Poilus, and farmers, pausing in their occupation, looked up to the flock of American planes, which were moving afar, covering scores of miles.

The German fled in the direction of Germany with the Spads on his tail. Finally all faded from view behind a cloud. The German's fate has not been reported as yet.

Wherever Liggett's men hit Sunday they drove through. They continued hitting along their twenty-mile front. One corps captured 4,000 prisoners in the last twenty-four hours, including a couple of dignified majors with their staffs. The majors punctiliously saluted all passing American officers as they marched back to a prison cage, getting salutes in return.

One man who was captured was a messenger who had been sent back from a point eighteen miles in the rear of the German lines with orders to discover why the line was breaking. Two other messengers were gathered in while hunting their battalion's post of command.

Early in the morning the enemy was sending high explosives against the American troops in the vicinity of Buzancy. He also tried to get up on them with machine guns but failed. Buzancy is well behind our lines.

There was a big artilleryman working one of the American guns, which was throwing chunks of metal into the German lines Sunday afternoon beyond Buzancy. Every time he pulled the lanyard he was heard to say something that was lost in the roar of the gun. A curious chap got over close enough to catch the Negro's words, and this is what he was saying with each shot:

"Mistah Kaisah, count youah men!"

November 3, 1918. With the American First Army

Along the battle lines in France tonight and stretching back behind that front, at the fighting wall, are bivouacking nearly 1,000,000 American veterans.

This statement has no reference to the total number of American soldiers overseas, which is more than twice 1,000,000. It means men tried and tempered by fire, desperate and confident. It means what it says—veterans.

They constitute one of the most formidable fighting machines the world has ever seen. They form the greatest army of experienced warriors America has had since the sixties.

It may be difficult for mothers and fathers in America to realize that the boys they saw leaving home and hearth a little more than a year ago, wholly unversed in the business of war and unsophisticated in the ways of the world, today are classed as crack battle troops. But such is the case.

They served their apprenticeship on the field. They have become historic in the annals of the greatest war ever fought. They are master hands at the game.

Half a dozen American divisions, made up of boys and men, who a few short months ago were clerks, artisans, bartenders, waiters, collegians, teamsters, brokers, messenger boys, ballplayers, and newspapermen, are rated by military experts and their enemies, who ought to know, along with the flower of the continental soldiery.

One German, who has fought against nearly all Allied crusaders, declared the other day when he was captured by the Americans that the German veterans would rather meet any troops than the American First Division.

The First Division has been through all the big shows, as the fights are called, in which the Americans have figured. It is the old fox of the Yankee divisions at fighting the Germans.

This story is written to impress upon American readers the fact that our army, which is opposed tonight by the pick of the Kaiser's troops, is respected by the Germans as an army of real veterans which has long since passed the days of experimentation and doubt.

It is true that it is steadily fed from the reservoirs of recruits who are pouring into France by boatloads daily, but it is sinewed and muscled by men who have been through all those pathways of hell which led through Soissons and Chateau Thierry to the Marne, on up through the Argonne to the Meuse.

It is an army plentifully bestrewn with Distinguished Service Crosses, Croix de Guerre, and other marks of great valor. It is a war-wise army. The men are a counterpart of the men who followed Jackson, Lee, Longstreet, Grant, Sherman, and Meade a half century ago.

They have seen comrades die beside them. They have been through mud and blood, filth, cold, and hunger. They have seen suffering. They have experienced suffering. They are veterans. They know how to fight methodically and effectively. They know all the oldest established ways of fighting. They have introduced many innovations. Moreover, they fight with a dash and spirit that has astounded the enemy.

Nothing ever seems to dampen their enthusiasm. It is always the strongest ingredient of their work. They are for the most part men who will return promptly to civil life, to their old peaceful pursuits, once the war is over. But now they are soldiers, with an amazing discipline, devoted to soldiering with the same whole-heartedness with which they followed whatever occupations they had before the war.

No one would have believed you could take an East Side paper-box maker who had never been off Manhattan Island and inside of a year make him into an expert modern soldier.

It has been done. Bookkeepers have been transformed into some of the greatest machine gunners ever seen. Artillerymen have been made out of Wall Street clerks. Over these have been placed officers who but recently followed employments as prosaic as the men, and they are admitted to be among the best officers in any part of the world where soldiering is more than a profession.

They are American veterans. Big trucks go rumbling down the roads apparently packed with new recruits. They wear uniforms manifestly new and most manifestly poor fitting. They are newly shod with clumsy footgear for the trenches. Their puttees are new. They seem brand new in every respect.

One marvels at the tenacity with which the Americans are rushing such crude material forward. Closer examination discloses V-shaped service stripes on the left arm indicating at least six months, frequently a year or a year and a half of service.[66]

Many wear wound stripes on the other arm. Some have two. Then the observer realizes this is a division of American veterans going back in after it has been refitted back of the lines. Only the fact that many of the men carry new French canteens indicates that they are other than recruits. This in itself proves that the "vets'" supply of American canteens is temporarily exhausted, so the men who lost their water bottles in battle are refitted with the queer French containers.

The Frenchmen generally use them for wine. The division I saw pass by was the famous [deleted by censor]. Its good clothes were all worn out months since. Those most recently from the States wear some insignia on their uniforms to indicate their division. One has a red diamond patch on the shoulder.[67] Another has a wildcat.[68]

The veterans are taking up this practice to some extent, but few divisions that have seen much service are called by nicknames. They are known by numbers. The "Rainbow Division" is never called anything but the Forty-Second. New England's Twenty-Sixth insists upon the nickname "Yankee Division."

Some old divisions have changed entirely from their original personnel, as for instance the Manhattan Seventy-Seventh, which is now made up of men from Montana and Oregon as well as New York but remains in popular mind the "Big Town's own."

The replacements are now given final battle preparations behind the lines. The last few days have been sunshiny and pleasant. The country close to the front presented scenes reminiscent of Upton, Dix, and other training camps in the States.

Recruits were being instructed in machine gunnery and how to take cover by men who were themselves raw hands a short time back. Between breaks in their own gunfire practice the rookies could hear the mumble of the guns at real work. Occasionally they could see puffs of smoke against the clear sky where shrapnel and shells were seeking hostile planes. Around them they could see crosses marking the resting places of gallant soldiers, for generally a training field of a battalion has been fought over time and again.

Always there is rumbling past them a procession of troops, trucks, tanks, and ambulances.

November 4, 1918. [Delayed] With the American First Army

"Old Pound-'em" Liggett's men Monday night held the heights commanding the towns of Montmedy and Longuyon, as well as Conflans. These are railroad centers of vast importance to the Germans. They are piled high with German supplies. They are alive with German troops.

Tonight they are within reach of the fiery lash of the American big artillery pieces. Strung along the hills dominating these towns and across the flatlands on either side are men from Texas, Oklahoma, Kansas, Missouri, Colorado, New Mexico, New York, the District of Columbia, and Maryland. The old rebel yell was heard over the fields of France as the boys from Virginia climbed the heights along with the rest. They are all a part of the army which Germany said would never get here in time—the army which Germany admitted today in her communique had "broken" the German line and caused a German retreat.

They sleep in dugouts still littered with German belongings and in shell holes still warm from German bodies. When it comes time for bivouac, Liggett's men find it easier to chase the Germans out of their positions than to build new ones. Men of the National Army[69] made up the line which rushed the heights Monday.

This time a year ago, most of the latter were wearing derby hats instead of the steel helmets under which they fought today and which make hard pillows for their heads tonight.

In three days they have shoved the Germans back twelve miles on an eighteen-mile front. They have taken about twenty villages. Most of these villages are being made into roads by American pioneers, as one of them explained today. They used shell-crushed stones, which once formed picturesque old houses, to pound into the highways and to provide a firm foundation for the interminable American caravans of trucks bearing supplies, trying desperately to keep up with the flying troops.

Many historic towns are ground into the roads now. The men in the front line are caked with mud from head to foot. It was clear again overhead today, but the path of war again led over soft ooze. The infantrymen went along kicking huge hunks of mud from their feet between shots. Occasionally they would have to stop and "unshell" themselves from their coating, made of the soil of France. One lone doughboy came down the road just behind the battle line, herding a bunch of German prisoners.[70] One of the prisoners accidentally dropped a photograph from his pocket. It proved to be a photograph of the Kaiser. The doughboy glanced at it, then gave it a kick.

Another prisoner raised and looked at the picture, then proceeded carefully to stamp the features of his beloved ruler deep into the mud with his heavy military boots.[71] It was such tough going over the fields that many soldiers threw off about everything they carried except rifles and ammunition.

Private Stephan Doyle, former Washington-Jefferson baseball player from Sharon, Pennsylvania, was discovered snoozing in a hole which had been carved out of the mud by a huge shell. His

A column of mule-drawn wagons stuck in the mud. *Courtesy of Library of Congress*

main topic of conversation was the bravery of his captain, a former Presbyterian minister from Culpeper, Virginia, named Hooper.[72]

Steve's admiration for this valiant man of God was so great he could not talk of anything else, but when the ex-Reverend Hooper was located in another watery shell hole he spoke enthusiastically of Steve. Fighting is so intimate along the American line, even battalion headquarters are pitched in shell holes. By day it snows machine gun bullets up there. By night the German artillery holds ear-splitting conferences with the American guns. A bunch of American soldiers were sleeping last night in a small shed in a town just taken by them. They were of the National Army. A big shell screamed through the shed. No man woke up. Only the chaplain had his eyes open to testify to the occurrence.

Lieutenant William W. Dawson,[73] of Cleveland, graduate of Ohio Wesleyan College, was following the troops as an observer, having been assigned to that duty for the purpose of completing his education as an officer. He had only a pistol. A gang of German machine gunners rushed up to him while the line was advancing and surrendered to him, much to his astonishment. Some Germans seem only too anxious to give up whenever they had a chance.

There was a detachment of them handling a machine gun in front of one town taken today when our soldiers swung up across the field. While fully 3,000 yards away, when the Germans were vague dots against the horizon, our snipers took pot shots at them. The Germans suddenly took on the appearance of shadows outlined against the distant trees. They had their hands in the air and were yelling "Kamerad." When the Americans reached them they found the snipers' shots had killed three. In the dugouts from which the Germans were routed, the Americans found all manner of stuff looted from towns. At one place there were a lot of French books dating back centuries, gorgeously bound. They probably came from some old chateau and must have been very valuable.

"Reggie" Foster's pioneers, moving up with the line, have collected 500 suits of steel armor used by the German snipers. The armor will turn away machine gun or rifle bullets. It protects the body from the neck to the knees.[74] An enormous mass of German military supplies is being piled up.

November 4, 1918. With the American First Army

It was a long crawl to the summit of Hill 360. But the American foot soldiers got there. They reached it yard by yard, moving much of the way on their bellies. Hill 360 will not loom in future histories of this war, but it has supplied one of the most demonical combats east of the Meuse.

It is a timbered hummock north of Belleau Wood. It looks much the same as scores of other hills rising out of the landscape in this section of France. Most of these hills have no particular name, so they are numbered for war map purposes.

Hill 360 has an elevation commanding the country for miles around. The Germans had done enough digging on it to provide the foundation for a Woolworth building.[75] They had turned it into a fort, ribbing its sides with steel and concrete. They lived there under the ground.

It was like a great hive. They delved deep into the hills with dugouts. They freckled the hills with shell-proofs. Trenches furrowed its wooded sides.

In front of all this the Germans hung a curtain of machine gun fire, which was rarely lifted. Seven times one day the Americans assaulted this position. Again and again they moved out of the mist from the flatlands below and started creeping up the sides, each time gaining a little more ground. It was slow work.

It was like rooting up a prairie dog village one hole at a time. Steadily the Yankees gained, however. They went up hand over hand, fairly springing the Germans out of their subterranean defenses with gun and grenade fire until finally they swarmed to the top of the ridge. There they are now.[76]

November 6, 1918. With the American First Army

One division of General Hunter Liggett's corps, which is whaling away at the Germans over a flaming front of twenty miles, encountered some old neighbors today.

They found themselves fighting the same division of German Regulars which they had met in the Soissons battle.

It is a matter of record that the Americans now hold two decisions over their opponents. Neither side was quite the same today as on the occasion of their first meeting. Both presented new faces, but there were rough old-timers left to recall the initial encounter.

The Americans were comparatively inexperienced at Soissons, while the Germans were veteran hands at the game. Today the Americans were as much sophisticated in the business of battle as the Kaiser's Regulars. It was quite a struggle when they hooked up again.

Hunter Liggett saw his great army "kick off" this morning. He is a big paunchy man, with a big mustache such as the old-time officers of the cavalry used to wear. The mustache is now frosted by years. So is his hair. He is a jovial soul and is the idol of the men who have followed him from Chateau-Thierry to the Argonne.

The American artillery built a smoke barrage in front of the Germans before the foot soldiers went across. It broke shells the size of a cuspidor over the German lines, these shells vomiting thick, black smoke.

Presently they had a smoky wall painted along the horizon almost the entire length of the line. Before the echoes of the bursting shells had died away into the minor throbbing of rifle and machine gun fire, the American infantry were popping out of the smoke upon the Germans.

It was a middling tough job on the front line, but it was almost as tough for the men back in reserve. The Germans dropped high explosives back that way by the wagon loads.

Our men moved around smoking cigarettes. Most of them had on new yellow jerkins,[77] which has recently been issued to the soldiers. They are sleeveless jackets of leather worn over the coats. Some men were in the replacements who had but recently joined their outfits. They were seeing their first big fight. But the majority was enacting a scene quite familiar to them.

There is all the difference in the world between green troops and old-timers. Wounded "green-uns" when brought back to the dressing stations always have the wildest tales of battalions and even whole divisions cut to pieces or wiped out. They are telling up at the front of a story of a dialogue between a chaplain of an Irish-American regiment and an old sergeant who was carried in on a litter.

"How's fighting, O'Malley?" asked the chaplain.

"Not bad, Father," said the sergeant.

"It's lucky you only got a wound in the leg," said the chaplain.

"Well, Father, you see it's the pack that protects you," said the sergeant.

"Then why did you throw yours away?" demanded the priest.

"I didn't throw it away."

"Now, O'Malley, where's that pack?" persisted the chaplain.

"If you must know," said the sergeant, "they shot it off me. But it took them a devil o' a lot o' shots to do it."

November 6, 1918. With the American First Army

American soldiers in the hands of the Germans as prisoners of war are worked daily from 9 to 12 and from 2 to 6, according to some German deserters, who have drifted over from the enemy lines. They say they deserted because they heard the Americans give their prisoners good treatment. The Germans don't hold many Americans, but the deserters say there is a cage at the town of Montmedy containing a few. They say the cage is about ten minutes' walk from the railroad station at Montmedy.

The American prisoners are housed in barracks, according to the deserters' story. They have no markings aside from oval disks made of metal, which they wear on their caps. These disks are numbered. They are given two German blankets and get about the same food the German soldiers get, which is none too good, judging from what the prisoners in American hands say. The American prisoners have German mess kits and sleep in double-tiered bunks.

The deserters state the Americans are interrogated by German officers as they are cleared through the cages. One American who had handled a machine gun was closely questioned by a German artillery colonel as to the working of our guns. The officer commented that it was obviously not as good as the German make. The deserters say when they left, the Americans were building some neat barracks.

November 6, 1918. With the American First Army

Smith's Thirty-Sixth Division comes from Texas and Oklahoma. After Le Jeune's[78] famous American division had played an important part with Gouraud's French army in smashing the Germans east of Vouziers, the men from the Lone Star State relieved it.

Since then the Texans have been having a good-sized section of war all to themselves. Little has been printed about them because little comes out. But they've had tough fighting for breakfast, dinner, and supper during the past few weeks. They have captured numerous important little positions, including some heights greatly desired by the corps commander.

He was so delighted with the work of the Southwesterners that he has commended them in his orders.

November 7, 1918. [Delayed] With the American First Army

The shade of Old Stonewall Jackson must have gazed down on the burning town of Sedan tonight (Thursday) with grim satisfaction. The military tactics evolved by the bulldog of the Confederacy and passed on by him through the Virginia Military Institute to this generation of American fighting men have brought the mud-caked doughboys from God's country to the outskirts of this ancient town. Even as the German agents were hurrying from Berlin with their white flag, Hunter Liggett's iron brigades were trampling triumphantly over the old battlefield of Sedan, clutching eagerly at the historic city itself.

Now they lie in Sedan, awaiting another dawn. Towers of flame rise from a score of great fires all over the city. In the yellowish light, gray old buildings stand out in weird light against the darkness before the eyes of Liggett's men. They are the same men, or exactly like the same men, who for forty-three days have been pushing the Germans out of France. They have reached the apex of the decisive battle of four years of war.

Many years separate Sedan and Yorktown, but just as the French played an important part of the winning of the decisive battle in the American Revolution, so the Americans have played an extremely important part in the decisive conflict for France.

Lineal descendants of men who fought at Yorktown with Rochambeau's regiment were in Sedan tonight, with the light of the burning town glinting on their bayonets.

These are men of the famous Rainbow Division, drawn from nearly every state in the Union.

On the same battle line with them is Manhattan Island's polyglot Seventy-Seventh Division, the heroes of the Argonne Forest. It is the Forty-Second, or Rainbow Division, however, which is actually in the town celebrated as the place where the Germans once swaggered truculently as victor over France.

Long, long ago Stonewall Jackson put into effect the idea of using infantry practically the same as cavalry, without horses, pushing it over the ground at great speed to the very limit of human endurance.

There's never been any infantry like Jackson's until Hunter Liggett's soldiers came along and tramped over twenty-five miles for seven days across man-murdering country, through a living wall of opposition, ribbed with artillery, upholstered by machine guns.

There is a mild-looking, retiring man at American headquarters named Colonel George C. Marshall Jr.,[79] who comes from Pittsburgh, Pennsylvania, who was graduated from the Virginia Military Institute, where Stonewall Jackson was a teacher.

This man Marshall was chief of operations of Liggett's forces. It was Marshall who had much to do with the planning of operations against Sedan, and he turned to the great master of all infantrymen for the general scheme.

"Drive the infantry" was the word. They picked all of Liggett's crack divisions for the driving. They became, in effect, flying columns. The infantry movement, it is apparent, must be slow on account of the difficulty of keeping up the supply trains. Liggett's men were given emergency rations and told to hang on to them because if they didn't they might have to go hungry.

When the American soldier gets into battle he generally unburdens himself, and the field rations go with the rest when he unloads. Liggett's men lugged their "cuisines" on their backs. American officers figured they had a big advantage in the fact their divisions were fresh and better than the Germans, which theory proved correct.

The American army on the move. *Courtesy of National World War I Museum and Memorial, Kansas City, Missouri, USA*

Day by day, Liggett's men out-marched and outfought the Germans. Motor trucks were constantly utilized to push them forward. The first day this scheme was tried it caused a big sensation, then a laugh, throughout the army. The idea of chasing the enemy with trucks struck the American sense of humor, but it was a big success.

Another system used is called "leap frogging." When one division got fagged out or scattered so it was hard to handle, another division was rolled up ahead without interruption and the fagged division followed in reserve.

Not until the night of November 4–5 did they have to pass the first division through. Another was passed along the following night. Still another went through in daylight, November 6. It was this system that gained twenty-five miles toward Sedan and resulted in the liberation of a couple of thousand French citizens who had been penned up in the towns for months and even years, besides freeing 700 square kilometers of French territory.

Meantime the Americans took 7,000 prisoners and a vast amount of swag of war. When it first started, the American front was eighteen kilometers (eleven and one-quarter miles) wide. Now it is forty-eight kilometers, or about thirty miles, wide.

This is due to the fact that it extends along the river Meuse, which winds in and out. The mass of the attack was directed at Sedan, though as a matter of fact Sedan is not in the American sector. It will have to be turned over to the French as soon as they get there.

Our men pushed up there first. Three of Liggett's divisions, made up largely of veterans of the long drive up from the Marne, converged on Sedan. They were the famous First, the Forty-Second, and New York's Seventy-Seventh. There never was any doubt as to the result after the first day.

The decisive battle of the seven days was at the Bois de Barricourt, which was taken by the Eighty-Ninth Division. This division is made of National Army men from Kansas and Missouri. The Jayhawkers and the Missourians had a terrific fight. The town of Barricourt had been taken with the bayonet.

Then the drive on to Sedan started. About two-thirds or three-fourths of the town is north of the Meuse. Most of the big buildings are on that side. The river bends in a sort of loop, and in the arm of this loop are a lot of buildings. The Germans had destroyed all bridges across the river and dynamited the roads.

At 4 o'clock yesterday the Forty-Second reached Wadelincourt, in the southern outskirts of Sedan. There they are now. The Germans are in the northern part. They have many troops there. On the heights northeast of the town is a lot of artillery. The enemy appears determined to make strong resistance, but the "Rainbows" have a foothold that it not likely to be shaken loose. The flatlands along the river have been flooded. The "Rainbows" got bridges across under tremendous difficulties. The Seventy-Seventh is beyond the river from the towns of Autrecourt to Allicourt.

All American troops have from two to three days' rations and plenty of ammunition. Liggett's men have practically cut the German armies on the Western Front in two. The Germans now have only one line of communication left between them.

November 7, 1918. With the American First Army

In old Sedan tonight they can hear the rumble of the American guns. General Hunter Liggett's army today drove far through the dripping hills of France toward the ancient stronghold, where one of the famous battles of history was fought, and where the Germans exacted the arbitrary terms of France that may be coming home to roost.

Sedan is now not over [deleted] miles beyond the muzzles of the forward American guns. The German fights with his back to the wall. These have been big days for America. They have been big days for all the Allies' arms. Every day General Hunter Liggett's men began at dawn where they had left off the night before. By dusk last Saturday they had ripped through what is known as the Freya Stellung, which is believed to be the last organized defense the Germans have in France. They had crushed all enemy opposition along the whole line.[80]

So fast did the Germans fall back before Liggett's columns on Saturday, the leathery doughboys finally grew leg-weary from pushing over the grassy ground, made slushy by the rain.

One division commander had a happy inspiration. Up came a strong battery of muddy motor trucks driven by almond-eyed French Cochin Chinamen and devil-may-care American chauffeurs. The tired-footed soldiers were loaded in, bag and baggage. They were packed in with their rifles and rig and soon found themselves much like the passengers of a Bronx subway express during the rush hour.

Then away went the trucks, reeling along the spongy roads in pursuit of the German infantrymen, showing white teeth in a wide grin. It was like a caravan of elephants lumbering off into the rain and fog toward the borderland of Germany. The last heard from the strange cavalry that day was that it had been unable to catch up with the Germans.

"Eddie" Rickenbacker, the American flying ace, came in this evening with a baffled expression on his countenance. He said he had not seen them, even from the air, and he had flown pretty well over the German lines, or at least where they're supposed to be.

Pershing[81] once chased Villa[82] 500 miles with his infantry in motor trucks. Gallieni[83] saved Paris by hustling all hands out in taxicabs. But probably never before was a whole army pursued by another army under gasoline power.

The headquarters of the different army corps engaged in the chase suddenly found themselves marooned. They had to make quick shifts to get somewhere near the troops.

Old Hunter Liggett himself was seen in the afternoon hurrying forward in the direction of his flying army. He rode in a big, gray, open automobile. It was doing sixty miles an hour over a road as slippery as a soaped chute.

The famous American leader bulked in the tonneau with one aide. The windshield of the car carried three stars, the insignia of Liggett's new rank as lieutenant general. The grizzled fighter passed big bunches of trophies testifying to the prowess of his men. German prisoners fresh from the front stood along the road, stolidly waiting for orders from the guards.

It was a pretty good trick to catch prisoners in this sort of fighting. They could not be surrounded. They had to be bagged in the open like rabbits.

The country over which Liggett's army fought is mainly wooded, with inevitable hills cropping up at frequent intervals. The shrubbery is now all brown and gold. It is not as thick as that in the Argonne. It's more like a park that has not been carefully tended for years.

Here and there they had to sneak away and hide themselves from the monster—war. Most of them failed.

From behind the hills and trees the Germans worked their machine guns against the oncoming Americans. Liggett's men hunted them like boys hunting squirrels. They moved from tree to tree, from cover to cover, silently, relentlessly.

Their forms showed faint and shadowy in the rain. There were brisk spells of fighting through the early part of the battle, but presently the Americans discovered that it would take a Houdini[84] to find the enemy.

The Germans were on the jump. In what is called the Bois de Barricourt, which is a section of thick woods, the Germans made a machine gun stand, but the Americans scarcely hesitated. They brought their line up to Barricourt itself. To the right of that village stands what is left of the town of Villers-Devant-Dun. Here the Germans stopped, rallied briefly, and started to counterattack.

Vague lines of gray figures in round caps and funny long-tailed coats bobbed up against the skyline like gnomes. But suddenly they melted and vanished before the chattering machine guns and carefully aimed rifles of the Americans.

Far behind the Yankee infantrymen thumped the big Yankee guns. Our artillery was tossing shells through the trees into the German lines. These shells broke with a muffled sound, as if the rain had affected the voices of the cannon.

The country over which Liggett's troops advanced was cluttered with the garbage of war. German overcoats hung on the bushes. German rifles, broken and bent, were found half-buried in mud. German knapsacks, canteens, and boxes of rations could be gathered up by the basketfuls.

There were the dead, of course. However, the dead vanish rapidly from the battlefields nowadays. Burying parties are prompt. It is better so.

The American casualties were amazingly light—so light, in fact, it seemed as if some special grace had watched over Liggett's men as they drove through the rain.

Particular attention had been paid to the arrangements for handling the wounded. They were hurried back to the field hospitals in speedy little motor ambulances of a celebrated American make that dodged about through the welter of traffic behind the lines with astonishing rapidity.

Undated. With the American First Army

The long riders of the American Second Cavalry were galloping after the retreating Germans on the final stage of the fierce pursuit which swept Liggett's men close to Sedan.

Cavalry hasn't been used much by the Americans in France. The Second was in action at St. Mihiel. Part of the Third, which with the Sixth constitutes about all the horsemen there are here, has also seen service, but not until the Germans began to make a race of it could they be utilized in the battle which will probably go down in history as the battle of the Argonne and Meuse.

The Second was then hurried up. The Germans were going back so fast it was getting hard to keep contact with them. It was about the third period, when Liggett began loading his infantrymen in motor trucks. The cavalry were the first Americans to enter the town of Beaumont, which is practically the beginning of the battlefield of Sedan.

A young lieutenant went in with a bunch of mounted scouts. The Germans opened on them with machine guns and shot several horses under riders. They all dismounted and took cover and fought the Germans off until the infantry arrived. Liggett has withdrawn his troops which made the rush to Sedan. He has turned the sector over entirely to the French.[85]

The French were moving up into Torcy, which is practically in Sedan, while the Americans were going in by another way. It was a combination affair between the two armies. Now that Sedan sector is occupied by the French.

November 9, 1918. [Delayed] With the First American Army

There is a battered old hotel in a little town close behind the American lines, into which all the news of the day floats out of the air. It's a town so churned up by shells they'll not be able to sort it out and piece it together again in years. It is the temporary headquarters of an outfit. There the guns are parked along the cluttered street, each gun with its name painted in large letters on the shields, after a whimsical custom of the American artillery.

"Maggie O'Leary" has "Old Dutch Cleanser" for a neighbor. They say "Maggie" has raised a considerable amount of Hades with the Germans in her day. Upstairs in the hotel, artillery officers have their rooms, whose paneless windows overlook the street through which the great parade of war passes in the muddy pomp of clouds and losswords every minute of the day and night.[86]

Several officers are slim-limbed fellows late of the polo-playing social stratum of Long Island. Their existence since coming out in the lines a few days ago has been rather hum-drum but would be still worse did they not get their news regularly, as if a boy were dashing in every few minutes with the latest "extras."

The wireless operators sit in dugouts when the batteries are in position. They get firing orders from observers and keep up their headpieces these days plucking news from the ether as it passes over the air waves from point to point. The headpieces are strange-looking contraptions, suggesting divers' caps. There is nothing that the artilleryman can do to hear all the war news as it trickles in upon the front line. They know all about what the peace parliamentaires are doing, even before it is heard at headquarters. They get both German and French news.

In spite of this, however, they were somewhat discontented today because no news concerning the American election had passed through the air, which is given over almost exclusively to war matters.

Some Negro soldiers gathered in a wrong rumor concerning the matter of peace last night. They didn't get it from the artillerymen, because the news secured by the artillerymen is uniformly correct. The Negroes heard that it was all over and time for shouting. Whereupon they proceeded to start a celebration.

They had gathered up a lot of flares and Very light[87] shells and explosives of one kind or another which had been discarded by the Germans in their hurried retreat and began turning them loose.

For a time, the sky in their immediate vicinity was ablaze, and it sounded as if new battles had started back of the lines.

The celebration was, however, suppressed before the alarm became very general.

November 10, 1918. Nancy, France

Heloise, the beautiful waitress at the Café Liegeoise, left a party of cash customers flat when the first bomb went off.

They had just finished their soup course. The Café Liegeoise is a sort of local "Jack's"[88] in Nancy.[89] At the second bomb the customers forgot their peevishness over Heloise's rash departure and hastily decided to locate in an abri or cave, in which she had found sanctuary.

They saved money by not waiting to pay for the soup. No one was left to receive it, anyway. Thus, night life in Nancy came to temporary halt. There's only a couple hours of it, anyway, these nights. "Jerry" is too apt to drive over the town and let fall some of his pet bombs.

He hadn't been over it lately until this night in question. He appeared around 5:30, which is about the time the night life begins. Before it was safe for the folks to come out of the cellars, it was too late for dinner.

In the old days Nancy was one of the gayest cities in France, not barring Paris. German officers used to flock over from the famous stronghold of Metz, which is only about twenty-five miles away, and infest the cafés.

For the past four years Nancy has always been within sound of the guns. The Germans have bombed it rather frequently, but the damage has been slight as compared with other towns. This night one bomb set fire to and burned the library of the university.

Old Stanislas, King of Poland, whose gigantic bronze statue[90] stands in the center of the town, looking out upon his gorgeous palace, made Nancy one of the most beautiful cities in the world. The café life has always been a feature of Nancy.

As the Liegeoise has been likened to "Jack's," so the restaurant Stanislas might be compared to Delmonico's.[91] It is one of four famous restaurants in the world.[92] It is not as gay as others. Its waiters are staid old chaps, most of whom have seen military service.

Young aviator princes of the American army flaunt their new fur-lined coats around the Liegeoise. The older officers affect the Stanislas. You can knock a hole through a twenty-dollar bill with a dinner at either place without much trouble. Yet, the prices, generally speaking, are not higher, if as high, as those of Broadway's gilded palaces. They are much lower in some respects.

Only Rockefeller[93] could pay a Broadway check for dinner with champagne that can be had in Nancy at a fairly reasonable figure. They hook you for a cover charge of ten cents in both the Stanislas and Liegeoise. A fellow blew into Stanislas the other night and had a dozen oysters at ninety cents a dozen; a portion of fried sole, for the same amount; roast partridge at $2.80; green peas for sixty cents; potatoes, forty cents; salad, fifteen cents; ice cream, fifty; and coffee, ten.

He was a hearty eater. The average fish portion runs around a dollar, according to the way it's cooked. Entrees vary from brains in butter at sixty cents, to pigeon with green peas at $1.25. These figures, of course, are translated from French.

For sixty cents in the Stanislas one can get a piece of beef steak with fried potatoes that would cost twice as much in the States. A ham omelet costs eighty cents. Brussels sprouts are thirty-five cents. Ices are largely made of substitutes for the usual ingredients, but it's hard to tell the difference. They are cheap.

The best brands of champagne cost less than half of what they do in the States. The prices in the Liegeoise run about the same as those in the Stanislas.[94]

There is no dancing at either place. There is no dancing anywhere in France. For music, guests in a Nancy café have the distant sound of the guns. It has been going on steadily for four years. It is marvelous how the restaurant people dig up supplies. They say the boss of the Stanislas hustles around all over France for that purpose. You can get most anything you order there, but often it represents a lot of research on the part of the owner. Still he is able to give you omelet with mushrooms for sixty cents, boiled lamb kidney with fried potatoes for sixty, veal or pork chops for seventy-five, and all soups for twenty cents.

No American troops are stationed at Nancy. They have few American military police here. There is a big Y.M.C.A. for soldiers.

They buried the Bishop of Nancy[95] last week. He was a very venerable and a very much loved man. Dignitaries from the Catholic Church from all over France were here for the funeral. They marched in a big procession through the narrow streets one rainy day.

There was a long line of very old priests, many carrying umbrellas. There was almost a solid block of nuns of various orders. There were hundreds of women and little children. On the sidewalk watching the somber procession were a few American doughboys. They stood at salute when the great black hearse, with the hooded horses dressed up in enormous black plumes, went past. Last Sunday Nancy held a memorial service and decorated not only the graves of the French soldiers but the graves of three Americans who were the first of Pershing's expeditionary force to fall for France.[96]

November 11, 1918. [Delayed] With the American First Army in France

On the dot of 11 o'clock this (Monday) morning, Band Sergeant Herman C. Miller led all that is left of the band of the One Hundred and Twenty-Second Field Artillery into a grove of trees on the battlefield of Laneuville and Stenay. There were about eighteen men. All come from Chicago. Miller himself in time of peace lives at No. 2615 Payne Street, Evanston, Illinois. With a switch for a baton, he gave the signal. The band struck up the "Hail to the President" march.[97]

The echo of the last shot had scarcely died away on the American front as the artillery bandsmen struck up the music. One hundred yards from the grove, Battery C, Fifty-Sixth Heavy Artillery, had just thrown a shell, the size of a baby, into the German lines from a French 155-millimeter piece. They let it go at 0:50.

There probably will be interminable arguments as to the distinction of firing the last shot at the Germans.[98] All along the line they claim to have waited until 11:59 o'clock before cutting loose. One battery rushed into position with the intention of firing the final salvo, and it seemed

Soldiers of the 105th Field Artillery after firing their last shot, November 11, 1918. *Courtesy of United States Army Heritage and Education Center*

as though the big guns were disconsolate because they could not reach the position in time.

Miller had a hard time mustering enough bandsmen to make much music. Some musicians have been killed or wounded. Others are serving as litter bearers. The band is attached to the Eighty-Ninth Division, which had rushed into Stenay a few hours before. The road over which they passed was still littered with dead horses, horribly torn by the artillery fire, and by wrecked guns and trucks.

There also were dead men on the road. Close together, almost as if they had been engaged in a hand-to-hand combat even as hostilities ceased, were a dead American officer and a German soldier.[99]

After blaring forth the march, Miller's band swung into "Watch Your Step" and "The Girlie You Love." Farther back down the line at a supply station of New York's Seventy-Seventh, another band was going full blast. This was a Negro band, attached to an engineer outfit, led by one Ferguson, a gold-toothed musician of Cincinnati. They played Sousa's[100] "Stars and Stripes Forever" with a saxophone putting in a lot of jazz.

Tonight on the front line, American soldiers are dejectedly watching the Germans in a wild celebration. The German soldiers are firing off ammunition by the ton, lighting the sky with rockets and flares. The Americans are not permitted to celebrate in that fashion.

Farther back of the lines a few flares were set off and an occasional shot was heard, but the front line regiments silently held the positions they had when hostilities ceased. They have patrols out as usual.

During the day at several places along the line, especially in the St. Mihiel sector, Germans came over to the American outposts with outstretched hands. They were all smiling jubilantly.

Doughboys loved European children.
Courtesy of United States Army Heritage and Education Center

They traded Iron Crosses, knives, helmets, and other belongings for American cigarettes. Americans talked with them frequently, but no Americans left their lines to go to the Germans. They were not allowed.

It was a curious situation, with the victors so quiet and the losers so feverishly celebrating their defeat.[101] One German said he expected to be home by Sunday. They were all unutterably and sincerely glad that the business of killing was ended. So are the Americans, for that matter, but the men in the front lines were not giving as much vociferous expression to their gladness today as the Germans.

They seemed to take it as a matter of course.

There were a few very old men and few young children in the town. A big soldier who said his name was A. C. Larsen snatched up one as soon as the order "fall out" was given and kissed it. He said he had kids of his own. The first American flag displayed at Stenay was a little one, carried by a Y.M.C.A. man, who was with the first line troops. He showed it to an old woman, who gazed at it wonderingly. Some of them obviously don't believe everything that was told them as true. They had been practically prisoners for four years.

The chateau, which was owned by Mme. Henri de Verdier, widow of a Frenchman who was famous in that part of the country, was undamaged, but all rooms were littered with belongings of German officers. While the Americans were looking the town over, a number of French officers scrambled across the Meuse and entered the town. Many houses at Stenay displayed French flags.

A woman storekeeper, who had a stock of them, insisted on giving them away to the soldiers. She wouldn't take any pay.

Company F, Sixteenth Infantry, which had the first engagement of any unit in the American army in this war, marched out of the battle line this morning, with the rest of the regiment, past the place where Miller's band was playing. There are not a great many veterans of that first engagement, which was just a raid. A fresh division was marching in as the Sixteenth came out. The old soldiers kidded the new men. They knew fighting had been suspended and were in a jovial mood.

Battery C, Sixth Field Artillery, which fired the first shot in the war, as far as the Americans are concerned, was not in the line when the finish came.

Sergeant Arch was the man who pulled the lanyard on that occasion. So far as known, he is still alive.[102]

The men of the Eighty-Ninth Division were walking through Stenay in skirmish line when 11 o'clock came this morning.[103] Stenay was about the largest town along the American front

A French woman and her daughter display their handmade flag, sewn secretly while Germans occupied the town. Never having seen an American flag, the stars are wrong and the stripes are vertical. *History of the Third Division United States Army*

for which the Yankees were fighting when the hour of the cessation of hostilities arrived. It was the headquarters of the German Crown Prince[104] during the campaign around Verdun.

The Eighty-Ninth is the division which the chief of operations of the American army credits with having broken the German line when it took the Boise de Barricourt, assuring the success of the American operations that day. It is a crack division of drafted men made up of whole regiments from Kansas and Missouri and units from Nebraska, Minnesota, Colorado, New Mexico, and other mid-Western Rocky Mountain states.

The boys knew last night, with the rest of the American forces, that hostilities would end at 11, but they went right on after Stenay.[105] The Germans had opened the floodgates of the canal there and widened the Meuse to 1,000 yards. The Eighty-Ninth crossed the footbridges. On that particular front the Germans put up a terrific fight to the last. Their artillery fire was vicious and quite accurate. They threw over heavy stuff. The last shell came along about 8 o'clock this morning.

It looked as if they had made an effort to hold Stenay until 11 o'clock. But when the American patrols got in, they found only four Germans. They were made prisoners and allowed to roam around for a time at will.

Every fresh detachment of Americans that entered the town recaptured them. Finally one became querulous about the matter and said he was sick of being taken prisoner. At 11 o'clock sharp the platoon commanders re-assembled their men in the streets of the town, in column formation. They scattered out and began finding quarters for themselves. That's about the only formality there was at the stopping of the war on that front.

Stenay was a city of old folks. A bunch of bent crones, with a doubting air about them, came out and greeted the Americans volubly. They said the Germans had taken most of the inhabitants away or scared them out by telling them that the Americans would bombard the town. This one thing the Americans studiously avoid.

They did not want to do any further damage to French cities. Stenay was scarcely touched by shells and undamaged aside from a giant causeway connecting with Launeville, which was cut in a score of places. The interior of the houses were a mess, the Germans having apparently looted everything. The first soldiers in prowled through the wonderful chateau that was the headquarters of the German Crown Prince.

Old Madame Hazard, the caretaker, was glad to see them. A number of other women were hiding in the chateau. They said the German soldiers had come to take them away, too, but a German officer, who had lived in the chateau, had told them no one was there. Tonight French soldiers marched arm in arm through the streets, singing and shouting. Some towns were lighted up for the first time in four years.

Doughboys in Stenay at 10:59 a.m., November 11, 1918. *Courtesy of United States Army Heritage and Education Center*

November 12, 1918. With the American First Army

For the benefit of certain historians, some remarks by American soldiers, uttered at one of the greatest moments in all history, are here set down. They were collected while a column of infantrymen was standing in a deserted street in the town of Stenay yesterday (Monday, November 11).

The captain in command of the troops had just glanced at his wristwatch. It was 11 o'clock. The officer called the war off for the time being. The men were looking around empty houses, kicking the mud off their shoes. Then they spoke dramatically as follows:

"Well, she's off. I wonder when they'll send us home?"

"This is a helluva-looking town. I wonder if we get anything to eat?"

"Who's got cigarettes?"

"Somebody gimme a match."

"That stuff in them bottles in that joint over there looks as if it might be good to drink."

"I wouldn't trade Topeka for this burg."

"I wish there was a first-class restaurant here."

"I wonder if that stuff in them bottles is beer? Them Heinies certainly know how to make beer."

"Well, the old war's over. I hope we hit nothing but the high places till we get back to St. Louis."

"They tell me the old Crown Prince hung out in this burg. I wonder which way that guy's running now."

"Guess I'll see what's in them bottles at that. It might be easy to take."

About that time the order came to "fall out." Then someone changed his mind and another order "fall in" was shouted:

"Hell's fire!" mumbled one man disgustedly. "I've got so all I know about this war is 'fall in' 'fall out,' and 'forward march.'"

Thus dramatically passed the most dramatic moment in that section of the American front.[106]

Twenty years ago this writer saw the end of another war in which the Americans were engaged. That was when the Eighth Corps marched into Manila. It is a coincidence that yesterday he saw men from the states represented in the lines which entered Manila among the troops that brought the Americans' part in this war to a temporary pause, at least in Stenay, the largest town before which the Yankees were fighting when the great "halt" came.

There was quite a contrast between the two scenes. Twenty years ago Coloradoans, Minnesotans, Pennsylvanians, Nebraskans, and other mid-Western and Rocky Mountain States tramped into the teeming town where some 20,000 Spaniards had laid down their arms. There was a big flag-raising and much ceremony. They went into the city in columns. They had their generals at the head.

Peyton March,[107] now one of the highest American commanders, was in a column heading the Astor Battery[108] with its funny little mountain guns. March was a captain then.

There weren't as many soldiers in the whole corps that marched imposingly into Manila that day as there are in one of the numerous veteran American divisions which rest on their arms along the wide front in France tonight.

Half a dozen machine gun companies still facing the beaten Germans could probably have taken care of the whole Manila army of occupation, minus the support of Dewey's[109] fleet.

Yet, in the main, the soldiers were much the same soldiers who entered Stenay without any ceremony whatever, coming from the same sections of the country and acting much the same. They walked into the town like skirmishers instead of a column. They were mightily unconcerned. They went in like a bunch of plumbers who had come to repair that leak.

The difference between Manila and Stenay was that Stenay was deserted save for a very few old inhabitants who came out of their houses, batting their eyes as if they had just been aroused from a long sleep.

After retaking a village, Americans celebrate with German beer and cigars. *Courtesy of United States Army Heritage and Education Center*

The steel-clad shoes of the infantrymen yesterday woke echoes for block after block of deserted houses.

Twenty years ago the streets of Manila were thick with people. Yet, twenty years ago, when the first conquering column came first to a halt in that town, the soldiers of the day looked around them, mildly curious, and one fellow gave articulation to the general thought which permeated the minds of American soldiers then as now: "Well, she's over. I wonder when in hell they'll send us home?"

November 12, 1918. With the American Armies in France

The great guns of the war still stand in their old positions among the trees behind the hills, their smooth flanks blotched with colorful efforts, now somewhat faded, of the camouflage artists.

They suggest a lot of tired, painted old women with nothing to do.

There is still much sound of war, without the effect, however, along the front. It is furnished by American and German soldiers burning up powder—most of it German—in celebrations.

The Germans started last night, the Americans being mere onlookers. Finally the Yanks, especially those in the Verdun region, decided the enemy was stealing their own Fourth of July stuff, so they cut loose themselves.

It went on all day and most of tonight. Rockets and flares kept the sky aflame, while the noise was provided by the exploding grenades and other ammunition.

Everywhere giant campfires were burning. For weeks and months the soldiers had been denied their fires until they fairly longed for them. When the opportunity came they built them extra hot.

Fires tonight run along the skyline for fully twenty miles, giving the effect of a great forest fire. At some points on the front the Germans have fallen back so far that quite a distance separates them from the Americans. At other points the opposing forces are close together.

Near Verdun the dividing line is marked by a string of campfires, with soldiers of the two armies only a few yards apart. The Americans and Germans are yelling in their lines. The military police have a lonely job just now.

One of the German officers was quite squiffy about his men fraternizing or rather attempting to fraternize with Americans.

Some German soldiers had approached the American lines with hands raised to barter for American tobacco, about which they seem fairly crazy. The doughboys were talking with them

Soldier holding a German Luger pistol.
Courtesy of Library of Congress

when a German officer appeared. At his sharp command the Germans humbly hurried away. Then the officer announced formally to an American officer, using very good English:

"There is your line and here is our line. We will keep to our respective lines."

An American soldier grumbled:

"He knows what he can do with his line. I had almost traded that Heinie out of a good Luetger pistol[110] for a sack of 'Bull.'[111] That Luetger would have been worth showing back in Portland, Maine."

November 14. 1918. [Delayed] With the American First Army

A brisk youth went bustling down the road leading to the town of Stenay this morning. He was full of business. In one hand he carried a hammer. Under his arm he had a bundle of wooden signs bearing such admonitions as:

"Do your bit."

"To the right."

"Route—Play the game. Obey the men."

These signs are seen by the hundreds along every road in the war area of France. They are for the benefit of truck drivers and teamsters. The youth's part in the great war is to tack the signs to trees and poles as fast as new routes are opened by the army. He was performing his task with enthusiasm this morning. A doughboy, who was one of the many little groups of doughboys strung along the road to Stenay, stopped the youth.

"Where are you going?" he demanded.

"I'm going into that town to tack up my signs," said the youth.

"Well, maybe you'd better wait a few minutes until we take it" was the mild suggestion of the doughboy.

Liggett's patrols are rummaging within five-eighths of a mile of Stenay tonight, but so far the town hasn't officially fallen. The patrol's job is to snoop around ahead of the columns and see what's doing. It's about as unhealthy a job as there is in the army. But patrols always get the first look at things.

There was a devilish tough job to be done in front of Stenay this morning. It fell to the engineers. The infantry has a song which runs:

"The cavalry and artillery,
And the lousy engineers,
They couldn't lick the doughboys
In a hundred thousand years."

But when the foot soldiers come to a place and they can't get over, under or around, it's always the engineers who give them a boost.

The town of Stenay is beyond the river Meuse. The river is normally about as wide as the Arkansas but it can spread out most abnormally. It is now nearly 1,000 yards wide. The Germans had knocked out some of the flood gates, anticipating our arrival. Besides, they had destroyed all bridges. Liggett's infantrymen, who are becoming semi-amphibious what with rain and mud and rivers to cross, first made bold to attempt wading the stream. They found that impracticable. The water was too deep.

The Handy Andys of the American armies got one pontoon down. A shell knocked it into splinters. The wreckage went bobbing off piecemeal down the river. The engineers got another pontoon into position, American guns putting a canopy of machine gun bullets over them while they worked. The instant there was a footing from bank to bank, advance platoons of National Army regiments rushed across under a smart fire from the Germans.

Finally three pontoon bridges were thrown over the river, and on these whole American divisions trampled across the Meuse.

Tonight Liggett's patrols are rummaging the country within five-eighths of a mile of Stenay. This is a little old provincial border town that used to have some pretense of an industrial "burg." The Germans have made it one of their important military centers. Military experts before the war believed that if Germany ever tried to break through into France without violating the neutrality of Belgium and Luxemburg, it would be at Stenay. After the engineers had given the infantrymen a lift at Stenay today, the doughboys ran into some hard fighting. The Germans are trying to hold in that vicinity but are making a poor fight of it in the face of Liggett's rush. Indications are that Stenay will be behind the American lines before many hours.

Further up the river is Sedan. It is a historic but rusty old town. Our lines are about twenty miles from there. The "casino" or club for German officers is said to be about the most important establishment in the town, but Sedan has a tremendous sentimental value.

Unless they have been sent out in the last few days, the civilians are still there. Near the town of Baulny a column of 100 German prisoners was sent back from the lines under guard of a single soldier, an Italian from New York, who spoke little English. An American officer was trying to explain to him by use of a map how to get the prisoners to a prison cage. But the Italian could not understand him.

The officer noticed a German major listening to the colloquy, smiling.

"Do you speak English?" asked the American officer.

"I do," replied the German.

"Can you understand this map?" asked the American.

"I can," nodded the major.

"Well, will you take charge of this bunch and march them to the cage?" inquired the American.

"I will," said the German, saluting.

Then he gave the commands in his own language to the prisoners, and they fell into a column of twos and tramped off to the cage. There the German major turned them over to the astonished American officers.

November 15, 1918. [Delayed] With the American-French Army

Fifteen thousand prisoners of war, just released by the Germans, marched into Verdun. It was a strange procession. Most of them were French, but there also were Russians, Italians, and some Americans. They came from all parts of the front. They wore all manner of attire. One man had on a green hat and red pants. Some even had on women's clothes. A lot of them had been prisoners for years.

They were given a great ovation by the garrison when they came in and were fed and clothed, as far as possible, at once. They didn't have to tell of their treatment by the Germans. Their very appearance related the story more eloquently than words. All prisoners held by the Germans will soon be back in their own lines, including all Americans.

Just how many Americans there are is not known, but the number is not large compared with others. It is certainly smaller by many thousands than the number taken by the Americans.

These prisoners are now employed on the roads, clearing up rubbish of war in the back areas. German prisoners can be seen on the roads almost as far back as Paris. The prisoners held the longest are easily distinguished by the fact they wear uniforms of grass green. These are old uniforms dyed with that color by the French, and issued as fast to prisoners as the clothes they had wore out.

Some Germans were prisoners so long they had not much left in the way of original uniforms except for a cap. It is understood the American Red Cross and Y.M.C.A. are planning to get through to the German prison camps and look after the American prisoners as fast as they are released.

November 15, 1918. [Delayed] Bar le Duc, France

One form of American invasion probably never contemplated by the Germans is now mobilizing in this town of Bar le Duc, famous for that species of jam which costs fifty cents a portion in the best regulated Broadway cafes. You couldn't lift fifty cents worth of jam in Bar le Duc now.

The forces assembling here constitute the press division attached to the American army in France. They are otherwise known as "Bulger's flying circus," the commander of the press division being Major Bozeman Bulger,[112] former widely known New York baseball writer. He is the chief press officer of the army.

While hostilities were on, he had his headquarters at whatever place was nearest the lines and also nearest a convenient telegraph wire. The press division has chased the army from the Marne to the Meuse. Now it follows the fighting forces on into Germany. It is reasonable to assume that the Germans are going to be considerably astonished when they get a view of the "flying circus."

The Germans are bound to make eyes when they see the press division in all its glory. The parade moves tomorrow. The roll will be twenty correspondents travelling in fifteen automobiles. With them will be ten army officers and thirty-four enlisted men.

The officers are in charge of the censorship. They included beside Bulger, Captain Gerald Morgan[113] of the field artillery, chief red pencil wielder of the department. Morgan was never able to find a blue pencil in France, so a red one had to answer his purpose. It wrought havoc in the ranks of hostile words during the last few months.

Lieutenant Arthur Hartzell,[114] formerly cable editor of the *Sun* and later with the *Times*, is assistant censor. Hartzell was acting as conducting officer with Floyd Gibbons,[115] the Chicago correspondent, when Gibbons was badly wounded in Belleau Wood. Hartzell could have escaped immediately but heroically lay with Gibbons in the wheat field for three hours to get the wounded man back.

Lieutenant Arthur John Delaney,[116] a New Yorker, is another officer in the press division. Lieutenant Conger Reynolds[117] of Iowa is still another. The division is nominally an offshoot of the intelligence department commanded by General Dennis Nolan,[118] but it works pretty independently. Probably never before in the history of American journalism has such an organized "covering" of a story been launched as the expedition which pulls out tomorrow in the wake of the army.

An American correspondent with his vehicle and personal gear. *Courtesy of Library of Congress*

The "flying circus" carries all its own paraphernalia. It has kitchen and cooks for its division mess. Every man carries his own bedding in a roll for use in the field, as it will be a couple of weeks before the army reaches a German town. Trucks will follow the division cars with the luggage of the outfit.

James P. Wilson,[119] formerly of the *St. Louis Republic*, remains behind in Bar le Duc with Glen D. Merriman,[120] a gilt-edged press operator from Pittsburgh and Chicago, to send out the product of the folding typewriters as it is relayed back by courier. Wilson and Merriman were imported by the division to handle the press. They are both enlisted men.

Fifteen thousand words a night were a cinch for them. They use American "bugs" in sending while the French operators pick away on queer contraptions that look like piano keyboards.

November 16, 1918. With the American First Army

The war is over, but many a good "inside" story that will make part of the history of America's share remains yet to be told. Here is one of them.

"You must secure a foothold on the other bank of the river immediately. The whole army is waiting on it. You must get over at all hazards."

This, in substance, was what the big wigs of the American army told the rugged old Regular with two silver stars on his shoulder who commanded a division upon the Meuse some ten days ago.

"I'll get over," was the laconic answer.

This is not an imaginary conversation. He said it. Moreover, he did what he said, for now follows the story of one of the most desperate and sanguinary struggles of the American army in France—the crossing of the Meuse.

It was what strategy experts, who pore with heavily furrowed brows over maps in every headquarters behind the line, sticking pins and little flags here and there, call a "pivotal blow."

It was, in plain language, a punch in the stomach.

Two nights later, Sedan was burning. Our troops, in the language of the military, were "sitting on Stenay" and could take it at will. Mouson was afire. A vast amount of war swag had been gathered in by the Americans. Many civilians in towns long held by the Germans had been released from the invaders' domination and were wandering about the streets of their little home towns, blinking their eyes in bewilderment like prisoners suddenly given freedom.

The German retreat beyond the Meuse was in full swing. Much of this American success goes back to the crossing of the famous crimson-tinged stream by troops of the division commander with whom this story has to do. Surely some small credit for that crossing is due to the thoughtful-looking young man with the wispy blonde "brain duster" on his upper lip.

To the headquarters of an old division commander came this young man with his hands full of blueprints and his mind full of ideas. He is Captain S. M. Smith, from the west end of St. Louis. They made him a captain not long ago for having ideas. He had traveled far over a muddy road to reach general headquarters.

The general was quartered in a wine cellar under a building in a shattered town well up to the front. Cobwebs a foot long hung from the ceiling. This general has a passion for dwelling right among his guns. His batteries encircled his headquarters. They were not a few hundred yards away either, but right close by.

There was little sleep in the neighborhood. He required his regimental commanders to have their posts of command very close to the front line. His brigade commanders were not far away. He argued that this effects a saving of life in runners and messengers.

He said he followed that system when he commanded a regiment. The old soldier has something of a reputation as a man saver. There was not much chance to economize greatly in that respect in the operation on the Meuse. The thoughtful young man laid his blueprints out on the rough table, which, with an army cot, constituted all the furnishings of the general's dugout. The prints showed in detail an invention by Colonel J. G. B. Lampert[121] of the engineers for getting troops across uncrossable rivers. Young Captain Smith represented the colonel.

Besides the prints he had notes describing the invention as a "canvas-type-portable-footbridge." It was on such a footbridge that the old general got across the Meuse. It was the first time that Lampert's invention was ever used in actual warfare; the experiments had been made on the Moselle a short time before. Smith is one of Lampert's experts on these bridges. He can produce ideas and drawings from his pockets and haversacks like a magician pulling rabbits from a hat.

No one analyzed the desperate nature of the Meuse undertaking better than the division commander. He could not pick his time with the whole army waiting. He had to move at once. He impressed upon his brigade and regimental commanders the imperative nature of the project. They, in turn, passed the word down the line. Even the enlisted men knew what was expected.

It was decided to make the crossing somewhere near a town called Dun-sur-Meuse, below Stenay. The river there is 160 feet wide. It is shallow at some parts and quite deep at others. There is a ford below the town. On the other side of the river paralleling the stream is a canal sixty feet wide and eight feet deep.

The banks of the canal are high, steep, and slippery. They afford no foothold. It is five-eighths of one mile from the river to the canal. This ground is flat and very muddy. The Germans had machine guns in position to enfilade all parts of the river and canal. Farther back on the line of hills they had artillery which could pour fire into the whole region.

At 4 o'clock in the afternoon of November 4, the American infantry rushed up to the river in an effort to make a crossing at the ford. With the whole awaiting on the result, time was an important factor. They waded into the water, but the Germans had this point immersed with machine gun fire. The test was impracticable. The infantry then waited until dusk, and about 6:30 o'clock thoughtful young Captain Smith's evolution of Lampert's invention came into effect. At a point further up the river toward the town, twenty engineers, working under fire, laid a 200-foot foot bridge in twenty minutes.

The foot bridge is formed of floats made of canvas stretched on folding frames. To cross them is like running over a narrow sidewalk.

Machine gun bullets perforated the first few floats put into the water by the engineers and sank them. When the foot bridge finally was placed across to the other bank, some of the engineers and some infantrymen went over in single file.

The bridge is a noiseless affair. Once across, the engineers established connections for heavier pontoon bridges, while the infantry went on fighting. They were in a deadly No Man's Land on a stretch between the river and the canal. They dug "fox holes" in the soft mud until they got a chance to rush up the banks of the canal. Then they jumped into the water and swam for the other side, all this time under terrific fire. Some were wounded in the water and were drowned.

The survivors, after crossing, could not get up the other bank. They clutched at the muddy, slippery sides, only to fall back into the water. Finally some carried ropes over between their teeth, with iron picket pins used for tethering horses stuck in one end of the ropes, and drove these pins into the banks. Then they went up hand over hand and dug themselves in.

More troops kept coming across the river on pontoons which had been established by the engineers. Soon the canal was also bridged and the general was able to report complete success. While they were lying between the river and the canal, our artillery could not fire because it would hit them. Neither could the German guns on the heights behind, because the German soldiers were so close to the Americans in that little valley of death that both sides were exchanging hand grenades.

November 17, 1918. With the American First Army

It is now permissible to tell a detailed story of the "beginning of the end" of the great war.

On the morning of November 5, General Pershing was notified in his private train up near the American front of the arrival of the German parlementaires. The American commander-in-chief usually sleeps on the train, which is constantly on the move. All division commands along the front had been keeping a lookout for the parlementaires in case they should appear before the American lines. Late Wednesday night our wireless intercepted a German wireless saying the parlementaires had left Berlin. The messages were not coded. The Germans probably wanted them intercepted. All through that night the French had been sending out wireless messages across the front addressed to German general headquarters, telling the envoys to go to Guise and even specifying the roads for them to follow. Evidently they had received no acknowledgment from the Germans, for at 6 o'clock Thursday a message was sent out from Marshal Foch's[122] headquarters, which was received at American First Army headquarters, saying: "The following message from Marshal Foch's headquarters is transmitted for necessary action.

"If the parlementaires present themselves at any point on the front to submit a request to Marshal Foch, they will be stopped at the front line division.

"This division will immediately inform Marshal Foch of their status and the objects of their mission. They will be detained at the division headquarters until Marshal Foch has made his reply."

The final word in this message was "acknowledge."

A short time after, a wireless message came from a group of French armies of the center saying that the parlementaires had presented themselves at La Capelle. A little later, Major Forsyth Wickes,[123] of New York, who was our liaison officer with the French, called up American headquarters by telephone and confirmed the news. General Pershing was immediately notified. Word was sent on to the division commands to keep an eye open for the envoys. The word was accompanied by information that the arrival of the envoys would probably be preceded by a cessation of firing by the Germans.

The German fire had not ceased, so far as the American fronts were concerned, up to Wednesday night, which was the turning night of the war. Up there the artillery was still pretty active, and patrols were still feeling their way through the blackness which smothered the land that night.

American front line troops had not been officially informed of the peace proceedings, one reason being that they were going along so fast that even the news could not catch up with them. However, there is an underground rumor system in every army through which reports travel even faster than by wireless. It is by no means improbable that our troops had some inkling of affairs.

Certainly it was pretty well known back of the lines. For several weeks the American army had been thoroughly satisfied that the collapse of the Germans was imminent. That conviction, however, made no difference in their fighting, as the results show. The Germans had been just as satisfied of their impending doom, judging from what prisoners said.

In the American camps, where all the details of the situation are known as far as anybody at the front can know, there was undoubtedly a feeling of relief that the bloody business was nearing its end.

Yet at the same time the Americans were prepared to go on if necessary. In fact, there had not been the slightest abatement of the armies' efforts in any respect. Men and guns were still moving forward. Lead and steel still whistled along the front line where Liggett's veterans were bivouacking, waiting for the coming dawn to resume their triumphant march that began three weeks ago.

The people in the French towns behind the American army were greeting their friends from across the seas with "la guerre est fini," meaning "the war is finished," an expression they have been using for some days past. They were as convinced as the Americans that Germany was through. The first thing that the girl waitress in the officer club at the town where the headquarters is located asked of one of her patrons Thursday night was whether the Germans had sent parlementaires to the Americans or the French. When told it was the French she was intensely delighted. She exemplified the quite natural feeling on the part of the French people that the enemy who had ravaged this brave country finally bent his knee in supplication to it.

November 17, 1918. With the American Armies on the March to the Rhine

For an hour we had been running through traffic on the road to the town of Etain. It was like traveling along a narrow lane with moving escalators on either side going in opposite directions.

One was formed by the Americans' new Third Army—"the Army of the Lord," someone has called it—marching to Germany. The other was made up of strangely garbed prisoners of war, just liberated from the Germans. They were Frenchmen, Russians, Italians, and even Serbians, with dingy sheep's wool shakos on their heads. They carried pitifully few belongings in packs on their backs or trundled them in wheelbarrows or little carts. They kept well on their side of the road, tramping to Verdun, where mile after mile of the American artillery and long truck and wagon trains passed within a few yards of them.[124]

They were seeing, though they probably didn't realize it, the famous First Division, probably one of the greatest organizations of trained foot soldiers on the face of the globe today. There had been little conversation in the car for some time. Now and then Cameron MacKenzie,[125] of the *London Daily Chronicle*, lifted his voice in querulous accents, wondering if it wouldn't be a good idea to try to get something to eat from one of the wayside messes.

MPs were the Army's traffic cops. *Courtesy of United States Army Heritage and Education Center*

Rolling kitchens[126] were setting up in business everywhere as the noon hour approached, shedding savory odors. It was bitterly cold, though clear. The infantrymen went along, their guns swung across their shoulders, slapping their hands like a village hackman waiting at the depot for the train. Clouds of steam spurted from the horses' nostrils. There was not much pomp of war about this procession of conquering heroes, although for the first time in many a day the brilliant guidons of the regimental standards of good Old Glory fluttered at the heads of some columns.

On the front seat of our car, practically buried under wrappings, sat Monsieur Gaston des Champs,[127] of the Paris *Le Temps*, one of the oldest and most famous political writers in all France. Up to the time we reached Fleville, a small roadside town, M. des Champs had not said a word. His repression was admirable. It is reasonable to conclude he would have maintained it to the end had we not lost our road.

Someone suddenly noticed that the American columns had dwindled away to a few stray soldiers and that the thoroughfare ahead was quite empty. Then we took a look at the next signboard and discovered we were within a very short distance of Fleville. So we rolled on into Fleville. One street of the town displayed quite a number of French flags. At the approach of our car a lot of women and children came running out of the houses with shrieks of delight. It dawned on us then that we were a sort of involuntary advance guard in the army for which they were waiting. They had not yet seen an American.

They climbed on the running boards of the car with outstretched hands, babbling in French. Richardson, our driver, specially imported by Uncle Sam from Worcester, Massachusetts, worried for the safety of the running boards. Then Monsieur des Champs began discharging volleys of "bon jours" right and left. Some of the women almost wept as they grasped his hand. His own eyes were filled with tears.

We knew just two words of French, and "bon jour" is neither of them. So the talking was left to Monsieur des Champs and to Burr Price,[128] of the *New York Herald*, who unveiled himself from many wrappings and joined in the conversation.

Cameron MacKenzie eyed the town speculatively.

"Wonder if we could get anything to eat here," he pondered.

The women said the Germans had just left the town the day before. Furthermore, they said Briey, which is one of the biggest towns on the American line of march and one of the most important, was only a few miles away. So we went on to Briey.

That town is the center of the great iron ore region of France, from which Germany got eighty-five per cent of her iron ore for which she fought against the Americans so desperately in the Argonne-Meuse battle. It is a little town of about 3,500 souls, set in the hills, much like any American town. French flags were flying from every house, but Richardson's horn awoke echoes in almost deserted streets.

Presently, however, people came running forth. All were dressed in their Sunday best. They had on white linen shirts and collars, which it seems, they had jealously guarded for many days for the time when they would celebrate their liberation from German domination.

Briey itself was never shot up. It was merely in the path of war and through it passed the German war machine without pausing. About 1,500 civilians are left there. Most of them got around our car. They, too, were getting their first sight of Americans, or at least of Americans who might be said to be ex officio advance agents of the coming army. Here it was the Monsieur des Champs cast aside all repression, journalistic and otherwise. He broke into a barrage of "bon jours" and the people almost shook his arm off. There were more tears here.

"Looks like there ought to be a hotel at this place," suggested MacKenzie.

"What's that chap saying now?" he asked Price, who was parleyvousing with a citizen of Briey.

"He says they had their first meat yesterday in two years," said Price. The people said the ore mines were up the road half a mile further, in the town called Moutiers. They said they were never permitted to go there without a pass all the time the Germans were in the region. Richardson tooted his horn for a while and finally got clearance room for the car. On we went up the narrow road between high hills, M. des Champs leaving worlds of "bon jours" behind him. He shouted them at every passerby and there were many of them, including men, women, and children. They responded fervently.

In Moutiers, which is a tiny place with tiny streets, stuck along the hillsides, we found more French flags, with one American flag among them. It is very hard to get American flags in this part of France.

Here again the car met with a wild reception. Here again M. des Champs had a wide field for his "bon jours." When the people found we were hunting for information about the mines, they pointed out a tall dignified gentleman with white mustache and little goatees whose name is Monsieur Rebel. He received us with many bows. His face was aglow with pleasure. Yes, he knew all about the mines, he said. The Germans had destroyed much machinery when they left; only two motors were working.

Would we like to see them? Well, he was sorry we hadn't the time. He said in normal times the mines produced millions of tons of ore every year. Not until 1916 did the Germans start working them systematically. Then they used their own men and Russian prisoners, but none of the French people.

He said they had got out 600,000 tons in 1918 up to the time they evacuated the region.

Before that they had not produced so much. The whole population of the town was now collected about the car, listening to the colloquy. To the right and left M. des Champs extended his hands and his "bon jours."

The hungry MacKenzie ran his orbs ruminatively over the situation but made no comment. It seemed incredible even to him that there could be a great deal to eat at that place. Finally it was time to go. Monsieur Rebel, who had been most dignified and even as repressed M. des Champs in the beginning, stepped back into the road, lifted his hat, and roared:

"Vive la France!"

All the people, including the very littlest of children, joined in answering the shout that rang though the hills. M des Champ's voice was easily heard. So were the voices of Price and MacKenzie. So, too, was even the voice of this writer. After a momentary silence, M. Rebel again thundered up into the hills:

"Vive l'Amerique!"

Everybody joined in that one. Then Richardson got his car going back and we went through Briey, leaving a trail of "bon jours." We were all getting the habit by now. Back along the vacant roads we went to Fleville, then down where we encountered the head of Dickman's[129] advancing columns of the First, Second, Third, Forty-Second, and Thirty-Second Divisions, all moving by different roads in the general direction of Luxemburg.

They were now getting ready to bivouac for the night. Campfires were blazing along the horizon. Savory odors of cooking were filling the air.

"Well, we'll soon be where we can get something to eat," said MacKenzie, triumphantly. When we unloaded our chilled bodies at Verdun, the new headquarters of the press division, where the reporters are living under the ground in the old citadel, Monsieur des Champs bowed along and said something in French. Maybe it was "bon jour" again. It was neither of the two French words we knew, at least.

But having seen into his good old heart and having peered behind his tears, so to speak, there was only thing to say, and we said—or thought—it.

And that was "Vive la France!"

November 20, 1918. With the First American Army in France

Two hundred and fifteen American soldiers who had been held prisoners of war by the Germans were brought into the town of Revigny yesterday.

"You ought to have heard us give them Heinies the old raspberry,[130] when we left up yonder," said Sergeant Walter Sampson, of No. 112 North Robert Street, Chicago, who was one of two men left of his platoon of Company E, One Hundred and Thirty-Sixth Infantry, after a charge.

"They had us at Montmedy first," said Sampson, "but our bombers came over and bombed hell out of the place, so we went on strike and refused to work around a railhead that bombers were aiming at. So they took us to Gorcy. That's where we were when the fighting stopped.

"We knew the finish was in sight, because the German privates kept telling us what was going on outside. Every day they'd be around saying the war was going to end next day; they were tickled to death about it, too.

"There was one ornery Prussian sergeant—a little, short guy—who was always yelling at us, 'Raus Amerikaner,' and we started a song for his benefit."

"I wish I had that son of a gun at the end of a bayonet right now," interrupted Fred Sena, of No. 164 Astor Street, New York, who was with the One Hundred and Thirteenth Infantry. "He was certainly onery."

"None of them liked our song very much, but the sergeant hated it most of all," Sampson went on. "So we sang it whenever he came around. We sang it when they marched us out of Gorcy down the roadways toward the American lines and turned us loose. Here, I'll sing it for you. It goes like this:

> Raus mit him. Just hear that funny noise.
> Raus mit him. Just let him have it, boys.
> We'll turn the old place inside out;
> We'll turn it inside in.
> Treat every Dutchman just alike,
> And raus mit him.

You could hear us whooping and hollering for a mile, all right."

Milton Horter, of Malta, Montana, who comes from the Ninetieth Division, said: "We knew it was over, because the flags were flying all over Gorcy when we went out. They certainly looked great."

"Yes, if it hadn't been for the people of Gorcy we would have starved to death on what food we got," said Lewis Morris, of Barnesville, Ohio, who comes from the Twenty-Ninth Division. "They gave us lots of bread. What the Germans issued to us wouldn't have lasted long."

"They didn't have much to eat themselves, them Dutchmen didn't," said John Powell, of Campbellsville, Ohio, the only man from the First Division in the party, which represented about fifteen American divisions on the line in the Argonne-Meuse drive.

"I'm going to dream about Dan Patch[131] stew and barley soup as long as I live—Dan Patch stew is horse meat," he explained. "It was meat from horses that had been killed in battle. You could see how it had been torn by shells."

"They treated us better than they treated the Russians or French," said Sergeant Herbert Birchard, of No. 209 South Twentieth Street, Omaha, who was a member of the Eighty-Ninth Division. "They had about a thousand Russians there. They booted them around pretty fierce all the time, even though Russia was supposed to be at peace with them."

"How was I captured?" Birchard grinned. "Well, I strayed over into the German lines one night. I saw a lot of guys laying on the ground sleeping and I thought they were our own men, so I went around shaking them and telling them to wake up. Finally I heard one guy say, "Vot iss?" The next thing I knew about forty Dutchmen were around me."

"Those Russians certainly got a rough deal," said Corporal E. Barfoot, of Richmond, Virginia, from the One Hundred and Sixteenth Infantry. "When we refused to work around the railroad where the bombers were dropping explosives, the French prisoners also struck, so the Russians had to do all the work there. They worked us on the roads, and when they did work us they paid us six cents a day.

"You worked a week for one mark, then they charged you four marks for a loaf of bread. We didn't have any blankets until a couple of days before we left. We slept in a church, on the concrete floor. That is, we tried to sleep there. Generally we sat up all night. The cooties wouldn't let us sleep much."

"Them German cooties are terrible," averred Frank Kochrek, of No. 235 South Halstead Street, Chicago, who was captured from the Thirty-Third Division. "They can bite worse than any I ever saw. We had a stove in the church, so it wasn't so awful cold there. I worked in the kitchen myself.

"I'm the only cook in this outfit," he added proudly. "I managed one of John Thompson's[132] restaurants, and who do you think I found in that prison camp when I got there? Why, this fellow here—one of my old customers."

He dragged forth Jack Morton Seaman, of No. 1443 Van Buren Street, Chicago.

Sanford R. Howton, of Johns, Alabama, just outside of Birmingham, who belongs to the Twenty-Ninth Division, wore a German cap cocked stylishly on the side of his head. He had a pair of German eagles taken from a Prussian helmet pinned to his breast.

Some of the others wore the helmets themselves. They are the most prized of all war souvenirs.[133] Several had Belgian caps given to them by the people of Gorcy, which is not far from the Belgian border.

"They asked us all manner of questions when they first got us," said Howton, who is a tall, gangling, serious-looking chap. "They would take us before the German officer, who would try to get information out of us about the army.

"He asked us how many men we had over here. I said I wasn't sure but thought about 5,000,000. Then he got out his notebook and said, 'You have a little over 2,000,000 men.'

"He showed me maps of our lines that showed just what American divisions were in the line and where they were. He told me the name of my battalion commander was Major Kick.[134] He wasn't correct about that, however. Major Kick had been away several days."

"Yes, one of them told me what date our division had sailed from America and said we'd been attacked by a submarine, giving the date," said another man. "I don't know whether he was right about the date or not, because I don't remember it myself. He had the rest down pat, though. I caught the date of our landing and arrival in line."

"Yes," said John Howton again, "when they told me how much they knew about us, I asked them what in hell they were asking me for. One guy said I was a great man."

"They took everything off us we had," said Corporal James Valodiska, of No. 3007 South Trumbull Avenue, Chicago, who comes from the Seventy-Eighth Division. "They took any jewelry we had and our knives and everything else. They snatched a wristwatch off me. They even grabbed our raincoats. Their officers wouldn't let them take things like that if they caught them, but they got them just the same. They cleaned us good."

"One thing they all kept asking us about was what they called our Edison gas,"[135] said Teddy Toughas, of Tower City, North Dakota, from the Ninetieth Division, who was captured on the right.

"Yes," chorused others, "they were daffy on the subject of Edison gas. They said it was something invented by old man Edison. They claimed it ate away everything like it was paper. They said they had seen their own guns and the bodies of their men eaten up by it."

"They didn't get much satisfaction out of us," declared Homer Milligan, of Decatur, Illinois, who was captured from the One Hundred and Twenty-Fourth Machine Gun Battalion of the Thirty-Third Division. He is a very tall fellow and is called "Big Boy" by the others. They say he impressed the Germans greatly by his size.

"They were pretty much scared of the Americans," said Sergeant Pat J. Long of No. 48 Village Street, Reading, Massachusetts, who was taken from the Twenty-Sixth Division in the bitter fight in Belleau Wood. It took fifty Germans to capture Long, who is a serious, efficient-looking, middle-aged chap.

"They said, 'You Americans are wicked fellows,'" he continued. "They were all mighty glad the war was ending. We had three American lieutenants with us when we marched out. They were James Sweeney of the Thirty-Sixth Division (Texas and Oklahoma men); Charley Hurley, of Boston, from the Seventy-Ninth; and Leary Fowler of Dallas, Texas.

"I don't know how long they had been prisoners. There was also an aviator named Kelton.[136] They took command of us and got us back to the American lines. We marched fifty kilometers one day. We were finally picked up by ambulances.

"The civilians in Gorcy treated us wonderfully well. They went without food one day, so we could have enough. Down at Montmedy we were under shell fire for five days. We were always trying to signal our aviators when they flew over the town, but I guess we didn't succeed."

"The most fun we had was when we found a German spy dressed up like a French prisoner," said Charles M. Ticer, of Albert, Oklahoma, of the Ninetieth Division (Texas and Oklahoma men). "Say, we led him the life of Riley; even the French threw bricks at him and everything else."

"And we certainly gave them the raspberry going out," put in Sergeant Sampson.

"All together now, boys, let's sing 'Raus Mit Him' just for old times' sake."

November 20, 1918. [Delayed] On the March to the Rhine

Bozeman Bulger's "flying circus," otherwise known as the press division of the American army, is commencing to function, as they say in the army, by courier. Since leaving the town of Bar-le-Duc[137] the noble correspondents have been cut off from their wire base. They have been living in modern catacombs known as the citadel of Verdun, where 45,000 soldiers can be quartered underground.

Fifteen or twenty thousand prisoners of war[138] and refugees have been sallying forth each morning to the now peaceful "front." Tomorrow they will move en masse to the town of Luxemburg.

From Verdun, motorcycle "copy boys" have been carrying the valuable manuscripts donated by the journalists back to Bar-le-Duc, where James Patrick Wilson and Glen D. Merriman, operators, remained as our "rear echelon."

Tomorrow the telegraph department will be transferred to the city of Nancy. Couriers will lug "copy" from Luxemburg to Nancy, Bar-le-Duc being finally abandoned for good by the writers.

American troops on the bridge leading into Germany from Luxembourg. *Courtesy of Library of Congress*

Just how "copy" is going to be sent from Germany, when the army gets there, is a question which is keeping those in charge of the outfit awake o'nights.

With them from the dungeon dwellings of Verdun the crypts are carrying a new brand of "cooties." They embody the best cootie blood on the western front, being a careful mixture of all breeds which have passed through the Verdun citadel in the last four years.[139]

Leo Donnelly,[140] actor, paid a visit to the "circus" in its dungeon last night. He has been working with the Y.M.C.A. theatrical unit on the west front for months. Dorothy Donnelly,[141] the famous creator of Madame X, and Patsy Henshaw,[142] a young actress from the coast, are among the other theatrical people still in the field.

Brink Thorne,[143] the noted Yale football player, found his way into the citadel tonight.

November 20, 1918. [Delayed] On the March to the Rhine through Luxemburg

The little children of Luxemburg are having a wonderful time these days. The coming of Dickman's soldiers is as good as Christmas to them. In their eyes an American doughboy is something obvious to climb all over and play with. Therefore, today, in every town along the white roads that crisscross the green countryside like the yard line markings on a football field were American infantrymen fairly festooned with kiddies.

In Petang, on a bench beside the famous Hotel du Chateau, sat one soldier with three youngsters on his lap, one hanging around his neck and half a dozen others pushing and shoving one another to get closer to him. He was alternately talking French and German to them, larding in a little English now and then. They were playing with his gas mask and steel helmet and examining his wristwatch and identification tag. He had emptied his pockets for their benefit.

Most of them were little girls. The wee girls of Luxemburg are less timid than the boys. The big girls of the famous old Grand Duchy are not so bashful, either. It was a common sight in all the towns, most of which were gaily decorated with flags, and even the miniature arches of lights, to see soldiers walking arm in arm with new-found feminine acquaintances who were laughing and blushing prodigiously.[144]

You can back the American soldier against the world for getting along with the ladies anywhere you put him.

It is the children of the Grand Duchy, however, who were the first to make friends with the newcomers. They did not hesitate a minute in making up to the big men who came tramping into their towns with guns on their shoulders. The streets of the average Luxemburg town look like a thoroughfare on the east side of New York when it comes to children. There are thousands of them. Many American soldiers speak German better than they do French. In fact, they were conversationally right at home immediately.

Those who could not speak German found their French handy because the Luxemburgers are mighty cosmopolitan when it comes to languages.[145]

At some places women showered flowers on the marching men. One mounted man went galloping down the street with a big bouquet stuck in the muzzle of his gun.

Many marching infantrymen had brand new helmets of the Prussian Guard slung over their backs. These are patent leather affairs, gorgeously set off with Prussian eagles in silver or brass. They were rare. The souvenir hunting is an American national habit, and the soldiers are no exception. It was necessary to issue strict orders against tampering with guns or other war material left behind by the Germans, as some over-zealous collectors were inclined to pick up loose bits such as breech blocks for relics.

November 21, 1918. Luxemburg

"The Army of the Lord" marched through Luxemburg this afternoon, and great was the stir in this capital of the Grand Duchy. "Black Jack" Pershing was at the head of his doughboy hosts. He was not mounted on a flaming charger, after the manner of conquering heroes of pictured memory. He entered the town, which is just a way station for him en route to Germany, boxed up in an army limousine.

"Black Jack" had got pretty gray and has developed a bit around his middle since the days when he commonly bestrode a charger. He wore his new decoration, the Distinguished Conduct Medal. He reviewed his troops from the balcony of the palace of the Grand Duchess of Luxemburg, with the Duchess[146] standing beside him.

She is a young woman, only about twenty-four, and quite pretty. A couple of weeks ago the Chamber of Luxemburg voted whether to continue her regime or adopt a republican form of government. Maria Adelaide is still in office, by grace of one vote. How long her term will endure seems to be an open question.

In the old town of Luxemburg there is a strong feeling in favor of a republic, but in the country districts of the little land they have a fondness for her. She seemed rather a patriotic figure in many ways as she stood on the balcony today, slim and girlish-looking, between two big American generals. Pershing was on one side. Major General "Jack" Hines,[147] a burly fellow who commanded the Third Corps and who is one of the best American leaders developed in this war, stood on the other.

General Hines was obviously conscious of his hands. He finally wrapped them together and held them in front of him. General "Joe" Dickman, commander of the army which is marching into Germany, and General Preston Brown,[148] another of America's new fighting men who flashed up out of comparative obscurity to heights during the war, were also on the balcony, with Colonel Boyd[149] and a couple of aides.

A captain of the Luxemburg army, which numbers 200 men, and one of his lieutenants stood with the American contingent. The Grand Duchess, or, rather, Princess, as she is generally called by her subjects, wore a suit of some sort of black material. It looked like velvet, but maybe it wasn't. None of the generals could remember what it was when they were interrogated after the ceremony.

American troops marching through the streets of Luxembourg. *Courtesy of Library of Congress*

Duchess Marie Adelaide of Luxembourg.
Courtesy of Library of Congress

Anyway it was a two-piece suit. The coat was trimmed around the bottom with gray squirrel fur. The trimming was a band about twelve inches wide. The collar of the coat was also of gray fur. She carried a gray squirrel muff with ermine edging. On her head was a wide hat trimmed with white feathers. She wore no jewelry.

Her sister, Antoinette, was her only attendant. She wore a black suit, with white linen collars and cuffs somewhere.[150]

Only part of the Eighteenth Regular Infantry appeared in the review. The Thirty-Second Division, consisting of Michigan and Wisconsin troops, marched toward Luxemburg in the last week, but the main body is swinging around the town.

Immediately after the review, the soldiers were marched out of the city again, and they are bivouacking on the outskirts.[151] It was like showing the doughboys the Promised Land, then dropping the curtain on it immediately. The only American soldiers allowed in Luxemburg are the military police and the men whose duties actually require their presence.

Tonight the streets of the town were jammed with people and brilliantly lighted. The few doughboys fortunate enough to be in the city were surrounded by crowds. Everywhere, Americans were greeted with cheers. Everybody speaks to them, and most of the folks raise their hats. Girls pin flowers to their uniforms. It is a pity for the soldiers who are camping in sight of these myriad delights to be unable to enjoy them.

The last of the Germans left Luxemburg yesterday. There was quite a bunch of them. It is said they were reviewed by a German general on their departure and the enemy had two bands, both of which went out playing "The Star Spangled Banner." Furthermore, it is said, some German soldiers were carrying red flags.[152] They are still marching on Luxemburg soil on the way back home. But there was none here this morning when the first Americans arrived.

A lot of British aviators, who had once been interned in Luxemburg, were among the early arrivals. They were so well treated by the people here during their long internment that they came back as visitors.

There are still some British soldiers here who were once interned and haven't yet been returned to their homes.

The whole town was gaily decorated with flags and bunting this morning. There were many real American flags, but the home-made article was still much in evidence. Storekeepers put up signs reading: "WELCOME TO THE AMERICAN SOLDIERS!"[153]

There were also signs of "English spoken here."[154] One enterprising café announced real dry martini cocktails. This was interesting but unimportant to the doughboys, as the café proprietors were requested not to sell liquor to American soldiers. Every door or two is a café in Luxemburg. They teach English in the schools of this Grand Duchy, as nearly all the people can speak that language about as a school-taught American speaks French.

French is about the most commonly spoken language here, though one hears a lot of German, too. However, there is plenty of real hatred for the Germans in Luxemburg, and the relief of the people over the departure of their oppressors is very genuine.

For more than four years, the men of the armies under Generals von Gallwitz[155] and von der Marwitz[156] were goose-stepping across the land, and the burden of war lay heavily upon the little country. They say they have not had much to eat, and what they have had has been very expensive. To the men who have been living and fighting on army grub back in France, the food here is apparently abundant and certainly mighty appealing, but maybe the Americans' idea of plenty is different from that of the Luxemburgers.

A number of French officers took part with the American army in the entry today and got a tremendous reception. Marshal Foch is expected here tomorrow. Many people say they would prefer to be made part of France to anything else.

The Eighteenth Infantry entered the town about 2:30. About that time the narrow street was so jammed with people it was hard for the military to chisel lanes through wide enough for the column squads. "Pompiers," or firemen, from a dozen nearby towns and villages were in the escort of honor. They wore gay uniforms.

There were choral societies and sporting societies, all uniformed. There were high-hatted citizens in open carriages. There were what seemed to be women's auxiliaries. There were unions of working men of one kind or another from the neighboring cities.

It was just such a parade as we have seen time and again on the Fourth of July, or other notable occasions back in the good old States. It was just such a parade, barring only the setting.

Every organization today had its own flag. They splashed the streets with gay coloring. There were half a dozen bands, including one big band, handsomely uniformed, which can play American march music. It did well with "Stars and Stripes Forever" after the review.

The people jammed together along the sidewalks were bubbling with good spirits. It was a great holiday for them. The writer saw the entry of the French troops into Metz, after a lapse of forty-eight years, the other day. While that occasion was more spectacular as a purely military show, it had no more warmth of feeling from the people than was displayed today. It must be remembered that Luxemburg has been a purely neutral state, and the entry of American troops meant nothing more than a passing show to them. There is no doubt that the French have more a sense of the theatrical about these things than the Americans anyway.

Our doughboys came in with Colonel Hunt[157] riding in front of the column. They had reached the edge of the city only a short time before, after a long march, and were pretty tired. They carried their big packs on their backs. They had their steel helmets on their heads. This was the only added touch to their appearance.

They have been carrying these helmets slung to their packs on the hike toward Germany up to today. Their bayonets were not fixed, but they looked mighty businesslike, and mighty good, as they swung into the main thoroughfare, with the long, loping, ground-eating stride of the American infantry. It is not as thrilling, as quick, and as jerky a step as that of the French foot soldiers marching behind a band, but it is impressive. It "gets" you. And it gets the American whither he is going.

The Eighteenth's band was booming away on familiar American march music. Old Glory fluttered in the chilly breeze beside the regimental standard as the little command tramped between rows of excited people, and it was good to hear that music and to see those colors so far away from home.

The "vives" began when General Pershing's automobile rolled into view, followed by a number of other cars carrying staff officers. They continued until a late hour tonight. Flowers began flying when the head of the doughboys' column showed up. A Luxemburg band struck up "Sambre et Meuse," a great marching song of the Poilus. It is a wonderful piece of music and just fits the Poilus. But it is a bit too abbreviated for the American leg action.

The doughboys grinned from under their helmets at the reception and began taking a peek at the town of which they had heard so much. There were girls in every window of the business buildings. There were small boys running their small legs off to keep up with the procession. Many a word in English was shouted at the men.

There was something strongly reminiscent about America about the whole affair. There was something homely about it. And all this time, while Luxemburg and her 20,000 inhabitants were buzzing with excitement over the entry, the rest of Dickman's army was still tramping the hard highroads beyond the city to Germany.

November 21, 1918. [Delayed] With the American Press Division Headed for the Rhine

It was our lot today to see the last armed German quit the north of France, which he has occupied for more than four years.

The thing came to pass quite by accident. It was really not our intention to get mixed up with the Germans, especially armed ones. In fact, nothing could have been further from our thoughts. But we missed the road to Longwy. That was the beginning of our relations with the last of the Germans.

We had been buzzing pleasantly along beside the Thirty-Second Division of General "Joe" Dickman's conquering host, which is marching to Germany. The Thirty-Second Division (Michigan–Wisconsin) is one of the crack divisions of the American army and was trained at Waco, Texas.

We greatly desired to see Longwy. We passed a band with its instruments, squatting at the side of the road, eating their midday corned "Willie" and bread. It occurred to us this must be the head of the column or close to it. However, American soldiers were still going down the road beyond, so we went too.

Part of Longwy lay in a valley below the hill, on the road along which we were moving. It looked most peaceful and pleasant with its pieces sparkling in the sun of a clear winter day. Part of it lay all about the hills in small pieces. It was scattered by the German guns early in the war. We passed over the road through the ruins and came again into open country. As far as we knew we were headed for the main part of Longwy, all right, although it struck us that American soldiers were conspicuous by their absence.

Suddenly Monsieur Gaston des Champs, veteran director of the Paris newspaper *Le Temps*, our guest, riding in the front seat with Richardson, the Worcester, Massachusetts, driver, because we thought it would be warmer for him there, began coming out of his head wrappings, layer by layer, showing signs of interest in the civilians going past. All showed white lines above their overcoat collars. They were waving.

Murmurings of "bon jour" began issuing from M. des Champs' lips. Suddenly, too, came Cameron MacKenzie, of the *London Daily Chronicle*, who had been dozing in the back seat, doubtless dreamily conjuring up visions of a large luncheon in Longwy. He took a long squint ahead and remarked casually: "There's a bunch of German prisoners headed the wrong way."

Sure enough, just beyond, a gray file was moving down the road. More suddenly then anything that had previously transpired, however, came a whoop from Tom Johnson[158] of the *New York Sun*.

"Hell's fire!" he said, "It's the German army!"

Richardson jammed on the brakes. Our car came to a jarring stop in the middle of the road, right at the heels of a column of heavily laden, heavily booted German infantrymen with their guns slung over their backs. They were marching in a column of twos. At the rear of the column was a little cart with all sorts of camp equipment. Behind the cart trudged two bland-looking German privates, one much begoggled.

They turned at the sound of the car and stared. The rest of the soldiers also turned and stared. From around the head of the column came a slim German officer in long overcoat, riding boots and spurs, a cane swung over one arm. He also stared. They didn't stop but went on down the road.

Out of our car we piled, Johnson and Burr Price, of the *New York Herald*, unslinging their cameras with glad shouts. "Champs" remained in the car with Arthur Hartzell, assistant censor of the press division. They felt the situation might develop certain complications, as far as they were concerned.

There was a little town ahead with flags flying from every window. There were some French flags, but the rest of them were unfamiliar to us. One look at them caused us to inquire the name of the town. Only then did it dawn on us that we were at the Belgian border.[159] Further inquiry developed that the boundary line itself was only a few yards beyond, with the German file bearing down on it.

Away went all hands on a gallop to get ahead of the Germans. Johnson and Price were set on sighting them as they crossed the border. They couldn't quite get ahead of the columns in time, but MacKenzie managed to clutch the last two men and halted them right on the line.

They stared in wonder, but as soon as they saw the cameras, they got the idea and posed with wide grins on their faces. Then they lifted their heavy feet across the line, and the last German was out of France.

Then we all resumed the gallop after the columns. The German officer turned as we ranged alongside him. He gazed for a moment, then he said, in perfect English, "Ah, you want to take a picture."

We allowed we did. One word led to another, and finally he stopped to have a conversation with us. He said a word to the men, and they moved to the side of the road, halted, and laid down their packs, stacked their arms, and gathered around us. The officer turned out to be quite a pleasant fellow. He was Rittmeister (captain of cavalry) Ihsson,[160] of Constanz, Germany, he said.

He had thirty men of the Thirty-Third Landstrum[161] with him. They were the rear guard. He said the rest of his command was on ahead some distance. He had remained to turn over an aerial station and other property to the Americans. He said he had heard about the Kaiser's leaving Germany but didn't believe he had abdicated. Neither did he believe the tales of the revolution in Germany. He said he had fought on nearly all fronts as a machine gun commander and was glad to hear the war was over.

"Everything will be all right in Germany when the army gets home," he said, confidently.

Meantime M. des Champs was having his day back with the car. The populace had gathered around him, and he made a speech. Putting his hand on Hartzell's shoulder, he told them the blushing lieutenant was the forerunner of the great American army that was coming up the road.

He told them, furthermore, they must give the army the proper reception. Everybody cheered vociferously.

We distributed cigarettes among the German soldiers, most of whom wore the ribbon Iron Cross. They snatched eagerly at the smokes. They hadn't had much tobacco. The captain declared they had always had plenty to eat because they took it with them. Then we left him reassembling his command in the road and went back to M. des Champs.

The Frenchman was leaning far out of the car, dropping "bon jours" lavishly. It was noticed that at no time did he go near the Germans. It is not to be wondered at. He lost a son in this war.[162]

In about twenty jerks of the big car we were out of Belgium over the border line of Luxemburg, through the town of Athus.[163]

There were a lot of German soldiers still there tugging their stuff out of the billets. Some of them saluted the car. An armed German stood on the bridge leading out, but paid no attention to us.

Belgian flags fluttered from the windows along with the flag of Luxemburg, which is the same as that of Holland. Here and there were homemade American flags done with colored chalk. There was one big, real American flag floating from a store in Athus. They were hoisting it as we passed. They had probably just heard the Americans were coming.

M. des Champs did his best to let them all know. He shouted the news at every group of loungers on the corners and the people on the road. Athus is a pretty, prosperous-looking place.

Cameron MacKenzie eyed a butcher shop window filled with meat. He eyed it longingly. A fat butcher stood in front of the place and waved as we passed. Now we were in a town called Petange, a clean, brisk-looking little place where there was an inviting-looking café called "Hotel Du Chateau."

Afterward we learned it is the famous eating place of the Grand Duchy of Luxemburg. We had halted there. Just as we passed, a vehicle exactly like an old-time American town hack passed, with two German soldiers on the seat beside the driver. German officers followed by orderlies galloped down the road on good-looking horses. Occasionally a column of German infantry went by. In the Café Du Chateau we were greeted by a young woman who said she was the wife of the proprietor. He was away, she said.

She almost wept at sight of us. They had seen no Americans yet. They had heard of their coming only by rumor. She brought forward a little girl, who kissed each member of the party solemnly.

Meantime the population of the town was gathered about the car, forcing its way into the café. Several German officers came in, looked us over casually, and sat down, ordering drinks.

Monsieur des Champs was the center of attraction as he was narrating the news of the day, interrupting himself now and then to "bon jour" some newcomer. Lieutenant Hartzell, who talks very good French, was also surrounded.

A telegraph message came from a nearby town called Rodange, saying they had heard of the arrival of our party and wanted us to stop there and have a reception. Hartzell had all he could do to prevent the burgomaster from getting out the band and starting a celebration at Petange. They had even sent for the chief of musicians, who came bringing his cornet to consult about the matter.

There were rumors of food from the kitchen, much to the delight of MacKenzie. Presently it came on, such a banquet as was never before a king—in wartime, anyway. It included meat, but blackish German bread went with it. There were also vegetables. Madame herself set up a round of champagne. She had it served by her little daughter, whom she had dressed in a French costume for the occasion.

People gathered around and told us some of their troubles during the war. They said the Germans had worked everybody up to sixty years. The German officers sitting at the table listened to the conversation stoically.

When it was time to go, Richardson had a hard time getting his car out of the mob of people surrounding it. There were old men and young men, mere boys, young women and old women, and little girls. M. des Champs' hand must be lame from waving. The gigantic gendarmes in Donald Brian[164] costumes towered over the heads of all others.

We passed out of Petange while the crowd cheered, and went back down the roads laden with blocks of German guns and other equipment which they had left in accordance with the terms of the armistice. We hadn't gone far before someone was struck by a horrible thought.

"My God!" they said, "that dinner we've got in us probably was fixed for General Pershing or General Dickman or somebody."

"I don't give a damn," said MacKenzie sleepily. "I'd like to see them get it away from me now."

"Bon jour!" called M. des Champs at a passing group. "Bon jour!" they yelled. "Bon jour" said all of us in unison.

The last German was out of France.

November 21, 1918. [Delayed] With the American Army of Occupation

On the march to the Rhine, American soldiers are dividing their conversation between what they will see in Germany and what happened during the dying hours of the war. There is still a wealth of untold stories of the last lap of America's victorious drive in the great war.

After the American troops in front of Sedan had been pulled back two weeks ago and the sector had been turned over to its rightful owners, the French, Company D, One Hundred and

Sixty-Sixth Infantry, an Ohio regiment of the Rainbow Division, reported to a French colonel in a stately old chateau which was his headquarters at Fernois.

This company was commanded by Captain Russell Baker,[165] of Delaware, Ohio. It had been invited by the French to act as guard of honor for the French troops, if they moved on the town. That night the French commander gave a dinner in honor of the American officers in the dining room, lighted only by candles.

It was a most dramatic scene. Every man present was fresh from the battlefield. The dinner over, Lieutenant Alison Reppy,[166] graduate of the University of Missouri, rose to speak on behalf of the Americans. He paid homage to France and her soldiers. Then taking from his pocket a little silk flag which his wife had sent him, he presented it to the colonel.

The Frenchman sat silent for a moment, deeply moved. Then, holding the fragment of color aloft in his clenched hand, he shouted:

"The blood of the world!"

Up sprang the assemblage, hundreds of booted feet resounding on the floor, while from hundreds of throats came the shout:

"Vive L'Amerique!"

This scene was enacted within 400 yards of the spot where forty-eight years ago, Napoleon III had signed his abject surrender.[167]

Later in the night two platoons of Company D slipped down to the outskirts on the west bank of the Meuse, opposite Sedan, and peered into the old town.

They got so close the Germans sprayed them with machine gun fire. They were probably the closest to Sedan of any Americans. In the years to come, the favorite subject for argument at the meetings of Pershing Post No. 1, Veterans of the American Expeditionary Force, or whatever they will be calling the organizations of the men who served in this war, is apt to be:

"What outfit got closest to Sedan?"

It will furnish many stirring debates. History will record that no considerable force of American troops really entered the historic old town; because, sentimentally, it did not belong to them. But many got very close. They got so close, in fact, that at one time it was reported that they were in the outskirts. But, as a matter of truth, they were far from taking the city itself, when they were pulled back to let the French take over the sector. It belonged to the French, anyway.

Our First Division and the famous Rainbow Division had pushed over, eager to take the town. American troops were not so mixed up together, as it was said at the time. It was once even reported that there had been fist fights between members of rival outfits. Members of the First and Rainbow Divisions were vastly surprised when they heard of these tales as they came out.

The Americans did take Wadelincourt, which is on the west bank of the River Meuse, right across from Sedan, but it is not Sedan. They reached the heights commanding the city and undoubtedly would have taken the ancient town had they been permitted to do so. However, no American claims taking the place now. As near as anybody can determine, a battalion of New York's Irish Sixty-Ninth got as far north as any battalion.

There will be many a battle fought over again after the war. The battle of Sedan is one of them. The First and Forty-Second Divisions made a wonderful campaign, getting in front of the town. The fact that they weren't allowed to take it detracts in no way from their work. They were aching to go in when they were pulled back. They moved so fast that they out-stripped their own ammunition carts. They took a hill, barbed with ten machine guns, at the point of the bayonet.

At sundown one evening, some troops of the Second Division reached a forest hedged in with machine guns. The Germans manning these guns had retired into the woods to sleep and wait for dawn to attack, which was their custom. The men of the Second Division formed a single file, each man hanging on to the other's coattail. Thus they tiptoed through the woods so that by daylight they were ready to attack all sides. This exploit was a mere episode in the fight that will live long in history of any engaged in by the Americans in the long drive from the Marne to the Meuse.

November 23, 1918. [Delayed] Luxemburg

In the big casino on the river front where all Luxemburg gathers of an evening to eat, drink, and talk, the orchestra struck up an American two-step last night. Not a one-step, but a two-step.

There is a big difference. It's the difference of a decade at least. It was something of Sousa's. They haven't advanced much beyond "El Capitaine" and "Washington Post" days in Luxemburg, as far as American music is concerned.

"Down in Jungle Town" is considered an exceptionally modern ditty here. As the strains of the old air floated over the crowds gathered around the tables, there was a momentary hush in the babble of conversation. The crowds included scores of American officers in field uniforms, American newspapermen, French officers in new uniforms of horizon blue with rows of medals on their chests, officers of the Luxemburg army in gorgeous military habiliments, and beautiful women in evening gowns, as well as citizens of the town in civilian apparel.

Through the great windows of the casino you can see rows of giant trees, marching along the river in soldierly fashion, with the moon sprinkling a soft silvery light over the branches.

Occasionally, above the gentle rhythm of music could be heard cries from the streets of the town where people were calling "Vive l'Amerique!" at every passing soldier.

They have another cry, too, taught them by the newly arrived doughboys, "Hoop, hoop, hooray."

As the orchestra reached the swing, swing of the Sousa melody, there was a sudden scraping of chairs on the floor of the casino, and out of the crews around the tables stalked a big figure in an American uniform, with the two silver stars of the major general glittering on his shoulders. It was "Big Jack" Hines, and at his side was one of the belles of Luxemburg. As the picturesque leader of the Third Corps stepped off with his partner, other Americans followed suit.

Bert Ford,[168] staff correspondent of the International News Service, in a pair of brand new field boots, was one of the terpsichorean kings of the evening. Gray colonels of the line, pudgy majors, and gallant lieutenants were among those on the floor. It was a gay scene. It fitted in with the surroundings. It's a great thing to be an American in Luxemburg these days. It's a great thing to be living through this period in the little Grand Duchy. It is something one is not going to forget even when the great war is becoming a trifle vague against the horizon of memory.

One feels like an onlooker in Graustark of Zenda.[169] It is all like in a novel. In the cafés, they sit and drink coffee or quetsch,[170] which is a local drink, until the early hours of the morning. Quetsch, by the way, is a white fluid which has the odor of anisette. It is a sort of after dinner cordial. They say the record for drinking quetsch is two drinks and a reach.

Beer is perhaps the most popular form of refreshments. It's the kind of beer that American beer heads will recall dimly as in vogue over there before the war.

Every house in town is open to Americans, and in the hallway of every house you can find an American overseas cap hung to the hat rack. In fact, in Luxemburg families regard an American guest for dinner as something of a prize. Part of the city has been restricted to the Americans. Officers and enlisted men, with few exceptions, are not permitted in the main part of the town.

They are on the other side of the river, in the new section of the city, and military police guard the bridges to keep them from crossing without passes. The rather limited number of soldiers in old Luxemburg are certainly lords of the earth for a spell.

French troops entered the town yesterday in a formal manner, getting a tremendous reception. About the same program was carried out in their honor as when the Eighteenth Infantry came in, with the exception that there was no Rupert of Hentzau[171] scene on the balcony of the grand duchess' palace such as was presented by General Pershing with Marie Adelaide the other day.

Marshal Foch did not appear, but it is said he will be there later.

"Diamond Jim" Brady's[172] old friend Alexis Brasseur,[173] one of the leading residents of Luxemburg, looked us up today. He showed us the identical table at which "Diamond Jim" sat

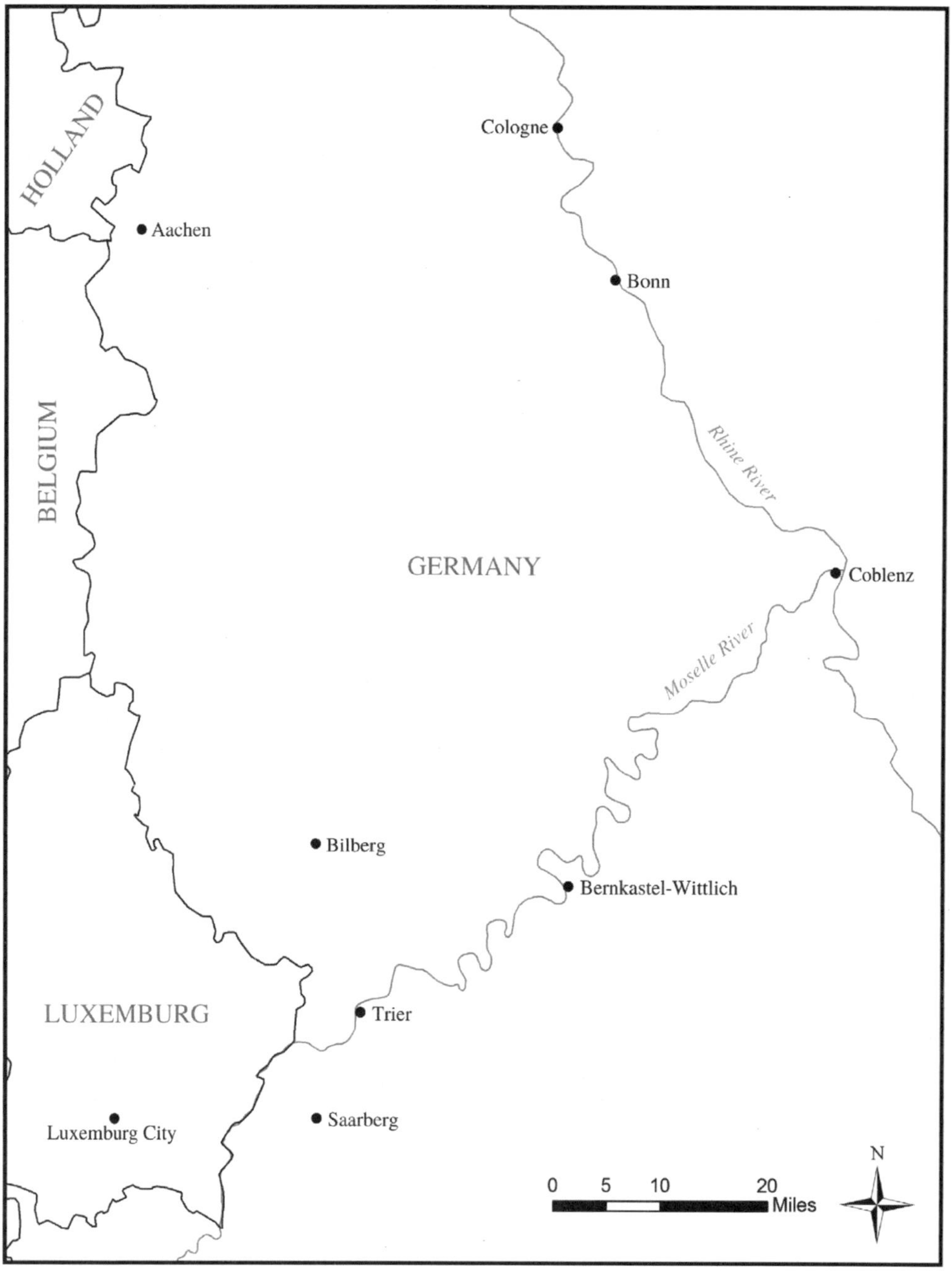

Western Germany

in the dining room of the grand Hotel Brasseur[174] when he was here. The hotel has the same name as M. Alexis, but there is no relationship between the two. In those days, as always, "Diamond Jim" was selling steel cars and M. Alexis helped him sell certain patents in Germany.

It is on M. Alexis that a famous old-time poker story originated. He was in America visiting "Diamond Jim" some years ago and went to Washington with Brady and party of friends.

"Diamond Jim" and his friends were playing poker on the train. M. Alexis asked if he could sit in.

"Sure," said Brady, "how much money you got?"

"About $500," replied M. Alexis.

Brady turned to a distinguished railroad financier, who was acting as banker for the game, and said:

"Give him a white chip, John."

It sounds mighty ancient now, but it was considered a great line when it was first pulled.

M. Alexis once lived in Central City, Colorado, where he was interested in the Frontenac mine. Now he resides quietly here and wears long white whiskers. His most pleasant memories are of the great time when "Diamond Jim" showed him Broadway.

November 23, 1918. Luxemburg

John Soldier will eat his Thanksgiving dinner[175] in Germany or thereabouts, six months to a day after the capture of Cantigny, which marked America's first scrap in the big war and eighteen months to a day since General John J. Pershing started for the scene of the trouble.

It probably will not be an elaborate dinner. Turkeys are scarce in this part of the world. Corned "William" will have to serve as a substitute in many cases; the beef is fairly plentiful.

These are rather pleasant days for the "Army of the Lord." They are days of hiking, it is true, and hiking is never a particularly pleasing function, no matter what the circumstances, but this hike goes through wonderfully beautiful country and over wonderfully good roads.

Moreover, the weather has been perfect. It is a little cold but always clear. In the mornings there is a white frost on the ground, which disappears as soon as the sun gets up. With such weather it is reasonable to assume the Allies would have had the Germans back on their own defenses in Germany by this time but for the armistice. They were going mighty fast when the order "halt" came.

Now "Jerry" retreats somewhat leisurely. Often during the present advance our men have been in sight of the last German. Sometimes the Germans left a town only half an hour or so before our men got in.

The natives would still be putting new flags in place of the German bunting. That, and the change in the price lists, to read francs instead of marks, represents the transition from German to Ally or American in some cases. They still charge in marks, however.

In Luxemburg and the surrounding country they ask something like a franc and a half for one mark, though francs are going up and marks are going down. The prices for food are very high. In hotels and restaurants they are higher than in New York. In a hotel they will make a very moderate price for an exceptional room, but the charge for food runs the cost of living away up.

Late yesterday it was possible to go down to the Moselle River, not a great distance from Luxemburg, and see the retreat of part of the German army.[176] They had their wagons decorated with evergreen boughs gathered on the hillsides, and little German flags. Their horses looked in pretty good condition. German guards were posted on the bridges, but they paid no attention to anybody who came their way.

Frequently American motorcycles or automobiles would go weaving in and out throughout the columns of German wagons, guns, and foot soldiers. The machines were bearing officers on their way to German territory to make the preliminary arrangements for the coming of the

American troops. When they had to halt, German officers would post guards over their vehicles to keep the crowds away.

It is said the Germans have not only shown no hostility to Americans but rather seem glad to see them. They seem to think the arrival of the Americans will mean they are going to get more food.

November 26, 1918. With the American Army of Occupation

We dreamed we were in the beautiful city of Luxemburg yesterday. It couldn't have been more than a dream, of course, because no correspondent could have actually been in the city of Luxemburg without violating an army order. This order was to the effect that no one could enter that particular town, or any other town for that matter, ahead of the American troops.

The American troops have not entered Luxemburg. Consequently no reporters have been there. Captain Gerald Morgan, chief censor of the army, took his famous red pencil in hand this evening to see that no correspondents had been there. However, there is no rule prohibiting a man from dreaming that he was there or from quoting facts from old Karl Balaker Dijon, reporter of his era, so this is the dream we dreamed.

It seemed to us in our dream that Luxemburg was the original spotless town. Furthermore, it seemed to us that it was the prettiest town we had ever seen anywhere on God's green footstool. We seemed to see in this dream of ours beautiful women beautifully gowned, walking in the streets of the great town with men well dressed in civilian pants of white linen. It struck us that this was a relief from crumpled olive drab breeches and flannel shirts.

We seemed to be one of a party riding in a gray auto down along a smooth white road into the suburbs of the town, past dwelling houses that wore an aspect of prosperity. They had nice yards. Clean-looking little children played before them. Great shade trees brooded over wide avenues.

Presently it seemed to us that our car was passing through crowded, bustling streets where everybody was in civilian apparel instead of habiliments of war. American, French, Belgian, British, and Italian flags hung from the fronts of business houses, so it seemed to us in our dreams, along with the flag of the Grand Duchy of Luxemburg, where once, early in the war, the girl ruler of the land drove her automobile down to the German border, as the soldiers of the Kaiser were pushing forward, and presented a solemn pact given by Germany against violating her land.

It seemed to us that there was an air of expectancy. Cries of "Vivent les allies!" came to our ears. We thought the car came to a halt and that immediately great crowds of people pressed about it with shouts of welcome. It seemed that someone in the car inquired for the Grand Hotel, which is one of the best hotels in Luxemburg, and that immediately half a dozen citizens leaped on the running boards and offered to act as escorts.

There passed along the filmy scenery of our dreams a vision of cafés and great windows, behind which sat people eating and drinking and chatting, people who seemed to halt in their gustatory occupation to wave their hands at the automobile. Then we dreamed someone in the car got conscience stricken, remembering that Major James, chief of the press division, was due in Luxemburg that afternoon to make arrangements for billets for his outfit, and that there had been rumors that General Pershing might enter the town officially.

It seemed to us that the car's nose was turned the other way, and that the driver was instructed to put on all speed. And from what we recall of the dream, he did.

The car was just a thin gray streak across our mental register. It appeared to us that about a mile out of the town we passed another car, standing by the road, and that that car contained "movie" men of the Signal Corps, with their picture apparatus; that further on we whipped by a truckload of Signal Corps men going in to install telephone wires for headquarters, but that was all undoubtedly nothing but a dream. Doubtless, Luxemburg is quite different.

December 1918

December 1, 1918. With the American Army of Occupation at Trier (Treves)

As these items are written a burst of barber-shop chords comes floating up through the narrow streets of this old town, which the Germans call Trier and which the French call Treves.[177]

By any name it would be pretty ancient, pretty much shoved together. Members of General "Joe" Dickman's Third American Army are doing a bit of close harmonizing somewhere outside. They are singing the familiar lullaby which runs:

"That's How I Miss You."

Thus does history move with giant stride along the "Strassen" of Trier. Peer from a window and you can see in the shadowed nooks up and down the quiet streets, persons indubitably specimens of American doughboy, chatting somewhat lately with persons as indubitably specimens of the German "fraulein." Their conversation is interlarded with "wee, wee" and "yah."

If they continue on into any more different countries, the doughboys will have a tough time getting their various languages straightened out.[178]

History is certainly doing well in Trier already. The American flag was not exactly planted on the soil of Germany today, but it was hung in front of various German buildings picked out as headquarters by various American generals, which amounts to the same thing. American automobiles are parked all over the town, surrounded by children, while American sentries

Trier (Treves), France. *Courtesy of Library of Congress*

walk their posts with hordes of little boys and girls almost clinging to their coat tails. The German youngsters seem to regard the coming of the soldiers today and the soldiers themselves as something gotten up exclusively for their benefit.

Trier is being governed by members of the soldiers' and workmen's council.[179] Former soldiers of the German army in civilian attire, with guns on their shoulders, are acting as policemen, but about their only duty today was to keep the kids from breaking the American automobiles by the sheer weight of numbers.

Thousands of the people of Trier gathered along the roads leading into town this morning to watch the coming of the American troops. They stood silent as the first columns went by. The silence of any big crowd is an uncanny thing. The people talk in undertones, but if there is not vocal outburst the quiet becomes oppressive.[180]

"I thought I saw some bands down the road," remarked an American officer who was watching the march. "I wish they'd hurry up and give us some music."

"Why, if you'll listen, you'll hear some pretty good music," replied another officer. "Don't you hear it? Listen!"[181]

They stood in a harking attitude in the midst of the big, silent crowd as the long lines of American doughboys trudged past. Now came the infantry, bending under their packs. Now the machine gun outfit with lop-eared mules dragging little gun carts, soldiers yanking at the bridles. Now the rolling kitchens with pots steaming and emitting fragrant odors. The soldiers scarcely looked to the right or left as they passed the lines of silent people.

When they did glance up, the doughboys did not change their expressions. It was a tremendous change for them after traversing a land of cheers of "vive" which is Luxemburg and France, but they had anticipated just something. There were no hostile remarks from the people, not even hostile glances, so far as that goes, but assuredly there was no warmth. They were the people of a beaten country gazing on the victors. They were most studiously silent. So were the soldiers.

Occasionally a command came from some officer, or a sergeant gave the marching men a staccato, "Left! Left!" Now and then a driver yelled at his mules. But generally the men went along almost noiselessly.

"I don't hear a damn thing," said the listening officer restlessly. "What do you mean, music? All I hear is that 'crunch, crunch' of their big feet on that gravel road."

"Well, that's the music," said the other, triumphantly. "That old 'crunch, crunch' ought to sound mighty swell to your ears. It does to mine, because, man, they're marching on German territory."

Presently came the band of the Sixth Infantry with a mighty blast of instruments.[182] Right here the crowd surged forward, proving that under the skin it was like all crowds. Right here the children of Trier proved that they're like all children the world over. They spurted out through chinks in the crowds by hundreds and started following the band down the street, across the bridge, into the main part of the town, somewhat disarranging the order of the troops following close behind.

This was the veteran First Division, which entered Trier. It was headed by General Preston Brown, a rather imperious officer of the new regime, who set up headquarters at the best hotel.[183] Going through the town, the band almost blew the narrow streets apart with the volume of its sound.

People poked their heads out from behind blinds, which seemed drawn with more than ordinary care, and gazed down upon the steel helmeted columns going past. They looked well today, our men—wonderfully well. They couldn't help commenting on it in this war-warped place. They are vastly impressed by the appearance of the army which the Kaiser had told them could never get here.

"We couldn't get here, but we're here," as a soldier put it tonight.

They most assuredly are and it's Trier what knows it.

December 2, 1918. With the American Army of Occupation

Under the heading of "local," the Trier (Treves) newspapers today had the following item:

"The American troops arrived in the city yesterday."

That was all. All day the streets of the town resounded to the tread of Dickman's soldiers passing through on the way to the Rhine. Americans are now so numerous in Trier and in the towns beyond they are losing their novelty to the German civil population.

General A. H. Smith,[184] American civil governor of the occupied district, is not recognizing the new soldiers' and workmen's government as yet. He called on the old burgomaster of the town, who almost cried over the unexpectedly decent treatment of the people by the Americans. As long as the civilians conduct themselves decorously, the American regime will be confined largely to military policemen regulating the traffic.

So far there has not been the slightest ripple of hostility. The older people are reported to be bitter, but the younger elements accept the new order without resentment.

Notices were printed in the newspapers of Trier today by the Soldiers' and Workmen's Council warning the people against demonstrations while the Americans are in their midst, also threatening punishment for overcharging for supplies by shopkeepers.

General Smith says reports from the surrounding country indicate that there is abundant food, but that certain articles, such as fats, are extremely scarce. Good meals are obtainable at hotels for prices lower than those charged in France and Luxemburg.[185] However, there are many little evidences of privations.

Mothers say there has been no milk for children for a long time. Many youngsters are wearing shoes with wooden soles.

December 4, 1918. With the American Army of Occupation, Trier (Treves), Germany

Frau Fleiner conducts a store in Trier. We were in there today buying socks. We bought the cheapest she had, at eighteen marks per pair, about $4.50 under the present rate of German money. Frau Fleiner explained in English that wools are pretty scarce in Germany.

Did we know her brother, Henry Belig, who runs a saloon in Melrose Park, Chicago? Excuse her English, please; it hadn't been used much in over four years. Would he like to look at some nice woolen undergarments at about $10 per garment?

She had visited her brother at the time of the World's Fair. Would we be interested in chopped silk underwear at $20 per copy? It would wear well. No, she didn't have shirts and drawers to match in either wool or silk case. There had been lots of military around in the last four years; they had bought it up in assorted lots pretty much.

She hadn't heard from Henry for a long time. It was hard to get mail in or out of Trier during the war. Did we know R. C. Richter, of Denver, Colorado, who has a ranch? He visited in Trier years ago. Lots of Americans used to come to Trier, but they were mainly tourists. Yes, those garments did look like violet bathing suits, but people don't wear their undergarments where they can be seen.

She had two sons in the war. One of them was killed in a battle in France. She hadn't heard from him in a long time either. What about some silk stockings? She had a very few left. The war had been very hard on the poor people of Germany.

What did they think about the Americans being here? Well, they were not bitter against the Americans being here. The Americans would understand the Germans better. No, she didn't think there would be any trouble between the soldiers and the civilian population, but, of course, it was hard on Germany to have a foreign army within her borders. Yes, it probably was just as hard on France when Germany's soldiers were over there.

About this time, Junius B. Wood,[186] of the *Chicago Daily News*, drifted in to assist us in the purchase of socks. Junius owns a little fat dog and lives in constant mortal terror of the small boys of Trier, who are constantly running their hands over the canine in a most suggestive manner.

Junius feels sure they are contemplating the dog from the standpoint of a potential sausage.

When Frau Fleiner heard Junius was from Chicago, she asked him if it is possible for him to get word to her brother, Henry. Junius said he would do it, at which the old woman wept tears of joy.

December 4, 1918. With the American Army of Occupation

We adventured today into the land of little children. Never did anyone see so many kiddies as there are in that section of Germany through which the American army is passing. Junius B. Wood, of the *Chicago Daily News*, argued that they must grow them on vines as much as they grow grapes all along the sunny slopes and hillsides of the Moselle. How else, he debated, could they be so numerous?

Tom Johnson, of the *New York Sun*, held to the theory that it probably rains children instead of raindrops in frequent showers which fall over this region. Neither Mr. Johnson nor Mr. Wood has any children, wherefore it struck us their ideas on the subject were rather vague. With the authority of a father of two, we undertook to put them in their place. From Trier to Bernkastel, every little village along the Moselle fairly boiled with adolescence.

There are many villages. When the horn of our automobile sounded in a narrow street in one of the small towns, out popped children. They leaked out of doors. They scurried from around houses. They bulged from windows, ranging in size from knee high to a grasshopper on up. They rushed after the slow-moving car trying to hook behind. We felt like a lot of journalistic pied pipers.

Mr. Johnson began observing the children with some interest and spoke of them as pink-cheeked little ones, obviously dwelling on this phrase with regard to its potentialities in a story about the matter. We pointed out with parental authoritativeness that some of them seemed pale and under-nourished, venturing the theory that it was probably due to lack of milk.

Mr. Wood stoutly contended that children shouldn't be raised on milk, anyhow, citing Chicago evidence to bear out his contention. However, we repeat, Mr. Wood has no children.

The streets of the lower East Side of New York are thinly populated compared to some of the German towns. There were little round-faced, cotton-topped boys in quaint smocks and voluminous panties, and tiny girls with flaxen hair hanging in pigtails down their backs, peering excitedly along the curbs to see the cars go by

It was a thrilling scene for them. It was a thrilling event for us. Once our car stopped in the middle of the street in one of the larger towns, and a great flock of youngsters promptly swarmed all over it. Mr. Wood viewed these manifestations with some alarm. Mr. Wood cannot disenfranchise himself from the idea that the plumpness of his wholly black dog, "Vesle,"[187] which always rides in the seat beside him, appeals to the gustatory thoughts of the youngsters.

"Vesle" himself is getting that idea. He cringes under the friendliest hands. Mr. Johnson began taking a gloomy view of the number of children.

"Just think what a job old Santa Claus would have if he tried to see all these kids on Christmas," he said. "It's taking advantage of an old guy."

One chubby little fellow in his papa's discarded soldier's cap shrilled: "Heep, heep, hooray," as we entered a town.

"The doughboys are here," observed Mr. Wood with Sherlockian astuteness. He was in there with crowds of youngsters tagging at his heels. We passed several companies at mess, and every company had its fringe of children.

Junius Wood with his famous dog, Vesle. *Courtesy of Chicago History Museum,* Chicago Daily News *negatives collection, DN-0071499*

Now and then he saw a little one happily munching on a chunk of American white bread smothered with jam. It has been a few days since German children saw white bread. They regard it as cake.[188] George Pattullo,[189] the magazine writer, was discovered standing in front of the First Division headquarters, gravely conversing with little people playing in the street.

"Come in and see General McGlachlin,"[190] he invited. "Say, did you ever see so many kids in your life?"

General McGlachlin is commander of the First Division.

"Our men are getting along with the German people fine," he said. "One reason is that the American soldier is kind to children. Say, did you ever see so many children?"

We hadn't, and then went on to the town of Wittlich. It is the seat of the civil authorities. There we had to run with extra caution through the streets to avoid the children. We finally wound up in front of a hotel where the veteran Sixteenth Infantry had its regimental headquarters. There was a big crowd of kids in front. Out came the grizzled commander of the regiment, almost stumbling over some youngsters on the steps.

"Say," he said, "did you ever see so many kids in your life?"

"I guess," added the commander, rather proudly, "we've got more kids in this town than any other place, its size, on earth."

"Poor old Santa Claus," sighed Mr. Johnson as we headed toward Bernkastel. Mr. Wood remained silent.

Near Bernkastel, one of the most picturesque river towns in the world, topped by the ruins of an ancient castle on a high hill, we found Lieutenant Colonel Theodore Roosevelt Jr.,[191] commanding the Twenty-Sixth Infantry, limping about with the aid of a cane. Here, at last, was a man who by right of heritage, anyway, ought to be authority on certain matters.

"Say," he began, "did you ever see—–"

"We never did," we replied hurriedly. "But Mr. Wood here claims that they don't necessarily have to have milk. He has no children himself, remember that."

There was much of the emphasis of the old colonel in the young colonel's voice as it came to us as a final memory of the trip.

"There are more children in this town than in any town in the country. Why, there are families here who have as many as ten children."

"Well," said Mr. Wood, breaking a long stretch of silence on the homeward journey, "I guess they ought to have more milk at that."

"Well," said Mr. Johnson, after another conversational hiatus, "just the same, Old Santa Claus hasn't got any cinch any way you look at it."

December 5, 1918. With the American Army of Occupation

John Soldier is getting pretty much bored by this occupation business, and that's a fact. It's all right to argue that technically we are still at war until the peace pact is definitely signed, but "that don't go" with John. As far as he is personally concerned, the war is over and he would like to get home.

This "marching to the Rhine" sounds romantic, but romance can't ride on shanks' mare[192] more than a couple of kilometers on a frosty morning. Then she falls off, and the rest of the day's journey is just a plain old-time hike.

"How long do you think they'll keep us up there?" is the question John asks the world at large.

Back in France there are veteran divisions querulously complaining because they were not selected for the Army of Occupation, which is the American Third Army, and the members of the Third Army probably would be just as fretful if they hadn't come. But now that they have seen Germany, they are dead willing to have someone else have a peek at her if it will get them back across the Atlantic any sooner.

In the years to come, it will be many a man's boast that he hiked with Dickman to the Rhine, but it would be a hard job to convince him of that along about noon these days when a sixty-five-pound load is tugging at his heartstrings.

Since time immemorial the Americans suddenly converted into soldiers have loathed police work, which is, after all, what their occupation now amounts to. When the fighting stops, John Soldier wants to get back to his old business, whatever it may have been.

It takes us back to a matter of twenty years to go around with a soldier's outfit these days and liven up the conversation. We can close our eyes and almost imagine we were back in the Philippines with Christmas coming on and thousands of American boys marking time, so to speak, in their billets after the war had ended.

Everybody's thoughts then were of home, just as everybody's thoughts are now. They were eagerly discussing rumors of orders back to the States for demobilization, and they are eagerly discussing such rumors this very minute.

Wherever two or more soldiers are gathered together, such rumors are eagerly discussed. Twenty years ago, they sang a song which they are singing now with a slight variation. It's a song almost as old as the American army. It was certainly mighty old twenty years ago. There are dozens of verses to it, which are altered from war to war to suit occasions, but the tune is always the same and it's never much of a tune at that. Twenty years ago the refrain ran like this:

> "It's home, boys, it's home, I want to be
> It's home, boys, home; back in God's country—
> Where the ash and the oak and budding maple grow—
> To hell with Manila, boys; it's home we want to go."

Today they merely substitute "Germany" for "Manila."

It's a great song. This jaunt is going to be mighty useful for conversation purposes at meetings of Dickman Post No. 1, Veterans of the American Expeditionary Forces, in the future years. But just at present, doing the Edward Weston[193] through the Rhineland runs for Sweeney with the Johns.[194]

In the towns along the way the windows are filled with toys. These things carry the boys' memory across the seas. There are almost as many toy stores in Germany as there are children. The toys are not up to the old German quality, but there is a great variety. Lots of mechanical toys are seen, but gimcracks made of wood are more common. Most of them were evidently manufactured before the end of the war was in sight. Regiments of tin Prussian guards stand stolidly in every window. Toy guns and soldiers' outfits are numerous. Even Christmas tree ornaments are made with Iron Crosses worked on them

Then there are thousands of dolls for little girls. These dolls are dressed in German styles. You see no doll characters representing anything but German, but then you see probably no German doll characters in the Allied countries.

Scores of children stand with their little noses pressed against every store window just as they do at home. Toys are one thing fairly cheap. However, you can get better dolls in America for what they cost here.

Big doughboys are seen in every store buying presents for the folks at home. There are numerous candy stores, but mighty little candy. The windows are filled with the most elaborate boxes, but inside they have little in the way of sweets to sell.

They make pies which look wonderful but which taste like compressed air. They are all fluff. The Germans are great hands to fill windows with marvelous imitations of candy and fruit which are made of papier mâché and which seem to serve no purpose but to tantalize the memory. They have plenty of picture books and Christmas cards and Christmas trees, anyway. It ought to be a fairly merry Christmas on the Rhine.

December 8, 1918. With the American Army of Occupation

When John Soldier repaired to his favorite "gasthaus" or café in Trier at 9 o'clock Saturday night, he beckoned to Carla, the beautiful waitress, and ordered up "ein," "zwei," or "drei" beer as the case might be.

She began talking like one of the signs so familiar throughout Germany. The gist of her conversation was "verboten." Naturally, John fretfully queried "Why?" Carla spread her hands wide and repeated her song with the refrain "verboten." John could have lemonade but not "ein," "zwei," or "drei" beers.

It was "verboten."

While John debated the matter with many gesticulations and numerous "wast ist los" (wast ist los meaning what's the matter), 9 o'clock and 10 o'clock came along. The door opened and in popped a big military policeman looking extra military-policeish.

"Raus!" he said laconically.

So there was nothing for John to do except "raus," and away he went to his quarters to dream of that dear France and that dearer Luxemburg, when "ein," "zwei," or "drei" beers, not to mention light wines, were most fluent. Thus a new order of things came to the Army of Occupation.

"Verboten" is a new idea when it comes to the matter of liquor and late hours for John. As Carla delivered herself of the dictum transferred to her by the military authorities last night, former German soldiers sitting at other tables with their "frauleins" and their "ein-zwei-drei" beers listened with some amazement.

They could not quite grasp the situation at first. When it dawned upon them that John cannot have his beer, they emitted loud Teutonic snorts. Some French colonials, who are uniformed somewhat similar to the Americans, had a narrow escape last night. Carla couldn't distinguish them from the Americans at first, so she "verbotened" them also.

Cries of great distress rose from the Frenchmen, but Carla was obdurate. Then the American officers went around and explained that Frenchmen are not Americans and Americans are not Frenchmen.

Carla gave the Frenchmen their beer, and so international complication was avoided.

It seems the new "dry" order didn't apply to the American officers. They were pushing over tall ones with white collars on them as John went away from there. It is understood, however, that the enlisted men of the expedition have gone on prohibition for the rest of their jaunt to the Rhine at 9 o'clock at night.

"I don't give a damn," said John Soldier, sourly, as he slammed the door of his recent favorite "gasthaus."

"There ain't any more to it than near-beer anyway."[195]

December 9, 1918. With the American Army of Occupation, Trier, Germany

Nearly every small boy in Trier and in the little country towns on up toward the Rhine now wears one of those round caps with a red band, which became so familiar to the Americans soldiers in France as the headgear of the enemy.

It is proof that the German boy's "daddy" has come home from the war. Some of the youngsters wear their daddy's old goat hide campaign boots and even part of their father's uniform if "daddy" isn't wearing these articles himself, which is not infrequently the case.

The male part of the population in this section of Germany is now half soldier, half civilian, as far as apparel is concerned. The men are going about their daily tasks with the old military coats and civilian trousers or vice versa. Out in the country districts the farmers are still wearing entire uniforms, but in most cases they have stripped them of the soldiers' buttons. They are wearing them because they have nothing else to wear. Around town, however, there are many former officers of the German army who are still in their resplendent uniforms as a matter of choice. Some of them can be seen lolling around the hotels with all their old imperious manner. It is pretty hard to believe that this particular species of German is repentant.

Trains arrive in Trier now and then from various parts of Germany. Most of them are loaded with soldiers returning home. Men and officers alike tramp along the streets and down the country roads, carrying their luggage on their backs. Many of them are attended by their womenfolk who have met them at the trains.

Practically every man in Trier, no matter how civilized he may be in the matter of dress, bears some unmistakable mark of having served in the army. The most common form is the military haircut, which has not yet had time to wear off. Military bearing is another. Their hands jerk up halfway to their foreheads involuntarily when a man in officer's uniform passes.

Former soldiers are eager to talk to Americans. Frequent instances are related of Americans and Germans discovering in the course of their conversations that they were opposed to each other in the same sector in France. One German was found today who was in the German forces that beleaguered Whittlesey's "lost battalion" in the Argonne.[196]

Without exception the German soldiers declare that the Americans are amazing fighters, and they generally add that if it had not been for the Yankees, Germany would have won the war.

The civilian population has had an easy time at the hands of the Americans so far. No onerous rules have been imposed. It is mighty different from the way the Germans treated the people of the regions in Belgium and France where they were in power. In turn, the German civilians seem rather to be going out of their way to make friends with the American troops.

It is pretty hard and indubitably wrong to feel vengeful toward a people who have undoubtedly suffered much. But at the same time it is equally hard to reconcile their present attitude with their demeanor of a year or so ago; it's pretty hard to forget the ruined towns and homeless women and children in France in this most German town, which has in no way been damaged by the war.

It still has its tree-lined streets. Its beautiful dwellings haven't been piled into masses of debris by shells and fires in wantonness. Its soldiers are coming home war-worn and weary, but they have homes to come to. That isn't so with a great many soldiers of France and Belgium. Their homes were blotted out in many instances by the very hands now stretched out conciliatorily.

American soldiers would be incapable of treating the people of a beaten country any less humanely then they are treating the people in this region. They would be incapable of manifesting vengeance, especially when the manifestations might fall upon women and children.

The fight is over. They have won, and there is no bitterness in them toward a beaten country and a beaten people, but in the light of the German soldiers' conduct in France and Belgium, it is interesting to contemplate what the conditions would have been in Trier tonight, where a group of men and women just passed the hotel where this dispatch is being written, singing songs and making merry, had this been an American town and had the soldier occupants been victorious Germans.

December 12, 1918. [Delayed] With the American Army of Occupation at Coblenz[197]

A blast of music on the edge of Coblenz about 10 o'clock this morning woke the echoes for blocks around and set thousands of little children of the town running in the direction of the sound. German citizens moving about in the streets stopped in their tracks and stood stolidly staring. Hausfraus began popping their heads out of windows.

The music came steadily on flowing into the narrow streets until it seemed to be closing them with the great volume of melody.

Certainly it choked the throats of many listening Americans with great emotion, for it was not difficult to identify the air as "Here's to You, Uncle Sammy," nor was it difficult to identify the occasion as the official entry into Coblenz of the American "Army of the Lord."

Old "Joe" Dickman's troops are tonight resting all along the Rhine. You can't go anywhere in the city which was once the favorite summer resort of Kaiser Wilhelm without bumping into representatives of that country from which Wilhelm said he would stand no foolishness "after this war."

All day today, McLachlin's veteran First Division, which licked the Germans on a dozen different bloody fields, was pouring into Coblenz in seemingly interminable lines of olive drab. Over the cobblestones of the principal streets of the town tramped America's peerless infantry hour after hour, followed by rumbling wagons, drawn by fat, lop-eared mules from Missouri, while kids in pa's discarded soldier caps ran along almost under the feet of the good-natured

American troops marching through Coblenz. *Courtesy of United States Army Heritage and Education Center*

doughboys, and startled frauleins peered from shop windows. Former German soldiers, now appareled in the height of German civilian fashion—which is not so high as it may sound—but with the inevitable cockade feathers in their new Alpine fedoras, stood on the yard-wide sidewalks critically eyeing their conquerors.

It was the Twenty-Eighth Infantry which first entered the town. They marched as if on parade. Their brown faces were shaded by steel helmets. They bore their heavy packs as lightly as if they were pillows. All the way through the town, the band knocked all quiet out of the atmosphere with a steady "boom-pah." It played "Hail to the President"—the same march with which the band of the One Hundred and Twenty-Second Artillery played out of the war that morning of November 11 back of the Meuse. Then it played another march which an excited Bostonian insisted was "Fair Harvard." It would have been somewhat appropriate at that, for not far behind the Twenty-Eighth Infantry a famous Harvardian was leading the Twenty-Sixth Infantry into the outskirts of the town. He is Lieutenant Colonel Theodore Roosevelt Jr. Besides the Twenty-Eighth, the Sixteenth and Eighteenth Regiments are also in the First Division.

At noon today the companies passing through the city stopped right where they happened to be and had dinner from rolling kitchens.[198]

One outfit located itself in a public square right in the heart of the business district. As each man of the mess got his plate full of steaming grub, he sat down on the curbing and started to eat. Presently they were all surrounded by children and even adults. It was a great object lesson. White bread was especially an object of comment, and soon some children were in the happy possession of pieces.

There is one thing the Germans have not had, however much they may have had of other things, and that is chocolate. The children seem to have an idea that every American goes around loaded with sweets, and are constantly appealing for it.[199]

All the principal hotels were quickly taken over today for rooms for headquarters and for officers.

Up to this morning the American occupation of Coblenz has been entirely informal, and the Germans gathered a slightly mistaken impression. They evidently thought the whole occupation would be what you might call "self-effacing" as the policing has been.[200]

Tonight, however, burly signal corps men began stringing wires into hotels without saying much about the matter to the proprietors, while military policemen took charge of the traffic, and the whole city found itself under complete control of business-like Americans.[201]

The Rhine here is lined with beautiful homes. Some officers were billeted in houses.

Tomorrow the troops cross the river and take over that section of the town, probably including the fortress of Ehrenbreitstein.[202]

Fortress of Ehrenbreitstein. *Courtesy of Library of Congress*

There was a great race yesterday among war workers to get into Coblenz. Two stalwart members of the Knights of Columbus came galloping in first. They were Fred Riler,[203] of Torrington, Connecticut, and John J. Donovan,[204] of Boston. They brought five tons of gumdrops and other supplies.[205]

Soon afterward the first American women to reach the Rhine arrived. They were, of course, girls of the Salvation Army. God bless 'em. Miss Eddie Hodges,[206] of Richmond, Virginia, and Miss Florence Tarkington,[207] of South Manchester, Connecticut, are their names. They came in with Fred Anderson,[208] of Tacoma, Washington, and were three days and three nights on the road.

The war workers were not allowed to remain in town yesterday, because they got here too soon. Our army is quite squiffy about those matters. But they came back today.

The Salvation Army made a record in this war which will never be forgotten. You may not have heard much about it so far, but you'll hear plenty when the boys get home. Someone once asked an old colonel commanding the organization in France why he didn't hire a press agent.

"Why," he said innocently, "I never thought of it."

The Knights of Columbus, too, have done great work. It is about a toss-up between them and the Salvationists.

December 12, 1918. [Delayed] With the American Army of Occupation in the Rhineland

In Coblenz there is an enormous bronze equestrian statue of old William the Great, towering over the end of the esplanade where the Moselle flows into the Rhine here.

Two privates of Lieutenant Colonel Lockett's[209] advance guard were gazing up at it Thursday morning, trying to read the inscription on it, when a young German soldier who speaks a little English came along and one of the doughboys asked him to interpret the sign.

The German made several attempts but could not give the literal translation.

"I can't read the exact words but I can tell you what it means," he said.

"It says that Germany can never be beaten."

For the next five minutes the hoarse gurgle of American laughter rolled out over the Rhine.

Nearly all advanced elements of the "Army of the Lord" have arrived at different points along the river. Formal entrance into Coblenz will probably be made Friday. Lockett's outfit is still the only troop unit here. The soldiers patrol the town in detachments of three or four with rifles slung across their backs. Their bayonets are always fixed.

Thursday night some restrictions were placed on the night life of Coblenz. Cafés were ordered to close at 9 o'clock. The order came from the burgomaster, said to be due to lack of coal. Up to now the cafés have stayed open about as late as they pleased.

"It's pretty hard on us to have to close so early," one proprietor remarked to an American officer.

"If just one-fourth of the restrictions you laid on the French and Belgians were put on you now, you'd still have it mighty easy," was the reply.

They sang "Mignon" at the opera here Wednesday night. The audience was not large and was made up of almost as many American officers and soldiers as of German civilians. One of the numbers played by the orchestra was George Cohan's[210] "Popularity." They don't have much opera these days in such towns in France as Rheims and Verdun.

German officers still were going around Thursday in full uniform, although it is said they will not be allowed to wear them later. Others who were fighting against the Americans in the Argonne and along the Meuse only a few weeks ago walk the boulevards in new civilian attire, swinging canes, and lifting their hats to one another. In the afternoon the tearooms are crowded.

Christmas shopping is in full swing, and the stores are filled with people making purchases. The proprietor of a jewelry store told us Thursday that business had been very good last year. He said people had plenty of money and nothing else to spend it on, so bought freely of jewelry. However, the jewelry offered for sale was not particularly elaborate, compared with that to be seen in Fifth Avenue shops. Prices are very high.

Among the troops arriving at the Rhine Thursday were the First, Second, and Third Divisions and the Thirty-Second, the pride of Michigan and Wisconsin. The railroaders, the Nineteenth of Texas, and the Fourth are coming up behind. Well back, the Eighty-Ninth from Kansas, Missouri, Nebraska, and Colorado is moving along.

The roads all around Coblenz are now reminiscent of the early stages of the last drive in France. They are choked with traffic.

The old Duchy of Luxemburg, through which the "Army of the Lord" is passing, is getting the impression that all Americans are moving into Germany, but the children there haven't lost the habit of shrieking "vive" to the passing troops. It is a big relief to go to Luxemburg, where the Americans are genuinely welcome, from Coblenz, where the people are inhospitable—to put it very gently. This is assuredly Germany. Even down by the borders, it is a pleasant change from this Rhine town. The atmosphere there is much different.

Of course, it must be remembered that Coblenz is not yet formally occupied by the American men, who are here merely as a sort of preliminary police. When our forces really take over the city it is likely there will be numerous changes in civil conditions generally.

No Americans are yet allowed across the bridge to the right bank of the Rhine, where the fortress Ehrenbreitstein frowns over the city. All day Thursday that bank was quivering under the movement of German wagons and other transports moving an army on its way back into the interior.[211]

Americans are not permitted to wander into the suburbs, where gorgeous dwelling houses line the Rhine and where German children play.

The former German soldier who lived in the States is bobbing up in Coblenz these days with stories of how he was visiting Germany when the war broke out and he was forced into service by the German government. Most of them want some kind of assistance from American officers.

December 13, 1918. With the American Army of Occupation in the Rhineland

If a person had come direct to this section of Germany, since the signing of the armistice, and mingled with the people and heard their story without having seen anything of the war as waged by the Germans in France and Belgium, it is quite conceivable that he might develop a compassion that would warp his viewpoint to some extent.

He might forget for a moment that he is seeing in his humility that same German who swaggered so truculently about the world only a few short months ago. He has merely changed his shirt. It seems to the writer that there is food for reflection in the thought that the Germans here are glad that Americans came instead of the French, the people against whom the Germans have sinned most.

It is idle to say that they really welcome the soldiers, it would be idle to say that any country would welcome enemy soldiers, but as long as they had to have some troops in their midst, there is no doubt that it gratifies the Germans hereabouts that those troops are Americans instead of those of the Allies, particularly the French.

The French would have treated them not a whit differently from the Americans, but they seem to feel that the Americans understand them because the regulations in the occupied zones are the same as has been applied to their own soldiers. At many places they have to be off the streets at 9 o'clock. The civilians and former German soldiers stayed out as long as they pleased.

It was different when the Germans were in France. Although American soldiers are frequently billeted in German homes and maintain friendly relations with the German families, there is no social intercourse between them and German civilians, nor is there likely to be.

Never by word or manner does an American soldier display any feeling against the Germans. He just goes along minding his own business. Of course, you're never going to get any American displaying any feeling against children and women—no matter what the circumstances—but even toward the men or soldiers observe this policy of reserve.

A large number of Americans speak German, and many Germans here speak English. Many have been in America, or have relatives there. In their hearts, the Germans doubtless resent the presence of our troops, but on the surface there is no sign of bitterness or hostility, such as their attitude toward America in the early part of the war led some Americans to expect.

It is no exaggeration to say they are pretty lucky in many respects. They are chiefly lucky that their country was not invaded by their own people, had those people conducted themselves as they did when they invaded France.

The Americans have so far preserved the highest grade of discipline, and they are tolerant and kindly. In fact, it is doubtful if an American who fought the Germans from the Marne to the Meuse feels any of the bitterness that is reflected by the people who never heard a gun fired.

Soldiers are generally that way.

The American fighting man despises the things the Germans did, and he is by no means disposed to make friends of the doers, but he doesn't go around in the hour of victory voicing hatred.

One of the officers was expressing surprise Thursday at the rather fawning attitude of some of the former German officers. The house of one of them had been taken by Americans for billets, and the owner looked after all their arrangements, trying to make them comfortable. He kept coming around asking if he couldn't do something more. It was a far cry from the old attitude of the German officers.

The Sixteenth Infantry found one fellow just the reverse, however. His name was Well. He runs the Well hotel at Wittlich. He was demobilized a few days ago and quietly resumed the management of his business.

One of the American officers asked him if he was glad the war was over.

"I am not," said Well.

"Why not?" asked the American.

"Because we lost," said Well. "Why should I be glad when it ended with us as the loser?"

The Americans said they thought better of him for his frankness at that.

December 14, 1918. [Delayed] With the American Army of Occupation, Coblenz

One hundred years hence the school children of America will be reading in their histories of how on Friday, December 13, 1918, an American army marched across the River Rhine.

This thought struck us with dramatic force, as we lay in bed, early that morning, in the palatial Hotel Coblenzerhof and listened to the comments of our roommate, Miller,[212] of the press bunch, who stood at the window and, gazing down into the street, made fragmentary reports on events below while putting on his shirt.

"Here comes General Frank Parker[213] on horseback and he is getting all wet," said Miller, jubilantly.

Our thought, combined with the prospect of seeing a wet general, proved to be alluring. We arose. Up to this moment it had been our intention of covering the historic occasion by the simple expedient of turning over in bed and looking out of the window from the shelter of sheets.

The Hotel Coblenzerhof fronts on the Rhine, is only a few yards from the river, in fact. A crossing at the most important point was handily arranged to take place on a bridge right beneath the hotel windows. Many a military notable probably witnessed the event as we ourselves had planned.

Crossing rivers has become more or less of an incident with the American Expeditionary Forces. Filled with our thoughts, however, we hurried forth into the street. It was shortly before 7 o'clock, army time. The crossing was set for 7 o'clock, army time, which made it 8 o'clock, German time. Armies have got in the habit of being forehanded with the Germans.

At either 7 or 8 o'clock, anybody's time, it is still dark in this country. Also it was raining this morning.

The Eighteenth Infantry of the First Division was standing in column squads in the streets, shedding water from its steel helmets. The band was waiting patiently at the head of the column, with raindrops trickling into its instruments.

The wet General Parker was humped up on a horse, looking at his wristwatch. All the officers around him were looking at their wristwatches. On the sidewalks stood a few German civilians, watching the scene. We sidled up alongside a dripping doughboy of our acquaintance.

"Do you realize," we said importantly, "that one hundred years hence the school children of America will be reading in their histories about what you are about to do?"

"That so?" he remarked casually. "Well, what of it?"

Then, the wristwatches all having apparently arrived at 7 o'clock, army time, officers shouted orders, the Eighteenth shouldered arms, General Parker booted his horse with his heels, and history began marching along.

We hurried across the bridge, ahead of the column, to view the formal entrance into the town on that side, which is called Ehrenbreitstein after the old fortress, which frowns on the heights above. A Cincinnati soldier kept insisting today that the name sounds like some old-time Red battery.

Arriving slightly ahead of the troops was Junius Wood's war dog, "Vesle."[214] Next came Junius Wood himself. Then a Y.M.C.A. girl. Then General Parker and his staff. Our army simply will not be dramatic. This is especially true of John Soldier. We went back down the line to confide a new thought to our friend.

"This is the first time in over a century that hostile troops have crossed this river," we informed him.

"That so?" he said, calmly. "Well, what do you hear about us going home?"

They had to march the troops over out of step. This particular bridge is an ancient structure on steel pontoons. It lies close to the water. They pick it apart every few minutes to let steamboats, which move in an interminable line up and down the Rhine, through.

When the soldiers were marching in step, they shook the bridge until it had threatening palpitation. Once in passage the band struck up a marching tune and put all the men back in step again. The musicians had to be suppressed.

Going across, the troops met a stream of German civilians who live in Ehrenbreitstein, who were coming over to Coblenz to their daily work. It reminded one of the rush off the Oakland boat at Frisco ferry. There were men and women in the stream. Some of them scarcely looked up at the passing soldiers. Others, faces expressionless, gazed at the troops their Kaiser said would never get here.

Over in the Hotel Riesen-Fuerstenhof in Coblenz, where many Americans were billeted, a German officer, in uniform, stood at a window of the dining room, watching the crossing. He cried openly, without restraint. There was a German private soldier in the street. When the American colors passed, he did not change from his stolid attitude. An American stepped up quietly behind him and said something in his ear. Forthwith the German faded from view.

The Americans did not attempt to enforce any salute of the colors by civilians, and the few men left around in town in German uniforms salute of their own volition when the occasion arises. Only German officers on a special mission here will be allowed in uniform hereafter.

Just as soon as the troops had crossed the bridge, some of them were stationed around Ehrenbreitstein. Others moved on about ten kilometers. Later some troops probably will be installed in the fortress, where, according to the now ironical Baedeker, "no foreign officers are permitted."[215]

While the Eighteenth, Colonel Theodore Roosevelt Jr.'s Twenty-Sixth, and other troops of the division were crossing at Coblenz, over the old pontoon, another bridge a little way farther up the stream, the Thirty-Second was going over at Engers and the Second at Linz, using ferry boats.

For several days the Second Division has been hobnobbing at Maria Laach[216] with Brother Lucas, who is in charge of the 150 monks in the monastery here. They are guarding what is said to be the largest store of the oldest and rarest wine[217] in all Germany. It was one of the pleasantest places on the Rhine for anybody.

December 14, 1918. [Delayed] With the American Army of Occupation, Coblenz

There passed over the Rhine Saturday several miles of cogent reasons why Germany couldn't win the war. Two regiments of the greatest field artillery in all the world rumbled through the streets of Coblenz and across the teetering pontoon bridge to Ehrenbreitstein. They were the Fifth and Seventh.

They provided a real show. It was something the Germans could well understand because it represented military force to the 'nth degree. They stood along the sidewalks, watching with eyes fairly bulging. It would have been interesting to read the Boche mind, as gun after gun went past, their sinister muzzles protruding from their canvas blankets.

Many of the Germans who watched could narrate personal experiences with the Fifty-Seventh Battalion at the Marne and the Meuse. The guns were the 155 shorts—the bulldogs of battle. Until recently they were splotched with camouflage, but when the march to the Rhine was commenced, the Fifty-Seventh repainted all its equipment in gray.

It was a bright morning, as brightness goes in this region, when the artillery column hit the bridge. There was but a glimpse of the sun showing the band of the Seventh, which was the first to cross, its horns gleaming in the vague sunlight. It kept up a thumping tune every yard of the way over.

Long after the old bridge was swaying under the wheels of the guns, the fortified hills of Ehrenbreitstein still were sending echoes of American music back across the Rhine. At the head of the column, fluttering bravely in the morning breeze, were the good colors—the red, white, and blue, with the red-blood standard of the artillery flowing along beside them.

It was like a sign from heaven. It made one thank the Lord he was an American. It made one's heart swell with emotions too sacred to attempt to write about.

Good old fat Padre Joyce,[218] one of the famous chaplains of the Regular Army, who was with the field guns for years but who now has apologetically explained that he has been demoted to looking after the spiritual interests of the machine gunners, stood with us on the Coblenz side of the bridge, watching the march.

Old Padre Joyce once advanced the jocose theory that the only real hope for an artilleryman is to baptize him and then shoot him, but he loves the field gunners as a child loves its dolls.

And the gunners all know Padre Joyce.

He began puffing up with pride as the Seventh approached. He used to serve with the Seventh.

"Here's the real Mick outfit," he announced. Then for the next hour he was kept busy answering nods and verbal salutations from helmeted drivers bobbing past on shaggy leaders and shaggier wheelers, and from cannoneers answering from the tails of guns. He told scores of stories as the procession went by.

"There goes Murphy," he said, "that tough-looking Tad there. I married him at Fort Russell, Cheyenne. Hello, Murphy! Hello, Clancy! Did I ever tell you the story of–Hello, Fred–"

Now and then he returned a real military salute. Padre Joyce's salute has no equal in all the army. It starts from his hip and reaches up about as far as his waist. There you might think he was merely scratching himself. But he knows the guns.

"Here comes another Mick outfit," he declared, as the Fifth succeeded the Seventh. "Look at them."

They were worth looking at. Most of the men in the two regiments are veterans. They wear their steel hats cocked sidewise—as only men who understand steel hats can wear them—and they ride along like men sitting on top of the world. They regarded their German audience quizzically. Most of the drivers wore big quids of tobacco in their cheeks after the manner of men who associate with horses. They delivered themselves of streams of juice occasionally with expertness and precision.

They were mainly young men with eyes of youth and hearts of youth and God. How good they looked as they rode through this old hostile town Saturday morning with sullen Germans watching! No wonder the Boche hates von Tirpitz.[219] No wonder they hate Ludendorff[220] for telling them the Americans could never get men across the sea.

There was one German woman opposite who stood bareheaded for two solid hours, so close to the curb that the wheels of passing guns splattered mud on her skirt. She never changed expression. She seemed to study every gunner and every gun minutely.

One marching artilleryman went by with a small box on either side clinging to his belt. The guns were drawn by heavy-footed French horses with short tails. Artillery horses have to have short tails here to keep them out of the mud. Some of the French stock dragging artillery have been so shortened behind that it would give the humane society the fantods to see them. Their hair grows amazingly long.

The Fifth and Seventh had brushed up their steeds for this occasion. Following the guns came supply wagons, pulled in many cases by six or eight Missouri mules. They were nearly all big, fat mules, too.

Every outfit in the army has some insignia painted on its wagons and camions. One outfit in the line this morning has for its trademark the picture of a German helmet with a big ax sunk in its crown. The audience did not miss this.

"Muleskinners" peered from under canvas canopies at the people like drivers of old prairie schooners scanning the horizon for Indians. They keyed their conversation with the mules to a low pitch while passing through the city for fear some German woman might understand English.

Rolling kitchens went along, their fires blazing and potatoes steaming. All this went right through the heart of the town and over the river.

After it came a long remount outfit with new horses and mules. Then a regiment of infantry tramped across the bridge. Then a regiment of engineers with its transport.

By night, Coblenz was convinced that von Tirpitz and Ludendorff were mistaken even more than they had been suspecting.

While the Americans were crossing one bridge, two French divisions were crossing another bridge in a different part of the town.

There appeared on the streets today, encased in a prodigious grin, an individual who excited intense interest from all native beholders. He was Gabe Jewell, of Louisville, Kentucky, with the complexion and color of new charcoal.

He is the first American Negro soldier to reach the Rhine. Gabe came as a cook with one of the headquarters outfits. No colored units are connected with the Army of Occupation, so Gabe and his companions have a unique distinction.

It seems that colored folks are not common in this region. Gabe was followed about by small knots of people, much to his annoyance. Some civilians tried to talk to him, but Gabe is no linguist.

Undated. [Published December 17, 1918] With the American Army of Occupation

There is always an argument in our car. Generally it's over the question whether we shall turn to the left or right at cross-roads, although anything else will do. As a rule we generally agree on the turn, and it proves the wrong one after we've gone a few kilometers, as we did on this night when we were returning from a visit to the Eighteenth Infantry, away up toward the Rhine. After we had discovered the mistake we journeyed on a few kilometers further. As usual, we debated the responsibility for the error.

"There's a German up the road there," said Mr. Wood, of the *Chicago News*, peering through the fog, rain, and mist. "Let's ask him which way's the right one. He's sure to have a brother in Chicago."

"No," argued Mr. Johnson, of the *New York Sun*, "he has a sister in Brooklyn."

"It'll be an uncle in Milwaukee," we averred, positively, having made a secret study of the ramifications of local family trees. We ranged alongside the figure, which bulked big out of the darkness. It proved to be an old man with a cloak wrapped around him.

"Nach Trier," we demanded, waving wildly in the direction ahead. He said, "Nein." Then he said some more words which Mr. Johnson interpreted as meaning that if we kept on we'd run right into the Moselle River. Unless the car could float, he advised against such a course.

We invited him into the car to show us the road.

"You have a brother in Chicago," observed Mr. Wood, confidently, as the old man settled down in the seat beside us.

"Tell him that in German," he directed Mr. Johnson.

"You have a sister in Brooklyn?" said Mr. Johnson, correctly. The old man exploded into a string of "Neins."

"It's an uncle in Burlington, Iowa," said Mr. Johnson. "His name is Wilhelm something, and he's very old and feeble. You see you're wrong again."

Mr. Wood was for pressing the inquiry to make sure the old man hadn't overlooked at least one sister in Chicago, but by this time we had reached the ferry. It was dark, but we could dimly see some kind of boat out in the river. A broad voice answered our yells. "There's one man who's sure to have a brother in Chicago," declared Mr. Wood, with great satisfaction. "It will be an aunt in Dubuque, Iowa," said Mr. Johnson, hedging a little. "An uncle in Milwaukee," we announced firmly. There proved to be two men in the boat. One of them was a Charon with whiskers. The other was a young German soldier in uniform. The boat was a flat scow, and we doubted if it could hold the automobile, so the driver ran the machine aboard to see it did not sink. Meanwhile, Mr. Wood was addressing himself to the Charon. "I am from Chicago, where your brother resides," he announced. Mr. Johnson changed his remarks. "He means your aunt who lives in Kansas City." Mr. Johnson was hedging again. The old fellow "Neined" them promptly. It was an uncle in Madison, Wisconsin.

We were getting close. The German soldier had been listening to the colloquy. He spoke up in English: "I also have an uncle in Philadelphia." We nodded, only we said: "We thought it should be in Milwaukee."

The Charon and the soldier were shoving off the boat when we heard shrill cries. Out of the darkness came running a young woman with a basket on her arm. She desired passage over the river. As she scrambled aboard the boat, she caught us in the glow of the automobile lights.

"Americans," she murmured.

Messrs. Wood and Johnson moved forward expectantly. "I have people in America," she said naively in German. "A brother," began Mr. Wood. "A sister," interrupted Mr. Johnson. "Nein," she said somewhat startled. "An uncle in Milwaukee."

But how should Mr. Wood or Mr. Johnson know, not being betting men that the local prices on an inhabitant in this particular region are:

Brother or other relative in Chicago: 4 to 1.

Brother or sister in some other part of America: 50 to 1.

Uncle in Milwaukee: 100 to 1.

December 17, 1918. With the American Army of Occupation at Coblenz on the Rhine

At 3:30 o'clock this afternoon, four American doughboys were sitting on the west bank of a very famous river in Germany, laying their aching feet in its cooling waters and idly squirting the juice of horseshoe plug into the stream.

They got to debating the merits of the river. One scoffed at it as a puny affair. "She ain't nigh as wide as the Mississippi down Natchez way," he asserted stoutly. Another admitted grudgingly that it is wider than the Oregon, but promptly added that it's not half as pretty.

"I wouldn't trade the Hudson for her," said the third, picking up a pebble and chucking it into the water

"No, nor the Harlem, neither, for that matter," said the fourth man, reflectively, looking at a dapper passing steamboat.

"Buddies,"[221] he said solemnly, "when it comes to rivers, just gimme the old Rock River back there in Illinois for mine. That's some crick, that is. Mebbe it ain't got as many bum old castles and wine orchards and all that damn foolishness, but she's some crick, she is."

Thus the "Army of the Lord" reached the Rhine. Nineteen months from the time it started it arrived.

It is a little ahead of its own schedule. It is considerably ahead of the schedule of the German High Command, which said it would never get here at all.

Tonight, gruff American voices were floating out over the bosom of the water as American soldiers strolled along the banks under great trees, watching the lights both up and down the stream, and passing many joyful remarks about keeping the "watch on the Rhine."

In many a café overlooking the river, American soldiers had their big American feet under German tables, drinking German beer, and listening to the music of German orchestras, while citizens and soldiers of the tumbling empire sat about with their women folk, watching them with curiosity. Waiters with closely cropped heads rushed about serving newcomers. Most of them had fed German machine guns somewhere between the Marne and the Meuse against their new patrons.

On the walls of cafés still hang pictures that bring the memories back to the old regime. One, showing the Kaiser and his six sons in military array, must have been once quite popular. Throughout the town of Coblenz there is an atmosphere of pre-holiday spirit amounting to downright gaiety as the invaders from overseas stamp along the streets.

Assuredly there is night life in abundance. It is quite a town in one way and another, this bridgehead of the Rhine, now held by the American army. It was one highly esteemed by the Kaiser and his family. In the restaurant of the Riesen-Fuerstenhof Hotel, on the river front, of which hotel Herr Hohansen is proprietor, the orchestra leader displayed much astuteness.

After a program of German musical noises, his orchestra struck up "The Stars and Stripes Forever."

Lieutenants Arthur John Delaney, of New York; George Ifft,[222] of Pocatello, Idaho; Conger Reynolds, of Des Moines, Iowa; and Henri Muller,[223] an instructor at Columbia, who has been with the French army throughout the war, were sitting at a table together.

They let go a volley of applause that sounded like a machine gun barrage. The Germans stared in amazement. Applause is not "au fait" in Germany apparently.

Only the advance guard of General Dickman's Third Army is on the Rhine today. American troops were not due in Coblenz for some days, but the German officers themselves asked for enough soldiers to police the town, as they are pulling out entirely.

Colonel C. O. Sherrill,[224] Chief of Staff of New York's Seventy-Seventh Division, came here a few days ago with a number of other officers to inspect the bridgehead and establish headquarters.

Colonel Sherrill got here just in time to see the German Seventy-Sixth Division moving over the Rhine. It was this division which fought the Seventy-Seventh throughout the battle of the Argonne Forest.

A young German lieutenant who was assigned to Colonel Sherrill as interpreter turned out to be the officer who wrote the note calling upon Major Whittlesey to surrender his beleaguered battalions in the epic of the defense of the Argonne.

This note was given by the officer to Private Hollingshead, one of Whittlesey's men who had been captured by the Germans and was sent back with the demand. How the note was received is history.

The Second Battalion of the Thirty-Ninth Infantry of the Fourth Division under command of Lieutenant Colonel James W. Lockett was selected as advance guard to occupy Coblenz last night. It has about 1,000 men. The Thirty-Ninth saw a great deal of fighting throughout the war and has had many replacements, so the majority of the troops who are the first to reach the Rhine are drafted men.

Lieutenant Colonel Frank C. Bolles[225] commands the regiment. Major Fred W. Hackett,[226] of Champlain, New York, is second in command. One of the lieutenants who came with the detachment today is George Hannigan,[227] former ball player with the Kansas City Federal League. The battalion was marched in from three miles out of Trier last night and loaded on a German train this morning. It was the first real troop movement of Americans by rail since the army started for Germany.[228]

Besides the advance guard, the entire "flying circus" of the press division was loaded, consisting of more than 20 correspondents. There was no chance of the occupation of Coblenz lacking publicity.

Lockett's battalion took all its personal effects. When it was all completed, the train, with flat cars filled with rolling kitchens and light carts, and an ambulance to the rear, was nearly a half mile long and looked like a circus outfit. The cars were all fourth-class coaches. The German coaches are not unlike box cars divided into compartments. The seats are board benches, which are harder than bankers' hearts.

The train was scheduled to leave at 8:15, but being a troop train, of course it didn't leave until a couple of hours later. Then it went winding cautiously down the valley of the Moselle toward the Rhine. The Moselle merges with the Rhine at Coblenz. That's why they call it Coblenz. It means confluence. All correspondents and most of the soldiers promptly draped themselves out of the car windows to see the sights. The road drifts along the edge of the river between towering hills, all of which bristle with vineyards, now spiders' tangles and dry of vines, past quaint little white German towns which are so close together that they stumble into each other.

With a Baedeker in hand and with a pair of auto goggles over his eyes, Herbert Bailey,[229] English member of the press platoon, hung precariously from a window, earnestly endeavoring to locate the ruined castles for the benefit of interested soldiers, but the train got past them before "Herb" could get set.

Bad to relate, on the historic occasion a poker game started.[230] In another car a man was piteously rattling a pair of African golf balls[231] appealing for action.

People in the little towns were going to Sunday school or church. Many a German soldier haircut was concealed under fedora hats.

The congregations halted at the church doors to watch the train go past. At every station small crowds were collected. The people knew the train was coming. In the station crowds and all along the right-of-way were hundreds of little children. They waved and shrieked at the soldiers. Now and then a civilian plodding along the road would stare at the train and then feebly waggle his hand.

Compared to Trier it was almost a warm reception. Certainly the kids were enthusiastic. Coblenz was reached shortly before 2 o'clock. The long train was stopped in the railroad yards, where it was met by American officers from general headquarters and German officers, resplendent in uniforms, Iron Crosses, and other decorations on their chests. They were there to turn matters over to the Americans.[232]

Colonel Lockett formed the battalion beside the train and then marched it into the street and up the street a few blocks to the German barracks. There was no ceremony about the matter. Lockett had no band. A small crowd of German civilians were gathered to watch the detraining. They remained perfectly silent as the soldiers went past. Windows flew open and heads popped out along the short line of march, but the people made no comment. The only sounds were the sharp commands of the officers and the tramp of feet. The men were fresh and marched briskly with their packs. As in the entry into Trier, they hardly turned their eyes.[233]

At the gates to the barracks a bunch of German officers, including one colonel with impressive whiskers, stood at attention as they entered. In another hour American soldiers were looking after affairs around town. German soldiers still patrol the streets with rifles, but they are getting ready to depart. Meantime, Americans are finding Coblenz a good-sized and very beautiful city, which seems to have plenty to eat, if a person has the price, and plenty to wear.

Meantime, too, Mr. Bailey is making a further study of the ruined castles, so that presently he will have all at his fingers' ends, so he can conduct parties of doughboys up and down the Rhine.

December 17, 1918. With the American Army of Occupation, Coblenz

"Eddie" Rickenbacker, the American flying ace and former auto racer, arrived here last night. He is figuring on moving his First Pursuit Squadron from Longuyon as soon as he can get a field around Coblenz.

Among other arrivals was an infuriated poet, to wit, Lieutenant Grantland Rice. He was assigned to a billet by a billeting officer. After traveling a long way to reach the place, going without breakfast and dinner, he discovered that the number was—a vacant lot.[234]

Café life in Coblenz is getting brisker every night. At its very briskest, however, it's not very speedy. It is confined largely to music and beer drinking. Every café has a pretty good orchestra. Most of the music is heavily classical.

There is probably not much café life in Louvain and Arras.

One of the biggest cafés here is run by a former German aviator named Wahle, who once flew with Beachey[235] and other American flyers in New York.

We were asking him last night about Walter Rutt,[236] the famous German six-day racer, who was supposed to have been killed while flying for Germany. Wahle says Rutt was never a flyer, except in a motorcycle. He was attached to the army motorcycle corps. As far as Wahle knows, Rutt is still alive.

Wahle's place has suddenly become a favorite resort for Americans, chiefly because it is about the best place. There's mighty little gaiety about German cafés. Germans rarely applaud the music, no matter how hard the orchestra work. They seldom laugh. They just sit around stolidly, drinking. The atmosphere is really depressing, and Americans do not linger at any place.

December 20, 1918. With the American Army of Occupation, Coblenz

In the lee of some ruined castles, along the other side of the Rhine, American soldiers were forming their mess lines for supper Friday night, and while the great moon played up and down the river, they messed for miles beyond the stream.

Patches of military policemen are already commencing to show in the queer little towns nestling in the deep valleys between the hills, where one looks instinctively for gnomes to appear

Red Cross workers handing out a Christmas package. *Courtesy of United States Army Heritage and Education Center*

suddenly. Mile after mile, our armies are spreading over the sector, which they will occupy beyond the river ford—who knows how long?

Christmas on the Rhine sounds poetic, but soldiers of Dickman's Army of Occupation would rather spend it back home.

Most of the soldiers of the Third Army haven't had any pay for some time. Christmas anywhere in the world without one's paycheck is bound to be most un-Christmasy.[237]

December 20, 1918. With the American Army of Occupation, Coblenz

It was quite some evening in Coblenz Wednesday evening; it was the largest eve, in fact, since the American occupation. There was nothing special doing, but the population of the city reverted unanimously to the old custom of infesting the cafés. Jim Churchill,[238] the Savarin,[239] and the Shanleys[240] would have turned green with envy at the business local institutions were transacting.

Tables could not be had at Weiner's. Wahle's was jammed. The Traube was packed. These are widely known places along the Coblenz path of pleasure. All other cafés, of which there are a score or more in the town, had full quotas of cash customers.

In every place there were fully as many Americans as Germans, and in some places the Americans had the Germans outnumbered. It was a singular scene, when one stopped to reflect that the shadow of the great war is just lifting from this part of the world.

Lights were blazing, orchestras were going, and there was a continual babel of talk and laughter until 11 o'clock. Coblenz has adopted American army time, which gives it another hour.

Some real "live ones" from down around American general headquarters in France blew in yesterday. They had stout bankrolls, which is more than most members of the Third Army have because the paymaster hasn't visited these parts yet.[241]

Furthermore they were as loose as the proverbial ashes. One round for them would involve as much currency of the country as a whole evening of rounds for the average German party. Ubiquitous German café proprietors raked in the money with enigmatic smiles.

Americans and Germans were not mixing their evening entertainment to any extent. Here and there might be a party which included both soldiers and civilians, and they would be exchanging polite conversation, but in the main they kept apart.

In Wahle's after the place got pretty well jammed, the proprietor himself was going around seating Americans at any tables which happened to be occupied by only a couple of Germans. The expedient will be recognized by veteran New York café owners.

Wahle is an aviator veteran. He is an affable, hand-shaking soul who apparently recognizes every person who enters the café, and personally attends to their comfort. In short, he is a natural-born café owner. He would get by in any land.

His place was dying before the advent of the Americans. Last night he set aside one room, where only wine could be purchased. Next he will probably admit only those who can purchase wine. And next he will probably admit only people in evening clothes. It is a big place, but the smoke was so thick last night it looked as if the premises were afire.

Over in Weiner's along toward the closing hour the orchestra was playing and everybody was singing "She's Got Rings on Her Fingers and Bells on Her Toes" in German.

In one or two places the horizon blue uniforms of French officers were seen. They were visitors from the French sector. The Germans stare constantly at Frenchmen. They seem ill at ease in their presence. They also stare at Americans but do not appear to be under the same restraint when they are around.

We may be oversensitive, but in the atmosphere of the places where the Germans congregate and in the undercurrent of that atmosphere, we are unable to sense but one feeling, and it is not exactly that friendly feeling which some people profess to find. It seems to us that there is always a covert sneer.

John Soldier is not fooled, either. We asked an enlisted man in Wahle's last night his analysis of the atmosphere, and he said:

"It's the old raz."

Of course it is quite likely that were conditions reversed, that were German soldiers swarming through American cafés, there would result an atmosphere prickly with resentment—that is, if Americans remained in that atmosphere, which we don't believe they would.

It is only natural for soldiers to seek diversion wherever they may be, and they have it coming to them, but one marvels somewhat that supposedly naughty people of an occupied town will flock to places where they know their conquerors are going to be in large numbers. We don't believe that even one careless, gay old Broadway café would get much local play were it packed by the soldiers of an enemy nation.

However, there are some proud Germans left. An American was seeking an appointment to rest because he needed something more than the billeting officer was likely to assign him. He was willing to pay a big price. Someone told him of a place he might secure, and when he went there the door was opened by a fine-looking, white-haired woman of the patrician type. He says he never will forget the picture of her standing haughtily in the doorway while behind her he caught a glimpse of a beautiful room.

She said she spoke French, and he stated his mission in that language.

"What?" she said, her voice trembling with indignation.

"Rent my house to an American! I, the wife of a German officer!"

He bowed low, respectfully. He had been ignorant of that fact, he explained. She thawed somewhat as he started to leave, and asked him many questions.

"Are you married?" she inquired.

"Yes," he said, "my wife is in Norfolk, Virginia."

"Supposing Norfolk were occupied by Germans and my husband went around to your wife and tried to rent her home. What would have happened to him?" she asked curiously.

"Madame," said the American thoughtfully, "I am of the opinion that he would have run some risk of having a kettle of hot water tipped over on him."

December 21, 1918. With the American Army of Occupation

It is rumored that our local Broadway-on-the-Rhine will not be as sprightly as heretofore. The ubiquitous "gold brick," who is the military policeman, is circulating about looking matters over, and when the M.P. goes abroad in the land it is just the same as a new mayor being elected on a reform ticket back home.

Not that Coblenz needs any reforming. Four Seidels[242] make up a wild night here. However, Coblenz Seidels are so tall that it requires several hours of steady sitting to encompass them, and Mother Grundy[243] has it that the time for consumption should be shortened.

Boulevardiers are wearing furrowed brows over the situation. It looks as if the Army of Occupation is going to have a lot of sleep.

Last night, ubiquitous men—which is short for military police—were peering about the cafés, and where they saw soldiers or officers talking with Germans they politely collected the names of the members of our military establishment overseas.

It seems the theory of our army is that our secret service representatives can take ample care of all the light conversation in these parts.

Furthermore, M.P.'s were seen to approach groups of young gentlemen who might chance to be standing along the streets engaging in neat repartee with natives—who not infrequently happened to be fair to gaze upon.[244] Presently these groups would dissolve. What the M.P.'s asked has never been made quite clear, but it seems they wanted to know in a general way why the conversation was being held. Naturally nobody wants to take an M.P. into his confidence.

Thus Coblenz is commencing to feel the weight of military occupation. As compared with the weight it has known before under its own military people, it is about as heavy as a straw hat so far. However, orders against fraternization were included in the original orders to the Army of Occupation.[245] That stricter rules by the government of the city for the regulation of its inhabitants will be issued seems almost inevitable as the army settles down in the American sector.[246]

The M.P. follows the flag and frequently gets ahead of it. Right now he is everywhere in Coblenz. It is rapidly becoming the typical army headquarters town, where rules bob up right and left. On every corner there is an M.P. regulating traffic with arm and whistle. He walks the streets looking after the peace and quiet. Incidentally, patrols with fixed bayonets still cover the city, but they are distinct from the M.P.'s. The latter attend to such matters as seeing that officers and enlisted men keep their coats buttoned and comport themselves perfectly. The patrol's business is sterner trouble. But they haven't had any heavy business yet. Coblenz is certainly well policed.

December 22, 1918. [Delayed] With the American Army of Occupation

When you drop into a dugout around meal time and find a general and his ear glued to a telephone, issuing battle orders, and stand around until, prompted by fear of personal starvation, he invites you to eat, it's an incident. He often has bum mess, anyway, and you can do much better by hunting up some friendly captain.

When a fat staff major comes around with a formal invitation, however, the matter takes on the aspect of a function. Such, in a manner, was the dinner given by General Pershing to newspaper correspondents with the American Army of Occupation on the Rhine, in his private car Saturday night.

Veterans of the days of the punitive expedition with Pershing in Mexico were not much dazzled. "He doesn't eat much himself," warned Junius Wood solemnly. "When the second helping comes around he don't take anything, so naturally nobody else dasts do it. I am going to load up with beans in advance, myself."

Others snobbishly took occasion to drop around headquarters during the day to casually let out the news in an off-hand way that they were on the verge of dining with the commander-in-chief, causing a profound impression among the colonels thereabouts. In colonel circles, it's considered no small honor to put on the nosebag at the general's table, but Junius Wood remained pessimistic.

"He pecks at one dish, then they snatch it away before you can get more," he said.

Alarmed by Mr. Wood's forebodings, George Pattullo went out and ate a full course meal.

Gen. John J. Pershing's arrival in France.
Courtesy of Library of Congress

There are only ten correspondents left with the army. That's fewer than there have been for some time. Several had been summoned from divisions far from Coblenz. One was speeding for a holiday in the flesh pots of Paris, when he encountered the general's entourage at Trier (Treves) and was turned back.

The general himself came from Trier to Coblenz by automobile, so he could see more of the country his army occupied. It was his first visit to the Rhine. His private train, made up of French sleepers and a diner, came up later and was laid out at the principal depot at Coblenz, where the correspondents were conveyed in a body. One wore the only white collar and set of white cuffs owned by anybody in the Third Army below the rank of lieutenant colonel.

There was a long table down the center of the diner, with seats on either side. They even had place cards so no correspondent could get lost. Besides General Pershing and the newspaper correspondents, the only other persons present were General Preston Brown, deputy chief of staff at Trier, and General Smith, the civil governor of the occupied area.

The commander-in-chief was naturally in a much-lighter mood than when he used to receive the correspondents in the bloody days between the Marne and the Meuse. He looked pretty tired, but then he had just finished a long journey. On his breast he wore the bar of a new Distinguished Service Cross medal and the decoration of the French Legion of Honor. His hair is now perfectly white, but he has lost nothing of that bearing which always made him the most distinguished-looking officer in the American army. He is one general who absolutely looks the part.

It has always been his custom to talk very freely to correspondents attached to his army on all subjects, though frequently he may not be talking for publication, and this occasion was no exception to the rule. However, the talk was mainly social.

Even Mr. Wood cheered up when it became evident the general was inclined to linger over the food. Someone mentioned the fact that they had heard Sam Dreben,[247] an acquaintance of the general's from El Paso, who came over here as a first sergeant in the First Infantry, had been killed in action. It was about this same Sam Dreben the writer wrote a story called "The Fighting Jew," when Sam landed in New York, en route to France, some months ago.

"I am sure that report isn't true," said General Pershing.

"I get a list of killed every day, and I would have noticed it. I did see where he had been awarded the Distinguished Service Cross for gallantry, however."

The statement that he looked over the casualty lists with such care indicates his thoroughness. He has a marvelous memory for names and personalities. Just before the party broke up, he made a short talk without rising from his seat, in which he said he thanked the newspapers of America for their assistance to the army, and also thanked the correspondents.

He then went off to a chateau up the Rhine to spend the night with his old friend and comrade, General "Jack" Hines, one of the most picturesque characters produced by America in this war, while the correspondents drifted out into the night.

"I was right about the second helping though, wasn't I?" demanded Mr. Wood, triumphantly, and everybody had to admit that he was.

December 22, 1918. [Delayed] With the American Army of Occupation, Coblenz

There was a fire in Coblenz today. Everybody went. It was a true touch of home. The local firemen were togged out in thick helmets and perfectly appointed uniforms. All city employees of Coblenz wear elaborate apparel. When our soldiers first arrived they thought the street car conductors were generals in the army. Even now, new M.P.s feel a strong impulse to arrest mail carriers for violating the rule against German soldiers wearing uniforms.

All the Americans in town who could get away were present at the fire. It was in the opera house—no ornate structure reared by the government which looks like an American city auditorium—but a more modern temple of Thespis where they have been producing "The Rose of Stamboul," "Mignon," and the like lately. All the children in the town were there, along with most of the grown folks. A fire is a fire in Coblenz, same as in Pueblo, Colorado.

The firemen came with a lot of apparatus, which caused the Americans, many of whom had formerly been firemen themselves, to shake their heads. Naturally our boys offered advice. They offered it in loud tones. Naturally the firemen didn't take it. It certainly was a touch of home. The street got so congested with people that the M.P.s took charge of that end of the situation. They shoved the people back, yelling, "Go on, now!," accompanied by violent motions which the people understood perfectly. There was much hollering and much excitement. It was a real breath from the homeland.

Finally, the firemen opened little trapdoors in the streets, disclosing underground fire plugs, much to the astonishment of the Americans, who debated the efficiency of that system gravely. Finally they got a stream playing on the blaze.[248] In the meantime some American soldiers had clambered to the roof of the building in which the fire was located, and began yelling directions from there. Others rushed in and lent a hand close up.

Eventually the blaze died down to a gentle smolder, and everybody went away talking about the fire. It was assuredly a touch of home.

A staff captain came around later and saw the result of the fire.

"My general's going to be pretty mad about this," he said. "He wanted to go to the show tonight."

December 22, 1918. With the American Army of Occupation, Coblenz

In great awe we approached the beautiful chateau Rolandseck[249] on the Rhine, marveling as we drew near at its splendor.

It is a sort of a cross between Senator Clark's[250] Fifth Avenue house and the Colorado State Capitol, set in grounds that suggest Golden Gate Park in San Francisco.

We half expected to see a stately duchess walking about among the trees, followed by trains of ladies-in-waiting. As we came on the lee side of the gorgeous pile, we became aware of a querulous voice lifting itself from the premises.

"Ah," we thought, "the duke is bawling out his vassals."

"It ain't right," the voice was saying. "It's a damn shame, that's what it is."

For no apparent reason, then we found our memory floating back across quite some months. The old Rhine, slugging in lethargic way between its storied hills, suddenly faded from view. We again saw the Polo Grounds and felt again the heat of a broiling summer's day. There popped before our mind's eye a little picture of a tall, tow-headed fellow in baseball uniform towering over the dumpy form of William Klem[251] and mumbling in William's ear:

"It ain't right, Bill. It's a damn shame, that's what it is."

Connection between that scene and the voice from the chateau was immediately established in our recollection. It was the fretful accent. We knew now we were not mistaken.

We entered the chateau and gasped for a few minutes at its inward magnificence, then trailed with peevishness to the luxurious chamber where sat the junior color sergeant of the One Hundred and Sixty-Sixth Infantry of the Rainbow Division, Ohio's own, Henry Gowdy. Otherwise, Lankus Hankus.[252]

Sgt. Hank Gowdy with manager John McGraw.
Courtesy of Library of Congress

"Are they any better than me?" Henry was saying. "No. Do they make any more money than I do when I'm making it? No. Then, why the hell can they snatch off my bedclothes—especially a good counterpane? It's a fine way to run a war."

The one-time hero of a World Series was sitting on the edge of a magnificent carved bedstead which seemed quite denuded of all covering save a skimpy army blanket and a half shelter tent. He was obviously low in his mind, but otherwise the same old Hank. He was addressing his plaintive remarks to a gentleman who seemed most sympathetic and who turned out to be his buddy, George Forrester, senior color sergeant of the One Hundred and Sixty-Sixth.

Not since a fleeting glimpse of him in the parlous days of the Argonne had we seen Henry, but he was most casual.

"Oh, hello," he said, extending one of his hands which wrung the baseball bat with deadly effect for the Boston Braves back in 1914, and which was also one of the same hands which carried the American flag over the Rhine. He was too depressed, however, to rise to either of the two feet on which he recently trudged 300 kilometers to get to Germany.

"I'm talking about officers," he said. "You see this bed? Well, me and George here and several other fellows are billeted here, and when we first got in it this bed had a lot of swell bedclothes on it—big fat sort of silk comforts, thick blankets, and a lace counterpane. I hear it took several hundred women several hundred years to make that counterpane. It was a pippin. I never did see such a bed. It made me sleepy just to look at it. After sleeping with them cows, rooming with them pigs and horses back in the French billets, it was like Christmas every night to me. That big joint across the river there belongs to the Anheuser-Busches[253] of St. Louis, and I could lay in my bed mornings and look at it and wonder why them St. Louis clubs don't do no better.

"Then what happens? Well, some officer comes along, sees my bed clothes, gets jealous of them—especially my counterpane—and tears off the whole works. Ain't that a disgusting way to run a war?

"You know who owns this joint? A guy by the name of Schnitzel. No kidding. They say he's one of the rich merchants at Cologne. Got more dough than some folks have got hay.

"You wouldn't figure that a guy named Schnitzel would know much about beds, but this bird was a regular bed shark. I wish you could have seen the counterpane. It would have made you sore the rest of your life.

"If you think this is a swell dump though, you ought to see two chateaux our General McArthur's got at Sinzig. Either one makes this look silly, and this one's got the Deshler Hotel[254] in Columbus skinned for size and accommodations.

"I wish I was a general. No one can cop a general's bedclothes, not in this army, anyway. I'm too upset. All I know about it is that they won't stand for nobody turning a good guy off for his bedclothes—especially if he was hitting. The league wouldn't allow it. Man! What a counterpane that was."[255]

And we left him still sitting on the bedstead, moodily contemplating the lost glories of its departed raiment—as sad a figure as we've encountered in many days.

December 22, 1918. With the American Army of Occupation

Over at general headquarters they have been anticipating a visit from the commander-in-chief for some days; therefore the atmosphere of the big stone building fronting the Rhine, which used to be some sort of German government edifice, has been buzzing with activity.

The interior of this building is decorated in barbaric fashion, which is probably splendid from the German viewpoint, but which is rather depressing to some callous young American officers, who have to work there. Their depression is increased by the sudden military rigidity which always afflicts a headquarters town once headquarters gets to functioning thoroughly.

Romance and frivolity got up and dusted out as soon as the first roll tops were wheeled into action. Bright spurs and highly polished shines appear on boots and shoes. Uniforms take on a varied aspect. General staff colonels and majors clutter up the premises.

The careless glory of the fighting front is replaced by military pomp. There is vast, widespread saluting. Voices become ceremonious. Laughter is infrequent unless some general should spring a wheeze. Then it is quite in order for all hands to let a guffaw. Nobody knows what would happen if a man should fail to laugh when a general cracks a joke, because the point has never come up.

Coblenz is thoroughly headquartered. They have a formal mount of evenings in the public square. Bands play. There is talk of drill for the troops in the field. This news is about as popular as if you told the soldiers an epidemic of smallpox was about to break out. There are rules for every little thing. Over at headquarters the officers have to register when they go out and when they come in, detailing the purpose of their absence, no matter how long.

You will find written in the book the truthful assertion of one young man that he absented himself for the evening to look at a movie show. They have also been ordered to take regular exercise certain hours every day. Another youth recorded in the book the fact that he had gone out for exercise and that his exercise consisted of "punching the bag."

Then he went to press headquarters and spent the morning in blithe conversation.

Second only to general headquarters in its rigid atmosphere is the big Coblenzhof Hotel, next door. The rooms have ornate signs on the doors, reading:

"This is not a public hotel. It is reserved for field officers of general headquarters."

No one below the rank of major is allowed in the hotel.

Lesser officers go by and gaze up with envy. With all its apparently good officers' outfit, headquarters, after all, can't help its being headquarters, can it? They are always about the same. This headquarters is the best we've seen, and it is certainly full-cocked and ready for a visit from General Pershing.

"Remember, if he finds anything to criticize, I'll accept no excuse," warned one of the high officers the other day.

Today some automobiles suddenly buzzed up to the entrance.

There was a wild clatter of booted feet over the tiled floors. There was a hasty shuffling of papers on the desks. There was a shutting of doors and a lowering of voices. The general had arrived.

Up the steps he came, while backbones for blocks around stiffened perceptibly. You could fairly hear the salutes snap as he went past. He vanished indoors. He was closeted with General "Joe" Dickman for a short time. Presently he reappeared under a barrage of salutes and re-entered his automobile. Zip—and he was gone.

Slowly but surely the tension exhaled.

"Gosh," muttered a sentry outside, surreptitiously mopping his brow. However, they are still punching the time clock over at headquarters.

In the doorway of the press division's dining rooms in a hotel on the Rhine, there appeared tonight the tall, gawky figure of a soldier who was evidently suffering from stage fright. He wore a uniform which did not fit. His coat collar wasn't high enough to conceal more than a foot of his neck. It had a "seemore" effect in the back.

His pants were so tight that stooping suddenly would have been a hazardous proceeding. Moreover, the face of the uniform had fuzzy whiskers where the nap had been rubbed the wrong way. The rude machinery of the delousing stations will do that to any uniform. The piece de resistance to the soldier's make-up, however, was his cap. It was not a regulation army cap. It was a cap with a fore beak. It had dewlaps to keep the ears warm. It rode high on the soldier's head and gave him the appearance of a duck hunter.

There was sudden overturning of chairs down the long table, and shouts of greeting, and the bunch of correspondents and officers jumped up at the appearance of the strange figure. About the same moment there arrived in the doorway behind a tall, embarrassed soldier in a group of trim-looking chaps in officers' uniforms. They had the silver wings of the aviation corps spread across their chests. They also wore significant little bars betoking the ownership of the Croix de Guerre of France and the Distinguished Service Crosses of America, awarded for deeds of bravery on the field of battle.

The embarrassed officer wore no decorations save one on the left sleeve of the coat. There he had a tri-colored patch of silk of scrambled eggs, which betokened him one of the famous fighting army divisions—the Rainbow Division. It's a pretty good decoration at that. It is hard to say who got the warmest welcome, the aviation officers or the lone bashful soldier. But in the midst of the general confusion, somebody pulled the soldier over in front of the man who wore two silver bars on his shoulder and said:

"Captain Rickenbacker, have you ever met Sergeant Hank Gowdy?"

"Well—"I'll—be—damned!" remarked Eddie Rickenbacker, American's aerial ace, as he grasped the hand of perhaps the best known man in the army. "So will I," said Hank.

It seems that they had never met before, though they were born and raised in the same town—Columbus, Ohio.

"I've got a newspaper photograph of your mother and my mother," said Hank, reaching for his pocket.

"I've got the same picture," said Rickenbacker, fumbling in his bosom. Then the two who started from Columbus about the same time to gain fame in the sporting world, one as a baseball catcher, the other as an automobile racer, sat down and talked over the home town folks.

Gowdy had come here from the Forty-Second Division, stationed down the River Rhine, to spend the holidays with old friends of his baseball days, Major Bohemian Bulger and Lieutenant Grantland Rice, the writer.[256]

Rickenbacker came in from the air camp at Trier with Jimmy Meissner,[257] of Brooklyn, the twenty-two-year-old major of aviation, who is probably the youngest officer of that rank in the army, Captain Douglas Campbell,[258] the famous flyer from California, and Captain Fauntleroy.[259]

They are all ordered back to the States. Rickenbacker was telling Hank about it while the homesick Henry uttered plaintive moans because he wasn't going. Later in the evening in a box at the opera house, they presented a singular picture, this group of dapper, much-decorated officers of various rank, seated around the blushing, campaign-stained sergeant of infantry in the fuzzy uniform. Between the acts the voices of either Edward Rickenbacker or Henry Gowdy could be heard saying:

"Well, do you know old so-and-so?"

December 23, 1918. With the American Army of Occupation, Coblenz

There was a strangely familiar clang of a bell in the streets of Coblenz Monday morning. It is rumored that four American correspondents and two Y.M.C.A. men instinctively started running violently in the opposite direction without even looking to confirm the sound. It is claimed a couple of censors also were seen ducking into a convenient alleyway—but this is not confirmed.

Germans along the sidewalks stared in amazement as a big covered motor van came rumbling over the cobblestones. In the van, which had once been an army ambulance, were seated two stern-looking military policemen with their arms folded across their chests. On the sides of the van was painted in big letters: "Military Police Patrol."[260]

Thus our little city on the Rhine was made complete in all details. It is just like living in New York.

Besides a patrol wagon we also have a navy. Eleven German boats which used to ply on the Rhine for various purposes have been taken over by the Americans and converted into a gunboat flotilla. They will be equipped with light guns and manned by Jackies and Marines.[261]

The first of these boats came up the river Monday with the American flag flying at the stern. It looked mighty good. The old flag always looks mighty good.

This has been a tremendous week for Coblenz shopkeepers. It would be interesting to know how much money American soldiers have spent with them for Christmas gifts for homefolks. The early arrivals ransacked the stores for military souvenirs. New stocks of Iron Crosses, helmets, and the like are appearing in the stores in almost suspicious quantities.[262]

One thing must be said in favor of the German storekeepers. They are keeping their prices level. So far there seems to be no attempt to gouge Americans, which is rather a refreshing novelty. One public square in the town was filled with Christmas trees for sale. For a week past you could see people of all classes going home lugging trees under their arms or over their shoulders.[263]

The shops were filled with women bearing long written lists which they were checking over just as the womenfolks back home probably have been doing for the last ten days.

Among them would be big American soldiers struggling with the German language in an attempt to make the shop girls understand what they wanted.

December 26, 1918. [Delayed] With the American Army of Occupation, Coblenz

There was a mighty hubbub in the land of little children today. Out into the snow-dusted streets the wee inhabitants trooped this morning, gleefully bearing all the wonderful things old Kris Kringle had left in their stockings.

There were an unbelievable number of wee women with braided blond hair pushing wobbly baby buggies along the esplanade and making frequent stops to peer with motherly solicitude at the wide-eyed dolls within.

Big American military policeman, keeping watch and ward of the traffic at cross corners, found a new and engrossing duty in righting these small vehicles and assisting the tiny mammas in gathering up their precious contents when buggies teetered too far at the turns.

There were myriads of boys in short pants and with marvelously shiny faces, lugging toys of various kinds in their arms. Everywhere you went you saw groups of them roaming about like bands of marauding gypsies with newly acquired loot. In every group there was at least one proud possessor of a toy drum keeping up a steady rub-r-dub-dub, and no drum owner lacked an admiring following.

There was one small lad who had a cornet. Strangely enough, he had no personal audience. He wandered about the streets, extracting the most singular sounds from his cornet for all the world to hear, but he moved alone. We are unable to explain this phenomenon save on the ground that he was regarded as a sort of musical Ishmael. Cornet players are friendless the world over.

And now there rose in this land of little children a new Napoleon—or perhaps we might better say a new von Hindenburg.[264] Down the esplanade there came marching in regal grandeur a boy no taller than a walking stick who was panoplied in wondrous fashion. On his head was a little spiked helmet. Around his small torso was a suit of glittering tin armor. In his hand he bore a tin sword. He moved with the step of a conqueror.[265]

December 27, 1918. With the American Army of Occupation, Coblenz

"Der Kleine Flieger,"[266] by which description we sought him yesterday, hunted us up this morning. He had heard that we had been paging him. What was wanted were the four feet of him, measuring from top to bottom. He was swathed in a fur coat and much dignity. "Der Kleine Flieger" admitted that he weighs all of ninety-four pounds. Some of it is chest.

In mingled German, French, and English he explained to us that most of the information we had about him was true except his name. That his was Christian Donhauser,[267] not Taske. Edward Taske, he explained, is his comrade.

"Taske's a good man," said "Der Kleine Flieger," with ten planes to his credit, but he, Christian Donhauser, has thirty. He got them all between July 1 last and November 11, the day the war stopped.

Taske's here with him, he said, to help fly the Fokker planes which will be delivered to the Americans.[268]

They start the flying tests tomorrow. "Der Kleine Flieger" said that afterward he wants to get to America to join the American army flyers. He said Sweden had invited him to go there as an instructor, but he is anxious to go to America, as he has relatives in Michigan.

Donhauser displayed a gold medal on his bosom given him by the former Kaiser. Only thirty men in all Deutschland have such a medal, he said. He also wears Iron Crosses of the first and second class and badges indicating that he had been wounded quite a number of times.

Once he was shot down by Guynemer,[269] the great French ace, and once by Navarre.[270]

Yes, he had met Eddie Rickenbacker, the American ace. A fine flyer! But he thought some of the American airmen lacked—here "Der Kleine Flieger" struggled for a word, finally producing "practice." They were getting mighty good toward the close of the war.

Yes, they had told him that the flyer he shot down in the air duel over Fere-en-Tardenois was Quentin Roosevelt.[271] He didn't know at the time, of course.

He, Donhauser, was leading his squadron of half a dozen Fokkers when they encountered the same number of American planes. Four of the Americans started back, with Germans in pursuit.

With his companion, Donhauser engaged one of the remaining planes. His companion's gun became jammed; then Donhauser and the American fought it out alone.

He said he could tell the American hadn't had a great deal of experience from his maneuvering, but he was most brave.

There were a couple of times, too, when the American got over him and had him in such a position that he, Christian Donhauser, thought strongly of "going home."

He had the better fighting luck of the two, however. The American plane went spiraling to the ground.

Its pilot was undoubtedly killed by a machine gun bullet, said "Der Kleine Flieger." The Germans recovered the body and buried it with all honors. It was then, he said, they informed him as to the identity of his brave opponent, and he wanted to attend the funeral, but his superior officers thought it was better not.

When he examined his own plane after the fighting, he found twenty bullet holes in it. They were all from young Roosevelt's gun.

"Der Kleine Flieger" is twenty-three years old. His home is in Heinburg. Before the war he was a civilian airplane pilot. He has a wallet filled with citations for various deeds, and pictures and stories of himself from German magazines. And yet "Der Kleine Flieger" is not even a commissioned officer—still an aspirant or student officer. He explained this on the ground that he had been shifted so often and so far that his promotion never caught up with him.

As conversation lagged somewhat, "Der Kleine Flieger" gathered up his blue cap and hoisted his fur collar preparatory to departure. Then somebody asked him what about those times when German aviators, for no particular reason or military advantage, drifted close to the earth, splattering machine gun bullets into streets where walked women and even innocent children.

He spread his small hands and shrugged his small shoulders. He hadn't done those things himself. If they had been done it was by order of higher officers. If a flyer did not obey orders, they said he was no good and sent him home. So!

"Der Kleine Flieger" spread his hands wider than before, shrugged his shoulders up to his ears, and stalked out—if a man only four feet tall can be said to stalk.

December 28, 1918. With the American Army of Occupation, Coblenz

It is now nutting time on the Rhine. One by one the filberts are commencing to drop in—congressmen, lecturers, poets, sightseers, whatnot. There are even rumors of the rapid approach of a delegation of lady authors.[272]

Trains are running between Coblenz and Paris, and passes to the "front" seem easy to obtain. One eminent gent who has some fame among the American people as a public speaker blew in the day before yesterday. He was greatly excited. He had a pass good for two days in Coblenz and said he was gathering material for a series of lectures upon his return to the States.

He spent the first day drawing correspondents aside and whispering in their ears:

"What is the one big sensational message I can carry back to the people at home?"

None of the correspondents knew of any very sensational messages or they probably would carry them themselves—at least as far as the censor's office. Then the eminent gent produced a new thought.

"I understand," he said, "several people, including some Regular Army officers, claim the Plattsburg training camps were a failure."

"Is that so," remarked one officer with interest. "Well, if it hadn't been for Plattsburg, you wouldn't be nutting around on this river right now."

What this bird and this species of bird will probably tell the folks back home will probably be most thrilling.

However, the sightseeing pest is something the American army has always had and probably always will have. It could not evade him at home and likewise here, when it went 10,000 miles away to the other side of the world. It couldn't dodge him when it lost itself in the deserts of Mexico. How then could it hope to duck them with only the Atlantic Ocean between it and them.

It is more than likely that Washington's troops along the Delaware were being pestered similarwise 142 years ago. One wonders in what particular guise the sightseer of that period went, whether as an alleged war worker, an entertainer, a writer for some mythical publication, an artist, a student of psychology, a scientific researcher, a politician, or what?

They have all brands on the American front. They trailed the artillery into the mazes of the Argonne Forest. They pursued it to Luxemburg. Now they are alighting on the Rhine.

So far the flights have been scattering, but indications are that the main flock will be in presently.

Someone has tipped off the local merchants. They are real worried about the delayed shipments of Iron Crosses.

December 29, 1918. With the American Army of Occupation, Coblenz

Flaming crosses of electric lights glow tonight from the peaks of all the American army headquarters along the Rhine. It is the holiday symbol of the "Army of the Lord."

The first cross was placed on top of General Dickman's headquarters in Coblenz. When the blazing cross suddenly leaped out of the darkness, Germans from far and near gathered in crowds and gazed at the spectacle.

Our army secret service generally couldn't understand why the people suddenly seemed so interested. Detectives were sent to find out. Detectives are sent out to ascertain every little thing that isn't clear to the secret service department. Their report on the matter of the lights is not known, but one correspondent took it upon himself to ask the reason of the curiosity.

"Why, I guess it's because it's a beautiful sight," was the reply.

The crosses were put up by official army order. They certainly made a deep impression on the Germans. Some of them wanted to know if there is any connection between the crosses and the idea that the Americans came in the role of crusaders.

Judging from the reports that are drifting in from various headquarters on the tongues of enthusiastic souls who went visiting on Christmas, the goose was the general piece de resistance of all the banqueting along the Rhine. Everybody had goose. You can get a goose in Germany when you can't get much of anything else.[273] With a goose for a background the rest was comparatively easy, for there isn't a cook in an American sector who can't do more tricks with a goose than Houdini.

A truckload of Christmas packages for American troops. *Courtesy of Library of Congress*

There were Christmas trees galore. Some outfits got their Christmas boxes from the

States in the nick of time. Old Uncle Sam's ration issue, with its sugar, white bread, condensed milk, and jam, helped out, too, while vegetables were obtained from the surrounding country.

And there was goose. Plenty of goose. In years to come, soldiers will not be able to think of their Christmas on the Rhine without getting goose flesh.

December 31, 1918. With the American Army of Occupation

Lieutenant Donhauser, the German aviator, who is said to be the man who killed Lieutenant Quentin Roosevelt of the American army in an air duel, arrived at Coblenz Saturday.

He is one of a bunch of flyers sent by the German army to repair and deliver to the Americans about forty Chasse planes which have been turned over to them in accordance with the terms of the armistice.

The planes are all of the Fokker type. Before delivering them, Donhauser and his companions will make flying tests. The planes are now being assembled at what is known as the Spitzburg barracks, an old German military training camp on a picturesque hill overlooking Coblenz. There was no adequate flying field in this vicinity, but the Americans are constructing one there.

Donhauser is a little fellow, about the size of Tod Sloan.[274] Moreover, he is about as cocky as they come. He was strutting around town today in full uniform, with his blue cap slanted over his ear and his head half buried in a fur collar. On his chest he wears the gold insignia of a flyer, along with black and white ribbons indicating he has won the Iron Cross both of the first and second classes.

He attended the opera Saturday night, visiting the billeting officer and being assigned to the home of Herr Werner of 20 Cusaniesstrasse. But the following morning he became restless and moved out to the barracks at Spitzburg. They said at the Werner house that he was muttering something about his uniform when he left.

In the English sector, where he was located before coming here, Donhauser was not allowed to wear his uniform, but German officers actually on duty in Coblenz are permitted to retain their military apparel. There are not many of them left. They have to keep certain hours and report regularly.

Donhauser was down at American headquarters Sunday evening, reporting in. He seemed enthralled by the lighted Christmas tree which stands over the old fortress of Ehrenbreitstein, across the Rhine, like a beacon of hope.

It was sleeting tonight. The air was so thickly filled with particles of ice that it was hard to distinguish objects far away, but the glowing tree blazed out of the darkness as brilliantly as that star which guided the three wise men in the long ago.

Donhauser stared at the scene over his fur collar for some minutes. He is about twenty-four years old. He is said to admit frankly that he is the best flyer in the German army.

This was suggested to an older German officer who was among the party left at Coblenz to complete the delivery of material to the Americans. He shook his head. He said Donhauser is pretty well known, but hardly in the class with Hauptmann Max Müller,[275] or another fellow who started life as a roofer. The name of the last chap escaped us, but we gathered from what the officer said that he was famed throughout Deutschland. The officer kept laying stress on the fact that he was a roofer. Then he took pains to mention that Max Müller began as an under-officer, but someone reminded him that Eddie Rickenbacker, America's greatest ace, was originally a sergeant. Donhauser claims to have downed thirty-two British, French, and American planes.

Quentin Roosevelt was flying with a party of four or five other American aviators in the vicinity of Fere-en-Tardenois, in France, when they encountered a party of German machines. Roosevelt left his group and made a fearless dash at the bunch of Boches. One of them pulled off from the group and met him. This is supposed to have been Donhauser.

In the fight which followed, the young American was shot down. His body was later recovered, having been buried by the Germans, who have always expressed the greatest admiration for his bravery.

Quentin Roosevelt's elder brother, Theodore Roosevelt Jr., is tonight commanding the Twenty-Sixth Infantry across the Rhine.[276]

January 1919

January 4, 1919. With the American Army of Occupation, Coblenz

There used to be a story going the rounds of the American press to the effect that during the war, the German authorities were openly countenancing and encouraging illegitimacy.

We always rather doubted that yarn, but because of a statement made by one of the most intensely German women we have ever encountered, we are compelled to believe there was considerable truth in it.

She is about the last person who would make such a statement unless it were true. She is a woman who is still thoroughly loyal to her country. She attempts to justify every act of her people in the war. However, she is a frank critic of many things the government did.

"When a girl had an illegitimate child during the war, she received 100 marks," said this woman Friday night.

"The money was paid by the government. There was no secrecy about it. It was common knowledge that soldiers could secure leave by stating their intention of going home to contract what you might call war marriages—which were not marriages at all.

"However, all the clergymen preached marriage and the propagation of children. Any time a woman went to church she was cross-examined as to her status and the number of children she had. If she was married and had no children, she was rather chided. If she was single but of marriageable age, she was also rather rebuked for not marrying and having a family.

"If a woman lost her husband in the war, she got a pension of about fifteen marks a month. If she remarried she got 1,000 marks in a lump sum, the monthly payments ceasing."

"Did knowledge of the government's attitude regarding illegitimates increase the number of that kind of children?" she was asked.

"Do you think the German women are crazy?" she said with great heat.

January 5, 1919. [Delayed] With the American Army of Occupation, Coblenz

When old George Sightseer comes to have his peek at the Rhine these piping days of the American occupation, he requires first one army automobile. You can commence to figure from there the high cost. An army automobile—even the old gray car which can do everything but talk—requires gasoline. And it's not easy to transport gasoline to the Rhineland, especially when the army is needing every pound of transportation for food, shoes, clothes, and other supplies.

However, George must see his sights. He might walk ten miles to save a dollar taxicab hire back home, but he really appreciates a thirty-, sixty-, or ninety-mile breeze in an army auto, with plenty of scenery thrown in. Such matters as tire wear do not weigh on his soul.

With the automobile he has a driver, of course. The driver is an enlisted man. His upkeep and salary and what it cost to get him over here to Germany might be figured in as one of the items of the cost of George's jaunt.

Then there must be a conducting officer. He is a lieutenant or a captain who has a family and business waiting for him back home and who is so tarnation anxious to get back there now that the war's over, and whose very remotest thought, when he started out to make the world safe for democracy, was his job as boss of a sightseeing car. No censor would pass his innermost reflections.

Sometimes George comes all the way from Paris, nearly 300 miles, so that he can take in the battlefields en route. Every yard of the way he's escorted and drivered.

However he comes, he takes up bed room in a town where they're none too plentiful. He takes up the time of people who might be more advantageously employed. All in all, he assuredly costs somebody something.

And who is old George Sightseer? Well, sometimes he's a congressman or maybe he is an author or a preacher of something. Then again, maybe he's just a fellow with the old familiar pull. George Wots-him-well of political devices. Often he's himself a political device.

If in that bill which is being charged against Germany for the maintenance of the Army of Occupation[277] there is to be included that item which might be laid down as "To seeing the Rhine"—it's nobody's right to complain—except, of course, Deutschland. And that does not count.

If, however, it is to be settled by America, then it seems to us it is a matter of passing interest to the taxpayer. Then, it seems to us, that a long-whiskered old boy out in Iowa, who has been paying heavy taxes, buying Liberty Bonds[278] and War Savings Stamps,[279] and whose son or maybe two sons have been sloshing about in the mud of France, has a right to be consulted.

Maybe he doesn't care to pay George's fare. Maybe he'd like the ride himself. Or maybe he'd like his sons to get the ride if there are any free rides going around—and you can bet they'd esteem some of that transportation after having hoofed it all over the continent. Let's cut out George.

January 5, 1919. With the American Army of Occupation, Coblenz

It's rumored that promotions are to be reopened in the American army. If that is true it will rectify what in our opinion is a most flagrant injustice against the soldiers. Immediately after the armistice went into effect, an order was issued stopping all further advancements. There may have been good reason for the order, but it certainly worked great injustice, nevertheless.

We know hundreds of officers who have been with combat divisions as first and second lieutenant for from a year to fifteen months, who have been all through the hardest part of the fighting, but who are still first and second lieutenants because their outfits were so busy campaigning that they had not time to think of promotions.

When the war stopped and everybody had the first chance to take a long breath, it was naturally the time when rewards would be passed around—but before this could transpire, out popped the order. It was a bitter disappointment to many of the most deserving men. It must have been a bitter disappointment, also, to the highest officers, who had looked forward to an opportunity of recognizing merit.

We know of a great many captains, majors, lieutenant colonels, or colonels who were taken out of the line against their desire and put into staff work because of their peculiar fitness for the job, who performed that work extremely well, only to remain stationary in rank while seeing men in the old line outfits go forward with a rush. Lieutenants have become majors of the fighting line, while majors have remained majors because they happened to possess unusual ability that made them valuable back of the line.

Meanwhile, before the order was issued, officers who had fought in the war were reading in the papers of the advancement of men back home who had never heard a gun fired.

We know officers who were beaten out of their promotion by no longer than twenty-four hours on account of the order.

A great many have no intention of remaining in the army after the war, to whom the matter of promotion makes little material difference, but they were entitled to it as a recognition of their services—and no man scorns such recognition.

It's a pretty tough break for a second lieutenant of say the First or Second Division, who has been fighting in the line from the Marne to the Meuse and maybe has been wounded a couple of times, then reads of some fellow back home who started his military career at the same time or later, but who remained in the States, becoming a major or a captain. And it's just as tough a break for him to read of the appointment of some famous athlete to a captaincy or a majorcy, not because of any singular ability for military labors, apparently, but because of his fame.

There are cases in mind that may become historic of several celebrated characters in the world of baseball who collected their last paychecks from baseball, then came over here as captains or majors, remained in the back areas for a period, and are now getting home not only in time for next spring's training, but even for late winter shooting. So far as can be learned, when they got their appointments they did not know the difference between a squad and a platoon. Maybe they don't know it now.

Meantime, old Henry Gowdy, who chanced to enlist early in the war, and who carried a set of regimental colors from the Champagne to the Rhine, squats morosely in his home up the river, gazing out over the placid water and wondering idly if there'd be enough corned "William" for all hands at dinner. Henry is still a sergeant.

January 5, 1919. With the American Army of Occupation

George W. Perkins,[280] representing the Y.M.C.A., gave a dinner last night to war cripples with the Army of Occupation. It seems Mr. Perkins is making an investigation into Y.M.C.A. conditions with reference to its work during the war.

We would say it is a sort of post-mortem. It was our offhand suggestion today that, instead of looking for views or information from newspapermen, Mr. Perkins simply send out into the

A typical YMCA library.
Courtesy of Library of Congress

street and have the first dozen soldiers who went by brought in. Don't pick them; any soldiers. If they are from "Big Bat" divisions, all the better. But any soldiers.

Here and there he would have found men from an outfit which happened to have an efficient worker. Then he would have learned that the Y is all right. Then he would have again discovered a chap from an outfit whose Y worker was the other kind, and would have heard that the Y is all wrong.

There you have the summing up of the Y.M.C.A. in this war.

It was purely a matter of personnel. We think it would be a great pity if the work of some of the earnest, high-minded, tireless persons we saw along the front, as well as in the back areas, should be forgotten or discredited in the slightest degree by a big row now that it is all over. But that is the way of the world.

And even while thinking that, we cannot help but think, too, that the other sort should not be allowed to get away with it. There were too many of them.

January 7, 1919. With the American Army of Occupation, Coblenz

Mr. George W. Perkins went seeking an earful about the Y.M.C.A. last night and received the same.[281]

He invited the war correspondents with the Army of Occupation to an official dinner along with some officers. The correspondents had been stirring uneasily in their cage at the Hotel Riesen-Fuerstenhof for several days, having been weather bound to some extent, so when they were led out they were r'arin to go.

Mr. Perkins fed them venison. This further invigorated them. Then he asked them what in their opinion had been the matter, if any, with the Y.M.C.A. and what it might do in the future.

He mentioned that the organization now has something like $80,000,000 and is trying to determine in what manner this money may be expended to the greatest benefit of the soldiers.

He requested the correspondents to be candid and we will say they were. In fact, there was probably more candor spread over the premises than there has been in this part of Germany in the last twenty years.

Most of the correspondents who spoke are men who have followed the army a long time and were talking from first hand observation. Furthermore, they are men who get the viewpoint and sentiment of the soldier pretty well.

They have known the things they told Mr. Perkins as the whole army has known them for months, but none of them ever bothered to put them in print because they all felt it would have been unfair to condemn the many for the shortcomings of the few. For, after all, it still goes back to a matter of personnel, as we have said before.

It developed that few of the things they told Mr. Perkins were news to him, for he had been making inquiries among a great many people other than newspapermen, and he is in no way deceived as to the situation. In fact, the object of his visit here is to correct as far as possible that situation.

He agreed that the fault had been largely in the personnel; then he pointed out the difficulties under which the Y.M.C.A. labored to amass 5,000 personnel from the limited class from which it was allowed to select.

He also pointed out the difficulties of Y.M.C.A. workers in getting supplies for canteens at the front, and there is much truth in what he says in that respect.

When supplies do not arrive the soldier doesn't inquire into the transportation difficulties. He simply blames the Y.M.C.A. and lets it go at that. The poor Y workers are helpless.

The correspondents told Mr. Perkins they thought the organization erred in trying to cover too much ground and in letting the army stake it to canteens without assurance of commissary supplies.

They also expressed the opinion that the publicity department had promised too much, and that charging soldiers for cigarettes and other supplies had been a grievous mistake.

Mr. Perkins said, however, that the army had insisted on the Y.M.C.A. charging. There was a time when it was common knowledge that the Y.M.C.A. charged more for supplies than they could be bought for at the commissaries, but this was rectified weeks ago.

The gathering and the discussion were purely informal, but Mr. Perkins's frankness and his evident desire to get at the bottom of matters indicate that the mistakes of the past will not be repeated.

The only regret is that Mr. Perkins did not come to France some months sooner; then a lot of hard-working, earnest, efficient people wouldn't now be feeling the results of the inefficient. It looks like a big time for the lads along the Rhine during the next few weeks.[282]

January 9, 1919. With the American Army of Occupation, Coblenz

One of the favorite sports on the Rhine these days is the rating or rather the attempted rating of different combat divisions, much after the fashion which sporting writers used to rate football teams at the close of the season.

What was the greatest division and which did the most notable work are questions which will be probably argued down through the ages, especially by members of the different fighting outfits, with but small chance that they shall ever agree.

Every soldier proudly maintains that his organization is the finest, and no one will ever be able to change that opinion. The very same debate was in the program twenty years ago after the Spanish-American War; only then the argument was narrowed down to regiments. We are one correspondent who doesn't happen to have a favorite division, probably because we were never attached to any particular outfit for any length of time but were thrown more or less in connection with the line divisions at different periods. Wherefore what we say on the subject is more the reflection of a consensus of opinion than a personal expression.

And while unanimity of any one phase of the situation is difficult to obtain, there is a proposition on which there seems to be a pretty general agreement.

It is that one of the best of the National Army or draft divisions, if not indeed the very best, is the Eighty-Ninth.

This doesn't necessarily mean that it was the best fighting division—there wasn't much difference in the whole American army in that respect—it means that in everything that goes to make up a fine military unit, it stands out. Many Regular Army men rate it among the best divisions of the whole army.

You can start a terrific conversational test any time by comparing the First and Second Divisions. You can get up a warm debate any moment by suggesting that this or that National Guard division is greatest.

But when the Eighty-Ninth is mentioned, both Regular Army and National Guardsmen nod their heads and say: "It's a fine outfit." They don't admit that it is better than their own, of course, but they agree upon its merit without cavil.

And now see how the Eighty-Ninth is grist in the mills of the gods that are said to grind with such exceeding fineness. It was sent to the war by General Leonard Wood,[283] no less. He started for France at the head of the division but was turned back. That was a bitter blow to him, but he ought to find some consolation in the record of his division. It fought from St. Mihiel to the Meuse. It was credited with one of the most important operations of the last drive. It was in line at the finish. Finally it was chosen among the American divisions sent to the Rhine. After all, army divisions are made by the officers, as the men themselves are exactly alike in the raw. Therefore, it is needless to add that the officers of the Eighty-Ninth are an exceptionally fine lot. We say this without knowing a single one of them personally.

The Eighty-Ninth was trained by General Wood at Camp Funston, in Kansas. It is made up of an all-Missouri and an all-Kansas regiment, with a scattering of members from Nebraska, New Mexico, Colorado, the Middle West, and the Rocky Mountain states.

You can tell a member of the Eighty-Ninth a block away by his snap and military bearing. As early as St. Mihiel the Germans reported it as a new but good division.

When you come to figure it out, several things in this war are tracing back to a lonely soldier in Kansas who was not allowed to come over. We do not know what they claim to have on Leonard Wood, though a couple of people have tried to tell us, but this fact remains:

There are many thousands of efficient officers in our victorious army who are, figuratively speaking, children of his brain, without whom we might not now have an Army of Occupation on the Rhine.

There is, moreover, in that Army of Occupation every division of fighting men who are products of his hands.

It seems to us that one man could not do very much more.

January 9, 1919. With the American Army of Occupation, Coblenz

According to reports printed over here, American officers and soldiers returning to the United States will not be permitted to wear many little items of apparel which will distinguish them as members not only of the overseas forces, but of combat divisions.

It is said that officers cannot wear Sam Browne belts,[284] trench overcoats, or overseas caps. This seems to the writer not only rather absurd, but a real hardship upon the officers.

Most of them will leave the army as soon after their return as it is possible to do so. Few of them have any other coats than trench coats. This is especially true of those who put in most of their time on the firing line. Not many of them have other headgear than overseas caps. The order means that they will have to go to the additional expense of buying new equipment, which they will be putting away in a few weeks, or perhaps days. Many of them, too, will have to buy new tunics if they abandon their Sam Browne belts, because months of wearing have either left indelible marks where leather came into contact with cloth or worn it out altogether.[285]

It is also declared that soldiers must leave off their army and division identification marks. If this is true, it means the First Division must rip off those meaningful figure ones from their left shoulders; the Rainbows must drop that scrambled-egg semicircle; the immortal Second must abandon the picturesque star and Indian head; the Seventy-Seventh must put away its Statue of Liberty; and all other tags of identification must depart. The striking big black letter "A" which designated Liggett's First Army during the days of Argonne would doubtless be included in the order, along with the gorgeous red, white, and blue target which the Third Army of Occupation sports on its shoulders.

Abolishing their various marks is not a matter of great importance as compared to the other proposition, but it would be a shame if the people of the States do not get to see their soldiers as they are now, not as they are refurnished by someone whose ideas may be sound enough from a military standpoint, but who obviously lacks sentiment.

Soldiers like little touches to their uniforms, such as divisional marks. They are very proud of them, and identify a man's outfit at a glance. It seems to us that officers and men ought to be permitted to come home just as they are. There is one thing that nobody will deny them wearing—that's their rewards for valor. Many a man will have a Distinguished Service Cross and the Croix de Guerre across his chest when he lands in America. Some of them have Legions of Honor and various British decorations, too. It will be pretty hard to disguise them by any order in such a way that they'll look anything but their true characters as members of divisions that won the war.

January 1919. Doughboy Dialogues: Voices of the Night

Scene: A heavily congested road in France and behind the front line on a dark and rainy night. Several miles of war traffic have been brought to a halt by some obstruction in the road.

First voice (from an ammunition truck, very petulantly)—Well, what in hell's the matter now?
Second voice (from truck just ahead)—I dunno. We've stopped again.
First voice (sarcastically)—Oh, have we? I thought we was going right along. What is it, anyway?
Second voice (dismally)—I dunno. I can't see nothin'. Gosh, she's wet.
Third voice (from an ambulance)—Hey, what in hell's the trouble up there? You dead, or what? Do you think I want to stay here all night?
Fourth voice (from a supply camion)—Come on now! Le's go! Ally! Ally! Ally!
First voice (bitterly)—Yeh, allyeh.
Chorus of voices (with sarcasm)—Ally! Ally!
Fifth voice (rising very authoritatively out of the darkness as somebody flashes on light, spraying entire column with the white glow)—Put out that light!
Sixth voice (as light suddenly vanishes)—Well, they's a military policeman around anyway. That'll help some.
Seventh voice (shrilly)—Who wins the war?

Routine traffic jams provided soldiers with the opportunity to gripe about the war. *Courtesy of United States Army Heritage and Education Center*

Muffled chorus of voices—The M.P.!
Fifth voice (deprecatingly)—Thas all right now! Thas all right!
First voice (consolingly)—Jerry won't be over a night like this, buddie. It's too dark.
Fifth voice—Nev' mind about Jerry. Just keep that light out.
Eighth voice (from another supply camion, very plaintively)—This is a hell of a way to run a war! Where are we at anyway? What's the name of this place? Don't nobody know?
First voice (peevishly)—Ah, it's Philadelphia. Where d'you suppose?
Eighth voice (in some distress)—How far's it to Buzancy? I gotta git to Buzancy tonight some time. I just gotta do it.
Ninth voice (from down the line)—Hey, what's the idea? Give us a chance!
First voice (derisively)—You gotta fat chance, you have, buddie!
Seventh voice (coming faintly and from far away)—Whoa, you—!
Second voice (admiringly)—Who's 'at guy? Sounds like a gen'rul.
First voice (also admiringly)—It's more likely some mule skinner. I'll say he kin cuss.
Second voice (warmly)—I claim he kin!
Tenth voice (from the interior of a truck, pensively)—I hope the square-heads don't start shovelin' no coal over this way till we git out of here. It'd be a little bit messy. You 'member that road to Montfaucon, Joe?
Eleventh voice (from seat of truck)—Aw, they ain't been shellin' this road for three hours. Gimme an Omar.[286]
Eighth voice (querulously)—That is cer'nly a hell of a way to run a war! How'm I ever goin' to get to Buzancy at this rate? What's the name of that last place we passed?
First voice (informatively)—Harrisburg.
Seventh voice (growing a little stronger)—Whoa, you d—! d—! d—!
Second voice—'At guy's cer'nly a bear!
Feminine voice (from interior of another truck)—I wonder if this is the best road to Buzancy?
Chorus of voices (whispering huskily all along the line)—Sh! Sh! Sh!
First voice (after startled silence)—Wasn't that some dame?
Second voice (hoarsely)—Sure! It's 'at Salvation Army gal. I see her back yonder today. She's the one what makes the flapjacks.
Ninth voice (from away back)—Well, what in hell—!
Chorus of voices (excitedly)—Sh—h—h—!
First voice (after clearing throat)—Yes, ma'am. This is about the only road there is. It's pretty bad. It's pretty bad but it might be worse. You ought to see the one to Cheppy.
Tenth voice (warmly)—Yes, or the one to Montfaucon.
Feminine voice (sweetly)—Is that so?
Second voice (softly)—She kin cer'nly make flapjacks.
First voice—If ever I run a war I'm goin' to have two roads to run it on. One for us and one for them Frenchmen. Then mebbe we'll git somewheres.
Eighth voice (sorrowfully)—Well, I don't like the way they're runnin' this war. I gotta git to Buzancy tonight and here I am tied up like this. I never see such a business. I wish Gen'rul Pershing hisself would come along and git stuck here. I bet he'd burn somebody up.
Eleventh voice (as owner comes splashing back thru dark)—Well, it ain't no frog after all. You know what it is? It's nothin' but one of them damn little ol' Fords[287] got crosswise in the road. They just got her brushed off.[288]
Eighth voice (gloomily)—Well, what d'you think of that? A Ford stoppin' the whole war for two hours! And I'm in a hurry to get to Buzancy, too! Well, here we go again! Ally! Ally!
Chorus (along line)—Ally! Ally!
Fifth voice (harshly)—PUT OUT THAT LIGHT!

January 13, 1919. With the American Army of Occupation, Coblenz

Soon after the United States entered the world conflict, the writer pounded out a two-column article speculating on whether this war—like all other wars in which America had engaged—would produce a man who later might become a towering figure in the political affairs of the nation. Washington, Jackson, Taylor, Grant, and Roosevelt[289] were born of battle, as it were. Would the war against the Boche bring forth another such man?

It was our general conclusion that the result suggested was highly probable. Furthermore, it was our deduction that the man most likely to attain to the gigantic proportions outlined was John J. Pershing.

Thus, we were, in a manner of speaking, the original "Pershing for President" fellow. Not that we have any great personal liking for Pershing.[290] We have a tremendous admiration for him, but no liking. We don't like generals as a class, in fact.[291] However, we admire a lot of people we don't like. And we argued naively that he rode like a man of destiny.

We argue now that he so continues to ride; we are a firm believer in destiny. We hold that the very stars in their forces seem to move for the big Missouri cavalryman who led the American army in France. For today we were reading dispatches from Americans in the London papers which drift into Coblenz that since the death of Theodore Roosevelt, Pershing's name is being mentioned in connection with the Republican nomination for the highest office in the land.

More than eighteen months ago, when we were attempting to trace the Pershing destiny, we pointed out certain rather obvious facts.

The country was manifesting signs of clamoring for Roosevelt to take our army overseas. To still this rising clamor and to take the limelight off Roosevelt, it seemed necessary for the administration to find some man who loomed impressively in the public eye as a soldier—a man in whom the nation would have confidence and, at the same time, a man who was not Roosevelt, or even Leonard Wood.

Many believe General Funston would have been the man. The writer so believes. Funston was esteemed by Americans as their greatest soldier. But Funston dropped dead. Pershing had just brought his punitive expedition out of Mexico after a long chase after the bandit Villa.

That expedition was a failure, but so far from bringing the slightest criticism to Pershing for that failure, it brought him into public regard as one of the nation's big fighting chiefs.

In passing let it be said that Pershing couldn't justly have been held responsible for the Mexico failure. It went back beyond him.

When Funston died, Pershing automatically moved still further forward in public regard. When he was named as leader of the expeditionary forces, America felt that our military fortunes were in good hands. The Missourian came to France in the position of honor and met with honors such as no American had ever known.

Many another general started out in this war during the last four years with a great flare, but four years is a long time, and many a general fell by the wayside. There were pessimists who predicted a similar end for Pershing. They said it would happen not necessarily because of any shortcomings on his part, but because our country, like other countries, would wax querulous if he failed to accomplish marvels. There are still some who hourly aver that had the war continued, their predictions would have been fulfilled—if only by the workings of the law of average.

But the war didn't continue. It is full of the glory of military successes, and no matter what anybody says, Pershing made that army. And no matter what anybody says, that army won the war. Why suppress the eagle's chortle now?

When all is said and done, America's very biggest figure in this war was John J. Pershing, and John J. Pershing did two things upon which he can securely rest his fame if he had done nothing else. One is the organization of the American Expeditionary Force. The other is the keeping of that force as a separate army instead of allowing it to be merged into other armies—for it was as separate that it won undying glory for America and changed the face of the earth.

The man who made Pershing had died. They say Theodore Roosevelt was playing politics when he singled out of our army a humble captain of cavalry and jumped him over many files to brigadiership. Maybe he was, but Pershing is one of his legacies to the nation. History shall estimate its value.

When, long after the Army of Occupation had settled down on the Rhine and long before we had read the political gossip from America, we canvassed our idea of the Pershing destiny to some extent among the soldiers.

We found, and still find, surprising as the statement may seem, that his name carries no magic appeal to men who fought that war. As far as that is concerned, no one big personality has been impressed on them. Some divisions have their own individual persons, as is the case of Douglas MacArthur[292] with the Forty-Second Division, but no great dominating individuality stands out in their minds.

Generals in this war did not come into very close contact with their men on the fighting line as a rule. "Joe" Dickman, Preston Brown, and a dozen other men other than the new and brilliant battle chief of the American army are probably unknown by sight to most of the men they led. Pershing visited his troops as often as he could, but that was necessarily infrequent when the big fighting arrived. Naturally his men couldn't get a line on his personality from actual contact.

In a way that was unfortunate, too, because, judging from the regard his old men had for him in the days when he was a troop commander, Pershing has a personality which carries an appeal to the enlisted personnel at all events. He was certainly always a great hand for protecting the rights of enlisted men—although that's a good old hackneyed saying when you're boosting an officer. We happen to know it's true in Pershing's case.

There has been much fulsome rot written about him in the last couple of years, so we don't want to wreck any illusions by an extended discussion of his personality. It is undeniable that he has expanded. His manner, once peremptory, is smoother; his once cold exterior seems brighter. His vision has broadened. His is the most soldierly figure among the high officials of all the armies. He is a poor speechmaker—he never will be a speechmaker—but he's a good conversationalist.

He says what he means, and means what he says, and he doesn't hesitate upon a decision. He keeps promises. He's fair and impartial. Once we used to think him the exact reverse but were afterward convinced that our opinion was based on a misunderstanding.

He has carried his old army friends with him as he has mounted the heights if they made good, but he has been ruthless with them if they failed.

He has been just as ruthless with incompetency everywhere that it came to his notice. He snatched major generals out of the fighting line during the fighting, if they weren't succeeding, just as quickly as he would have snatched out corporals.

In that snatching he wounded divisional pride now and then, and these hurts may still be smarting after the soldiers get home. But we are convinced that he never was animated by any motive other than the good of the service.

We say that when we might prefer saying otherwise if we could.

There are innumerable instances where Pershing could have avoided making mortal enemies by taking a course other than he did. But there are mighty few instances recorded in which he failed to do what ultimately proved to be a good thing.

Some divisions undoubtedly were asked to do what seemed more than their share of work in the line, but events have proved that had the Americans relieved their divisions as facilely as did the other armies, the war might be going on yet. It was rough on some divisions, but it won the war.

There are going to be great tubs of olive drab rinsed after this war, the same as after every war. For wars don't change and soldiers don't change. Dangers, hardships, and grievances all become different matters in perspective.

January 18, 1919. [Delayed] Trier, Germany

When you stand in the presence of a man whom you realize is perhaps one of the greatest men of all ages, you are bound to feel a certain amount of emotion, unless, indeed, you are most blasé. And not being blasé, we confess to being very deeply stirred a few days ago when we stood before that chunkily built, bright-eyed old man, who is the world's foremost soldier—Marshal Foch of France.

It was in his private car in the town of Trier, the first town of any size entered by the Americans after they crossed the German border. The car was one of a long train of cars which stood on a siding near the Trier depot.

There were only about eight of us. Four of our party were American correspondents. Two were English correspondents attached to the American army. Then there were a couple of officers of the American press division and Lieutenant Francois de Tessan[293] of the French army, who is one of the French liaison officers with the press division.

De Tessan arranged the interview. De Tessan is, by the way, half American, being related by marriage to the Verdiers of San Francisco,[294] who own a big store there. He was in America with Marshal Joffre.[295]

He had been working for some time to arrange an interview with Marshal Foch, so he was a proud and happy man when he stood beside the old marshal and introduced his American friends as they filed in one after another.

To an American correspondent, an interview with the average general is not a particularly momentous event. In fact, they are generally inclined to dodge such meetings. In campaign times, when they go around seeking news, the last person they want to see is a general. They'd much rather see his chief of staff because he's apt to have more items of interest.

It is different with French correspondents. They regard a reception by the general commanding any forces they happen to be visiting as not only most important, but a large feature of their story, but what a general usually says is a lot of platitudes, and while every man was delighted at an opportunity of just seeing Foch close up, that is what the Americans expected to hear from him Friday.

It's what the French correspondents would have expected to hear and undoubtedly would have heard from an American general. Platitudes are an old game over here. Wherefore, when the grizzled Marshal of France made that declaration which was detailed in the *Denver Post* last Saturday, it caused quite a stir among the newspapermen.

Originally the interview had been arranged for Limburg, where Foch maintains a headquarters, but he had to go to Trier to meet with members of the American commission there. Some

Marshal Ferdinand Foch. *Courtesy of Library of Congress*

of us went by train and some by motor from Coblenz over muddy roads, for damp, disagreeable weather has come to Rhenish Prussia. Trier itself is unutterably muddy and depressing at this period.

Lieutenant de Tessan had gone down the night before, and he met us fairly effervescing. Everything was all right, he said. The marshal would see us. Up to this moment we had thought everything was assured anyhow, but it seems de Tessan had been in doubt. One never knows about marshals. But he had just been over to the train. We could go there as soon as the marshal had finished luncheon.

Presently we filed off down the road, de Tessan at our head like a troop commander and glancing back nervously very minute to see that nobody strayed away. One never knows any more about American correspondents than about marshals. In good order we arrived at the train. It was a solid train of sleeping cars of French manufacture.

Through the windows we could see little rooms fitted with desk telephones, with French officers laboring diligently. Elaborately uniformed aides strolled alongside the train. Here and there were French sentries in steel helmets. De Tessan said after an investigation that the marshal was just finishing his coffee, so we whiled away the time hobnobbing with Ed Hurley,[296] chairman of the American Shipping Board, Admiral Benson,[297] and a few other odds and ends of notables who had a private car on the track, having come there for a conference.

Soon Lieutenant de Tessan was seen wildly waving from the platform of the car, and we hastened there. He vanished inside and we followed.

The Marshal of France stood by a table in the drawing room of the car, and it was a good-sized room, too, for a railroad car. It was furnished with a couple of plain mahogany tables, evidently designed for working purposes. There was a telephone on one table.

De Tessan called out each man's name and organization as he entered. Each man saluted, then shook hands with the general. Then they had a chance for a back survey of the marshal. They saw a solidly constructed old man of not quite medium height, but giving the impression, despite his manifest age, of great bodily strength and activity. He has quite a shock of gray hair. He wears a big gray mustache with ends. It hides most of his mouth, except when it is lifted in a smile. He smiles frequently. His face is heavily lined. There are many crow's-feet around his pleasant eyes.

De Tessan took us to see General Mangin[298] not long ago. Mangin is even shorter than Foch, but physically more impressive. He radiates virility. He's of the peppery type. Foch seems more deliberate.

Again de Tessan took this writer to see General Schuhler, the Alsatian—about the size of Benny Kauff[299]—who commands the great Algerian division. Schuhler is different from either Foch or Mangin. He's a twinkling sort of man, but beneath the twinkle you always catch a glint of fierceness. None of the three Frenchmen is as imposing physically as Pershing or some other American generals who might be named, but all three somehow convey to you an impression of amazing efficiency, and Foch more than any of them.

He began to talk as soon as we were grouped around him. He spoke in an ordinary conversational tone, with oratorical effect, but very clearly. De Tessan says he has a slight dialect, due to the fact of his being a South-of-France man. Most of us could understand in a general way what he was saying, but only a couple present, who happen to be particularly well versed in French, could get it all. There was no attempt to interpret his remarks at the moment, although de Tessan usually does that for us in such cases. He promised the full text later on.

At the end of each sentence Foch uses an ejaculation which sounds like "hah," with a rising inflection, but it's merely a habit of speech. He employs both hands in gesticulation as he talks. He employs them constantly. Now it's the left, now the right, but one or the other is going up or down all the time. None the less, he gesticulates with grace.

He was dressed in a dark blue uniform. On each sleeve were seven little gold stars. There was no insignia of rank on his collar or shoulders. On his left breast he wore twelve different ribbons indicating military decorations of one kind or another. One of them was a new American Distinguished Service Medal. His leather leggings did not match his shoes. His shoes were run down at the heels and generally pretty well worn. On his left wrist he wore a silver watch. On the third finger of his left hand he wore a wedding ring. Otherwise he had no adornments.

Many a lieutenant dresses more elaborately than the Marshal of France. He had no attendants with him when he received us. Not even some distinguished French correspondents with his party were admitted to the interview.

The Marshal's voice is very pleasing. He talks rapidly but enunciates clearly. He looked first one, then another, in the face as he talked. His eyes seem to reflect the soul of this old soldier. When he speaks of his beloved France, they light up with singular radiance. This is the truth. There are moments when they seem weary. Then the name of France crosses his lips, and his eyes burn with a holy fire.

An American interview differs from a French interview. When an American is interviewed, he is content merely to answer questions, without going beyond them. A Frenchman makes a sort of set speech. Once a correspondent interjected a question which Marshal Foch answered, presently, but it was the only one offered.

Frequently his big gray mustache was lifted in a smile at his own remarks, or, rather, at our thoughts.

It is not likely that Marshal Foch prepared his remarks in advance. They sounded to be extemporaneous. He spoke as a soldier. We shall not here attempt to analyze what he said. It seemed to all of us a most memorable statement. It seemed to us that its keynote was "Let us keep the watch on the Rhine."[300]

Generals are not as a rule as outspoken of thought and sentiment as this brave old soldier.

It was very hot in the steam-heated car, so hot that fog covered the windows. The figures of French officers, English naval men, and American notables in civil dress moving around outside seemed faint and ghostly.

The voice of Marshal Foch rose and fell in musical cadence, broken but occasionally by the inexplicable "hah!" for a quarter of an hour, then suddenly halted. He had said what he had to say. Lieutenant de Tessan again was all agog. It was time to go.

One by one the correspondents passed before Marshal Foch and shook hands with him again. To each of us he said a pleasing "Bon jour, monsieur." And inside of us, as we went out into the muggy air of Trier, there was a profound feeling of emotion akin to reverence that we had had the privilege of seeing and hearing this man whose name will pass down through centuries as one of the saviors of humanity.

January 18, 1919. With the American Army of Occupation, Coblenz

A pain, sharp and sinister, hit us in the left lung without warning. So we went away to the old hotel in the old town of Trier, which had been the original headquarters of the press division when it first came to Germany nearly two months ago.

Our arrival seemed to cause some excitement. Shrill feminine voices called. One of those Amerikaner correspondents had returned. He was sick. There was a fine flutter among the Zimmermadchens. Correspondents are never forgotten by the Zimmermadchens in any hotel in which they have stopped. We rather suspect it is because of the mess they leave behind.

The English-speaking wife of the proprietor came up duly solicitous. She had no vacant room, but assuredly she would find a room for a correspondent, especially for one who was kranke, which is to say ill. It was not a large room which she produced. In fact it was excessively small, but sick men cannot be choosers.

Its one window looked out on a dreary, dead wall. Through it came the sound of streetcar bells and the monotonous voices of aged newsboys crying their afternoon papers along with other noises of the town, which is at once one of the most picturesque, and at the same time most thoroughly Boche and most thoroughly depressing, of all Rhenish towns.

Two Zimmermadchens peered timidly into the room. Where had we been since we went away from there? What was the trouble? Ach! It was doubtless the Spanish fever.[301] There was much Spanish fever in Trier. We had better be careful. One of their brothers had died not long ago from Spanish fever, and so quick we would scarcely believe it. This was cheering news indeed!

And now came other members of the "flying circus," or press division. Never let it be said that they would permit a worthy brother to lack company in the hour of his illness, especially when he had the only spare room in town.

They each and severally delivered themselves of advice concerning remedies for our ailments, illustrating their remarks with narrations of personal experiences.[302] Then they took a viva voce vote and decided that a doctor might not be a bad scheme. After which they set up their folding typewriters, lighted cigarettes, and waited for Lieutenant Francois de Tessan, our French liaison officer, who had drawn up a text of the remarks of Marshal Foch during the interview with the French commander and had taken it back to the Marshal for his approval.

Captain Gerald Morgan, chief censor of the American army, arrived with his trusty red pencil in hand, took a look around the room, and then established a temporary office on a little table at the head of our bed.

Noble Hall,[303] of the *London Times*, came in with a fur-lined coat just presented to him by his paper, dangling clear to his heels. If he ever falls down in that coat he will never be able to get up again. He removed the extraordinary garment tenderly and piled it on top of us, fearful lest we might be cold.

By this time, fever had commenced to creep over us, and we had a hazy illusion that they were holding our wake. We conceived the horrible idea that Captain Morgan was slapping his familiar stamp, "passed by censor," on us and put us on the cable. Faces grew vague and indistinct through the fog of smoke. As an evidence of our feverish phantasies we thought we heard the voice of Herbert Bailey, of the *London Times*, ordering wine.

Presently Lieutenant de Tessan arrived with the precious manuscript of Foch's remarks. It was in French, and all hands save ours manned their typewriters while Noble Hall took a chair in the middle of the room and started to read the manuscript into English.

Becoming imbued with the spirit of the remarks, his voice took on a sonorous intonation. He waggled his left index finger by way of emphasis. The typewriters rattled fiercely into his lingual path. Now and then there was a pause for everybody to debate the exact shading of some Frenchy phrase.

Lieutenant de Tessan sat complacently regarding the activity, which was in a sense the result of his endeavors.

Occasionally, Bert Ford, of the International News Service, would arise solemnly and shake hands with de Tessan, so carried away was he by Foch's conversation and de Tessan being the nearest representative of the French nation.

Suddenly the door opened and we heard muffled voices saying, "Mein Gott!"

Batting his eyes behind a pair of thick specs as he tried to peer through the smoke which befogged the room was a young German doctor. His heavy shoes spoke eloquently of his recent vocation of soldier. His thoughts about the scene he was witnessing were doubtless most interesting, but having located his patient—which was us on the bed—he came over and produced a stethoscope and pocket electric light.

He put one or both down our throats—we have forgotten which—and listened through one or both of our lungs. Then he wrote out a sheaf of prescriptions, which Captain Morgan absent-mindedly stamped "passed by censor," and went away bubbling like a camel.

Two more Zimmermadchens peeked in but were promptly dispersed by Lieutenant de Tessan with a loud "raus," he holding that their presence interfered with business.

Once more the battery of typewriters resumed. Noble Hall's voice clambered to perorational cliffs. It was most soothing. We were dreaming that we were drifting lazily into print across leagues of ocean cables on golden strands of vocal music duly stamped "passed by censor," when out of the clear sky of contentment someone remarked that the censor would not release the story until Saturday; albeit, it would go by courier to the telegraph office at Nancy that night.

In the chilling silence which followed, our temperature fell two degrees. All eyes turned toward Captain Morgan. He nodded brutally.

We have a very hazy recollection of the three- or four-hour train ride in a foul compartment of a train back to Coblenz; of much turmoil and of a terrific amount of advice when we arrived at our hotel; and, finally, of a German doctor with a gray mustache and a uniform coat of the German army who shed bitter-tasting powders in great profusion. Then, we have still another dim recollection of hearing the voice of Major Bozeman Bulger saying outside our door, "Say, Captain Morgan, that telegram of yours shook us up around here. We thought you meant that this fellow was dying. What kind of a time did you have down there, captain?" And of the voice of Captain Morgan saying with similar sweetness, "We had a wonderful time. It was just like the good old days before the armistice."

Undated.

Paris is today the most expensive city in the world. In a Parisian hotel I paid $8.50 for a table d'hote dinner of watery soup, a mouthful of boiled fish, a boiled chicken leg, and an apple, with a pint of mediocre wine on the side.

In the Rue de la Paix one day I met a famous journalist.

"Where are you living now, old man?" I said.

"I'm not living at all," said he. "I'm dying by inches in the Hotel Blanc at the rate of about $19.75 an inch."

January 24, 1919. With the American Army of Occupation, Coblenz

(Author's note—the story which follows has been reposing for several weeks in the censor's pocket and has been withheld by him from immediate transmission—for what reason we know not. We have liked to think it was because he loved to take it to bed with him of an evening to read himself to sleep.

(This impression was dispelled to some extent today, however, by the condition of the manuscript when it was restored to us with permission to send it along. It was as sadly creased as a bank note from the pocket of Tad Dorgan,[304] giving rise to the theory that the censor had retained the document because it softened his seat for him whatever time he occupies a hard-bottomed chair when he's ruthlessly stabbing to the heart the literary endeavors of war correspondents.

(Anyway, here's the story just as it was at the beginning. We had worried no little about its stoppage, not because of its intrinsic merit, but because it clogged our hitherto pristine record of not yet having a narration abated by the censor.)

Aside from a little African golf[305] and a few indoor sports, there hasn't been much doing with athletic diversion since the Americans hit the Rhine. The football season is over. It's too cold for baseball.

Somebody forgot to bring the tennis racquets along. So sport has been pretty dead around here until yesterday, when some of the French dropped in and gave us a demonstration of a new pastime which is said to be most popular in the French sector around Mayence.[306] It is also said the British are fairly adept at it in Cologne and that the Belgians in Aix-les-Baines are really expert. The Americans had heard of it but never seen it played.

The game is played with a cane or sword and a German civilian hat. The idea is to knock off the German's hat if the German fails to salute the colors.

A battalion of French Algerian troops from the famous fighting corps came here by boat recently to be reviewed by General Dickman and the French general, Mangin. Quite a delegation of German civilians lined the esplanade along the Rhine River front as the troops landed with their picturesque red-fezzed band playing and bugles blaring. In the crowd were a lot of French officers and numerous Americans, including both officers and enlisted men.

As the French colors went past, the hands of all the soldiers flew to their caps in salute. The German civilians stood silently watching. Suddenly, bingo! Up went a German hat high in the air! A French officer had reached out with his cane and deftly flicked it off the astonished German's head. Zip! Up went another German cady into the ozone and toward the right field wall of the Rhine.

Zip! Zip! More German kellys hit the breeze.

Our soldiers at first were vastly surprised at the lid shower. They couldn't understand what made the hats fly. When they discovered the motive power they became greatly interested, but also intensely critical, after the characteristic manner of Americans toward any game they do not play.

They commented on the technique of some of the Frenchmen as it appealed to them, not realizing that they were seeing the best Hat-knockers-off in all Rhenish Prussia.

"There's one fellow there who's picking nothing but derbies," commented a doughboy. "I don't see nothing to knocking off them old iron dicers. I'd like to see him swing on a flat cap once just to see how good his eye is."

"Sir," said another soldier, accosting a French captain, "to settle an argument between me and my friend here, will you tell me whether a fedora hat counts more than a Yale crush?"

Captain Gerald Morgan of the press division became involved in a heated debate with Lieutenant Stern from Third Army headquarters, the former claiming that a cleek would be more efficacious in getting at a hat which was bunkered between a pair of large ears, the latter contending in favor of a brassic.

As for the Germans, they couldn't grasp the game at all. Germans aren't much on sport, anyway. They hadn't been advised by proclamation or otherwise that they'd have to salute French colors, and Americans hadn't been requiring salutes of American colors since occupation. Some people say it isn't the custom for Germans as civilians even to salute their own colors. So they were pretty soft for hat-knockers-off.

Junius Wood, of the *Chicago Daily News*, didn't think much about the ability of the supposed French experts. "There ain't one of them could hit old Joe Gans[307] in the head with a sack of peas," he allowed.

Hank Gowdy, who was spending the week in Coblenz, also was unimpressed.

"If them guys under the hats would duck now and then 'twouldn't be so easy for them Frenchmen," he said. "I'd like to see one of them knock my lid off if I knew he was going to try. Look at the times Poll Perritt[308] tried to dust me off when I was up there at the old home plate. It's no cinch to hit a swinging target."

Despite these carping criticisms, however, it must be said that the Frenchmen at times displayed rare form. Some Americans were around that night deprecating the exhibition on the ground that we have the exclusive hat-knocking-off privileges in this section and that it was a clear infringement of our copyright, yet the fact remains Americans had failed to exercise their rights in that respect so Frenchmen cannot be blamed for invading this territory.

If they're going to organize a hat-knocking-off league, however, Americans are unlikely to be tail-enders for a time until they get the hang of the game.

Meantime, tonight there was heard along the Rhine the sound of cyclonic sneezing. Many high-collared German haircuts were exposed to chill breezes yesterday. Hereafter, local hat styles are likely to be sun-bonnets, which you can tie under your chin.

And what the score was at the finish nobody knows, but it is rumored an American colonel wandering around with a camera in hand snapped a couple of young French officers attached to headquarters as they took their cracks a second time at the sky pieces, and these officers suddenly disappeared. Maybe they weren't sufficiently developed.

Also that night a couple of soldiers were heard arguing that, even if a man should become a regular Ty Cobb[309] at knocking off hats, he wouldn't get anywhere because the business really has no future.

January 26, 1919. With the American Army of Occupation, Coblenz

There have been opened in our little city two modern shoe-shining establishments. This, in itself, is not a matter of importance perhaps, save that heretofore getting one's shoes shined was not as easy as it sounds, but presiding over, or rather under, the chairs in those establishments are German frauleins. There are few, if any, Greeks in Coblenz.

Both institutions are located on Rhinestrasse, which is one of the main streets of the town. Both have hoisted signs reading:

"Shoe shining, American style."

Business is fine in both places. To them repair, in large numbers, stout genial doughboys. They were at first somewhat bashful and reluctant about the situation, and some still insist on wielding a brush and rag on their own shoes, much to the astonishment of the frauleins, but this natural embarrassment is falling off.

It is quite a scene to see a line of soldiers with their extensive pedal extremities propped up on foot rests while girls "shine 'em up." This proceeding obviously does not come within the purview of the anti-fraternization law. There is some conversation between customers and shoe shiners, but this, of course, no doubt is strictly along business lines. Most of the girls have already been taught the familiar cry of that particular mart of trade by their patrons, though they get a Weber & Fields[310] dialect into the old call.

They are fairly proficient in the art of polishing, though German shoe polish is a terrible thing. There is little or no brown or tan shoe polish in Germany, and what they use as a substitute seems to be founded on kerosene. It raises Ned with shoes in no time. As a result of the scarcity of this kind of polish, black shoes have reappeared in the American army for the first time in years.

It started with the provost guard. Soldiers of the latter organization took to polishing their weather-beaten tan shoes with black polish. Now nearly every soldier you see has black shoes.

While girls are invading this line that's supposed to be strictly man's domain, the leading manicurist of this town is a man. His name is Schwartz. He's a little blonde and efficient. Besides being a manicurist he also is a friseur, which is to say, barber. Moreover, he's a chiropodist.

He's back in his shop on Rhinestrasse after four years' absence, which he spent peering along a rifle barrel in the region of Apremont and Verdun. They say he was a pretty good shot, too. When he was in town, Hank Gowdy gave the first manicuring custom he's had in nearly two years to Schwartz.

"Chances are the last time I saw that guy, he was trying to pot me, too," said Hank.

One characteristic of Americans which causes no little comment among German women is the agility with which doughboys give up seats in crowded streetcars when females enter. Judging from the stir it creates, this was not done to any great extent by local masculinity. Furthermore, our soldiers have a habit acquired from long practice at home of helping women aboard cars. They do this unconsciously and it has also caused much gossip in feminine circles.

January 27, 1919. With the American Army, Coblenz

There's a pretty smart jeweler in this town by the name of Walter Mulke. He's a sort of local Tiffany[311] or Dreicer.[312] His store is one of the largest of many establishments of that kind in Coblenz. He has always carried a stock of rather high-grade goods for the tourist trade in the days when Coblenz was a big Rhine resort, but he probably never had the grade or line he now has.

It took Herr Mulke just about a week to size up the American soldiers. This was during the holidays when business was extremely brisk. Then he took his gripsack in hand and made a tedious journey up Frankfort way. When he returned he was staggering under a burden of new goods. He brought back a big assortment of expensive jewelry of one kind and another, with particular reference to stuff for women. Most of it is gone already, for Herr Mulke had noticed that what an American wants he buys and that generally an American wants high-class articles.

He brought back wonderful examples of enamel work in toilet articles, such as powder boxes and the like. It went in a twinkling. In would stalk a big soldier with mud on his shoes and wearing his campaign-soiled uniform and lay down $100 or $125 for some dainty trifle without batting an eye. They would go from $100 up to $300 or $400 with equal sang froid.

Herr Mulke sadly asserts that business is good, but that it would be better if he had more stock.

Never has such shopping been seen as goes on all over Coblenz every day. Each day sees new and different batches of soldiers come to town from what might be called the front lines. They seem to head direct for the stores. They are prodigal in their purchases of feminine articles, showing where their thoughts lie. They buy handkerchiefs, beaded bags, and lace things of every description. They also purchase freely of souvenirs.[313]

It is a pleasure to report as a sort of commercial note that our local factories seem to have caught up with the demand for Iron Crosses, there being now a surplus on the market.[314]

Herr Mulke has no corner on the jewelry trade, by any means. There are numerous other stores of that kind, as stated above, and they are all generally crowded. There is one big cutlery store here where you almost have to wait in line to get in. Articles of that kind are easily carried and so are in greatest demand. So far the German storekeepers seem to be sticking to the same scale of prices which prevailed when the troops first got here. They have a rather surprising code of ethics, too.

One jewelry store has two silver cigarette cases which are identically alike in every detail, but one is marked quite a bit higher than the other. The storekeeper explained this on the ground that he purchased them at different times and that silver had gone up since he bought the first one.

There are a lot of curio stores in Coblenz. These have been heavily invaded by soldiers. They have been buying up antiques for souvenirs, paying all kinds of prices for them, too. The curio dealers here are just as cagey as they are in the States, and their prices are very little cheaper. Any articles of gold or silver are much higher here than in America, and the same is true of nearly all kinds of jewelry, especially precious stones. Silks and laces are also higher. That goes for all articles to wear, however.

But regardless of prices, the soldiers buy and keep on buying because that is the most exciting sport in Coblenz. It is all very well to talk about amusements arranged for their benefit, but any soldier would rather go around town of his own free will, seeing and buying, than be chaperoned somewhere else. So would anybody for that matter.

This is probably the best-behaved town in the world today. The writer has been here continuously since the American occupation and has yet to see a soldier under the influence of liquor. We have yet to see a row involving soldiers. There is only one place in town where the soldiers cannot go, and that is a district in the heart of the city where reside certain ladies of no uncertain reputation.

The district is in charge of military police, and aside from them, no man can go through the district in uniform. It happens to be part of a very busy section, and German civilians are permitted to go about their business there without restrictions. They probably lose a lot by being automatically debarred from the soldier trade.

It is strange it never occurred to the local authorities to move the women and unlock the district.

February 1919

February 24, 1919. [Delayed] Brest

New York's Twenty-Seventh Division—the Empire State's own—will begin loading for home tomorrow.[315] It will first fill the gigantic *Leviathan*,[316] which got into Brest yesterday. This boat will carry at least 9,000 men.

Just what units will go on the *Leviathan* has not been definitely announced, but they will include General O'Ryan[317] and his headquarters staff.

The commander of the Twenty-Seventh got in last night. He did not leave the clearing area until he had seen his entire outfit aboard the train.

First to reach Brest were the One Hundred and Sixth Infantry and machine gun battalions. The First and Second Battalions of the One Hundred and Seventh Infantry arrived yesterday, and the rest of the division got in today.

It is at Pont-a-Nezen camp, a few miles outside of the city. This is one of the camps that have been subjected to considerable criticism back in America. The members of the Twenty-Seventh do not seem disposed to find any fault with their quarters. The date of the *Leviathan*'s sailing is not known, but as a rule the boat does not linger long in the harbor once she is loaded.

Some of the Twenty-Seventh engineers have already gone home, but it was thought that the rest of the outfit would get to New York in one bunch.

Februry 25, 1919. At Sea

This day has been a most momentous day in the lives of many thousands of young New Yorkers, this day being sailing day for the transport *Leviathan*, with the main body of New York's Twenty-Seventh Division—homeward bound!

For my story is begun with the gnarled coast of Brittany only a few miles astern, still dimly visible, in fact, through a gauzy rain. The story might indeed very properly take date of Brest, France, from which port the giant ship has just cleared—homeward bound.

Homeward bound! Lord love us, what a sweet-sounding term! Home! New York—Manhattan Island—Broadway—Buffalo—Newburgh—Poughkeepsie—Watertown—Jamestown—Binghamton—Utica—Ogdensburg—Malone—Hornellsville—Saratoga—Schenectady—you can hear the names uttered every minute all along the street-like decks of the great boat and all in the one connection—home!

The land these lads came to fight for is fading into the foggy knots of ocean distance and into the mists of memory as they chatter; each man of his own particular heart's desire, whether it be the Big Town or the Little Town of the Empire State, but in any and every case—home!

For over an hour the decks have been packed with men standing in full marching kit—all their belongings on their backs—waiting while some unexpected shift in quarters on the boat was being effected.

"Wonder how long we're gonnah stand here?" grouses one fellow, shrugging his heavy pack in an effort to ease his aching shoulders.

"I don't know and I don't care a whoop," replies another, with a world of cheer in his tones. "I don't care about nothin' so long's this old canoe got her nose pointed in the right direction."

It was about 1 o'clock—you will remember that this story is started on Wednesday, February 25, in the year of our Lord 1919—that a chap came by, saying to himself and to the world at large: "Well, she's coaled and we're getting ready to go."

All hands went out on deck and had a peek. It was as he said. The *Leviathan*, which used to be the *Vaterland*[318] and the pride of all Deutschland, is so all-fired big that it cannot get even close to a dock in Brest or much of anywhere else for that matter. So it lays pretty well out in the harbor, squatted down in the water like a half-submerged mountain ridge, and is coaled from lighters or barges.

The last barge was being yanked away from the side of the *Leviathan*, to which it had been clinging like a big black leech, by a dingy tow boat called the *San Luis*. It belongs to the United States Engineering Department at Brest. Ranged along the deck of the *San Luis* were the last of the coaling brigade, which had been working night and day for several days hurling coal into the bowels of the transport.

They were mainly Negroes. They were dressed in hip boots and slickers and sou'westers. Besides these garments they all wore extra wrappings of thick coal dust. They looked like a lot of hired hands of old Beelzebub, fresh from a job in Hades. The *San Luis* itself was coal-dusty from bow to stern. Even the flag floating out behind seemed sooty. But it was the coalers who gave the Twenty-Seventh its farewell from France, and they did it, appropriately enough, in French.

"Aw-vaw!" they bawled, with the true intonation that the Frenchman puts on "au revoir." They've been long in France—these coalers. Back from the towering ramparts of the *Leviathan* fell a spattering of "aw vaws" and more "good-byes," with a lot of airy persiflage, and the *San Luis* pulled away, leaving with those aboard the *Leviathan* a memory of white teeth flashing through masks of coal dust.

It was raining, of course. It's always raining in Brest or nearly always. There was an exception which we shall presently note. A strong representation of *Leviathan*'s population of about 12,000 people was on deck to personally observe the process known as getting under way.

It consists chiefly of a horrendous grumbling from somewhere away down in the innards of the vessel and then a movement of the surrounding landscape, as if somebody had commenced to shift the scenery. And then everybody says to everybody else, as they indubitably said in this particular case: "Well, we're off." And so we were.

Down a narrow aisle of water, hedged with sawed-off hills on either side, the *Leviathan* moved. There was no cheering on the boat, no open manifestations of exultation such as might have been expected on such a momentous occasion, but everyone was almighty glad and almighty thankful. Many a man who probably hasn't done any vast amount of praying in his lifetime muttered a semblance of prayer to himself as the shores of France began dropping away.

Men who have trod the roads through the Valley of Death and who have been singed by the fires of hell have a right to pray—and know the time to pray. There are a great many such men on board the *Leviathan*. Up on Deck A, high above the surface of the water, are a lot of them. There, half the deck had been given over to the wounded and the sick. They lie out on

USS *Leviathan*. Courtesy of Library of Congress

cots in the open air, sheltered by close-drawn awnings, or hobbled about on crutches and with the aid of canes.

Each man wears a tag—the same sort of tag that's put on baggage—describing him and the cause of his being there in minute detail. Not all are from the Twenty-Seventh Division. Many are casuals, forlorn fragments from other outfits which have, or haven't, gone home. They are the war-torn veterans of the Argonne and the Meuse, as well as the Hindenburg Line, where the Twenty-Seventh won undying glory.

Captain George W. Peppard,[319] supply officer of the New York Division, put the thoughts of a lot of people in words when he came along to where a group was standing watching the receding skyline of the Brittany coast.

"Gentlemen," said the captain, "This is the day I've been looking forward to for quite a spell. This is the one day. There was a time when I didn't think I was going to see this day, but—well, that's a matter of detail now."

On his right sleeve the captain wears the V-shaped wedge of gold, which is the mark of a man wounded by an enemy projectile. The members of the group nodded very thoughtfully. They, too, had all seen times when—

But now they were homeward bound!

The roar of the cannon; the ceaseless spatter of the machine guns; the mud, the hunger, the cold, the weary hikes; and the long days in camp were behind them. Before them was home and the joy of home going. Every man saw in his mind's eye the old Statue of Liberty waving a welcoming beacon.

It's the same Twenty-Seventh Division that marched away from New York many months ago—the lads from Fifth Avenue, Broadway, the Bronx, and the upper reaches of Harlem, from Brooklyn, and from the Upstate towns and hamlets. It's the same division less, alas, a couple of thousand boys who will never again march behind the colors of the old Empire State regiments.

It's the same and yet it is not the same. These lads who seemed so very, very young and untried when New York saw them last are different now. There's a difference in their way of carrying themselves, in the expressions in their eyes. They seem older; they are older. They have changed. No man can go through the crucible of fire in which they have been tempered and remain unchanged. They are veteran soldiers; they are the men of the new Grand Army of the Republic.

They have been many places and they have seen many things. They know much about life and a deal more about death. They are some of the new race of men that has arisen in the world. They are the new giants of the world!

And they are going home!

It's doubtful if any of the young crusaders had any regret as the ocean behemoth ploughed sluggishly downstream. Maybe some of them reflected on the occasional good times that were mixed in with the bad times in the quaint little old towns hiding beyond the distant cliffs and wondered if they'll ever see La Belle France again, but such reflections were undoubtedly very brief indeed. They'll never forget France, and France will never forget them—but this was no time for regret.

On one deck a group of girls were huddled against a rail watching, wild-eyed and a little wistful, the disappearing shoreline. They were the "war brides" who married American soldiers. There are five of these brides going to their new homes with their husbands, and there are some very pretty girls among them. This going to "Amerique" is a new and big adventure to them. The married names of the newlyweds are Mesdames Jeanne Alwin, Jane Abrahamson, Olive E. Posner, T. Jarvis, and A. Beaumont.

The boat had not been under way long before there was some impromptu dancing on deck. A couple of exuberant youngsters gave an exhibition of their agility, and looking at them with most singular expressions were some of the wounded. Against the crutches of a couple of these men, empty trouser legs flapped in the sea breeze. God only knew their thoughts!

On an upper deck, watching his men, was Major General John F. O'Ryan, commander of the Twenty-Seventh. He was a proud man this day. He had a right to be proud. He was taking home the division that he made, that he toiled with, and sat up nights over, and fought for—taking it home with a glorious record behind it.

While the *Leviathan* was being coaled, two bands "spelled" one another in matters musical. It seems that our government officers, by dint of vast research and inquiry, have discovered that when the Negro coal passers have music they work much faster. Therefore the bands. The coal goes into the esophagus of the transports to the tune of "How's Every Little Thing in Dixie?" or "The Dallas Blues." The more jazz the musicians get in, the harder the coal passers toil.

They could coal the *Leviathan* at Southampton in about a third of the time it takes to do it by hand at Brest, but for some reason the government does not see fit to employ the British station. The Brest system is reminiscent of a mediaeval era.

The loading wasn't going fast enough to suit the Twenty-Seventh, and a lot of the soldiers volunteered to help on the job. The S.O.S., otherwise the Service of Supply, wouldn't stand for their assistance because, it's said, the S.O.S. prefers doing those things itself. That didn't prevent some of the soldiers volunteering as stokers after the boat got started. The last heard of Udo Keppler,[320] famous Pennsylvania football player and wrestler, he was down in the boiler room stoking a mean stoke.

A transport was nothing new to the Twenty-Seventh, of course. The men lost no time looking around. They proceeded to get themselves "oriented," as they say in the army, or located with the businesslike efficiency of vets, finding the nearest routes to places they might want to go and disposing of their belongings.

The *Leviathan* is a steady old gargantuan. It's so big that it could scarcely wabble much if it wished. Seas that would stagger most any other vessel it just sort of trampled underfoot and just squashes 'em out into a smooth roadway. When the Boche started out to build himself a large boat, he built a large one. It's like sailing aboard the Grand Central Terminal.

Before they decided they had enough aboard, they had tucked away in the bosom of the boat all of the One Hundred and Fifth Infantry, all of the One Hundred and Sixth Infantry, the division headquarters, the headquarters troop, the One Hundred and Fifth Machine Gun Battalion, two battalions of the One Hundred and Seventh Infantry, and a big batch of casuals.

The One Hundred and Fifth used to be the Upstate Second Regiment, along with the Tenth and some of the Seventy-First. The One Hundred and Sixth was the old Twenty-Second and Fourteenth of Brooklyn. The One Hundred and Seventh was, of course, the old Seventh and the First. The One Hundred and Fifth Machine Gun Battalion is made up of part of the old First Cavalry and Squadron A.

The division left behind in Brest, bemoaning their lucklessness at not getting aboard the daddy of all the boats, was one battalion of the One Hundred and Seventh, the One Hundred and Eighth Infantry, the One Hundred and Fourth, One Hundred and Fifth, and One Hundred and Sixth Field Artillery (the whole artillery brigade), the One Hundred and Second Ammunition Train, the One Hundred and Second Supply Train, the One Hundred and Second Sanitary Train, the One Hundred and Fourth Machine Gun Battalion, the One Hundred and Sixth Machine Gun Battalion, the One Hundred and Second Field Signal Battalion, and the One Hundred and Second Military Police.[321]

It is understood that these outfits are to be cleared just as quickly as possible from Brest, and they ought, therefore, to ebb along in short order. In fact, it is said that the orders from General Headquarters of the Army were to clear the whole Twenty-Seventh Division before there was any other troop movement, and the facility with which the first bunch was shot through Brest indicates that this story is correct.

There are a great many casuals at Brest awaiting transportation to the States, and there was much of the proverbial weeping and wailing when the Empire State's Own went breezing through and aboard the *Leviathan*, as if the ways had been greased for it, which, in fact, they were. However, the casuals forgot that the Twenty-Seventh had been waiting in the embarkation area for many weary weeks.

After the heroes of the smash through the Hindenburg Line came out of action, they went to Corbie and Roisel, near Amiens. Then down to Montfort, in France, in what is known as the embarkation area, on November 23. They were told that they would embark about the middle of December. From that time on, they had been waiting, going through the dreary monotony of camp routine. It is that which tries the souls of men more than battle.

There was no waiting when they were once started out of the Montfort region, however. The advance outfits went into camp at Pontanezen, three and a half miles from Brest, coming down by train. It is this camp at Pontanezen which has been the object of numerous attacks by so-called investigators. It's said Napoleon once trained his army there, and some of the old barracks are still standing. As a matter of fact, Pontanezen is a pretty good camp, as camps go, and is so pronounced by the Twenty-Seventh.

I had a brief look at Pontanezen. However, the only person who can give an expert opinion on a camp is a man who has to live there. I don't believe much in these offhand judgments of investigators who merely gaze around a place, listen to a few explanations, and then render a verdict in writing. My judgment is that Pontanezen has been considerably maligned, but I wasn't stuck in Pontanezen for weeks.

It's muddy out there, but it's muddy everywhere around Brest. The man hasn't yet been discovered who can control the elements. Brest is one of the most colorful places in all the world just now, despite climatic conditions, and the Twenty-Seventh did a little sightseeing and quite a lot of shopping before it departed.

In the streets of Brest you see American, French, and British soldiers and sailors. A Chinese war boat was in harbor while the Twenty-Seventh was there, and the slant-eyed mariners from the Celestial Kingdom—or isn't it a republic?—wandered about, usually the center of little throngs of American soldiers who wanted to sell them souvenirs of the great war.

The division went into Pontanezen Sunday night. By that time it was generally rumored that the division would embark Tuesday morning on the *Leviathan*, although everybody refused to believe it until it was established by actual fact, which is the only way to believe anything in the army.

Tuesday was that day when it wasn't raining. We have mentioned it before. They say there are three such days in Brest. Providence doubtless arranged this particular day by way of special grace for the Twenty-Seventh.

The troops hiked down from Pontanezen over roads freshly curried with chopped rock, which is not good for the feet. However, it was a short hike. Many of the officers had spent the time in hotels in Brest. The men moved in full marching kit, and each man had an extra pair of brand-new trench shoes slung over his back. Much of the Twenty-Seventh's equipment is British, especially rifles, tin hats, and gas masks. They've painted their tin hats a fresh grass green and have added a snappy touch by painting the divisional emblem in front. They also wear this emblem on their shoulders.

It's the only outfit I have ever seen that has every emblem made exactly alike. In many divisions the men and particularly the officers get the emblems made the best they can, with the result that while alike in general design they are all different in manufacture. The New Yorkers have identically the same markings.

At the docks in Brest the men were loaded aboard lighters. Many of them had landed in Brest when they first came to France, and they had an opportunity of seeing with their own eyes the wondrous changes the Americans have wrought since then along the old waterfront. The Red Cross women were on the job at the dock, and as each man went aboard, he was given a pair of socks. In each sock was a batch of tobacco and candy. They draped these socks around their necks and went aboard the lighters, wearing them in that fashion.

The ancient, gray *Plattsburg*,[322] once the *New York*, was in harbor with the *Leviathan* waiting to take on troops. So was the big *Caronia*.[323] None of the Twenty-Seventh went on these boats, however. Most of the division had gone aboard the *Leviathan* before General O'Ryan reached the dock with his staff. It is O'Ryan's habit to stay behind until the last minute to see that everything is going all right.

The lighters laid alongside big openings in the cliff-like sides of the *Leviathan*, and the troops were poured into these openings. The big boat sopped up soldiers like a sponge soaking up water. Platoon after platoon, company after company, and regiment after regiment disappeared inside her and still there was room for more.

"Years and years after we've been mustered out, they'll be finding old guys with long whiskers down in that tub who'll be saying they belong to the Twenty-Seventh," averred one soldier.

They got to directing each other in terms of the city. They informed laggards that their quarters were "three blocks west." Scamp Montgomery's[324] famous line "some skiff" fits this Boche monster of the sea. Telling some fellow to look you up on the *Leviathan* is like asking a man to say hello to your uncle in Texas. The mark of the Boche is still visible in the permanent signs of one kind and another, but the Americans have changed many of his ideas. They use the famous swimming pool for storing baggage. Most of the cabins have been arranged so they will hold more men.

Heine had a printing office on the boat, and the Americans have improved it by putting in a linotype. They still use his old presses. Parts of them get lost, but they seem to run better than ever afterwards. The *Leviathan* is manned entirely by the Navy, and the soldiers immediately began digging up old pals from around New York among the "gobs."

After one meal aboard the boat, they began asserting loudly that in the next war they were going in the Navy, to which the sailors replied with the assurance that they were going to take the Army in theirs. There's no denying, however, that one certainly eats on board the good ship *Leviathan*. The men mess by units, as always. They march past huge containers of food, mess kits in hand, and having been provided with roast beef, potatoes, macaroni, beans, bread and butter, and what-not, they march to tables where they sit down and eat.

They got all they want to eat, which is an important detail because it is the first time they have had enough—really enough, understand—since they left the comforts of home. The mess hall is the old second-cabin dining room of the boat, and it's almost as elaborate as the first-cabin dining room, where the officers eat. Of an evening it is used for movie shows and accommodates several thousand men at a time.

The field officers eat in the old Ritz café[325] and the junior officers in the same room, but separated from their superiors by the balcony effect of the Ritz. Flo Ziegfeld[326] could put on his Follies in the dining room and have room for a bigger audience than he ever played to in New York. It's almost big enough for a national convention.

Lieutenant W. A. Halloran,[327] the division impresario, began making arrangements to put on a show almost as soon as the outfit came aboard. He has much the same troupe which produced "You Know Me, Al" in New York. Colonel Marshall, from General Headquarters of the A.E.F., started right out the first afternoon with a lecture on the Argonne-Meuse campaign to the officers and followed it up with moving pictures at night.

There were also movies for the men. The Red Cross, Y.M.C.A., and Knights of Columbus people, who have been with the division all the way through, came home with it, and they resumed just where they left off at camp. There are also a bunch of Red Cross, Y, and K of C casuals aboard. Quite a number of women are in these parties.

The soldiers were loaded so rapidly that the first night they hadn't all been quartered. On every deck they were rolled up in their blankets and sleeping on the floor. There are six officers in staterooms originally intended for four, but everybody seems comfortable. This is by no means a record boatload for the *Leviathan*. On one occasion, during active hostilities, they had nearly 14,000 men on board. None the less, 12,000 is quite a load.

March 1919

Nearing God's Country, Doughboy Dialogue

Scene—One of the troop decks on a United States army transport.

First soldier—You know why we're gittin' such good weather now? It's because we're over ha'f way acrost. We're on the American side of this ocean now. Ev'thing's better on this side than it is on the other—even the weather.
Second soldier (gloomily)—I nev' see but one kind of weather on the other side, and 'at was rotten weather. I see more sunshine today that I see in the last nine months. I ustuh git sore at the sun around New York, but I'm nev' gonnah say another word about it. I'm nev' gonnah open my trap about it, even if it shines at night. Can't have too much sun the rest of my life.
First soldier—Well, we're on the American side now, and thass why the ocean is so smooth.
Third soldier (plaintively)—I don't think she's so darn smooth. I don't like this ocean. Sometimes I can't hardly eat nothin' on this ocean, and when I can't eat they's somethin' the matter with me. I don't care hardly nothin' about oceans. I wouldn't give two francs for any ocean.

"I'd almost druther be in France than on this ocean."
Courtesy of Library of Congress

Fourth soldier (as plaintively)—Thass me, too. It joggles me all up inside. Look where I am, anyway—down there on H deck. If the bottom falls out o' this boat, I'll be the first to drown. I couldn't be no closer the water unless I was swimmin'.
Third soldier—I druther hike any day than ride in this vestul. It's always tippin' up 'n' down. The part I'm in is, anyway. I wisht I was a gen'rul an' could ride where she don't tip.
Fourth soldier—Yes, 'n' what with some guys down there on H deck not havin' no new socks lately, I tell you I ain't havin' so much fun. I wisht this ocean would stop squidin' around for a while.
Fifth soldier (derisively)—Lissen to them sod busters, will yuh? They think this is rough. Why, she's jus' like a bowl o' soup! I wouldn't mind ridin' in this big bus of a boat for a month if it wasn't that I'm anxious to git home. I got business at home, I have. I want to git to tendin' to it jus' quick's I can, but first, of course, I'm gonnah have me a good rest. 'N' the tooter the sweeter, like the frog says.
First soldier (promptly)—Thass exactly my idear, too. I'm gonnah have a rest.

I wonder how long it'll be before we're mustered out?
Sixth soldier (confidentially)—I got it pretty straight from a guy thass pretty close to people around headquarters that it's liable to take quite awhile. Mebbe a month. Mebbe longer. And then mebbe it won't take so long.
Third soldier (gloomily)—We had corn beef 'n' kebbage yesterday, and I ain't able to eat hardly any of it. When I ain't able to eat corn beef 'n' kebbage they's somethin' wrong with me. It's sure a sign I ain't Jake. I hope I nev' see any oceans any more, but if I do I hope I'm a gen'rul, so I kin have somethin' to say about where I ride on the boat.
Fourth soldier—Me too! When I git back to Malone, I'm nev' goin' near no more oceans. I'd almost druther be in France than on this ocean. I won't nev' go to no more wars unless they have 'em up on the Erie Canal or some place where they ain't no oceans to cross.
First soldier—I druther be any place except in France, unless, of course, it's in Belgium.
Seventh soldier (positively)—Say, I wouldn't trade li'l' old Newburgh for all o' France and Belgium! Especially not for Belgium! No, sir! When I git back to Newburgh, I'm gonnah stand on the corner o' Broadway and Grand and—
Fourth soldier (eagerly)—Newburgh? Say you ever bin to Malone? I wouldn't swop Malone for two Frances, and seven Belgiums. Well, I should say not! All I see to them countries is rain 'n' kilomeeters.
First soldier (casually)—I live in Brooklyn, myself. Thass a place to live! When yuh talk about tradin' places, I wouldn't trade no part o' Brooklyn for all o' Yurp. I ain't got nothin' agin' Yurp, but they kin have it! I'll take Brooklyn in mine! I wouldn't trade Prospect Park for the whole works over there!
Second soldier—Well, I guess Brooklyn's all right at that. I don't know, 'cause I don't go there if I can he'p it. I live in Hudson street, and I'll be there toot sweet as soon as I git off o' this boat. 'N' after I git there it's gonnah take more'n any Yurp to git me away from there again, if anybody asts yuh.
First soldier—I wonder where they're gonnah take us after we git home? I wonder if we're gonnah go to Upton? I hope we don't go to 'at joint, anyway. I got no use for Upton, though I nev' seen it. Some way I got a prejuduss agin' it.
Sixth soldier (lowering voice)—I got it from a guy who knows pretty much what's goin' on around this division 'at we're liable to be sent to Camp Merritt, or—
Second soldier—Merritt? Thass in Joisey. Thass great for me! I got a nuncle who lives in Paterson, and I kin hop over 'n' monjay with him. They have great chow at his mayson, too!
Sixth soldier—Or we'll be put in the armories right in town. Right in New York!
Eighth soldier (who has hitherto been quiet)—What's 'at? In New York? Right in town? Tell me 'at some more! But (pessimistically) chances are it ain't so. Chances are it's just news from the same ol' place.
Sixth soldier (warmly)—No, sir! I got it straight!
Eighth soldier (still pessimistic)—Well, chances are if it's so there's a lot o' new rules, or the town's gone plumb dry, or somethin' like 'at. Chances are it won't do me no good.
Fourth soldier (brightly)—I'd a lot druther they'd send me right on to Malone. I ain't got so much use for New York. I don't care if she is dry. They kin jus' check me right on through to Malone.
Third soldier—Well, they're gonnah give us big reception in New York, so I hear. I guess we'll git big receptions ev'where for 'at matter, nez par?
Eighth soldier (more pessimistic than ever)—Yeh, and after we bring home a week or so they'll be lookin' at us an' sayin' "Why in hell don't them guys go to work?"
First soldier (indignantly)—If they've dried up the ol' town on me already I'm gonnoh be good 'n' sore, I tell you those! Not 'at I care nothin' about drinkin', because I couldn't do none anyway, bein' in uniform, but I don't like the idear of them takin' advantage of me bein' way to war. I call it a dirty trick! I'll say so too, when I git home!

Fifth soldier (consolingly)—'At dry business don't come off until July. I read it in a paper. Anyway, it don't bother me. Just so they haven't done with hot cakes, 'n' maple surp, thass all I care.
Eighth soldier—Well, if thass true about us going to the armories, I'm a new man from now on!
Sixth soldier—Well, I got another tip, too. I hear they's a chance we may go to Camp Mills, down near Mineola.
Eighth soldier (sarcastically)—What else do you hear? Give us all the crepe at once!
Sixth soldier (soberly)—'N' of course we may get quarantined—
Eighth soldier—Well, I don't give a damn where we go, or what they do to us. We're nearly home, anyway. Thass enough for me! Nobody kin discourage me! We're almost home 'n' pretty soon I'll see my sweet patootie, 'n' all the gang. Thass good enough!
Third soldier—Jus' so I kin git back to where I kin enjoy my corn beef 'n' kebbage like I oughtuh. I ain't got no holler comin'.
Fourth soldier—But no more France 'n' Belgium for me unless they hold their wars handier to the docks. I don't mind goin' to 'em on streetcars, or railroad trains, but I couldn't stand this ocean, and H deck again. No, sir!
First soldier (very solemnly)—When I git off this uniform and back in civvies—Oo-lar-lar!
Chorus (from away down inside of them)—Ah-H-H-H-H!

March 4, 1919. On Board U.S.S. *Leviathan* at Sea (via Radio)

Three-quarters of the voyage of the transport *Leviathan*, bearing home General O'Ryan's headquarters detachment and 8,000 officers and men, making a total of 12,000 men on board, has been completed.

The big boat, perfectly handled by a Navy crew, will probably get into New York harbor Thursday around noon. She carries the One Hundred and Sixth Regiment of Infantry complete, two battalions of the One Hundred and Seventh Infantry, all of the headquarters outfit, and the One Hundred and Fifth Machine Gun Battalion.

It has been a remarkably pleasant journey so far. The sea has been calm and the weather clear.[328]

There have been theatrical performances by Twenty-Seventh Division performers, dances, movie shows, and other amusements every night since leaving Brest.[329]

Chips from the Log of the *Leviathan*

Took a turn along one of the lower decks of the *Leviathan* shortly before she reached New York. It was like walking down Main Street of some town where every face is familiar.

Here's Sergeant Howard McLellan.[330] Mac used to be a reporter on the *Evening World*. Been a mighty handy man for G-2 with the division in this war. Knows everybody and everything in the outfit. Top hole chap, Mac.

——————

Yonder's Private Russell Brown,[331] actor. His last appearance on the Broadway Rialto was as the star in the division's show, "You Know Me, Al." He was Al.

——————

Private Bill Breck[332] was going up in the avenue, as you might say, a boulevardier in an overseas cap, worn slightly askew. Bill drew the pictures for Dere Mable,[333] the love letters of a rookie, written by Lieutenant Ed Streeter.[334] They say the boys made $25,000 out of the book.

——————

Ed Streeter, by the way, is up with the Army of Occupation in Bocheland.

——————

See Private Lauren Stout[335] in the distance. Artist. Well known. Good soldat, ocey, which is not the way to spell also in French.

——————

Yonder's Private Stanislaus Stange Jr.[336] Made a name as division observer. Has written a show which Dave Belasco's[337] going to produce. It's called "June to November."

——————

The *Leviathan Press* is the local newspaper. It is printed daily and covers the field well. Two pages—one on either side of the sheet. In politics it seems to be neutral.

——————

Then there is the *Red Watch Mark*, printed weekly by the engineering department of the boat. It is a dandy little publication.

——————

Tommy Atkins never got over calling the New Yorkers Sammies, much to their intense disgust, but the Aussies and the Canucks called them Yanks.

——————

Tony Albany, who has local note in the Twenty-Seventh as an accomplished molester, is a brother-in-law to old "Black Hand" Dick Curley,[338] the sporting promoter.

——————

Gossip along the Boulevard de Deck D has it that the gang's going to get out a big edition of its paper, the *Gas Attack*, when it gets back to New York.

——————

Many a poet and many an artist within this division. Plenty of talent. Plenty of temperament, too. Young Cornelius Vanderbilt Jr.[339] was one of the best poets in the outfit. Went home some time ago. They speak of him as "Neeley."

——————

There's Raeburn Van Buren,[340] artist. Comes from Kansas City. Ted Beall[341] just breezed past. Another artist. Both gents privates.

——————

Who's this but Phin Deery.[342] Phin's the son of Bob Deery,[343] foreman of the *Morning World*, and one of the best known men along Park Row. Phin's brother, who is also named Bob,[344] was wounded in the Belgium show but is aboard, alive and well.

——————

Rob McCay[345] is easily identified as the son of Winsor McCay,[346] the famous cartoonist of the *American*. Rob was a dispatch rider and won the British Military Medal for bravery.

——————

Winsor McCay also has a son-in-law aboard the *Leviathan*. He is Major Raymond Moniz,[347] who is anxiously looking forward to meeting a little son whom he has never seen. He is assistant quartermaster of the division.

——————

Bill Halloran put on a vaudeville show Thursday night in the officers' mess hall. Martin Green,[348] of the *World*, had the only civilian hat aboard and loaned it for one of the props.

——————

Tough break for two soldats just before the boat was getting ready to pull out. They had put in applications a long time ago to remain in France for the Y.M.C.A. Then, when they had forgotten these applications and were all smoked up over the home going, notice was received that they had been accepted. So they had to go over the side of the *Leviathan* to a shore-bound lighter. Sore? Phew!

——————

Major Lucius Bigelow Jr.,[349] big and handsome as all outdoors, strolled along the deck eyeing the water. Bigelow was a mighty football player in his day at Yale.

——————

Ah, there's Captain Alwyn Ball 3d,[350] formerly of Princeton. He could play quite a few football, too.

——————

And Captain Ham Andrews,[351] formerly of Princeton. And Captain John Reynolds,[352] formerly of Harvard. They just passed. You could get up an imposing football squad from those aboard the papa of canoes.

——————

Or if you wanted to play a bit of hockey, what about Captain Bob Leake,[353] of Princeton.

——————

Music by the sailors' orchestra, with dinner in the officers' mess hall. No jazz. All heavy stuff.

——————

The "gobs," which is to say the sailors, toss a baseball profusely about a starboard deck of an afternoon.

——————

Brigadier General DeBevoise[354] is the only other general besides General O'Ryan aboard. He commands the Third Brigade.

——————

Captain H. T. Blythe[355] goes trudging along dreaming a sort of pleasant day dream of Newburgh, no less. Blythe has served in two wars with New York State outfits. In '98 he went out with the First Infantry. Now he is with the One Hundred and Seventh.

——————

There are suites, or young flats, aboard this yawl which cost passengers as high as $8,000 per voyage in the days when it was the *Vaterland*. Hot and cold water and all privileges with these apartments—in those days.

——————

This reporter does not have one of the suites. Neither has any private.

——————

Sergeant Major Hart,[356] General O'Ryan's orderly, drifts past every few minutes dragging a Belgian police dog.[357] The dog belongs to the general.

——————

Passed a Belgian relief ship Thursday while at abandon ship drill. The *Leviathan* gave her the old flag run-up as a salute.

——————

Nobody knows whether the *Leviathan*'s a her or a him. Most folks call it "it" and let it go at that.

——————

"Zu" on your water faucet means "on" and "auf" means just what it sounds—off. One gets to be quite a linguist riding around on these punts.

——————

Lonesome bird on board with the Statue of Liberty emblem of the Seventy-Seventh on his shoulder. There are quite a number of casuals from the Twenty-Eighth, the Rainbow, Seventy-Eighth, and Seventy-Ninth and other combat outfits, but he's the sole representative of the double sevens.

——————

Seventy-Seventh's starting to move down into the embarkation area in France, but that doesn't mean anything. It may be there until it has long whiskers.

——————

They've got a Boche truck[358] aboard that the Twenty-Seventh snatched in the Hindenburg affair. They're taking it back as a souvenir.

——————

Major T. Harry Shanton,[359] of White Plains, was left behind by the division. He's assistant provost marshal at Havre now. It's a big job. Shanton used to be a circus ringmaster. That's ideal training for an A.P.M.

——————

Lieutenant Colonel Sherman,[360] vice president of Sherman & Son, is another absentee. He's assistant deputy provost marshal general of the A.E.F.

——————

Everybody refers to the *Leviathan* as the "Levi Nathan."

——————

"Gobs" wait on the tables in the officers' mess. For gents not waiters by profession, they are very adept, too.

——————

Everybody who had any French money left changed it back into American dough just before the boat left Brest. The U.S.A. had a man at the dock loaded down with greenbacks for that purpose. Now the soldiers have to learn the Yank money language all over again. It's the prettiest money on the face of the globe.

——————

The Twenty-Seventh doesn't work as much French into its conversation as the average American division. That's because it wasn't around the French as much as the others. It understands and slings British pretty well, however. British is harder to learn than French.

——————

What used to be the ballroom on the *Leviathan* is now the hospital. It's about the size of Carnegie Hall. Has an illuminated ceiling, gorgeous paintings, and everything.

——————

"Gobs" serve as chambermaids. They can make up a bed toot sweet, which is to say durn fast. A "gob" can do most anything, apparently. A "gob" is a sailor, as we have said before.

——————

Why "gob," we don't know. Explanations of the derivation are as numerous and as confusing as the explanations for the origin of the word "boche" or "doughboy."

——————

As far as the Twenty-Seventh can remember, it was served with the British rum ration just twice while it was at the front, although the British served it to their own soldiers right along.

——————

"One jolt of that hooch would make a guy go over the top or over anything else," confides a Twenty-Seventher.

——————

It's a big relief to be able to sail around an ocean without the lights going out at night and no submarines to think about.

——————

Brest is one of the greatest places in the world to leave from. The leaving is particularly attractive.

——————

Lieutenant Jay Rogers[361] used to catch for the Yanks. He's now with A Company of the One Hundred and Seventh. Shoe business in Hornellsville when the war racket's off. He could pole 'em.

——————

They serve ice cream at the officers' mess nearly every other day. No spoofing. Ice cream.

——————

The Twenty-Seventh says the Australians are great guys. They claim the Aussies as pals. Think mighty well of the Canucks, too.

——————

"Well, Yank, it's up to you," was the greeting the British gave the New Yorkers when they landed on the Belgium front.

——————

Eggs for breakfast the other day. The scene almost paralyzed some of the men. An egg, not eggs, but an egg, costs you about one buck in Belgium.

——————

Two meals a day for the enlisted men. Three for the officers. The only thing to be in the war business is a General.

——————

Big cootie hunt, or "vermin inspection" as they call it, Friday. No results.

——————

Lots of folks on this tub used to pay money to hear Private Judson House[362] warble. He was a Metropolitan tenor.

——————

Private George Anderson,[363] whose wife is Fritzi Scheff[364] the famous prima donna, is a passenger on the Levi.

——————

Bill Holmes, field clerk, was out on deck reading *If I Were a King*. Bill is General O'Ryan's brother-in-law and can call the general "Jack"—if he wants to.

——————

Young Mike Donovan,[365] old Mike's[366] son, and himself once a well-known middleweight fighter, is with the Household Guards, otherwise the headquarters troop.

——————

Sergeant Dick Cotter,[367] of the One Hundred and Sixth Infantry, has been anxiously looking for the old lady with the lamp in her hand since the wagon left Brest. Dick used to catch for the Giants and the Yanks.

——————

War didn't cure the British of the tea habit, according to the Twenty-Seventh. No matter what happened, the Tommy had to have his tea. When it came 4 o'clock, he'd stop right wherever he happened to be, get out the tea caddy, and set 'er steaming.

——————

Incidentally, it was no easy task getting the British to issue coffee to the American contingents at first. They couldn't understand why the Yank was so squiffy about his Java when there was tea on tap.

——————

Then by the time the British got round to issuing the coffee, some of the Americans had acquired a yen for tea and, after a course of Arbuckle's,[368] they commenced to holler for Oolong.[369]

——————

Private Nick Gianakopolus,[370] "Nick the Greek," famous middle-distance runner, uses the deck largely for galloping purposes. Nick is doing a bit of training for the indoor championships. He's in the One Hundred and Sixth Infantry.

——————

Private Bob Johnson, machine gunner, is that same Bob Johnson who was once a football star at Dartmouth. Private Fred McKeen, old Cornell back, and Private Brewer, once of Colgate, are other former football stars of another day whose eyes are earnestly seeking the skyline of little old New York.

——————

Captain Glass,[371] of the One Hundred and Sixth Machine Gunners, stroked the Syracuse crew in his day.

——————

A name the Twenty-Seventh utters with veneration and love is the name of Father Kelly, the famous chaplain.[372] He has been decorated three times for gallantry. He is to the Twenty-Seventh what Father Duffy[373] is to the Forty-Second. Father Kelly comes from Albany.

"The Broadway Boys" is the title of the division's vaudeville performance. It's a bear, too.

Udo Keppler, the famous athlete, was around in a suit of dungaree, having volunteered as a stoker. They were hunting for two stowaways known to be aboard and leaped on Udo as a ride grafter. Udo had a terrible time explaining about himself.

March 7, 1919. New York

Home from war came 9,000 men of New York's Twenty-Seventh Division yesterday, and what a home-coming it was!

From the moment the transport *Leviathan*—eight days out of Brest—poked her big snout into the upper bay, until she eased her matronly girth, groaningly, into a berth at Hoboken, things happened with such amazing sequence that even now it is difficult to assemble them in coherent order.

They happened with such rapidity that they left the brown-clad men, stacked in tiers on the many decks of the great boat, a wee bit dazed—but fully cognizant of this one beautiful fact:

They were home! They were back in that God's country, for which their eager eyes had been straining since the dawn of the gorgeous day. They were back among the home folks, and the home folks were glad—are glad, I should say—to see them. For it was a God's country welcome!

It is not strange that some of these men who have looked on dire things, and have been in dire places the last ten months, suddenly found themselves batting their eyelashes to relieve them of salt-watery little drops that appeared on them in the most untoward manner. It is not strange that some of them found themselves a little choky-like in the region of the windpipe.

That familiar skyline yonder, standing up out of the morning, each building as clear cut as if carved from crystal; that towering greenish figure holding the old light on high and to which one remarked, perfunctorily, because he had been thinking of saying it for some time: "Old lady, if you see me again, you'll have to turn around"—these things, visualized, were only the realization of the dreams of every man aboard.

They had dreamt of them in the trenches, in the camps, the muck, and the mud and the wreck of war which has been their portion these long months; most of them—the New York bred—had every detail of the scene before him burned by fond association in his memory. But the welcome that came with these things was something not entirely anticipated.

They had expected that there would be some sort of "turnout," of course. They had idly speculated on it during the long days on the ocean from the land they went to fight for, and wondered just what form it would take, but it is doubtful if they looked for the greeting they received yesterday—a greeting from the great heart of all New York State throbbing in it.

They say the waterfront strike kept down the number of boats that went out to greet the *Leviathan*. Perhaps it was just as well. The navigators of the gigantic vessel were not entirely happy over the fleet that did show up.

To those on board the *Leviathan* it seemed as if the sea around and about was fairly boiling with boats of all descriptions as the big transport picked her precarious path up the channel, and surely each boat, skipping hither and yon, like so many water bugs, carried a band. Music welled up from all sides, and it was all grades and noises in music, but there was one band leader who knew something. His band kept playing a marvelous melody, and the name of this melody is "Home, Sweet Home!"

The men who broke the Hindenburg Line thought well of that tune. They disgorged cheers which came from the very bottoms of their souls.

On the bridge of the *Leviathan* as she came up the bay stood Major General John F. O'Ryan, who took the New York men away to war, and who is returning them, as he himself has put it, "the same clean and efficient young men who went away."

He wore a garrison cap, with the chin strap drawn down in under his square-cut jaw, his uniform was impeccable, as always, and on his feet were a pair of glistening boots. He was watching the reception and the approaching island of Manhattan, which seemed to be bearing down upon the transport with a whoop of joy, but mainly he watched his men.

With him was General DeBevoise, commanding the Fifty-Third Brigade, with a reputation born in battle beyond the seas almost as great as that of his now-celebrated chief. From their point of vantage they could see everything that was going on, and through the medium of aides they handled the boatload.

General O'Ryan does not bring back all the lads he took away ten months ago, of course. War is not that kind. Eight times the Twenty-Seventh Division hit the enemy, and those eight times cost it sixty officers and 1,435 men—killed in battle or died of wounds. There was an additional cost of 142 officers and 5,195 men wounded or gassed; three officers and 251 men missing; two officers and 174 men captured by the Germans.

But the Twenty-Seventh never failed to gain an objective—and it never had its full divisional strength of 27,000 when it went into the line, either. It had about 17,000 men at the most, and its losses were around 42½ per cent.

Those men piled on the decks of the *Leviathan* yesterday are members of one of the great combat divisions of the American army. They are the men of the One Hundred and Fifth and One Hundred and Sixth Regiments of Infantry, complete; the One Hundred and Fifth Machine Gun Battalion; two battalions of the One Hundred and Seventh Infantry and Headquarters; the Fifty-Third Brigade Headquarters; and the Headquarters Detachment.

Pilot McLaughlin[374] brought the *Leviathan* in. He is president of the Pilots' Association, and he has shown the big vessel up the channel and out again on nearly every journey she has made since the boat was changed from the *Vaterland* into the *Leviathan*. It was his appearance out by Ambrose Light[375] yesterday morning that made the Twenty-Seventh feel that it was really getting in touch with home.

But it was not until the ship got past quarantine, where it never hesitated by the way, and the boats loaded with the welcoming home folks showed up that they commenced to understand just how joyous they were themselves about coming home.

A torpedo boat destroyer circled them a couple of times down near Ambrose Light. A Spanish ship, outward bound and loaded to the gun'ls, gave them a big blast from its whistle; the liner *Panama*, filled with folks seeking the warmth of the tropics, lifted a cheer as the *Leviathan* moved stolidly along. Then the first of the boats labeled "Mayor's Committee," which finally became a veritable parade of boats labeled the same way, bobbed into view, and the soldiers, now formed on the decks, let out a whoop.

That "Home, Sweet Home" band was on the first boat. Then came a band with "Oh, How I Hate to Get Up in the Morning," which was not true of yesterday morning with the Twenty-Seventh, anyway. These boats were packed so tightly with people that it was a wonder they weren't gaping at the seams, and every person aboard them was cheering or waving.

A couple of hydroplanes, or flying boats, fluttered over the transport in what seemed dangerous proximity to the rigging. One fellow in particular was constantly flying very close, while a movie picture operator in the prow of the plane industriously ground away at a crank. The soldiers, who have seen a great many planes and a great many desperate aerial feats, could not help admiring their nerve, however much they questioned their judgment.

In the full glow of the silver morning the *Leviathan* went steadily forward, and now the shorelines could be seen lined with people. Governor's Island, down around the water's edge;

the Battery, which seemed like a gigantic anthill teeming with action; the pierheads and the roofs of buildings surrounding the route of the transport—all were packed.

The cheers came rolling out across the water in great gusts. The soldiers cheered their response. Flags fluttered everywhere. Now from the windows of the Whitehall Building and from the windows of surrounding buildings there came drifting downward in the cool breeze masses of torn paper and long, squirming lines of ticker tape. The air was so thick with paper that it looked like a small snowstorm.

A boat came out labeled "the Seventy-first Infantry." There were several boats loaded with soldiers of the Twenty-Seventh, who had come home ahead of the outfit, wounded or sick or otherwise. A band hit up "How Dry I Am" and the men on board the *Leviathan* roared. "Welcome to the Twenty-seventh and Sergeant Frank Conklin"[376] said a sign on one little boat. "Liberty Bell" was the popular air with the bands as the *Leviathan* passed the Statue of Liberty, which seemed to smile benignly. Anyway, some of the soldiers said "the old girl" was smiling.

There were 8,636 men of the Twenty-Seventh Division aboard that lumbering old slob of a ship. There were 271 officers of the division. But that was not the total population within the walls of the oceanic citadel that was reared by the Hun to the amazement of the maritime world, and subsequently to his own undoing.

There were 11,708 in all on the boat, including the crew, the officers, and "gobs" of the American Navy, which put the American Expeditionary Force in France and is now engaged in putting it back in America. If it hadn't been for the Navy, these delirious home-coming scenes might not now be possible. 'Mid all the hurrahing Jack has slipped into the background to some extent, but the soldier hasn't forgotten him. The soldier knows what he did—and what he is doing.

While the soldiers were getting all the cheers yesterday, Jack was laboring back of the scenes with the big boat. The *Leviathan* is what the sailors call "tender" going into New York harbor. She has to be very gently nursed. They are never able to get enough coal to load her sufficiently to make all the speed of which she is capable—about twenty-three knots—and she gobbles up what they do get on so rapidly that she reaches a destination very light below and very heavy above.

They could make the Brest–New York run in six days if they could get the coal. As it is, it takes eight. By that time the reduction in coal, to say nothing of the reduction in water and the stores, which are consumed by the soldiers, leaves little left below the ship's waistline, as you might say.

The Boche didn't think the Americans could ever operate the *Leviathan*. That was among the Boche's fatal mistakes. Lieutenant Commander V. V. Woodward,[377] a young engineering officer, is said to be the man largely responsible for the way the boat has been ferried back and forth across the Atlantic. He found out all her secrets in no time.

Captain Phelps,[378] one of our veteran maritime men, who is boss of the big ship, also got acquainted with the former *Vaterland* to such an extent that he probably knows more about her now than the Boche could ever learn. He was on the bridge yesterday morning getting the Twenty-Seventh in.

Some of the naval officers aboard the boat viewed askance the plan of having the soldiers on deck going into port. Heretofore, the men had been kept below decks, because soldiers are great hands for moving around in large numbers with great suddenness on such occasions as the arrival in port, and all coagulate on one side of the ship and run her aground.

However, Captain Phelps said he didn't have the heart to deprive a New Yorker of a look at his hometown—especially a Twenty-Seventh Division New Yorker—and he swore by Neptune that his boat would stand any new scheme in that respect the army figured out. So the Twenty-Seventh came in on deck. The sailors argued:

"They won't stay where they're put. They'll hear a band on one side of the boat, and they'll all want to rush over there. As some fellow will see his gal and start a stampede in that direction, and the poor, old boat will list all over the place."

"That might be true of some divisions," answered the soldiers, "but this is the Twenty-Seventh."

The divisional boast of its discipline was made good. There was very little confusion—never enough to be alarming. Naturally the soldiers were fairly bursting with excitement, but they did not shift around. Those on the port side had the worst of the deal. They could not see much of their beloved Manhattan for a time.

But they stood fast even when the bubbling on the other side told them things were doing yonder. The division went on deck with the units lined up just as usual. Someone suggested that the "apple knockers" be mobilized on the port side.

"Because," he contended, "they don't care a damn whether they are looking at New York City or Jersey."

This cruel suggestion found no supporters. The "apple knockers" were not separated from the "wise crackers."

The Twenty-Seventh calls its Upstate men "apple knockers," presumably because they come from the region of the succulent pippin. Sometimes they are called "sod busters." The "wise crackers" are the city men in the language of the division.

Coming up the bay the men were lined up along the decks on either side. They piled high on the life rafts forward, and still higher aft. Every foot of space from which a man might get a view of the surrounding water was occupied, and yet they left aisles for the sailors to carry on their work. Not a man stirred from the station assigned him throughout the exciting trip to the dock. It was a marvelous display of discipline.

Just before the *Leviathan* reached the dock and the tugs grabbed hold of her and began warping her alongside, "quarters" sounded, and the blobs of olive drab collected on the decks suddenly dissolved. The men went below and gathered up their equipment, not to reappear again until they began debarking.

Then they came in heavy marching order, ready for the next trip, which took the Fifty-Third Brigade to Camp Mills and the One Hundred and Seventh Infantry to Camp Merritt. The streets around the dock were packed with people eager to get a sight of some loved one in the ranks. A high fence separated them, but there were rapturous greetings none the less.

There was mighty little sleeping done on board the *Leviathan* Wednesday night. Everybody was too wrought up. Those who did doze off were up before dawn, peeping through portholes or over the rail for a light that betokened the approach to home. It was getting gray in the east, however, before any eye picked up the dancing spark far out on the water, which the sailors said was from one of the new emergency light ships off Fire Island. It was quite some time after that when the island itself reared its dusty-looking bulk out of the deep.

What a day it was! All sunshine and silver glow. What a day for men who have been living in a wet murk for months!

The men were supposed to be officially awake at 6 o'clock. They were given a breakfast of the good old reliable army beans. Then they set to work cleaning up their quarters. They left their part of the *Leviathan* spick and span. After that there was nothing to do but wait. Some of them gave their long-nosed English Enfield rifles, which distinguish the Twenty-Seventh from other American divisions, a final rub-up. Most of them, however, got out on deck as quickly as possible to look around. The first real cheer that the Twenty-Seventh lifted from the boat was along about 8:30 o'clock, when they picked up the yellowy old Ambrose lightship hunched down in the channel and saw the pot-bellied, slate-colored pilot boat coming up. The men aboard the pilot boat let out a whoop as their vessel ranged up alongside the monster troopship, one fellow jumping up and down and throwing his arms about with great violence. And now it was things commenced to happen.

The last day out, which was Wednesday, you could almost feel the *Leviathan* palpitate with excitement. That's the way it seemed, anyway, although the palpitation was in reality doubtless due to the throb of the great engines which were lifting the ex-Boche boat along the Atlantic at eighteen knots an hour.

Everybody was moving around at the same time. It was like the interior of a subway express station at rush hour. Little processions of soldiers were constantly marching along the corridors, carrying trunks and other baggage out of the cabins. Aides and orderlies dashed about with as much activity as if a barrage had opened, carrying orders here and there.

Every few minutes the familiar yell of burden-bearing sailors would be heard: "Here I come, soldier!," which is their way of imploring gangway through their cousins in olive drab aboard troopships. One very, very sad little cortege of bluejackets went down along deck during the afternoon. There were four of them. They carried a stretcher, on which was something covered with a white sheet.

It was the mortal remains of a poor soldier who had answered his last roll call. There were three deaths in the Twenty-Seventh Division after the *Leviathan* left Brest. Private Albert H. Lanzer, of Company B, One Hundred and Fifth Machine Gun Battalion, died of pneumonia; Gentof Anderson, of Company A, One Hundred and Sixth Infantry, died of the same cause. He lived at Badger, Minnesota, and came from Fort Dodge to the New York outfit.

Wednesday afternoon, almost in sight of home, Harry F. Dulhagen Jr., of Jersey City, another member of the One Hundred and Fifth Machine Gun Battalion, died. In this, as in the other cases, pneumonia was the cause.

There were two other deaths aboard the boat. Both were casuals.[379]

A casual, which is a soldier temporarily detached from his own outfit for one reason and another, is always a rather forlorn spectacle. He is to all intents and purposes a man without a home. Nobody wants to be bothered with him any more than is necessary.

I know, because I have been a casual.[380] A sick casual is downright pathetic, however tenderly the care of the nurses and doctors, for, after all, he is away from his own people.

Which is to say, his own outfit. He is a stranger in a strange land.

There were 1,172 enlisted men among the casuals on the *Leviathan*, which does not take account of fifty-five civilian war workers, sixty-eight officers, and seventeen plain, unadorned civilians. Some of the enlisted casuals live in New York, or nearby, but the majority are from far away. Wistfully they watched the jubilating New Yorkers and listened to their talking reeking with the accents of home.

True, the casuals were home themselves, for America in general is now home to the soldiers of the American Expeditionary Force, but they were not home in the same sense as the men of the Empire State. They were not yet in the bosom of their family, so to speak.

There are now quite a large number of men in the Twenty-Seventh who are not New Yorkers. They came to the division as replacements. Some of them are from Middle Western States and some from the Rocky Mountain region. They have seen very little of New York. But the New Yorkers have come to be fond of these new-found "buddies," delivered to them in the strange manner of modern war. Long before the skyline was sighted, the Big Towners had been telling them of the wonders of Gotham and promising to show them boys around—when they get the opportunity.

Physical examinations went on all over the boat Wednesday. There were examinations for communicable diseases and examinations to see that none of the lads brought back with them from France or Belgium any of those little strangers who gained great notoriety during the "guerre" as "cooties."

Some of the doctors conducted their examinations with a view to privacy, but most of them took place on the deck. The soldiers bared their noble torsos to the wild sea breezes, and the "cerakerb" looked them over.

On the port side of A Deck, where stretched orderly rows of cots, white faces that seemed to be all eyes peered from beneath the blankets with a world of longing in their expressions at the feverish preparations going on about them. These were among the saddest victims of the cruel war overseas. They come home in the shadow of the pale plague. The majority are casuals.

The hospital on the deck below, in what was the ornate ballroom of the *Vaterland*, was filled with patients suffering from diverse maladies, but there was joy among them. The doctors tell of men who were thought to be hovering very close to that mysterious home which the soldier describes as "west," but who shut their teeth down hard and battled so courageously to see home once more that they pulled through.

Wednesday morning was a gorgeous morning—a meteorological gift of the gods. It came on misty, and a rain developed toward evening, along with a breeze which corrugated the sea to come extent, but in the morning a bright sun shone. The men were sprawled out all over the decks, yearning and discussing the ship's rumors[381]—of which there are always many—or telling about what they intended to do the first thing when they got home.

Throughout the voyage, General O'Ryan required the men to be in the open air, because a bit of "flu" appeared on the boat, and "flu" does not like fresh air. The officers had to be out there with the men, too. So every yard of the decks presented an impromptu conversazione at all times, save only on Tuesday, when the ocean was fairly boiling with agitation.

An epidemic of animal mascots broke out as the boat was staggering up against the State of New Jersey, in a manner quite as amazing as if some magician had produced them from a high hat. There were all kinds of dogs, from German message dogs, as the sheep dogs used by the Boche to carry messages are called, to just plain yellow dogs. They are the property of different units and individuals of the Twenty-Seventh. Some of them were adorned with blankets bearing their names, along with service stripes and even wound stripes.[382]

There was only one bewhiskered red and very ruminative goat. He belongs to a supply company. He seemed in no manner impressed by the welcome. Most of the mascots were gathered up in France and Belgium, although some have made the round trip with the division. You can always get a good story out of soldier-mascots—from the soldiers, that is. Some of the stories are not infrequently founded on fact.

Wednesday night there was a farewell dance, and the ladies aboard the boat, who had been required to retire at 10 o'clock up to that night, were given an extra leeway. That is, they were permitted to stay up until 11 o'clock. The original order lifted one of the most palpable breezes of the passage, but the *Leviathan* is a military institution when it has troops aboard, and what the military says goes. And the military said for the femmes to retire.

They were all out Wednesday night, however, some of them in evening clothes, and the old *Leviathan* went rolling along the trough of the sea, ablaze with lights, and shedding jazz music far out over the water.

The stairs leading to the lounge where the dancing took place were packed with soldiers watching the gay scene and dreaming, no doubt, of the lights of Broadway and the dance floors of cafés on the big bright line.

I'll never think of the *Leviathan*, but what I'll think of those stairs, and the strange parade that has passed up and down them for the past week—the parade of the "crutch cases," as the medicos call men crippled in the legs, who are able to get about on crutches. The elevators on the boat were not working. The cripples had to go up and down the stairs to their meals.

It was a spectacle that squeezed the heart. Up and down they went, up and down, one step at a time, dragging their poor maimed limbs after them, and clinging to the stair rails, or to the arms of some companion. They are a lesson—and an inspiration—the wounded men coming back from the war. They are cheerful past belief. Many of the men aboard the *Leviathan* sustained leg wounds from machine gun fire and shells which will send them clumping about for months longer with awkward steel braces clamped about their limbs; some have lost their legs entirely; one lost a leg and an arm.

But they all speak of their misfortune with a world of philosophy. That chap who lost an arm and a leg always went around with a cigar gripped between his teeth and a smile on his face. Up and down the stairs they pegged yesterday morning to get to their stations on deck as the *Leviathan* grumbled into harbor, and they were as cheerful and bright-hearted as anybody in that great surge of happiness. What men they are—God, what men!

R. VAN BUREN
EN ROUTE

March 9, 1919. New York

When I left Paris a few weeks ago, there was some talk of engaging one of the principal parks for an open-air meeting of the members of "the American Association of Gents Who Are Trying to Sign Georges Carpentier."[383] The organization will return to this country in a body as soon as it can charter the *Leviathan* for the voyage. No other tub would be large enough.

It is easy to identify a member of the association in good standing. His badge will be a noticeable bulge in the hip pocket, and a wild glare in his eye. The bulge is caused by the package of contracts which he expects the celebrated French boxer to sign. The wild glare in the orb is the result of peering into Maxim's,[384] and other way stations, seeking personal and intimate friends of Georges who can introduce the member to the fighter.

The idea of the contracts which the lads want Georges to sign is, of course, to bring the Frenchman to Amerique. Some of the boys make the weird suggestion in their documents that Georges fight somebody or other, after he gets here. Others desire him merely for exhibition purposes. Large sums to be "in hand paid" to the said Carpentier, party of the first part, are mentioned in the contracts—very large sums indeed.

That Carpentier will sooner or later succumb to the wiles of the association members—or one of them, at least—goes without saying. They are mumbling about so many francs that he would be scarcely human did he resist. However, and in the meantime, he has an appointment for July 4 at Strasburg in reconquered Alsace, with one Dick Smith[385] of England. They are to box 20 rounds for a purse of $20,000. The fight is under the auspices of one of the big Parisian newspapers, and Carpentier is not likely to run out on the engagement. Therefore he will certainly not be in America before that time.

Maybe after the Strasburg row the American promoters will not be so much interested in Georges. He has been out of the ring for a long time, and while Smith is commonly regarded as rather a set-up for him, things have been known to happen in the best-regulated fistic families. Close friends of Carpentier doubt if he will ever show his old-time form. However, the Strasburg bout is bound to be a big money-getter, for Carpentier is very popular in France, and his reappearance in the ring is attracting a lot of attention.

Jack Curley[386] has a representative in Paris trying to land Georges for an American engagement, and he has about as good a chance to get him as the next man. It is said that one fellow, representing another well-known American promoter—Bill Gibson,[387] no less—had Carpentier's name to a contract, which contract he carried in his overcoat pocket. The "flogger" was stolen in a café, and with it went the contract.

It is assumed that if this yarn is true, Carpentier will sign a new contract with the same party, but he was not under contract at the time I left Paris, and, according to his friends, he was not wildly anxious to come to America, because he does not like traveling on the sea, a sentiment which shows he has pretty good judgment, anyway.

He can get plenty of matches in France and make plenty of money there, because boxing is highly relished by the French. The seed planted by Willie Lewis,[388] Danny McKetrick,[389] Joe Jeannette,[390] and all the other pioneers of the game over there has taken root. They hold big shows under the auspices of the different American war workers' associations in Paris almost nightly, with many French boxers taking part and the Frenchmen clamoring for admission along with the Americans. French boxing clubs were getting ready to resume operations when I left.

Of course, the French haven't had much opportunity in the past four years for developing a new generation of boxers to follow in the footsteps of Carpentier, Ledoux,[391] Balzac,[392] and others who were prominent before the war, but some promising lads are already commencing to appear over yonder. The best of them all seems to be a little fellow named Crique,[393] pronounced "Creek"— who was promptly dubbed "Battle Creek" by the Americans.

An army boxing match in the spring of 1919. *Courtesy of United States Army Heritage and Education Center*

The American army goes in very strong for boxing, of course. It has produced a few pretty good new men, but the best of the pounders over there are chaps who were more or less well known in the ring before they went into the army. Their past experience naturally helps them out. Up in the Rhine region, with the Army of Occupation, they have a huge hall in Coblenz where shows are frequently held, and the place is always packed.

"Biz" Mackey,[394] the old-time Middle Western lightweight, who is with the Knights of Columbus, attached to the famous Third Division, held forth at Polch, not far from Coblenz, and he was putting on some good shows. "Biz" was telling us that he had a couple of phenoms, too.

After the army got settled down along the Rhine, football was the big outdoor pastime, and every division had exceptionally strong teams—teams which I believe could have given good accounts of themselves against the best college elevens. Hamilton Fish[395] was coaching and playing with one of the best. Harry Legore,[396] the Yale back, was with another, and scores of other famous gridiron names dotted the different lineups.

Baseball had not reached the Army of Occupation to any extent, with the weather being down around zero a part of the time, or very rainy, but they were planning for the spring just the same.

When the Army of Occupation was breezing through the duchy of Luxemburg, an eager individual with a complete vocabulary of what the soldiers call "Luxembushwah" hung around the camp of the newspaper correspondents, making strange sounds out of his mouth. Nobody knew what it was all about for several days, but finally he got hold of Captain Billy McKenna,[397] the old Fordham runner and Rainbow divisioner, and spoke in Bill's ear at great length.

Bill listened but could make little of the matter until he got an interpreter, and then it transpired that the Luxemburger wanted to arrange a soccer football match with an American army team. Furthermore, it leaked out that Luxemburg has one of the greatest soccer teams in—well, in Luxemburg. It seems that it is the popular diversion in the duchy, in fact.

There were no soccer teams handy at the moment, and Bill didn't have time to organize one, but they popped out later on. There are a lot of pretty good ones in every division of the American army abroad. Up at Bonn and around Cologne—or Coln, as the Germans call it—every other vacant lot is a soccer field given over to the Canucks and the English.

But so far as the American army is concerned, baseball and boxing are the big games, just as over here, and just as they will probably always be wherever Americans gather. I agree with the view of other observers that the French will never take to baseball—and the English will never take to baseball—but France is going to be one of the great boxing countries of the world. England, of course, has always been one of the greatest.

March 16, 1919. New York City

The Fifty-Second Field Artillery of the Twenty-Seventh Division met with the usual fate of almost all of the artillery brigades of the combat divisions—immediate separation from its division and all the trials and tribulations that fall to the lot of an artillery brigade which is suddenly called upon to function as an independent unit both in the United States and in France. Happily, however, it had as its chief Brigadier General George A. Wingate,[398] not only an artillery officer of vast experience, but a man peculiarly equipped to command and one to whom the complex and colossal task of feeding, clothing, and fighting 6,000 eager and impetuous New Yorkers became a great game—a game that he made every one of his 6,000 soldiers feel he was bound to win.

This feeling of confidence in their chief and their own ability as artillerymen kept the brigade from the depths of despair when the infantry left for France without its artillery. Nevertheless, it was a blow to them. Left in Camp Stuart (Newport News, Virginia) for a long, weary month, the brigade heard nothing but the report, "They don't want artillery in France, they want infantry." And as regiment after regiment of infantry filed past the anxious brigade into ships and away, the hopes of the artillerymen were at the lowest ebb.

At this time the brigade was composed of the one-time First, Second, and Third Field Artillery, newly changed to the One Hundred and Fourth, One Hundred and Fifth, and One Hundred and Sixth United States Field Artillery; the One Hundred and Second Trench Mortar Battery; the One Hundred and Second Ammunition Train; and, for the purposes of administration until further disposition, the One Hundred and First Field Bakery, the One Hundred and Second Sanitary Train, and the One Hundred and Second Mobile Ordnance Repair Shop.

To make matters more interesting to the already sufficiently occupied brigade commander, the authorities sent to him 1,200 replacements for the division, which he formed into thirteen companies and whose chief function during the weeks at Camp Stuart seemed to be developing measles and thereby delaying the "Clean Bill of Health," without which no organization could depart for France.

This period is one that every member of the brigade tries to forget. The camp was quarantined and men were not allowed to leave its confines. Aside from the fact that there was a splendid view of Hampton Roads, and other soldiers departing for France and a few Y.M.C.A. entertainments and such shows as the men themselves organized for their own amusement, there was nothing to do but wait and occupy themselves with that very interesting pastime of the soldier—dissecting the latest rumor.

After one false start, in which the One Hundred and Second Ammunition Train had the heart-breaking experience of being ordered to go and then recalled, the brigade was finally furnished with ships and had cleared Camp Stuart by the end of June. As everyone knows, at that time there were many reports of submarine activity along the coast, and the trip over was an exciting one for the brigade. They were, however, convoyed by destroyers and battleships of our navy, and such submarines as were seen were either quickly dispatched by the 6-inch guns or depth bombs or else put to flight.

On September 9 the brigade marched from Noxeville, where it had rested two days, into the line beyond Verdun, taking over the artillery positions of the One Hundred and Fifty-Seventh and One Hundred and Twentieth divisions of the French army, and became part of the XVII French Corps in the celebrated Hill 304 and Mort Homme sectors.

At this time the One Hundred and Fourth Field Artillery was commanded by Colonel Merritt H. Smith,[399] of New York; the One Hundred and Fifth Field Artillery by Colonel Dewitt C. Weld Jr.,[400] of Brooklyn; the One Hundred and Sixth Field Artillery by Colonel Emery T. Smith;[401] the One Hundred and Second Ammunition Train by Major Lansford F. Sherry,[402] of New York City; and the One Hundred and Second Trench Mortar Battery by Captain Charles Pearson Jr.,[403] of Buffalo.

General Wingate had for his staff Major Isaac J. Lovell,[404] of Brooklyn, in charge of the Operations Department; Captain Walter H. Schoellkopf,[405] Buffalo, Intelligence Officer; Lieutenant Max L. Van Norden,[406] in charge of the Telephone and Radio Service; Lieutenant Harold H. Jones[407] commanded the Headquarters Detachment; Lieutenant Hector Turnbull,[408] Munitions Officer; Lieutenant Thomas H. S. Andrews,[409] Liaison Officer; Lieutenant Effingham Burnett,[410] Aide to General Wingate; Lieutenants North and Lloyd.[411] Captain Chauncey J. Hamlin,[412] of the One Hundred and Sixth Field Artillery, was temporarily detached from his regiment and attached to the Thirty-Third Division staff as Division Munitions Officer.

Here follows a plain and unvarnished account of the activities of the brigade, beginning with the St. Mihiel offensive and ending at 11 o'clock, November 11, when hostilities ended.

The brigade participated in the St. Mihiel offensive on September 12, firing from 1 a.m. to 6 p.m. at the maximum capacity of its guns. All the artillery of the XVII French Corps participated in the attack, in which the First American Army moved forward and reduced the St. Mihiel salient that had been held by the enemy for four years. The original sectors were held until the night of September 25–26, when the batteries changed positions and were concentrated on the west bank of the Meuse River in the Mort Homme sector, opposite the Brook of Forges from the Moulin de Raffecourt to the Meuse, in preparation for the Meuse-Argonne offensive.

The attack started with the bombardment of the army artillery of the First American Army at 11:30 p.m., the corps artillery joining at 3 a.m. on the morning of the 26 and the divisional artillery commencing its fire at 5:30 a.m. This was the commencement of the great attack of the entire First American Army along a front reaching from the western edge of the Forest of Argonne down to the Meuse River, in connection with a similar attack by the Allied armies on the left of the First American Army.

It extended practically along the whole American front and the Allied forces on the east bank of the Meuse. The Thirty-Third Division, which the brigade was supporting, held the right flank position of the First American Army and, as it advanced, executed a pivoting movement to the east and thereafter held the right flank of the salient formed by the advance of that army along the Meuse River.

The Third-Third Division had been assigned the task of crossing the Forges Brook and the swamps on each side thereof, reducing the strongly prepared positions in the Bois de Forges and capturing the towns of Forges, Gercourt, and Drillancourt and all territory intervening between the old French front lines and the west bank of the Meuse. It attained all these objectives on schedule time.

The Thirty-Third Division held the front attained by it and proceeded to organize it for defense, ultimately taking over the sector of the Eightieth Division on its left to just east of Brieulles, the artillery of the Eightieth Division being withdrawn from the line and this brigade covering the entire front, a distance of fourteen kilometers.

During this period, from October 3 to 7 inclusive, the brigade participated in the attack of the divisions on the left against the Trench du Teton, a strongly held field work just south of Brieulles, and on the town of Brieulles itself, which had withstood the attacks of the Eightieth Division for several days and held back the Fourth Division, which had been put in to relieve it. The reduction of these places enabled the First American Army on the left to advance toward Dun-sur-Meuse. From September 25 until October 7 the Thirty-Third Division and this brigade had been part of the Third Corps.

On October 8, the Thirty-Third Division and the brigade were attached to the XVII French Corps for the purpose of an attack by the units of the latter corps against the enemy, holding the sector on the right bank of the Meuse, immediately north of Verdun.

All that remained of the French town of Forges. *Courtesy of Library of Congress*

One battalion of the Thirty-Third Division crossed the Meuse River at Brabant on a foot bridge erected by the Engineers and took up the attack, which had been carried by the French to Consenvoye, and continued it until they reached a line opposite the enemy Giselher Stellung, extending from Sivry-sur-Meuse to the vicinity of Magenta Ferme.

On the way they reduced the enemy positions in the Bois de Chaume and Bois Plat-Chene. The Twenty-Ninth Division and the Twenty-Sixth Division (French), both to the right of the Thirty-Third Division, were stubbornly resisted by the enemy, and the positions gained by the battalion of the Thirty-Third Division were so heavily attacked that the entire Sixty-Sixth Infantry Brigade was ultimately sent in to hold the line. Later this brigade was relieved by the Sixty-Fifth Infantry Brigade, the former brigade taking over the positions of the latter on the west bank of the Meuse.

On October 14 the Twenty-Ninth Division and the Twenty-Sixth (French) Division attacked the heights of the Grande Montagne, and the brigade assisted that attack with its artillery fire. The lines remained unchanged, although there was great activity on both sides until October 21, when the Thirty-Third Division was relieved by the Fifteenth French Colonial Division, and the Fifty-Second Field Artillery Brigade was relieved by the divisional artillery. The brigade marched to cantonments in the vicinity of Dieue, just south of Verdun and in the Bois la Ville, preparatory to relieving the Seventy-Ninth Division in the Troyon sector. During this period it was under the II French Colonial Corps.

On October 25 the brigade was detached from the Thirty-Third Division and attached to the Seventy-Ninth Division.

On October 28 the brigade went into the line again with the Seventy-Ninth Division, which relieved the Twenty-Ninth Division north of Verdun, in the sector adjoining of the right the sector it had just left, the brigade relieving the One Hundred and Fifty-Eighth Field Artillery Brigade on the nights of October 28–29 and 29–30. The brigade came again under the XVII French Corps, which had been continuing its pressure against the enemy on the east bank of the Meuse.

On October 30 the Seventy-Ninth Division extended its front, taking over a portion of the front previously held by the Twenty-Sixth Division, and the brigade took over a portion of the sector held by the Fifty-First Field Artillery Brigade. The front of the new sector extended from Belleu Bois to Bois d'Ormont, inclusive. The Bois d'Ormont had been captured but had been partly retaken by the enemy after a terrific artillery bombardment that made it absolutely untenable for troops. It commanded the only line of approach and gave direct observation to the enemy.

On November 1, 2, and 3 the One Hundred and Eleventh Corps attacked along the line held by them on the Canel-Brieulles road and from Brieulles to Dun-sur-Meuse. This attack resulted in forcing the enemy off the heights on the west bank of the Meuse. The brigade participated with its fire.

General Claudel, commanding the XVII French Corps, in order to ascertain the strength of the enemy forces on the left, directed all his divisions to make reconnaissance in force on their immediate front, the Fifteenth French Colonial Division and the Seventy-Ninth Division cooperating with each other. The One Hundred and Fifty-Eighth Infantry Brigade, Seventy-Ninth Division, made its reconnaissance in force in the direction of Bois de la Grande Montagne, supported by the One Hundred and Fourth Field Artillery. The One Hundred and Sixth Field Artillery supported both these attacks. The Fifteenth French Colonial Division on the left attacked on the east bank of the Meuse in the direction of Villeneuve Ferme.

The One Hundred and Fifty-Seventh Infantry Brigade and the infantry of the Fifteenth French Colonel Division encountered such strong enemy opposition that they were unable to advance. The One Hundred and Fifty-Eighth Infantry Brigade succeeded in securing a foothold on the Borne de Cornouiller, and the corps commander directed that this advantage be maintained and that pressure be continued along the entire line, the attack being forced on the Borne du Cornouiller.

The entire One Hundred and Fifty-Eighth Brigade and a large part of the One Hundred and Fifty-Seventh Infantry Brigade were concentrated on the Borne du Cornouiller, and, after repeated attacks, the enemy was forced to retire. The Seventy-Ninth Division, pivoting on its right, advanced its left to Solderino Ferme, connecting up with the Fifteenth French Colonial Division, which had crossed the river at Vilosnes, taken Haraumont Ridge, and reached the farm. In this advance the Seventy-Ninth Division broke through the Giselher Stellung and the Kriemhild Stellung.[413]

March 23, 1919. New York City

Keeping the watch on the Rhine is a dreary business. It long ago palled on the soldiers of the American Army of Occupation—"the Army of No Occupation" they call it.

General John J. Pershing has been reviewing the troops up in the Rhine region, and, if you have been reading the dispatches about his visit, you must have noticed that wherever he goes he hears the one question, "When do we go home?"

That's the only thing that interests the soldiers of Dickman's Third Army. It's the only thing that has interested them since the signing of the armistice. It's the only thing that interests the American soldiers in France.

President Wilson has just ordered the speeding up of the return of the soldiers, showing he senses the feeling of the men still abroad. Someone is always ordering the "speeding up" of the return, but as a matter of fact the government has been bringing them back just as fast as possible since the armistice.

Those "speeding up" orders are probably by way of encouragement to the waiting soldiers. The administration is just as anxious to get them home as they are to get here.

An army of voters the size of the American force overseas, in repose so to speak, isn't good for politics. It doesn't tend to make the offices safe for the Democrats.

An inactive army doesn't have anything to do but sit around and talk, and invariably the talk becomes critical. Mainly it is apt to be critical of those in authority. They are not really to blame, but it's human nature to criticize those at the top, and the army is nothing if not human.

The divisions with the Army of Occupation which are to be brought home first are the Forty-Second, or Rainbow Division, and the Thirty-Second, which is composed of troops from Michigan and Wisconsin. Both are National Guard divisions and both are great combat units.

The Thirty-Second is across the Rhine with the First and Second Divisions, both composed of Regulars and Marines. The Rainbows are also on the Rhine, but they did not cross the river.

Starting very shortly, the Rainbows and, eventually, the Thirty-Second will proceed down the Rhine in barges and small boats to Antwerp or Rotterdam, where they will load for America according to the present plan. They will see a lot of scenery anyway, for the trip down the Rhine is through a very beautiful part of Germany.

When the Regular divisions will be started home is a question which depends on the plans of the Allies for the continued occupation of the Rhine bridgeheads. I doubt if the last of our army will be withdrawn from Rhenish Prussia inside of six months, if then. As always, the Regulars will be the very hindmost in the homecoming procession.

They may discharge a lot of the men in the First, Second, Third, and other Regular divisions who enlisted only for the duration of the war, and fill their places with men recruited specially for the Army of Occupation, but it looks now if some of those "duration" men are going to be overseas for quite a spell. Some of them want to stay away, but the great majority wants to come home.

The fellow in the Regular Army is out of luck in a case of this kind. The National Guarder, or even the National Army chap, have home delegations lifting joint cries for their return, which are bound to be heard by someone, but there's never anyone to yell for the Regular. That the authorities jolly well appreciate the difference is shown by the order in which the divisions are being sent home.

The fair way, of course, would have been to return them in the order of their going, but that would have brought the Regular First Division home first, and there were no delegations of congressmen standing around clamoring for the First.

As a matter of fact, probably there are just as many men in the First Division who went into the army only for the duration of the war and who are just as eager to get back to private life and their business as in any National Guard or National Army division, but they are classed as Regulars and that's the difference.

It was considered a great honor for a division to be selected for the Army of Occupation, and some divisions which thought they ought to be included were a bit piqued over their omission. But the glamor of the honor soon faded for the occupationer.

As between the chap in Germany and the fellow who stayed behind in France, I consider the latter the luckier, although there isn't a lot to choose between the two.

The fellow in France can at least mingle in the life of the community in which he is situated. That may not sound particularly attractive, but it breaks the monotony of existence to some extent. In Germany the soldiers are restricted in their movements. To all intents and purposes we are still at war with the Germans, and that status is maintained in the Army of Occupation.

I am inclined to doubt if the American would fraternize to any extent with the German even if it were permitted, whereas in France he can and does knock about among the people with perfect freedom and no little enjoyment. I've heard a lot about how the American soldier dislikes the Frenchman, but I don't believe that feeling is general throughout the American army.

Some of them say the French tradespeople robbed them, but in the same breath they will tell you how they were robbed by the American tradespeople in the camp towns at home. Things were not as comfortable in France for our soldiers during the fighting as they have been in Germany since the hostilities ceased, but even the comparative comfort enjoyed along the Rhine palled on our soldiers.

The German at home is a dull fellow. The Frenchman is rarely that. The American soldier is momentarily mighty weary of both and wants to get back home among his own people, but I venture to say that in the years to come, when his perspective is longer and better, he is going to see where Frenchy was pretty good company after all.

The Y.M.C.A. and the Knights of Columbus and the army itself have put forth tremendous efforts to afford entertainment on the Rhine. They have boxing shows and musical shows and shows of every description every night; they have field days; they have football and baseball; and all this diverts the soldier more or less. But, after all, it's a mere diversion and it doesn't take his thoughts away from home.

There is no cure for nostalgia, except home, and our soldiers have nostalgia in a highly developed form, as General Pershing is doubtless prepared to testify after his trip through the Army of Occupation.

March 26, 1919. New York City

"Tell me when the One Hundred and Seventh comes along," said the woman. "That was Joe's regiment, so be sure 'n tell me quick's you see it."

Over this old island lay God's good sunshine and the peace of God, as New York's Twenty-Seventh Division paraded yesterday for the last time in war array.

Between 2,000,000 and 3,000,000 persons saw the parade. Most of them were choked into what is normally that channel of stately residence and dignified commerce called Fifth Avenue, but which yesterday was a broad, flag-festooned chute, walled with human hearts and running bank high with cheers—and tears.

She was one of the millions. She was not old; her years were up to the lines in her face, but her eyes were very tired. Her dress was shabby and her gloveless hands showed the signs of great toil.

People cheered because they were glad and people cried for the very same reason. Then there were people who neither cheered nor cried. Their emotions had no voices, save inward whisperings of very great thankfulness, as the long columns of the soldiers went past, the sunlight spilling over them a silver glow and their steel helmets painted a grass green, undulating like the flaky scales of a big lizard.

The woman's old-fashioned hat was askew, and strands of hair, but lightly flecked with gray, strayed from beneath it. "I had to hurry to get here," she remarked. "I've been up since 5 this morning tryin' to get through with my work, and I thought I'd never make it."

"Jack" O'Ryan—Major General John Francis O'Ryan—rode at the head of his men as they marched up the avenue. He was on a big sorrel horse.[414] He carried his chin high, as befitted the commander of the division which broke old Hindenburg's line and has been praised by Pershing and Haig[415] and King Albert of Belgium and King George of Great Britain.

"I'd a-died if I hadn't got here," she said quietly. "I've been lookin' to it for weeks. It's a pretty long wait, isn't it? But then I know it's a big job handlin' all these men. My Joe used to tell me what a job 'tis. Yes, I'm pretty tired and my feet do ache a little, but I'm used to bein' on 'em, what with housework and all. And I had to come. I just had to. I want to see Joe's company. I want to see the boys he was with."

Behind the dapper leader of the Twenty-Seventh came not only the men who stopped the drive of the Germans for the channel ports; not only the Big Towners of the Manhattan Island and Greater City regiments and the sturdy Upstaters, but the artillerymen of Wingate's brigade, which backed up old Hunter Liggett's doughboys in the mighty dash of the American First Army through the Argonne and along the Meuse.

Wingate's outfit was detached from the Twenty-Seventh, like nearly all other divisional artillery outfits in this war, and served as a separate unit. It was not reunited with O'Ryan's men until after the signing of the armistice.

She was wedged into the deepest portion of the crowd which packed the little heights of Central Park behind the grandstands on Upper Fifth Avenue. "They sent me some tickets to one of the stands further down," she said, "but at the last minute I couldn't find 'em. And it's too late to be botherin' anyone about it. I don't like to be botherin' people anyhow. My Joe was the same way about things."

It's been two years since these men of the Twenty-Seventh—they were boys then—marched down Fifth Avenue, bound for the war from which they returned to the bosom of the Big Town yesterday. The tears of women and the grief of strong men flowed in the wake of those lads that

Massive crowds in New York City welcome the 27th Division. *The Pictorial Record of the 27th Division*

summer day they marched away. Many of them were so pitifully young; many were so pitifully untried—then.

They have come back steady-eyed, strong-limbed veterans of battle. They have come back older, aye, and better men—those who have come back. For at the peak of the column there rumbled a somber reminder that not all have come back. It was an artillery caisson, draped as a funeral carriage, in memory of the men of the Twenty-Seventh who died that the world might live.

There were horses with pathetically empty saddles, so well understood by those who know the military ways. Their former riders have gone galloping off on the long, long trail with the black horseman—Death. Then, too, there was a giant service flag[416] besprinkled with a great many gold stars. It was borne at the head of the procession.

By tip-toeing, the woman could get a fleeting glimpse of this flag over the shoulders of those in front of her. "One of them's for my Joe," she said, simply, as if we had not already divined her sorrow. "He was killed in the last big fight. I got a letter from him that very same day, and he said he was most thankful to get some socks I had knitted for him. I was goin' to make him some more, when–"

The men marched with the swing and sway of veterans. There was that old "uh-hah" in their marching motion that marks the sweep of the experienced hiker. They didn't have the same formation in which a division goes into the battle line, and they were not exactly adorned for such an event, but they had the nonchalance of an outfit that has been in and out several times.

The column was wrinkled with grins, so to speak, but being at attention and being most of all the Twenty-Seventh Division, which prides itself to the Nth degree on its discipline, the men marched with strict attention to marching. But the grins played over their faces as often and as joyously as the sunlight itself.

Of course, they heard the "Oh-you's" whooped at them from delighted personal acquaintances. or heard the shrill cries of well-nigh distracted kinfolk, but they went booming along over the asphalt with much military decorum. Strong-limbed policemen had to occasionally lumber along the marching flanks to compel women and other frenzied folks to unhand the soldiers.

"I got letters from my Joe's officers, and they said he was very brave," said the woman, gently. "I knew he would be. He was like his father. Joe's father was a soldier, too. He died four years ago. He said all along we was goin' to have a war and he was a'goin' himself, he said, but we never thought Joe'd be old enough. He was just a boy. I wonder which one of those stars was Joe's."

New York crowds will hereafter take date from the parade of the Twenty-Seventh.

There was never anything like it before. In some spots downtown it was a pretty tight squeeze. The soldiers could just barely get through. The policemen hurled veritable barrages of blue uniforms against the crowds, but it was like bumping themselves up against brick walls.

Only the front rows suffered. But when you get more than 2,000,000 people jammed into one street, what can you expect?

From every window not only along Fifth Avenue, but in every street crossing Fifth Avenue, there were blocks of heads. There were thousands of people on every roof. They climbed flagpoles to perilous heights. In every store window where the proprietor hadn't decided that his plate glass was too valuable to risk and hadn't put up a sort of retaining wall of timber, little grandstands had been built. Little grandstands had also been constructed in the windows of the upstairs places overlooking the avenue.[417]

"Joe's father went to the Spanish war with Colonel Roosevelt," said the woman. "We hadn't been married so very long before he went away, but he felt he had to go and I didn't try to stop him. I remember well when he came back. I went down to Montauk Point to see him and tell him about Joe, because Joe was born while his father was away. Joe's father had a fever when he came back, and it was a long time before he got well."

On the skyscrapers blocks distant from the avenue, but offering narrow little glimpses of the column as it passed the side streets or moved along between lower buildings, were observation posts where thousands of people saw what they could of the parade through field glasses.

If you were caught in the crowds on the sidewalk in Fifth Avenue—and you had to be up mighty early to get caught there—your activities were quite over until the parade passed. Women began fainting early and continued fainting late. Ambulances were constantly rattling up through the streets. Finally some army trucks were driven through the crowd and gave some elbow room.

Seats in the stands were selling for any price. As high as $100 for a single seat was reported. Seats on the buildings and in the windows also brought good prices if they were put on the market, though in such cases the proprietor generally elected to have a party of his own.

"Joe's father always said a boy ought to join the army if we had a war, and that's why I didn't try to stop Joe when he wanted to go," the woman continued. "If his father'd lived, he might have gone, too. He was that way and Joe was just like him. I want to see Joe's company and try to imagine just where Joe would be and how he would look."

Taxi-cabs were hard to charter because the drivers were struck with a desire to take their own families out. Everybody—about everybody—in all this Big Town and from parts far remote wanted to see the Twenty-Seventh. They came by the thousands from up the state. Fifth Avenue, blazing with glory, was last night almost as impassable as it was during the day.

Nearly every town in New York is represented to some extent in the Twenty-Seventh. Some towns have large contingents. They probably get still another reception when they get home. All along the line of march yesterday you could hear the Uticans, the Buffalonians—if that's the right word—the Syracuse folks, the Rochester delegates, and all the other Upstaters yelling at their townsmen in the procession.

But in the main, the townsmen just shot a quick glance from under the steel hat and went hoofing it along. The men's packs had been lightened to some extent for the parade. They didn't carry all the junk they used to take into action. They did not have their ammunition, either. Therefore, they stepped off the Fifth Avenue blocks as if they were out for a morning breeze.

The Twenty-Seventh's steel helmets are not painted just according to army Hoyle, but they look very nifty. A division would scarcely go into action with that big red insignia[418] painted on the sconce piece at a point where it would be mighty interesting to a German sniper.

"My Joe looked awfully handsome in his uniform. He was a good-looking boy anyway, and he made a fine soldier," said the woman. "And there never was a kinder lad lived. I wonder if I'll be able to pick out the place in his company where he'd be if he was there. I don't suppose I will because, when I saw them parade before, I had a terribly hard time picking out Joe. But I can imagine how he'd look. Oh, I can imagine that!"

The wounded men of the division were sent ahead of the main body in automobiles. They got a tremendous ovation. They were showered with flowers[419] that seemed to fall out of the very sky. They were driven by particularly handsome young women, in particularly stylish-looking cars, and they were all a-grin. Some of them couldn't even sit still in their seats but mounted the back of the seats, where they could see and be seen to better advantage.

They went buzzing up the avenue, waving their crutches or just their hands and responding to as many salutations as possible. Military discipline was not as strict with them as with their marching brethren. These men are the fragments of the bloody conflict overseas. Some of them are maimed for life. But the cheerful way they journeyed up Fifth Avenue ahead of their more active fellows did the heart good.

"My boy Joe said the Twenty-Seventh is the greatest division of them all," said the woman. "He always said that. He wrote it to me in every letter, and I knew it must be true. They are all such fine lads. They have been so kind to me. Joe had a great many friends in his regiment, and in a way it's a comfort to me to know he was so well liked."

Beyond the Plaza one came to the region of the park lined by the "swell" residences of the "swell" set. The "swell" set indubitably went to war in this war, no matter what else you may say about it, and it was decidedly interested in the Twenty-Seventh. Besides, a great many of the Twenty-Seventh belong to the "swell" set themselves.

Don't forget it includes the old Seventh, "the Dandy Seventh" they used to call it, and many members of "the Dandy Seventh" patronize upper Fifth Avenue as a place of residence. Only, of course, "the Dandy Seventh" as the One Hundred and Seventh Infantry, a great regiment in a great division, is something entirely different from what it used to be. But it's the old Seventh none the less.

Then Squadron A and some of the First Cavalry, who machine gunned their way through the war, appreciated the residential advantages of the avenue no end, so all in all the coming to Upper Fifth yesterday was rather a homecoming.

"My Joe's father would be a proud man today if Joe was alive and marchin' along with these boys," said the woman. "My Joe's father belonged to the State militia, both before and after he went with Colonel Roosevelt, and he always said there was nothing like the New York militia. I suppose Joe was just naturally bound to be a soldier. He came by it."

Folks went picnicking in the park. They took lunches and made a day of it. The driveway overlooking Upper Fifth Avenue was parked with automobiles so close together that it was impossible to crowd between them. Fat policemen had a merry time of it, dusting around trying to keep the populace off the grass, though why they wanted to keep people off that dusty park covering is a mystery. Anyway, they tried it, but that's all. Members of the police reserve valiantly assisted in looking after the crowd.

The inevitable serial speeder—the Hall Room Boys[420] of the air—we had with us as always. A couple of flyers kept circling down in dangerous proximity to the ground. There ought to be traffic rules in the air, but crowds attract aviators as surely as a tip attracts a waiter.

Vendors with flags and souvenirs interlaced the throng. Several veterans of the Civil War, with their badges indicating service in the Hindenburg Line smash of their day, walked about in the sun. The air was like rich wine. The sun warmed the very heart. The Twenty-Seventh nearly always has good weather. Providence loves the Twenty-Seventh.

"No, I'm not a bit tired," said the woman. "I don't understand how people can be so restless, especially if they've got somebody they know in the parade. I could stand here forever if I thought I was goin' to get to see my Joe in the end. My feet ache some, but I don't mind. I really don't. Only it's getting late and I ought to be back lookin' after things."

People clambered aboard the decks of their limousines, if they had 'em, hauled out lunch boxes and thermos bottles, and eyed the passing throngs disrespectfully. Young gentlemen climbed the trees and hurled down comical remarks. Camp stools were quite numerous. An intermittent band helped to while away the wait. A ball game involving juveniles went on in the park meadow.

The banks of the reservoir formed a fine bleacher in the sun for thousands. They sat there shading their heads with newspapers and giving the "raz" to horsemen and horsewomen who galloped along the bridle path oblivious to everything. Andrew Carnegie's[421] house had its tenants on roof and windows. Colonel "Jake" Ruppert[422] entertained a party on the balcony of his home.

The "help" in all the avenue houses had great viewpoints from the windows. There was one tremendously big house, with an exasperating number of windows and balconies, where just an old man and woman appeared on a balcony. They seemed incredibly lonely and incredibly selfish, but maybe they had a reason. However, most of the houses had their guests, and many of the guests were wounded soldiers.

"My Joe didn't like parades much," said the woman. "He said they were too much fuss, but he would a liked this one, I know. He didn't like fuss of any kind much. He was a quiet boy and he wouldn't even let me fuss over him. His father was the same way, too. My Joe took after his father a great deal."

Now and then some daring spirit would lead a mad rush for a point of vantage. A big crowd would follow and the police would labor breathlessly to get things adjusted, without much luck. A New York policeman[423] is normally the best-natured thing in the world, and never more so than on an occasion of this kind. He doesn't like to disturb a crowd's pleasure.

There are a lot of billboards along Upper Fifth Avenue, just beyond the region of the "swell" set. These billboards were perches for the youth of the community. Everybody expected them to give way, but Providence also looks after the youth. Mothers brought their babies and their nursing outfits and had their adolescent spreads on the grass. A Broadway bunch that had stayed up all night to see the show yawned in their automobiles. Women rushed here and there without any particular coherence, carrying flags and banners of welcome and chiding their escorts because it was warm and their feet were tired and they had no seats.

In a little corner saloon in the Nineties the hospitable liquor dealer had set up a tier of seats in his window and was entertaining a crowd of friends. Soldiers from every other division in the army—the Rainbow, the Seventy-Seventh, the Thirty-Second, and the Regular outfits—wandered around, envying their luckier comrades of the Twenty-Seventh this amazing to-do. There were numerous Jackies from the war boats, too.

"There's a boy there who reminds me of my Joe," said the woman. "He's got light hair, just like Joe had, only it isn't so curly. Joe's hair was always curly from the time he was born, and he hated it. I do hope I'll not miss his regiment when it goes by. Please watch good for it."

And now, after all the waiting and the crowding and the scrunching about to get a better position, now after all the expectation, a sound comes rolling up the avenue that is like not as if one were approaching a beach where a heavy surf is pounding, but as if the surf is coming on to where one waits.

It comes on and on, gradually growing stronger and stronger. There is a fierce forward movement in the crowd and a wild waving of flags and a great cheering. A band comes into sight. It is the great police band, and, obviously, the musicians are breathing heavily into their instruments, but no music can be heard. Not a note. It is drowned by the roaring of the crowd. The effect is most ludicrous. It looks as if the musicians are merely simulating play.

Who's this?

O'Ryan.

Sure enough, it's O'Ryan on his sorrel, with two orderlies, one the redoubtable Sergeant Major Hart, riding behind him, their helmets on their heads and their chin straps drawn around their chin, O'Ryan, as immaculate in attire as a veritable fashion plate, looking neither to the right nor left.

And behind O'Ryan comes O'Ryan's men—the Twenty-Seventh Division.

The columns of helmets come on and on, rising and falling, to the movement of the marching feet. It's for all the world as if they were being swept up the avenue on the crest of the vocal tidal wave.[424]

"You'll not forget," said the woman, almost pleadingly. "My Joe's regiment. It will be here soon. Oh, those wonderful boys! Those wonderful boys! If my Joe was only with them! I can't just see how he'd look. I've got his picture in a steel helmet that he had taken in France. My Joe! I wonder how many more are here like me, thinking about the boy who isn't here!"

POETRY

A Song of Hate

[June 3, 1917]

Now wealthy John P. Stubblefield
    Has neither kith nor kin,
But often speaks about the blood
    We'll pay the Germans in.
Then up goes John P. Stubblefield
    To the court house on the hill
To kick about his taxes
    While your son goes to drill
        And John P. stands where he can see,
        And hollers: "Give 'em hell for me!"

Now this same John P. Stubblefield
    Was young in Ninety-eight,
And hated Spain and Spaniards
    With a very savage hate.
Yes, this same John P. Stubblefield
    With wrath was 'most insane,
So some of us went marching off
    To help avenge the *Maine*.
        And John P. stood where he could see,
        And hollered: "Give 'em hell for me!"

Well, this same John P. Stubblefield,
    He started up a store,
And he was getting good and rich
    When we came back from war.
And some of us were broke and sick,
    And all were mighty slim,
But John P. Stubblefield was glad
    We gave 'em hell for him.
        And my old man, he said to me:
        "He's like his Pa in Sixty-three!"

Now that's been nineteen years ago,
    And John P.'s rich as mud,
But somehow he can't get away
    From that strange lust for blood.
He hated Mexicans a while,
    And yelled when Company B
Went hiking off to Mexico:
    "Boys, give 'em hell for me!"
        And John P. bid on army shoes
        As soon as he received the news!

So this same John P. Stubblefield
Is hating of the Huns;
He says he's sorry he can't send
A half a dozen sons.
Then up goes John P. Stubblefield
To the court house on the hill
To roar about taxation
As your boy goes to drill.
He raves about the horrid Hun,
While your son lugs a nine-pound gun!

Yes, this same John P. Stubblefield
Makes speeches by the yard;
He criticises congressmen,
And criticises hard.
He wears a flag upon his coat—
There's flags around his store;
He's raised the price of woolen yarn
Because of this here war.
My wife is knitting sox these days—
That's how I know about that raise.

When someone said we all should save,
Who was the first to send
A letter to the papers,
Advising folks to spend?
"For saving would hurt business—
In saving panic lurks"—
Why, this same John P. Stubblefield—
Then he laid off fifty clerks
And fifty teamsters at a clip,
While your son studies marksmanship!

Yes, this same John P. Stubblefield,
He burns with righteous rage.
He storms about the income tax
And cuts his chauffeur's wage.
He fought against preparedness—
Now he warns of army graft
And tells the war department
To hurry up the draft.
Well, my old man once said to me:
"He's like his Pa in Sixty-three!"

It's this same John P. Stubblefield,
With neither chick nor child,
Who hates those Germans with a hate
That's very hot and wild.
Of course, I hate the Germans, too,
For that is only fair—

But I do not hate them half as much
As I hate John P. there.
Now Lord forgive such thoughts, I pray—
Did your boy go to camp today?

Then up goes John P. Stubblefield
To the court house on the hill
To kick about his taxes
While your son goes to drill.
And when the transport's loaded,
And its nose swings to the sea,
With Sons of Men along the decks,
I know where John will be.
John P. will stand where he can see
And holler: "Give 'em hell for me!"

The Old "Leatherneck"

[September 1917]

Many a year my Uncle Joe
Served as a Private of Marines.
Got cut down by a bolo blow
On Waller's hike in the Philippines.
Little old brittle, old pappy guy,
With one flat wheel and a gray goatee.
Nights I read him the news of the war
And he sets and smokes and listens to me.

Sets and smokes, and rocks his chair,
And chews on his pipe, and rumples his hair,
When I read of a row, and begins to swear,
And says, "I bet the leathernecks was there!
If I say "no" to Uncle Joe, "this fight was in the air,"
Says, "Don't care where!" and rocks his chair—
"I bet the leathernecks was there!"

I read him the tale of Vimy Ridge,
The tale of the brave Canucks;
And he scrabbled his nose along the bridge,
And says: "Them's wonderful ducks!"
He says: "Them soldiers is doughboys, see?
And they's nothin' much they can't do—
But read me some more about this war—
What did the leathernecks do?"

"Yes," he says, "that's fine!," when I read of a fight,
And his eye lights up with a singular light.
Then he chuckles and says: "Well, hell's delight!
The leathernecks sure was there!"
If I say "no" to Uncle Joe, "it don't say so nowhere,"
Says: "Don't give a damn, if they was a jam,
The leathernecks must a-been there!"

I read him about the Mongolia's crew,
And their scrap with subsea sneak.
I read him about the Silvershell, too,
Which he says was a narrer squeak.
He says: "Them flatfeet behind them guns,
And a mighty good gang, that's true.
But read me some more about this war—
What did the leathernecks do?"

He says: "By Gosh!" as he listens to me,
And bites at his pipe with a singular glee
When I read of a fight, and he says, says he,
"I bet the leathernecks was there!"
If I say "no" to Uncle Joe, "this fight was under the sea,"
Says, "I don't care, if the fight was there,
That's where the leathernecks'd be!"

The Stay-Behind

[September 27, 1917]

How do you think I felt inside,
        When I stood on the sidewalk there,
And saw you stepping along the street
        To the drums and the bugle blare?
How do you think I felt inside—
        (I waved, but you didn't see)—
You, in your dust-stained khaki blouse;
How did I feel? Well, how does a louse?
(Her, and the two-year-old at the house—
        And the landlord lookin' to me!)

How do you think I felt inside—
        Me, in that old straw hat?
(Tied to a load of household junk
        And a lease on a Harlem flat.)
How do you think I felt inside
        When I saw the columns start?
(Her, and the little two-year-old—
Nary a dime does the bankbook hold)—
How did I feel? So cold, so cold
        'Way, 'way down in my heart!

How do you think I felt inside,
        Scroonched back there in the crowd?
Big horn cheaters upon my beak,
        And you stepped by so proud.
(Linen collar around my neck—
        And tied to a salary roll)—
How do you think I felt inside,
When you marched past in your khaki pride?
Why do you think it was I cried
        'Way, 'way down in my soul?

The Pride of Company A

[October 1, 1917]

Our cook he was a movie star; a million films he took—
(That guy down yonder lookin' like a scullion.)
The gals say he's so handsome, but I'll say he can cook—
There never was no slum like his slumgullion!
When he yells: "Come and get it!," we take it on the trot;
We don't know what he's got for us, but know it's good 'n' hot;
And I'll say he's the best cook ever straddle of a pot—
Our cookie, who was once a movie actor.

Our cookie standin' yonder a-holdin' back the crush
O' the mob that's after seconds, and a-sayin' not to rush;
Our cookie, who has kissed Miss Pickford right upon the mush—
Our cookie, who was once a movie actor!

Our captain is a millionaire, and plenty o' jack he's got—
(He'll stake a short guy any time to money.)
If I had half his sugar, or just his private yacht,
I'd laugh myself to death, I'd feel so funny!
We've got a first lieutenant who was raised up on a farm;
A sergeant from the Astor, where he dealt 'em off his arm—
But the guy we'd mourn the most for, if he should come to harm
Is our cookie, who was once a movie actor.

Our cookie, who has busted up black villains by the bale;
Our cookie, who has been close up to Betty Barriscale—
Our cookie, who at messtime was never known to fail—
Our cookie, who was once a movie star!

We've got a guy in my platoon who quarterbacked for Yale—
(You ought to hear him sing "Booly-booly.")
They say he was a bear cat with a long and fuzzy tail—
He bunks next to a guy named Johnny Dooley.
This Dooley done the best he could, and done it everywhere;
His racket was the wire game, but now he's on the square—
And we've got a Harvard tackle, but the guy by which we swear
Is our cookie, who was once a movie actor!

Our cookie, who was heroed by the hour on many screens;
Our cookie, who has hugged Pearl White, and all those movie queens—
Our cookie, out there yonder, stewing up some spinach greens—
Our cookie, who was once a movie actor!

We've got a guy in my platoon who was a dancing guy—
(They say he shook a mean hoof in the Frolic.)

Our corporal was a preacher, and he has a solemn eye
And acts as if he always had the colic.
We've got a Harvard tackle, and a husky Princeton guard;
A big, fat Irish rassler, who's a champ at no holds barred—
But the guy that we are strongest for, and who's our richest card,
Is our cookie, who was once a movie actor!

Our cookie, who has rescued several thousand dames, I guess;
Our cookie, who's a curly wolf for looks in evenin' dress—
Our cookie, out there yonder, gettin' up our daily mess—
Sweet cookie, who was once a movie actor!

Song of a Drafted Man

(The First Night at Camp Devens)

[October 5, 1917]

I'm here with two thin blankets,
As thin as a slice of ham.
A German spy was likely the guy
Who made 'em for Uncle Sam.
How did I sleep? Don't kid me!
My bedtick is filled with straw,
And lumps and humps and big fat humps
That punched me 'till I'm raw.

Me and my two thin blankets,
As thin as a last thin dime—
As thin, I guess, as a chorus girl's dress—
Well—I had one hell of a time!
I'd pull 'em up from the bottom—
(My nightie's by B.V.D.s.)
A couple of yanks to cover my shanks,
And then my dogs'd freeze!

You could use 'em for porous plasters,
Or maybe to strain the soup.
(My pillow's my shoes when I try to snooze—
And I've chilblains, caught the croup.)
Me and my two thin blankets,
Bundled up under my chin—
Yes, a German spy was likely the guy,
And, gosh, but he made 'em thin!

One of Runyon's popular poems was set to music in 1917. *Courtesy of Library of Congress*

"Hold 'em, Yale!"

[November 28, 1917]

There's a Bowl in old New Haven.
(There's seventy thousand paid.)
The sun looks down on a pop-eyed town
On the day that The Game is played.
"Hip!"
The signal passes!
"Hip! Hip!"
The ball flips true!
There's a whirl, and a swirl,
And the lean-flanked backs
In the jerseys blue plunge through!
Hark! There's a song from the bleachers!
Hark! It's the old, old hail—
"Bulldog! Bulldog!
Bow-wow-wow!
Eli Yale!"

There's a storm-ripped stretch of ocean
Where the Dutchman's U-boats trade.
There's a young patrol from the big, round Bowl
On the day that The Game is played.
"Aim!"
The signal passes!
"Fire!"
The shot goes true!
There's a swish, and a swash,
And a gurgling squash
As the lean-flanked backs drive through!
Hark! There's a song on the water
That floats from the victor's rail—
"Bulldog! Bulldog!
Bow-wow-wow!
Eli Yale!"

There's a mud-clogged field in Flanders,
                    There a trench by shrapnel flayed,
Where the doughboys blink at the dawn's first wink
          On the day that The Game is played.
"Hup!"
          The signal passes!
"Let's go!"
          The light turns blue!
There's a splash, and a crash
And a long, long smash
          As the lean-flanked backs drive through!
Hark! That's a song of triumph!
Hark! That's the old, old hail—
                              "Bulldog! Bulldog!
                              Bow-wow-wow!
                              Eli Yale!"

There's a street in old New Haven
                    That the sighing elm trees shade.
And they sigh, perhaps, for the lean-flanked chaps
          Of the day when The Game was played.
"Come!"
          The signal carried!
"Come! Come!
          The Flag needs you!"
Oh, a nation stirred at the magic word,
And the backs came plunging through.
Hark! That's a song from the nation!
Hark! That's a proud, proud hail—
                              "Bulldog! Bulldog!
                              Bow-wow-wow!
                              Eli Yale!"

The Little One-Star Flag

[November 23, 1917]

Oh, I used to hear the family
In the house across the way—
A father, and a mother, and a child.
And, Oh, the noise they used to make;
They'd keep the neighborhood awake—
I sometimes used to think they'd drive me wild!
I glanced across the way the other day;
It seemed too quiet over there, by far,
And hanging in the window of the house across the way
Is a little flag which bears a single star!

There's a Service Flag in El Paso,
And it flaunts two dozen stars.
Oh, it swings there to the glory
Of the soldiers and the tars.
But no star there in its beauty
Tells of stronger Love and Duty
Than the little one-star flag across the way.

Oh, I used to see them waiting
In the house across the way—
The mother, and a little girl, so sweet.
And, Oh, the way they used to shout;
And, Oh, the way they'd hurry out
When they saw Daddy coming up the street.
Now I miss the noise they made there as they played,
It seems too quiet over there by far—
Oh, they're watching from the window of the house across the way
By the little flag that bears a single star!

There's a Wonder Flag in the plaza,
Flying from a dizzy height,
Like a gorgeous patch of heaven
That was ripped from starry night.
But no star there in its beauty
Tells of stronger Love and Duty
Than the little one-star flag across the way!

The Little One-Star Flag

[December 1, 1917]

Oh, I used to hear the family
In the house across the way—
A father, and a mother, and a child.
And, Oh, the noise they used to make;
They'd keep the neighborhood awake—
I sometimes used to think they'd drive me wild!
I glanced across the way the other day;
It seemed too quiet over there, by far,
And hanging in the window of the house across the way
Is a little flag which bears a single star!

There's a Service Flag in Broadway,
And it flaunts two thousand stars.
Oh, it swings there to the glory
Of the soldiers and the tars.
But no star there in its beauty
Tells of stronger Love and Duty
Than the little one-star flag across the way.

Oh, I used to see them waiting
In the house across the way—
The mother, and a little girl, so sweet.
And, Oh, the way they used to shout;
And, Oh, the way they'd hurry out
When they saw Daddy coming up the street.
Now I miss the noise they made there as they played,
It seems too quiet over there by far—
Oh, they're watching from the window of the house across the way
By the little flag that bears a single star!

There's a Wonder Flag in Wall Street,
Flying from a dizzy height,
Like a gorgeous patch of heaven
That was ripped from starry night.
But no star there in its beauty
Tells of stronger Love and Duty
Than the little one-star flag across the way.

Baddest Boy

[December 2, 1917]

People said; yes, people said
That the baddest boy in town
Was a kid, a freckled kid,
By the name of Willie Brown.
He disappeared, people sneered,
And guessed it, with a frown—
"Gone to enlist—he won't be missed—
Why, he's the baddest boy in town!"

Baddest boy!
I saw him marching—
Marching
Down the avenue!
With a step so free and easy,
And his eyes so bright and blue!
Baddest boy!
Someone was watching—
Watching
Willie Brown!
And I knew that she was praying for
The baddest boy in town!

People say the other day
Came a message to our town.
They read it out—it was about
Private Willie Brown.
The message said that he was dead—
In action he went down.
And people say he saved the day—
The baddest boy in town!
Baddest boy!
I saw him marching—
Marching
Down the avenue!
Behind the colors of his regiment
And the old red, white and blue!
Baddest boy!
Someone was watching—
Watching
Willie Brown!
And I know that she'll be mourning for
The baddest boy in town!

How Do You Say—in French?

[December 2, 1917]

I wrote a letter to me pal,
Me old pal, Donohue.
He's over there across the sea
With all the gang in Company B—
I wrote: "I'm sending you a box of dainties, Donohue!
I'm sending you some sweets," I said;
"Some ham; some doo-dads for your bed."
I got an answer back today;
Says he: "Now, listen, you!

Never mind the jam;
Never mind the ham.
Never mind the doo-dads
For me bood-wars in a trench.
But here's a task for you—
Please ask," says Donohue,
"How do I say 'I love you' in French?

I met her in Bordeaux," says he,
Me old pal, Donohue.
"And over here across the sea
No speak the Irish much," says he—
"I understand her signs," says he,
"But do not parlay-voo.
So hustle around this very night,
Father Duffy will set you right—
Borrow a book from him
And send it on to Donohue!

Never mind the jam;
Never mind the ham.
How can I use doo-dads
When me bood-war's in a trench?
This is the job for you—
Find out," says Donohue,
"How do I say 'I love you' in French?"

Economy Is Nothing New to Me

[December 3, 1917]

I hear a lot of talk of Conservation;
Of Economy, and everything like that.
I understand they seek co-operation—
(Citizens, refrain from getting fat!)
Well, it won't affect the speakers' corporation;
Kindly listen to old George Authority;
To me it won't seem rare, for I'll tell the whole world, fair,
Economy is nothing new to me!

We have the wheatless Monday at my house—
(Gosh! If our icebox could speak!)
We have meatless Tuesday, Wednesday, Thursday—
And an eatless rest of the week.
I sit, and glance, in my seatless trousers
At a heatless grate, you see;
In a feetless chair; I'll tell the whole world fair,
Economy is nothing new to me!

Oh, I'm in favor of this move for Conservation,
But suggesting that poor I economize
Is like telling one of Uncle Sam's postmen
That he ought to take a little exercise.
When you open up on me on Conservation
I'd advise that you had best conserve your breath—
For if good old Mother Hubbard ever peeks into our cupboard
She will very likely laugh herself to death!

We've got a cheatless meter at our house;
We've got a neatless servant, brown.
I've got a greetless mate when I get in late
From a treatless tour of town.
Oh, I rest my head on a sheetless bed;
We've got a beatless landlord; he
Has a sweetless air, I'll tell the whole world, fair,
Economy is nothing new to me!

Although written in 1917, this poem was not set to music until 1921 when it was also retitled "Left." *Courtesy of Library of Congress*

Songs of a Selected Man

(A Marching Soliloquy)

[December 4, 1917]

"Left!
Left!"
Had a fine gal when I
"Left!
Left!"
Mighty good pal when I
"Left!"
"One! Two! Three! Four!"
How
many
miles
more?"
"Left!"

"Left!
Left!"
Booked for a wife when I
"Left!
Left!"
That was the life when I
"Left!"
"One! Two! Three! Four!"
Hear
old
Cap
Roar!
"Left!"

"Left!
Left!"
Had a good job when I
"Left!
Left!"
Left to a slob when I
"Left!"
"One! Two! One! Two!"
Close
up
there
you!
"Left!"

                                    "Left!
                                    Left!"
Many a day since I
                                    "Left!
                                    Left!"
Never no pay since I
                                    "Left!"
"One! Two! Hep! Hep!"
Hey
          you,
                    get
                                    step!
                                    "Left!"

                                    "Left!
                                    Left!"
Don't run around since I
                                    "Left!
                                    Left!"
Always am found where I'm
                                    "Left!"
"Hawfoot! Strawfoot!"
Stay
          where
                    I'm
                                    put!
                                    "Left!"

                                    "Left!
                                    Left!"
Had some good feet when I
                                    "Left!
                                    Left!"
Pair of good feet when I
                                    "Left!"
"One! Two! Three! Four!"
Which
          dog's
                    most
                                    sore?
                                    "Left!"

Lonesomest Town

(The Rainbow Division, Composed of National Guard Regiments, Has Arrived in France.)

[December 7, 1917]

There's a lonesome town in Dixieland,
There's a lonesome town in Maine;
On Dakota's plain, amid the waving grain,
They'll be lonesome till the gang comes home again
        But the lonesomest town in all the states—
        In all the world,
        I'll say—
From Arkansaw to Rome, it's the town that I call home.
        And it's the lo-o-one-som-est town of all!

Sat'day night in Colorado,
Sat'day night in my home town.
See the Main street arc lights
Winkin', winkin', winkin'.
        As they winter breezes toss 'em up and down.
Look into the poolroom on the corner—
                "Where's Jim?
                "Where's Slim?
                "Gone!—
Gone away to war—
Shorty, Buck, and forty more—
        Mister, this is the lonesomest, lo-o-o-one-som-est town!"

Sunday night in Colorado,
Sunday night in my home town.
Hear the Baptis' chuch bell
Ringin', ringin', ringin'.
        See the people walkin' up and down.
Peek into the church around the corner—
                        "Where's Nell?
                        "Where's Stell?
                        "Gone!—
Mary, Libby, Jess and Lois;
Gone away to nurse the boys—
        Mister, this is the lonesomest, lo-o-o-one-som-est town!"

There's a lonesome town in Michigan,
        In Iowa and Idaho.
And in the sunny land along the Rio Grande
        They'll be lonesome 'til the gang comes back, I know,
                But the lonesomest town in all the states—
                        In all the world,
                        I'll bet—
        From Oregon to Rome, it's the town that I call home,
                And it's the lo-o-o-one-som-est town of all!

The "Do Anything Guy"—U.S. Engineers

Dedicated to Captain Til Huston's[1] outfit, with the Expeditionary Forces in France.

[December 12, 1917]

Late of the Katy Flyer;
Late of the Homestake mine.
Mucker, or maybe a trammer,
Or a con on the Alton line.
Late of the New York subway
(Wise on electric gear);
He can lay track well from here to hell—
Dugan, the Engineer.
Old Do-Anything Dugan—
Dugan, the Engineer!

He can lay track well from here to hell,
Or bridge the breast of an ocean swell;
He can fight a spell, I'm here to tell—
Dugan, the Engineer!
Old Do-Anything, Dugan—
Dugan, the Engineer!

Late of the town of Dayton,
And a damn nice neighborhood.
Maybe from Cincinnati,
Where Houck's is drawn from the wood.
Maybe from old Chicago,
And holding that city dear;
He can lay that track to hell 'n' back—
Dugan, the Engineer!
Old Do-Anything Dugan—
Dugan, the Engineer!

He can lay that track to hell 'n' back;
Scrap at hand, he'll have his crack—
Railroad shack or lumber-jack
Is Dugan, the Engineer!
Old Do-Anything Dugan—
Dugan, the Engineer!

Late of a morning paper—
Joined in a state of fatigue.
Late of the forestry layout,
Or late of the Three Eye League.

Late of a job on Broadway,
And the work seems a trifle queer—
With a road to drench, or a fire to quench—
Dugan, the Engineer!
Old Do-Anything Dugan—
Dugan, the Engineer!

A fire to drench or a thirst to quench—
He can span a gap with a wooden bench;
He can build a trench with a monkey wrench—
Dugan, the Engineer!
Old Do-Anything Dugan—
Dugan, the Engineer!

Late of the truck department
Of a store on the Avenue.
Late of the O.K. chop house,
Or late of the Princeton crew.
Late of the Michigan Aggies—
Give him a Michigan cheer!
He can shoe a mule, or teach a school—
Dugan, the Engineer!
Old Do-Anything Dugan—
Dugan, the Engineer!

He can shoe a mule or teach a school;
Filter the water or find the fuel—
Any old tool or an army rule—
Dugan, the Engineer!
Old Do-Anything Dugan—
Dugan, the Engineer!

Hear of the gang at Cambrai?
Surely you must have heard?
That was his style at Cambrai—
(Or however you say the word).
That is the style of Dugan,
Keeping the roadway clear;
He can lay track well on the lid of hell—
Dugan, the Engineer!
Old Do-Anything Dugan—
Dugan, the Engineer!

He can lay track well on the lid of hell,
Or bridge the breast of an ocean swell—
He can fight a spell; I'm here to tell—
Dugan, the Engineer!
Old Do-Anything Dugan—
Dugan, the Engineer!

Old Boy

(On seeing a veteran of the Spanish-American War in his new uniform as a captain in the National Army.)

[December 22, 1917]

Old Boy, I saw you years ago;
Old Boy, your hair was brown,
Old Boy, your brow was smooth, I know,
When you marched through the town.
Old Boy, that was in ninety-eight;
Your waist was trim, your shoulders straight—
How proud, Old Boy, you were, Old Boy,
When she called you Old Boy!

Old Boy, I saw your long good-byes
There at the depot gate.
Old Boy, I heard your long, long sigh—
Old Boy, I knew your fate!
Law men, Old Boy, 'twas long ago—
How long, Old Boy, I ought to know!
How young, Old Boy, you were, Old Boy,
When she called you Old Boy!

Old Boy, I saw you yesterday;
Old Boy, you're not so slim.
Old Boy, you're getting rather gray;
Your waist is not so trim.
Old Boy, there's something in your eyes
That takes me back to those good-byes,
And says, Old Boy, your heart, Old Boy,
Is just as then, Old Boy!

Old Boy, your brow is touched by care;
Old Boy, some hair is gone.
Old Boy, a wrinkle here and there
Tells me you're getting on.
Old Boy, your step is not as spry
As then when you went marching by—
But still, Old Boy, you are, Old Boy,
To her the same Old Boy!

Winter at Camp Mills, 1917

[December 25, 1917]

I.

When I get back to old Cheyenne, in old Wyoming dear;
I'll probably wear a long moustache, and whiskers down to here.
I'll stand upon the corner, and I'll say: "How do you do—
These are the whiskers that the wind blew through!"

II.

"These are the whiskers that grew on Hempstead Plains,
The lilacs that sprouted 'mid the snowstorms and the rains.
These are the whiskers that the seaward breeze turned blue—
These are the whiskers that the wind blew through!"

III.

When I get back to old Cheyenne and yarns on weather start,
I'll mention weather colder than a quartermaster's heart.
I'll stroke my long lace curtains, and I'll say to folks: "Now, shoo!—
These are the whiskers that the wind blew through!"

IV.

"These are the whiskers that the breezes loved to tease.
They used to have an icy fringe that dangled 'round my knees.
When I'd get up at reveille to snatch my morning stew—
These are the whiskers that the wind blew through!"

V.

When I get back to old Cheyenne I'll tell 'em how I dream,
Of miles of radiators all a-radiating steam.
Of big base burners burning, and of blankets thick and new
To cover up the whiskers that the wind blows through!"

VI.

"These are the whiskers that bloomed by night and day;
These are the whiskers that the breezes loved to play—
The Long Island breezes that have nothing else to do—
These are the whiskers that the wind blew through."

VII.

When I get back to old Cheyenne I'll tell 'em how I'd read
Of guys hived up in barracks down at Upton, Dix, or Meade;
Around a big, pot-bellied stove; fire roaring up the flue—
When I raised whiskers in a tent that the wind blew through!

VIII.

"These are the whiskers the breezes loved to tease;
This is the spinach that breezes loved to freeze."
When I get back to old Cheyenne I'll say: "How do you do—
These are the whiskers that the wind blew through!"

The Fall of Beriah Bent

[January 7, 1918]

When the rags-and-bones-and-hanks-of-hair, or portly dames and fat,
Or ladies of the genius that is sometimes known as "cat,"
Or ladies bearing grievous marks of blighted heart romances,
Or ladies wearing camouflage upon their countenances,
Or ladies whose endearing charms had long ago decayed,
Or ladies large and masculine and masterful essayed
To peddle Red Cross memberships to old Beriah Bent,
He always clutched his pocketbook and answered, "Not a cent!"

I've joined it in Chicago, I've joined it in Duluth,
I've joined it twice in Hackensack, and that's the gospel truth.
I've joined it out in Fresno, Cal., and Providence, R. I.;
Nine times in seven different states I've joined since last July.
I've written on subscription sheets until I've dulled my pen,
So please don't ask me any more—I shall not join again.

When maids with figures svelte and trim, with wreaths of auburn hair,
And eyes like Maxine Elliott's, that smiled like Ina Claire;
When girls that talked like Billie Burke and looked like corpyhees
Would fix upon Beriah Bent their soft and childlike gaze,
And ask him if he didn't have a dollar he could spare
To purchase cots and comforts for the soldiers over there,
Although he held a dollar in superlative regard,
He never failed to loosen up, and loosen good and hard.

He joined again in Tuckahoe, he joined in New Rochelle;
He joined in Minneapolis and Butte and Kalispel;
He joined in Kansas City, Mo., and Chattanooga, Tenn.,
And every time a peach came by he joined it once again.
Which brings to light an axiom you'll never find in books:
"The Janes will always land 'em, if they've only got the looks."

The Spirit of You

[April 24, 1918]

McSweal, of the Battery, private; with a wound that he couldn't survive–
"Press hard on the blood-flow, fellow; we'll try to keep him alive!"
McSweal, of the Battery, speaking—a locket set turquoise blue–
"No chaplain to see me departing? Well, I'll pray to the spirit of You!

"There's a violet scent in my nostrils; there's a violet breath on my cheek;
I'm seeking no thin-worded parting, well knowing You never would speak.
Now the moments that waited run swiftly—Time was my friend, I knew,
And it's brought me at last to my altar to pray to the spirit of You!

"'Tis an old, old, helpless longing that quickens the stagnant veins;
'Tis a world-old crying for something that rouses the hidden pains.
'Tis a constant searching for surcease—I've called on the Gods that are true–
And now I recall my religion, and turn to the spirit of You!

"I've cursed in my moments of passion; besought with a heart contrite,
But never an answer to praying, though I'm having it answered to-night.
'Tis an old, old, cold, old longing—'tis a dreaming that never came true,
But the blessing of Faith is with me as I pray to the spirit of You!"

We left him out there as he wanted—McSweal, of the Battery, dead;
We left him wrapped in his blankets, with a white cross over his head.
With the locket still clasped in his fingers—we gave him a volley or two,
And left him out there as he wanted to talk to the spirit of You!

Shooting pool in a Red Cross hut. *Courtesy of Library of Congress*

Pool-Shootin' Roy

[May 22, 1918]

Son o' ol' Miz McAuliffe, the wider o' Box-Car Jack,
An ol' time shack on the Santa Fe, who run to Dodge and back.
He was killed in a wreck at La Junta, and he left the wife and boy—
A kid knee-high to a hop-toad, and tagged by the name o' Roy.

This Roy was sort o' ornery, and he never would go to school.
He spent the most o' childhood days in learnin' the game o' pool.
His shoulders grew somewhat rounded, and his chest it grew rather thin—
But, gosh, he grew to a marvel at knockin' them pool balls in!

Pool-Shootin' Roy we called him, and many a night I've set
Watchin' him clean the table, and puffin' his cigarette.
Sleeves rolled up to the elbow, and playin' so ca'm and cool—
If ever a lad was born for a thing, he was born for playin' this pool!

Fifteen balls was a cinch for him—fifteen balls from the break;
One ball loose from the bunch a bit, and the whole darned rack he'd take.
He was great on a combination, and great on a cut-shot, too—
He'd make those pool balls talk to him when he started handlin' a cue!

Days he's stand on the corners, battin' his eyes at the sun—
Nights he was busy at Dan McGuire's makin' some wonderful run.
His shoulders grew somewhat rounded, and his chest it grew rather thin,
But better'n better this Roy got at knockin' them pool balls in.

And some of us thought he'd be a champeen, but every one didn't agree,
For Doctor Wilcox wanted to bet he'd die of the old T.B.
But the war it settled the question, for the first of our kids to go
Was Pool-Shootin' Roy McAuliffe—our poolrooms suffered a blow.

What is that thing the Frenchmen give to a good game fightin' boy?
Say it again—the Croix de Guerre? Well, that's what they give to Roy.
It seems fifteen Germans were on him, and handlin' him rather mean,
When he got a machine gun to workin' and pocketed the hull fifteen!

Me—M'gee

[May 23, 1918]

Walter McGee, a prominent New York clubman, forty-five years old, made a desperate attempt to get into the service. Failing in that because of his age, and desirous of doing something, he has taken a job as dock laborer and is helping load boats for France.

There's a chair in a clubroom corner
        That's shaped to the shape o' McGee—
An easy chair that's stuffed with hair,
        With a place for a glass near the knee.
But he isn't there in that easy chair
        (Which, of course, is plain to see).
"They do not serve who sit and wait,"
        Said he: "that's me—McGee!"

Touch o' gray in his foretop—
        "A soldier I'll be," said he.
Plenty of room in the doughboys
        For the likes o' me—McGee."
Touch o' gray in his foretop—
        Creaky o' back and knee.
"Put on your duds," said the sawbones;
        "Rejected—W. McGee!"

Touch o' gray in his foretop—
        "Gee!" said W. McGee,
"Maybe, by gosh, there's a job awash
        For the middle-aged likes o' me."

"Keep on your duds," growled the doctor,
    "Too old to go to sea;
Stand aside for a younger man—
    Rejected—W. McGee!"

Creaked too much for the army—
    Too old to go to sea.
Said he: "I swear there's a job somewhere
    For the likes o' me—McGee!
I can wallop a dock to a frazzle,
    As good as the next man—me!"
"Take off your coat!" snarled a foreman—
    "Accepted—W. McGee!"

There's a chair in a clubroom corner
    That fitted him to a T;
There's an empty glass that the waiters pass
    Which belonged to W. McGee.
Touch o' gray to his foretop—
    But easy o' back and knee—
"Hi, lend a hand!" yells the foreman, grand—
    "Coming, boss! Me—McGee!"

Bundy's Men

(Major General Omar Bundy's[2] men, of the Second Division, were responsible for the American success at Vaux—General Peyton March's report.)

[June 8, 1918]

Bundy's men are from the south—
Bundy's Men! Bundy's Men!
From the Mississippi's mouth—
Bundy's Men! Bundy's Men!
Bundy's men breathe chivalry,
And Bundy's men are brave—
'Twas Bundy's men who won at Vaux,
Advancing wave on wave!

So here's a toast to Bundy's men,
And all of Bundy's crew—
To Bundy's, Omar Bundy's men,
And Omar Bundy, too!

Oh, Bundy's men are northern men—
Bundy's Men! Bundy's Men!
Valley, town, and mountain glen—
Bundy's Men! Bundy's Men!
Oh, Bundy's men are big and strong,
And gallant, and polite—
But ask the Boche who fought at Vaux
How Bundy's men can fight!

Bundy's men are western men—
Bundy's Men! Bundy's Men!
Cattle range and shearing pen—
Bundy's Men! Bundy's Men!
Oh, Bundy's men are foot and guns,
And Bundy's men can tell
How Bundy's men they won at Vaux
And gave old Heinie hell!

Bundy's men are eastern men—
Bundy's Men! Bundy's Men!
College, store, and broker's den—
Bundy's Men! Bundy's Men!
Oh, Bundy's men are handsome men,
And Bundy's men are swell,
And Bundy's men can step a bit,
As Heinie Boche can tell!

So here's a cheer for Bundy's men,
Who drove the long line through—
For Bundy's, Omar Bundy's men,
And Omar Bundy, too!

All Right

[July 21, 1918]

He's back on a leave of absence,
And his face seems drawn and gray,
It's hard to realize it's been
A year since he went away.
Grave he is in his manner,
But his voice has the old-time cheer:
"They're all right, over there, all right—
Are YOU all right, over here?

They're all right, over there, all right;
There's nothing at all that's wrong.
Sam, Joe, and Bill—I saw them all
And I left them well and strong.
They told me to tell you all hello,
And to tell you to have no fear
But that they're all right, over there, all right,
If YOU'RE all right, over here!

"Yes, there's lots of mud in the trenches,
But they're making the best of it.
The cooties are not much overdrawn,
Or none of the rest of it.
It's a big, new kind of business—
A business that's sad, and queer.
But they're all right, over there, all right—
Are YOU all right, over here?

"They're all right, over there, all right;
Yes, it's true about those rains.
It's true about the hardships, too,
And that never a man complains.
It's true that there's quite a task at hand,
And that Death is ever near—
But they're all right, over there, all right—
Are YOU all right, over here?

"If YOU'RE all right, over here," he said,
"And leaving no job undone,
They'll be all right, over there, all right,
Till they've ended the thing, and won.
If YOU'VE done YOUR share the best YOU can,
And YOUR conscience is sound and clear,
They'll be all right, over there, all right,
And YOU all right, over here"

He's back on a leave of absence,
And his face seems drawn and gray.
It's hard, indeed, to realize
It's a year that he's been away.
Grave he is in his manner,
But his voice has the old-time cheer:
"They're all right, over there, all right—
Are YOU all right, over here?"

Song of the Yankee Guns

[August 25, 1918]

I
The types that tell the story
Sing: Glory! Glory! Glory!
They seem to be an echo of the guns—
The Yankee guns!
Each line a bar of music—
Of sweeping, swelling music—
Glory! Glory! Glory!
To our God, and to our guns!

II
The guns in mighty choiring—
The guns freemen are firing;
The guns that pound on land and sea—
The guns, the Yankee guns!
Yea, this the mighty chorus,
The song that lifts before us—
Glory! Glory! Glory!
To our God, and to our guns!

III
The guns that spit and sputter,
The guns that whine and mutter;
The big guns, and the little guns—
The guns, the Yankee guns!
Their voices gently blending,
Their song is never ending—
Glory! Glory! Glory!
To our God, and to our guns!

IV
The guns that growl and grumble,
The guns that roar and rumble;
The guns that are our heartbeats—
The guns, the Yankee guns!
And old, old song repeating—
The faith of us repeating
Glory! Glory! Glory!
To our God, and to our guns!

V
The types that tell the story
Sing: Glory! Glory! Glory!
They seem to be an echo of the guns—
The Yankee guns!
This is the song they're singing,
In mighty chorus swinging—
Glory! Glory! Glory!
To our God, and to our guns!

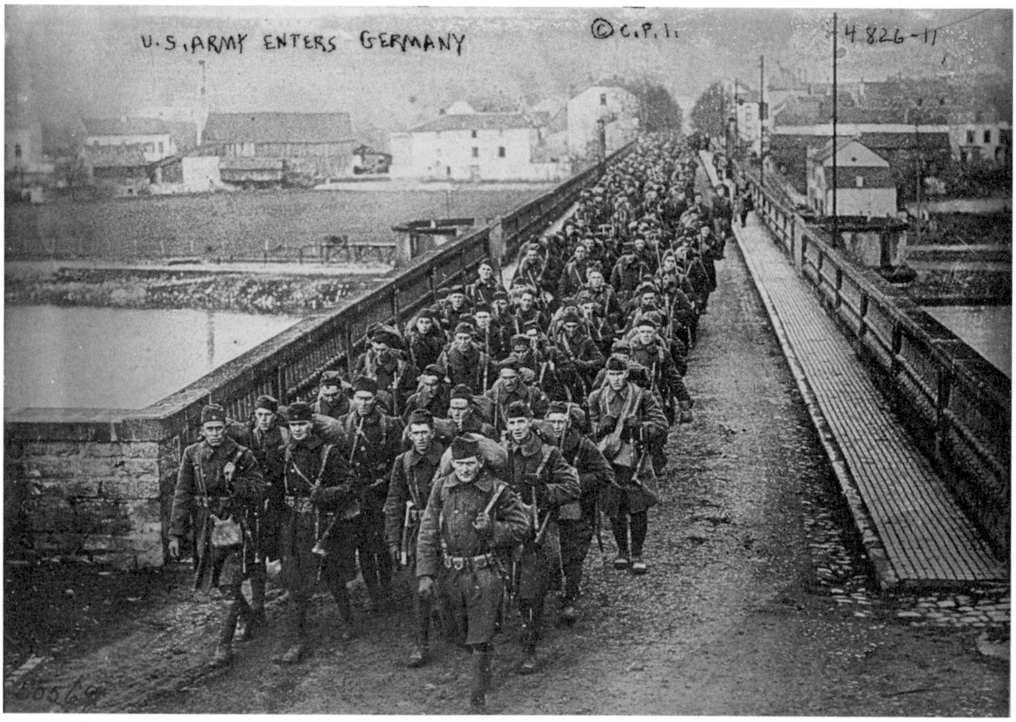

Gen. Dickman's soldiers crossing the Rhine.
Courtesy of Library of Congress

With Dickman to the Rhine

[January 6, 1919]

Yes, 'twas a wonderful trip, sir,
With wonderful sights to see;
Sights that I'll tell my kids about
When I take 'em upon my knee.

When I'm an old bird with whiskers
I'll lift up those kids of mine
And tell how I hiked with Dickman—
Old Joe Dickman—to the Rhine.

Many a thing I remember well,
Especially hearing someone yell:
"FALL OUT!"
"FALL IN!"
"FORWARD, MARCH!"

Scenery there was in plenty, sir, the like I never have seen;
Some of it struck me as brownish-like, and some of it mighty green.
Some of the roads were muddy, sir, and some of them pretty fine
As I hiked up with Dickman—old Joe Dickman—to the Rhine!

Went right through with all our hands,
And ran the army on three commands:
"FALL OUT!"
"FALL IN!"
"FORWARD, MARCH!"

We started from near Etain, sir, a most historic town–
It wasn't so very far from there our slum-gun busted down.
And we were short on eats, sir, from there on up the line,
When I hiked up with Dickman—old Joe Dickman—to the Rhine.

And the thing that I remember well
Was hearing our young captain yell:
"FALL OUT!"
"FALL IN!"
"FORWARD, MARCH!"

Yes, 'twas a long, hard trip, sir, as hard as I've ever found;
And often the seat of my pants, sir, sort o' dragging on the ground;
And sometimes I rather thought, sir, that it didn't seem quite so fine
To be hiking along with Dickman—old Joe Dickman—to the Rhine.

I wonder if old Joe's the bird
Who gave that war cry to the Third:
"FALL OUT!"
"FALL IN!"
"FORWARD, MARCH!"

Think of the things we saw, sir, and the history that we made,
Longwy? Why it was near there we struck a hell of a grade!
And there was a place in Athus that sold some pretty good wine,
As I hiked up with Dickman—old Joe Dickman—to the Rhine.

And what sticks in my memory
Is hearing someone yell at me:
"FALL OUT!"
"FALL IN!"
"FORWARD, MARCH!"

Remember the Moselle River? Well I should say I do.
'Twas there at Wasserbillig that I got a stone in my shoe.
And Trier? Why at Trier a fraulein was teaching me, "Yah and Nein,"
As I hiked up with Dickman—old Joe Dickman—to the Rhine.

And I was teaching her to say
The words that I heard every day:
"FALL OUT!"
"FALL IN!"
"FORWARD, MARCH!"

Castles? Well, yes some castles. The Boche was good at them arts;
But most of them all mussed up, sir, like castles get in these parts.
And many a roadside joint, sir, where I bought my beer in a stein
As I strike up with Dickman—old Joe Dickman—to the Rhine!

And the thing I never will forget
Was hearing as I hike and sweat:
"FALL OUT!"
"FALL IN!"
"FORWARD, MARCH!"

Yes, sir, I hiked with Dickman, sir, and I'll say I hiked far;
I say I hiked with Dickman, sir, though Dickman hiked by car—
No, sir, I never saw him, but I know he'll think it's fine
To hear that I was with him, sir—with Dickman to the Rhine!

And he'll be pleased to know that I
Will always recollect that cry:
"FALL OUT!"
"FALL IN!"
"FORWARD, MARCH!"

What the Shell Says

[January 12, 1919]

Cap'n say: You, Washington, you mine you pick en shubble;
'At shell she ain't uh-lukin' for no niggah pioneahs.
He tryin' to fine 'at gun back theah thass mekin him 'at trubble—
You wuk uh li'l fastah en doan lissen whut you heahs.
        But all uh time he talk
        Ah heah 'at ol' shell squawk:
You ain' un-goan back to
                Al-uh
                Bam
                Uh!

Cap'n mighty smaht man when hit come to buildin' bridges;
Cap'n he is quality in Bummenham—thass so!
Cap'n he know cullud folks en treats 'em mighty squidjuss,
But Cap'n doan' know shell talk lak u cullud pusson know;
        When dey come 'iss way
        He dons know 'at dey say:
You ain' un-goan back to
                Al-uh
                Bam
                Uh!

Boche he sen' nem airyplanes to fine out wheah ah'm wukkin—
Sneak eroun' away up high en show me to hes gun;
Gun he frows tin cans at me an gits mahs nuves to juhkin—
How dey spec ah'm evah goan to git 'iss railroad done
        When nem shells come heah
        En holleh in mah yeah:
You ain' un-goan back to
                Al-uh
                Bam
                Uh!

Cap'n say: You, Washington, 'at shell doan know you libbin'
Cap'n mighty nice man en he treats me good en fine—
Suttinly know hes bridges en hes railroad en hes cribbin'
But how he know whut dev-lishments am in a Boche shell's mine?
        How he know dey say,
        When dey come 'iss way:
You ain' un-goan back to
                Al-uh
                Bam
                Uh!

Doughboy Ditties

[1919]

At night, when we camped by the old chateau,
An' the yellow moon looked down,
I used to dream of a girl I know—
A girl in the old home town.
I dreamed o' the words she said to me
The day that we said good-bye,
When I left her to cross the rollin' sea—
But mostly I dreamed o' pie!

For there's girls in England and girls in France
And girls on the windin' Rhine;
You are always meetin' a lovin' glance
Anywheres up the line.
You can always sit in a game o' hearts
Where the ante's a gentle sigh,
But the scarcest thing in these foreign parts
Is a hunk o' reg'lar pie.

An' now that the packet is headed home
An' the lights fade on the shore,
As I watch the gloamin' begin to gloam,
I am dreamin' my dreams once more.
Again I dream o' that last good-bye
Ere I sailed o'er the rollin' brine,
But mostly I dream of the big mince pie
That soon will be mine—all mine.

There'll be always girls, if you look around,
Wherever your feet may stray;
Whether you're outward or homeward bound,
They'll never be far away.
But when you're guardin' a dreary post
Or watchin' the shrapnel fly,
The thing that you will miss the most
Is that good old home-made pie!

Here's the Twenty-Seventh

(Written for the Twenty-Seventh Division's paper, *Near Over*, printed on board the Transport *Leviathan*, at sea.)

[March 1919]

Here's the Twenty-Seventh, back from Over Yonder—
(Lady, with your lamp, we hope you're well!)
Meet the lads who did a chunk to make old Jerry ponder—
Last address the neighborhood of Somewhere-Close-to-Hell!
Here's the Twenty-Seventh—
The New York Twenty-Seventh!
With its memories of its battle deeds—and of its men who fell!

Here's the Twenty-Seventh, with its luggage in its lockers—
(Lady, with your light, how do you do?)
Albany and Utica, and Upstate Apple Knockers;
Brooklynites and Broadwayites, and of The Avenue.
Here's the Twenty-Seventh—
O'Ryan's Twenty-Seventh!
Drove against old Hindy's line, by God, and drove it through!

Here's the Twenty-Seventh, packs upon their shoulders—
(Lady, hear their line of British chaff!)
Ask the big Australian who's his pal among the soldiers—
Ask our neighbor, the Canuck, how Friend Yank stood the gaff!
Here's the Twenty-Seventh—
The New York Twenty-Seventh!
Hello, Lady, with the light—we want to hear you laugh!

Here's the Twenty-Seventh, back from 'cross the ocean—
(Lady, here is Tom and Joe and Dick!)
Meet the lads who did a heap to set the Boche in motion—
Busted right through Hindy's line and did it toot sweet—quick!
Here's the Twenty-Seventh—
And here's to the Twenty-Seventh!
Let 'em take the town apart to see what makes 'er tick!

Home Again

(On Board the United States Army Transport *Leviathan* with the Twenty-Seventh Division)

[March 1919]

There's a stir along the decks;
There's a light like Jerry's flare;
There's a line of craning necks—
"Won't be long until we're there!"
Someone's seen the far-off ground,
Faintly traced as by a pen,
And his heart begins to pound—
"Home again! Home again!"

Home again! Ah, God, how sweet
Down in his soul that rings!
Home again to the old home street,
And the old home things.
Don't ask him now of battles fought—
Of what he's seen and been;
Let him alone with just this thought:
"Home again!"

There's a mist before his eyes,
And it's not the ocean's foam.
From the starboard someone cries—
"Twenty-Seventh, yonder's home!"
Lord, he's heard it for a week
In the kicking of the screw;
In the old tub's every squeak—
"Home again and home to you!"

Home again! Ah, God, you know
What joy to him it means!
Home again to the old home glow,
And the old home scenes.
Home again to the old home walks;
The old home haunts and men;
Home again to the old home talks—
"Home again!"

There's a mist that makes him blink,
And it's not the salty spray;
Times there were he did not think
He would meet this blessed day.
"See it! See that light come on?
See that slowly widening streak?"
Lord, he's watched for it since dawn—
Lord, he's SMELT it for a week!

Home again! Ah, God, once more
To breathe the old home air.
Home to a familiar door—
And to the old home fare.
Ah, what recollections start,
What sweetest music when
He feels that thumping in his heart—
"HOME AGAIN!"

Endnotes

Preface

1. The *Fourth Estate*, February 15, 1919, 19.

Introduction

1. James Montague, "Rooting for Runyon," *Pittsburgh Post*, August 12, 1918, 6.
2. Phillip Knightley, *The First Casualty: The War Correspondent as Hero and Myth-Maker from Crimea to Iraq* (Baltimore: Johns Hopkins University Press, 2004), 134.
3. There is a great deal of confusion surrounding the date of birth and true age of Damon Runyon. Different biographies have different birth dates, and major reference works such as Bartlett's *Familiar Quotations* list incorrect years. The editors of this volume use October 3, 1880, since this was the date provided by Runyon himself both on his passport application from August 1918 and his draft registration from September 1918. The passport application includes a written statement from his family doctor in Kansas also confirming that date. Runyon may have been involved in misrepresenting his age; compare Jean Wagner, *Runyonese* (Paris: Stechert Hafner, 1965), 141, no. 1, on the controversy surrounding Runyon's proper age.
4. Edwin P. Hoyt, *A Gentleman of Broadway* (Boston: Little, Brown, 1964), 13.
5. Jimmy Breslin, *Damon Runyon* (New York: Ticknor & Fields, 1991), 43–44.
6. *Shamokin News-Dispatch*, March 13, 1941, 6.
7. Hoyt, *A Gentleman of Broadway*, 21; Kyle R. Ward, *In the Shadow of Glory: The Thirteenth Minnesota in the Spanish-American and Philippine-American Wars, 1898 to 1899* (St. Cloud, MN: North Star, 2000), 71.
8. Antona H. Richardson, ed., *Minnesotans in the Spanish-American War and the Philippine Insurrection* (St. Paul, MN: Paduan, 1998), 27, 48.
9. Ward, *In the Shadow of Glory*, 72.
10. *San Diego Evening Tribune*, January 17, 1917, 8.
11. *Canton Repository*, July 16, 1940, 4.
12. Wagner, *Runyonese*, 14, n. 142.
13. Breslin, *Damon Runyon*, 72–73; *Kansas City Times*, December 16, 1946, 18; *Berkshire Eagle*, December 17, 1946, 15.
14. *Denver Post*, February 18, 1914, 10.
15. Breslin's biography contains many specific details and lengthy dialogue from events Runyon is alleged to have observed or participated in. Some of the specifics of these events appear to be contradicted by other biographies or known fact. While referenced here, the editors feel Breslin's book should be used with care by future scholars. For an interesting review of the book, see "A Long-Winded Life of Damon Runyon" by Jack Shafer at www.ajrarchive.org.
16. Breslin, *Damon Runyon*, 171.
17. Ibid., 171–72.
18. Ibid., 174.
19. Hoyt, *A Gentleman of Broadway*, 141.
20. For a complete history of this famous episode, see Alan D. Gaff, *Blood in the Argonne: The "Lost Battalion" of World War I* (Norman: University of Oklahoma Press, 2005).
21. *Idaho State Journal*, May 30, 1968, 5; *Rockford Republic*, January 23, 1919; 3; *Harrisburg Evening News*, February 7, 1929, 24.
22. Hoyt, *A Gentleman of Broadway*, 146; *Kansas City Times*, December 16, 1946, 18.
23. Breslin, *Damon Runyon*, 180–81.
24. Hoyt, *A Gentleman of Broadway*, 149–50.
25. Ibid., 214–15.
26. "Our History" from www.damonrunyon.org.
27. Michael S. Sweeney, *The Military and the Press: An Uneasy Truce* (Evanston, IL: Northwestern University Press, 2006), 44–49; Knightley, *The First Casualty*, 131.
28. Knightley, *The First Casualty*, 133.
29. Thomas M. Johnson, *Without Censor* (Indianapolis, IN: Bobbs-Merrill, 1928), 293.
30. *Indiana Gazette*, February 22, 1943, 10.
31. *Delaware County Daily Times*, September 21, 1937, 3.
32. *El Paso Herald*, March 24, 1921, 3.
33. Knightley, *The First Casualty*, 138.
34. *Wichita Beacon*, October 10, 1918, 8.
35. *Brooklyn Daily Eagle*, January 12, 1919, III, 4.
36. *Olean Times Herald*, November 20, 1918, 8.
37. *Washington Herald*, December 1, 1918, 1.
38. *Canton Repository*, February 20, 1943, 6.
39. Sweeney, *The Military and the Press*, 52–59.
40. *Abilene Reporter-News*, December 21, 1946, 10.

41. *Oakland Tribune*, March 16, 1919, II, 40.

42. H. L. Mencken, *A Mencken Chrestomathy* (New York: Vintage Books, 1982), 592–96; H. L. Mencken, *Newspaper Days, 1899–1906* (New York: A. A. Knopf, 1941), 272–73, 265.

43. Breslin, *Damon Runyon*, 169–70.

44. Hoyt, *A Gentleman of Broadway*, 127.

45. Ibid., 128.

46. *Dallas Morning News*, January 3, 1934, 1.

47. *El Paso Herald*, August 31, 1918, II, 1.

48. Tom Clark, *The World of Damon Runyon* (New York: Harper & Row, 1978), 115.

49. Hoyt, *A Gentleman of Broadway*, 128, 141; Gaff, *Blood in the Argonne*, 120.

50. Clark Kinnaird, *A Treasury of Damon Runyon* (New York: Modern Library, 1958), xv.

51. *Lubbock Evening Journal*, December 20, 1949, II, 8.

52. *East Liverpool Evening Review*, December 10, 1940, 4.

53. Daniel R. Schwarz, *Broadway Boogie Woogie: Damon Runyon and the Making of New York City Culture* (New York: Palgrave Macmillan, 2003), 6.

54. Breslin, *Damon Runyon*, 60–61.

55. Patricia W. D'Itri, *Damon Runyon* (Boston: Twayne, 1982), 79.

56. Comparisons between Runyon's verse and that of Rudyard Kipling abound in contemporaneous sources. One example is a review of *Tents of Trouble* that reads "They elbow along—these verses—with a devil-may-care stride and an oath like one of Kipling's now and then." Another example refers to two recent poems published in *People's Magazine*: "They have become one of the features of *People's* and are making quite a hit, being compared by some people with Kipling's earlier work." A third review commented on "The Private Soldier": "Just as the barrack room ballads of Rudyard Kipling proclaimed the arrival of a spokesman for Tommy Atkins, so have the verses of Alfred Damon Runyon on American army post life proclaimed the spokesman of our own private soldier." *Denver Rocky Mountain News*, May 29, 1911, 6; *San Diego Evening Tribune*, April 15, 1908, 4; *Seattle Daily Times*, September 26, 1907, 6.

57. D'Itri, *Damon Runyon*, 79.

58. Ibid., 80.

59. Ibid., 85.

Reportage

1. Born in Muskau, Saxony, Karl Bruno Julius von Mudra joined the Prussian army in 1870. His early career was spent in the engineers, and he became chief of that department in 1911, embracing the newest technology relating to the attack and defense of fortifications. He was advanced to the nobility and was elevated to general of infantry and command of the XVI Army Corps in 1913. Von Mudra led his corps during the 1914 invasion of France and soon became recognized as one of the most able of the German generals. He became commander of the 8th Army in 1916, and the 1st Army in 1918. Although strongly in favor of continuing the war, von Mudra retired and died in 1931. David T. Zabecki, *Germany at War: 400 Years of Military History* (Santa Barbara, CA: ABC-CLIO, 2014), 2: 890.

2. The city of Rheims (now Reims) had always been a point of interest to Americans following the US entry into the war. William T. Fowler, president of Reed College and a member of the Red Cross mission to France, wrote of the famous cathedral on September 6, 1917: "Directly behind us, in the midst of a devastated city, was the sublimest and most tragic of all the ruins I have seen—the Rheims cathedral. It will stand there perhaps for centuries—a monument to German stupidity. It represents their attempt to kill a God with guns—their failure to understand how the spirit can triumph over crushed stone." *Oregon Journal*, October 7, 1917, 1, 10.

3. After graduating from Williams College, Charles White Whittlesey went on to Harvard and received a law degree in 1908. He left his New York City law practice to be among the first men accepted at the Plattsburgh Training Camp and joined the 308th Infantry at Camp Upton. Whittlesey went to France as a captain but had been promoted to major by the time of this incident described by Runyon. Following the relief of Whittlesey's cutoff command, he was promoted to lieutenant colonel and awarded the Medal of Honor. Whittlesey resumed his law practice but never adapted to civilian life. One of his law partners said, "The disabled, the jobless, the friendless, the widows of the war—all of them were on his mind constantly." Tormented by his wartime experiences and constant postwar reminders of what he and his men had endured, at the age of thirty-seven Charles Whittlesey committed suicide by stepping overboard from a steamer bound for Havana in 1921. *New York Tribune*, November 29, 1921, 1, 4; *New York Times*, November 29, 1921, 1, 4.

4. The Hudson Dusters were a gang of New York criminals whose headquarters was located on Hudson Street. The gang members seemed more enthusiastic than efficient. In June 1917, one group of Dusters bumped into another rival faction of Dusters on Carmine Street. Guns were drawn by both sides and some fifty shots were exchanged, leaving crowded Carmine Street "a screeching inferno." Four persons were wounded—all of them innocent bystanders. The Dusters were obviously in need of target practice. *New York Tribune*, June 24, 1917, 16.

5. The Gopher Gang was a New York group of street thugs from the Hell's Kitchen area of the city. When a group of these criminals were drafted and sent to training at Camp Upton, they carried a banner that read:

Hell's Kitchen.
What's the use?
We're out to cook
The Kaiser's goose.

What the men said in private was probably a little less elegant. Army life did have a positive impact on a low-level Gopher named Mickey Bell. He previously walked the streets carrying a blackjack but had been converted to carrying a New Testament while in the army. *New York Tribune*, September 21, 1917, 5; October 21, 1917, 8.

6. Yaphank was a small village on Long Island, near which would be constructed Camp Upton, a training camp for draftees from New York City and the surrounding area. The site "was known to the Indians as Wampmissick and to the farmers of the neighborhood as Crow's Nest." All men and supplies would be shipped by rail through Yaphank Station, "typical of the old tumble-down stations featured in vaudeville and novels." One newsman reported that the sixty-mile trip from New York City took "generally about two hours and a half, depending on the disposition of the wheezy, superannuated engine that slides along over flat land and through pine barrens." The 77th Division would be organized at Camp Upton. *New York Tribune*, July 9, 1917, 5.

7. Following the *Lusitania* disaster in 1915, a group of civilians, fearing future involvement in the European war, formed a reserve officers training camp at Plattsburgh, New York (the "h" in Plattsburgh was generally dropped when referencing the military camp). Candidates ranged from college age to men in their thirties, all receiving instruction in weapons and tactics. By the summer of 1916, some 40,000 candidates had finished a course in basic military training, most of whom served as officers during the war. Anne C. Venzon, ed., *The United States in the First World War* (New York: Garland, 1995), 464, 470.

8. George Gibson McMurtry Jr. was the son of George Gibson McMurtry Sr., who had founded the town of Vandergrift, Pennsylvania, and was influential in the steel business. The younger McMurtry was a Harvard student at the outbreak of the Spanish-American War but left his books to join the 1st United States Volunteer Cavalry, renowned in history as "the Rough Riders." McMurtry returned to New York, where he became a successful Wall Street broker before heading off to the Plattsburg Training Camp, emerging as a first lieutenant in the 308th Infantry. Following the war, McMurtry resumed his financial career and became the driving force behind the Lost Battalion Survivors Association, paying all the expenses for the yearly meetings until his death in 1958 at the age of eighty-two. *Pittsburgh Post-Gazette*, August 7, 1915, 8; *New York Tribune*, May 2, 1917, 4; L. Wardlaw Miles, *History of the 308th Infantry, 1917–1919* (New York: G. P. Putnam's Sons, 1927),140–41; *New York Times*, November 24, 1958, 1; Gaff, *Blood in the Argonne*, 291.

9. Pvt. Lowell R. Hollingshead of the 308th Infantry.

10. Another observer made a similar assessment: "The patch would baffle a rabbit, and the machine-guns are strewn through the woods like snakes in the grass, but somehow the infantry have pushed and fought and cut and chopped their way through." Alexander Woollcott, *The Command Is Forward: Tales of the AEF Battlefields as They Appeared in the* Stars and Stripes (New York: Century, 1919), 115.

11. Runyon's observation was confirmed by Alexander Woollcott, who wrote later: "Among the men who came alive out of that ravine was visible a fraternity that had not, and could not have, existed when they went in, the brotherhood of the besieged. Approach any one of them to-day and their first and last word on their experience is always a word in devoted praise of 'our major,' the officer around whom they rallied and whose steady, dauntless spirit saw them through." Maj. Whittlesey felt the same about the soldiers under his command, praising their stamina "in wonder and admiration." Woollcott, *Command Is Forward*, 128–29.

12. A graduate of Hamilton College in 1909, Woollcott became a reporter for the *New York Times*, one of his first assignments being to rewrite a story on the sinking of the *Titanic*. He eventually became a drama critic for a number of New York newspapers, in addition to dabbling in such careers as "actor, playwright, author, raconteur, and radio commentator." One Brooklyn paper said of his clout: "Woollcott was famous as an acid critic and a sharp-tongued raconteur, whose indorsement of a literary work virtually assured its success." Attempts to join the army and navy failed because of his flat feet and astigmatism, so Woollcott joined the medical department before taking up his pen for *Stars and Stripes*. One friend joked that this transfer saved countless doughboy lives, but, in fact, "the work that Woollcott did as a front-line correspondent is among the best in the wide range of American reporting." After the war he resumed his newspaper position and became a member of the famed Algonquin Round Table. His apartment, at the end of a street overlooking the East River, was the scene of famous breakfast parties for the literati of New York, leading Dorothy Parker to refer to it as "Wit's End." Woollcott died January 23, 1943 at the age of fifty-six. *Brooklyn Daily Eagle*, January 25, 1943, 7; *Boston Herald*, January 24, 1943, 1; *Syracuse Post-Standard*, July 8, 1951, 28; *Cleveland Plain Dealer*, January 25, 1943, 8.

13. Homer Alvan Rodeheaver was educated at Ohio Wesleyan University but did not graduate. Before the war, Rodeheaver began playing trombone with musical groups. In 1910, he began a two-decade association with Billy Sunday, the popular American evangelist. Described as a "consummate entertainer," Rodeheaver blended gospel music with popular tunes of the day but also added magic tricks, jokes, and humorous stories to his stage performances. By the time he parted ways with Billy Sunday, the well-known trombonist had created his own publishing house, which promoted gospel music to counter the evils of jazz. During World War II, he returned to Europe as a representative of the YMCA. After a successful business career, Homer Rodeheaver died in 1955. W. K. McNeil, *Encyclopedia of American Gospel Music* (New York: Routledge, 2005), 320–22.

14. William Ashley "Billy" Sunday had a major-league baseball career with the Chicago White Stockings, Pittsburgh Alleghenies, and Philadelphia Phillies that stretched from 1883 to 1890. He was a weak hitter but a terror on the base paths, although Sunday "had a hard time getting to first often enough to make his speed count." He later became the country's most famous evangelist; his trademark would be removing his coat and vest before starting his sermons with a baseball windup. One wartime sports writer compared Billy Sunday's enthusiastic evangelism to a boxing match with the devil: "Sunday uses the same style of leaping, jumping, erratic attack, swinging from all angles, ever boring in for more punishment, ducking, dodging, and side-stepping, and bouncing off the

ropes on one side across the ring to the other." Billy Sunday, "the man who saved a million souls," died in 1935 at age seventy-two. *Washington Evening Star*, November 7, 1935, 1, 11; *Washington Times*, January 11, 1918, 6.

15. Noted promoter of all things sports, from motorcycle racing to boxing, the war found William H. Wellman a sergeant in the 52nd Pioneer Infantry. Bill's stint in officers' training school did not result in a commission, only a diploma that stated he was eligible for promotion if a vacancy should occur. Not one to miss an opportunity, Wellman wrote in February 1919, "I am going to try to develop a boxing champion in the AEF." He had started his career by building the Brighton Beach Velodrome at the age of sixteen, followed shortly thereafter by managing the Sheepshead Bay Speedway. At the age of nineteen he leased Madison Square Garden for one year. He later moved on to auto and airplane racing, theatrical ventures, and oil drilling. *New York Tribune*, January 5, 1919, II, 6; *Charleston Evening Post*, February 21, 1919, 3; *Richmond Times-Dispatch*, October 25, 1931, II, 4.

16. Born in Hong Kong, Reginald Love Foster worked for the *New York Sun* and *World* before graduating from Yale in 1891. He rose through the ranks of the 12th Regiment, New York National Guard, and led it to France as a colonel when it was redesignated the 52nd Pioneer Regiment. Foster would later offer a synopsis of his regiment's service: "We escaped with marvelously few casualties. We were just behind the front lines and all the German misses got us, and there were many misses. We rebuilt bridges, made and mended roads and salvaged material thrown away or lost by the doughboys." Commissioned major in the Regular Army in 1920, Foster retired in 1932 and died at the age of seventy in 1940. *New York Sun*, April 14, 1919, 7; *Washington Evening Star*, June 13, 1940, 7; *San Francisco Chronicle*, June 15, 1940, 9.

17. A singing and dancing star in vaudeville from 1906 to 1920, Elizabeth Brice, born Bessie Shaler, had a starring role in the Ziegfeld Follies of 1913. One audience member wrote that "the roof threatens to come off the theatre when Elizabeth Brice comes dancing to the footlights, swinging her shoulders and putting all the pep in the world into her old songs." She sang "Buzz Around, Buzz Around" and "Come Let's Settle Down" until the doughboys "fairly split with their whistling." After the war, Brice teamed up with Will Morrissey to re-create their show under the name "The Overseas Review." Hundreds of veterans thronged these performances to show their affection and appreciation with bouquets of flowers. Her career eventually faded and she died in 1965. *New York Times*, January 26, 1965, 1; *Oregon Journal*, November 24, 1918, III, 4.

18. Margaret Mayo, born Lillian Slatten, was a Broadway actress known for her comedic ingénue roles around the turn of the twentieth century. She then became a playwright, her first big hit being "Polly of the Circus" in 1907. Her theatrical troupe, dubbed the Mayo Shock Unit, spent seven months in France, "playing with the boys applauding from the trees, playing in the rain and fog and the mud till they have no voices left." Mayo's Shock Unit played in any venue available, from a battered old theater to "a stranded truck, with a dressing room made out of a piece of tarpaulin." Her Broadway hits allowed Mayo to retire after the war with a fortune estimated at $2,000,000, although she was reported to have lost most of her wealth in the stock market crash of 1929. She died in 1951 at the age of sixty-seven. *Washington Evening Star*, February 26, 1951, 12; *Oregon Journal*, November 24, 1918, III, 4; *New York Evening World*, March 29, 1919, 6.

19. Thomas J. Gray came from an impoverished background, but by the age of twenty he advertised in *Variety* that "I have written for some of the lead people in the business and still have many original ideas left for Sketches, Acts, Monologues, Burlesques, etc." Among other stars, he provided lyrics for Mae West that "added to her naughty persona." After a brief stint as an actor, Gray continued to write musical numbers until 1917, when he began writing for movies. After the war he wrote a production called *The League of Notions*, which was performed in London. In 1921, he joined the staff of Buster Keaton and for the next three years was associated with that comic, as well as Charles Chaplin and Harold Lloyd, in writing movie comedies. Gray died in 1924. *Variety*, February 8, 1908, 25; *Boston Herald*, December 1, 1924, 5; Lisle Foote, *Buster Keaton's Crew: The Team behind His Silent Films* (Jefferson, NC: McFarland, 2014), 152–55.

20. Will Morrissey (William James Morrissey) died penniless in 1957 at the age of sixty-nine. The cigar-chomping comedian became a Broadway producer during the Depression but always seemed to operate on a shoestring budget and occasionally starred in his own productions. He once admitted, "I can't find another actor as talented and low-priced as I am." When called as a witness in a dispute between Milton Berle and his agent and asked how much he had paid the entertainer, Morrissey responded, "Evidently you know nothing about show business or you'd know that Morrissey never paid anybody." On another occasion the Marx Brothers appeared in one of his shows, but the brothers never appeared together on stage. It was rumored that one of them had to keep an eye on Morrissey and the box office receipts. Although associated with some of American's biggest stars, he continued to produce flop after flop, one obituary being so unkind as to note that he "produced more flop shows than Rogers and Hammerstein produced hits." *Long Beach Independent*, December 28, 1957, II, 6; *Bakersfield Californian*, December 19, 1957, 37.

21. One observer noted of these productions, "All the old hokum, jasbo and gravy known to vaudeville can be found in the show. It is easy to take the old jokes and dress them up in O.D. If you want to make fun of someone, call him a second lieutenant." In one skit Will Morrissey talked about having given shows for the doughboys in Italy. Margaret Mayo then asked innocently, "Ah! And when you were in Italy, did you touch Florence?" Amid the laughter and whistles, Morrissey said that he had not, "But it's a good idea!" Morrissey would then tell a story about a Frenchman who leaned a ladder in a corridor of a fashionable Paris hotel so that he could peak through the transom into a lady's room for over two hours. Appearing to be scandalized, Margaret Mayo would remark that she thought Frenchmen were always polite. Morrissey would respond: "Well, this fellow wasn't. Why, he stayed there all that time, and there were eighteen second lieutenants waiting at the foot of the ladder." Pandemonium would erupt. The shows were just like vaudeville back home except for the lack of peanuts. *Oregon Journal*, November 24, 1918, 34.

22. Hank Gowdy came up to the National League as a first baseman and outfielder through the Texas League. His first stop was with the New York Giants, where John McGraw converted the gangling Gowdy into a catcher before trading him to the Boston Braves. Gowdy, whose most-profane comments were "Gee Whiz" and "By Golly," became the hero of the 1914 World Series when he hit one home run, one triple, three doubles, and one single in eleven at bats. He was the first major-league player to enlist, joining the 166th Infantry and becoming a sergeant. After the war he returned to baseball and played until 1930, after which he coached for the Braves, Giants, and Cincinnati Reds through the 1948 season. "Sergeant Hank," as he was affectionately called, served as a captain in World War II and then worked with the Columbus Jets of the International League as director of youth activity. He died in 1966 at the age of seventy-six. *Washington Evening Star*, August 2, 1966, 12; *Boston Herald*, August 2, 1966, 25.

23. Christy Mathewson, known to baseball fans as "Matty" and "Big Six," was a Hall of Fame pitcher with seventeen years on the New York Giants roster. Prior to the war he served three years as manager of the Cincinnati Reds. Commissioned captain in the Chemical Weapons Service in 1918, Mathewson was assigned to the 28th Division. While in France he wrote that baseball would never be popular there, since French soldiers considered the game "too rough." He elaborated: "They are more afraid of a hard hit grounder or a liner than they are of a German shell. Their infield work is bad. They can run bases all right, but have little opportunity because they cannot bat. The thing which the French players cannot do is to stand up close behind the batsman and catch. Nothing can persuade them to stand up and get them right under the bat like our catchers do. They want to retreat about ten yards and catch the ball." Mathewson developed a serious lung disease as a result of being accidentally gassed during training, and died as a result in 1925 at the age of forty-five. *Brooklyn Daily Eagle*, October 22, 1918, II, 2; October 8, 1925, 18; *New York Times*, February 18, 1919, 12.

24. Harry H. Niemeyer had served in the 1st Light Battery of Missouri Volunteers in the Puerto Rico campaign of 1898. His service overlapped employment as a feature writer for the *St. Louis Post-Dispatch*, where he had written columns under the name "Nie." Niemeyer was employed in the drama department of the *New York Times*, where he was an assistant to Alexander Woollcott. He unsuccessfully attempted to enlist for overseas duty and settled on working in France for the YMCA. Niemeyer moved to Hollywood in 1934, where he worked in the motion picture industry until his death in 1940 at the age of sixty-three. Harry Niemeyer was credited with saying, "Never put off until tomorrow what you can put off until the day after tomorrow." *New York Times*, July 28, 1940, 30; *Franklin News-Herald*, November 30, 1940, 4; *Macon Telegraph*, August 2, 1940, 4.

25. A graduate of Indiana University, Scott was a bestselling author of mystery and underworld stories. With a background in publishing articles for a variety of newspapers and magazines, he made a seamless transition to novels, writing under the name Leroy Smith. His big break came in 1914 with the publication of *13, Washington Square*, which became a motion picture the following year under the new title of *33, Washington Square*. One reviewer, who could have made the same comments about Damon Runyon's future writing, said: "Every phase and craze of night life in New York is shown. There are crooks of amazing ilk, men whom one might elbow any hour in the corridors of many hotels." Leroy Scott drowned in 1929 at the age of fifty-four while swimming in Chateaugay Lake in Upstate New York. *Brooklyn Daily Eagle*, July 22, 1929, 5; *San Bernardino County Sun*, July 23, 1929, II, 1; *New York Times Book Review*, May 3, 1918, 88.

26. Born and educated in England, Herman Whitaker served in the Duke of Wellington's (West Riding) Regiment from 1883 to 1886 before he came to America as an employee of the Hudson Bay Company. Immigrating to California in 1895, he knocked around at a series of menial jobs and became friends with Jack London. Whitaker acted as a correspondent covering Pancho Villa's rebellion, then switched sides to cover Pershing's expedition to capture Villa. Gen. Pershing recommended him to cover the world war for the *Oakland Tribune*. Although recently released after being gassed at the front, Whitaker went right back to work: "On the morning the armistice was signed the regiment I was with was ordered to take hill No. 319, and I decided to go with them. I was armed only with a camera and I was obliged to take a cane owing to trouble with my leg." Suffering from what he thought was appendicitis, Whitaker sailed for America. In New York he was diagnosed with an intestinal infection, but an operation failed and he died in 1919 at the age of fifty-two. *Oakland Tribune*, November 14, 1918, 4; January 20, 1919, 1; *Oregon Journal*, November 23, 1918, 1.

27. Author of *Rich Man, Poor Man*, Maximilian Foster went to France as a correspondent for the *Saturday Evening Post*. Foster seemed to be "a slave to the map habit," or, as Sgt. Alexander Woollcott put it, "going over the top—ography." When the American Peace Mission arrived following the armistice, Joseph C. Crew was placed in charge of official transmissions to the United States, with Maximilian Foster as his assistant. Following his return to New York, Foster resumed his writing career with the *Saturday Evening Post* and various New York newspapers, in addition to work on several movie scripts. He died in 1943 at the age of seventy-one. *Washington Post*, December 17, 1918, 2; *New York Tribune*, January 21, 1919, 8; *Washington Evening Star*, September 22, 1943, 4.

28. Henry Grantland Rice graduated from Vanderbilt University in 1901 after playing baseball, basketball, and football (in order of ability). Following a series of sports-reporting jobs, he settled in New York, where he worked for the *Evening Mail* from 1911 to 1914 and then with the *Tribune*. He enlisted as a private in the 115th Artillery but rose through the ranks to become a first lieutenant and wrote for *Stars and Stripes*. Following the war, Rice, affectionately known as "Granny," became the preeminent sports writer in the country. His pen immortalized sports greats: Walter Johnson became "Big Train," Red Grange became "the Galloping Ghost," Christy Mathewson became "Big Six," and the Notre Dame 1924 backfield became "the Four Horsemen." Beloved by everyone who met him, Grantland Rice died in 1954 at the age of seventy-three. A friend said of him, "Much of our gold is hidden at Fort Knox, but the greater part of it lies buried at Woodlawn under a stone marked 'Grantland Rice.'" *Washington Evening Star*, July 14, 1954, III, 1, 3; *Brooklyn Daily Eagle*, November 3, 1954, 20.

29. Twenty years later, Runyon would write a column on cooties, recalling that the doughboys also referred to them as seam-wolves, shirt-rabbits, and lining-squirrels. He humorously wrote of his first encounter with these pests during the Spanish-American War: "In our own experience as a soldier we recollect a seam-wolf at Camp Merritt in San Francisco that was as big as a Jersey yearling and very tame. We called her Esther. Esther was real cute, but she developed kleptomania. She was found stealing cans of sardines from the commissary and we were ordered to get rid of her." *Canton Repository*, November 3, 1939, 4.

30. A Tennessean whose great-grandfather had served under Gen. Andrew Jackson, Luke Lea was appointed to the US Senate in 1911 by the state legislature but was defeated in the ensuing election. Six feet three inches tall, the towering Lea was appointed colonel of the 114th Field Artillery and served through the war. Following the armistice, Col. Lea led a small group of army officers, including future major-league baseball executive Larry MacPhail, in a "sort-of-authorized" attempt to kidnap the Kaiser from his estate in Holland. This plan to capture the German leader and take him to Paris for trial as a war criminal failed when Dutch police arrived. Holland protested this military invasion of a neutral country, but Gen. Pershing did nothing more than confine the Americans to base for a month. Described as "brilliant and colorful," Lea later became a powerful editor and financier but in the 1930s lost his newspaper interests and was jailed for conspiracy and bank fraud. Following his parole and eventual pardon, Lea retired and died in 1945 at the age of sixty-six. *Washington Evening Star*, November 19, 1945, 2; *Washington Times*, April 1, 1919, 1.

31. Newspaperman, playwright, and author, William H. "Will" Irwin grew up in San Francisco and graduated from Stanford University in 1899. After working for several San Francisco newspapers, Irwin joined the staff of the *New York Sun*. Following the 1906 earthquake, Irwin covered the story from his New York desk, combining his intimate knowledge of San Francisco with sketchy news reports from California. His amazingly accurate stories, although entirely faked from across the country, secured his fame as a reporter. He later joined *McClure's Magazine* and *Collier's* before becoming a freelance writer. In 1942, he published an autobiography titled *The Making of a Reporter*. Will Irwin died in 1948 at the age of seventy-four. *Brooklyn Daily Eagle*, February 25, 1948, 13.

32. Annette Kellerman, known as "the Million Dollar Mermaid," was a world-class swimmer and actress. Born in Australia in 1887, Kellerman performed in Aussie aquatic shows in tanks full of fish and eels. In 1907, she appeared on Revere Beach in Boston "in a brief one-piece swimsuit without the cumbersome skirt expected of women swimmers." Police charged her with indecent exposure and ran her off the beach. Esther Williams starred as Annette Kellerman in the aptly titled movie *The Million Dollar Mermaid*. She eventually returned to Australia and died in 1975 at the age of eighty-eight. *Boston Herald American*, November 6, 1975, 52.

33. Mules and cussing had a strange, symbiotic relationship in the American army. During World War II, Damon Runyon stated emphatically that "there are no new words in army cussology" and "the army's lexicon of cuss words has shrunk with the passing of the mule of the old army." He explained: "The mule was a great inspiration to new cuss words. Army mule skinners did not have to sit around thinking up the words—they would come to their lips unbidden when they were arguing with the mules. With few mules in the army nowadays, the cuss words a soldier can apply to a mule are useless, unless, of course, he wants to apply them (under his breath) to a general." *Idaho Statesman*, April 13, 1943, 4.

34. This regiment was the 3rd Grenadier Guards (Queen Elizabeth's).

35. The famous Knickerbocker Hotel, located at Broadway and 42nd Street in New York City, added to its exclusivity on June 5, 1918, when it opened Armenonville, billed as "New York's Smartest Restaurant." *New York Times*, June 5, 1918, 5.

36. By May 1919, waiters had lost their respected position in German society. A nationwide strike resulted in legislation imposing a 20 percent tax on hotel and restaurant bills in lieu of tipping. This so-called *zu-schlag* tax ruined the image of waiters, "who overnight changed from attentive, tip-seducing individuals, to bolsheviks in the business who cared not whether or not guests were satisfied." *Trenton Evening Times*, May 11, 1919, 10.

37. This observation was shared by Col. von Steibel, chief of staff of the German 27th Division, who told one American correspondent, "The Americans were too reckless, in too much of a hurry to get things done." The colonel, however, gave an example that this haste eventually worked to the Americans' advantage: "For instance, in attacking our machine guns—which are the best in the world—they utilized no scientific means. It seemed to us that the only way they knew to eliminate a machine gun nest was to keep coming until they got it. That was rather discouraging to the morale of our gunners. They knew that if they stayed long they would be killed or captured." *Springfield Daily News*, December 16, 1918, II, 5.

38. Following his graduation from Harvard in 1898, Albert A. Boyden joined *McClure's Magazine* and became its managing editor from 1903 to 1906. In that year he became managing editor of the newly established *American Magazine* and continued in that position until 1917, when he resigned to join the YMCA in France. After the war he served with the Red Cross in Poland and acted as secretary to the American Reparations Committee in Vienna. Boyden had been sick ever since the war and died of what was termed "pernicious anæmia" in 1925 at the age of fifty. *Washington Evening Star*, May 3, 1925, I, 26.

39. Initial peace overtures by the German government were greeted with derision in the New York press, which offered the public a journalistic interpretation of the offer: "We, Wilhelm II, by the Grace of God, King of Prussia and German Emperor, wishing to get away with the booty we have stolen from Belgium, France, Russia, Italy, Serbia, and Rumania, and wishing to escape punishment for the crimes we have perpetrated on the Sea, on Land and in the Air, and wishing to reorganize our armies for new and more terrible attacks upon the liberties of mankind do hereby proclaim to all the World that we are ready to TALK peace—but only to talk, in order that the free peoples of the World in alliance against us may be tricked into slackening their war efforts and quarreling amongst themselves." *New York Times*, October 9, 1918, 8; *Brooklyn Daily Eagle*, October 9, 1918, II, 5.

40. Grover Cleveland Alexander was at the peak of his pitching career prior to becoming a sergeant in the 352nd Field Artillery. He won ninety-five games for the Philadelphia Phillies during the 1915, 1916, and 1917 seasons. Despite the war, Alexander's thoughts always turned to baseball. At one point he confessed to Junius Wood, "A man can't play baseball all his life, and I wish I could get back in the game while I have the stuff in me." Sgt. Alexander was in charge of firing one of the company guns on the day the armistice went into effect. He returned to the National League after his wartime service, and his greatest day came during the 1926 World Series. Alexander had won the sixth game, which tied the Series with the New York Yankees. Some claim that the following day he was drunk as a skunk from partying, while others say he was ready to go again if necessary. With the Yankees trailing 3–2 in the seventh inning but with the bases loaded and two outs, Alexander was unexpectedly called in to pitch. He calmly struck out Tony Lazzeri, and the St. Louis Cardinals cruised to victory. He would later admit "that was just about the biggest kick of my career." Elected into the Baseball Hall of Fame in 1938, "Old Pete" retired to Nebraska and died in 1950. *Omaha World Herald*, March 3, 1919, 8; November 5, 1950, II, 3; *Canton Repository*, November 10, 1950, 35.

41. Spring 3100 was the telephone number of the New York City Police Department. *New York Times*, February 7, 1918, 12.

42. A graduate of Vanderbilt University in 1906, where he excelled at football, Innis White Brown was working as a sports editor for the *Atlanta Journal* when he journeyed east in 1916 to join the staff of the *New York Sun*. In the summer of 1917, he went through the Plattsburg camp and emerged as a first lieutenant. Brown went overseas as a captain in the 114th Field Artillery in the 30th Division and was wounded by shell splinters on October 2 while on an observation post. Upon returning home, he became an acknowledged authority on the rules of golf, although neither an instructor nor champion golfer. As editor of the *American Golfer*, Brown was said to be "the most sapient rule-addict in America." He continued his successful sports writing career and died in 1961. William J. Bacon, ed., *History of the Fifty-Fifth Field Artillery Brigade* (Nashville: Benson, 1920), 199, 229; *Atlanta Constitution*, April 14, 1916, 13; *New York Sun*, June 26, 1918, 3; *Columbus Ledger*, March 31, 1919, 6; New York State Adjutant's General's Office, Abstracts of World War I Military Service, 1917–1919 (Albany: New York State Archives); US NARA, Record Group 92, Records of the Office of the Quartermaster General, 1774–1985, Interment Control Forms, 1928–1962.

43. Frank Cavanaugh's football career began at Dartmouth, where he was an All-American end. He became a successful coach at the University of Cincinnati, Holy Cross, and Dartmouth prior to his enlistment in the 102nd Field Artillery, despite leaving a wife and six children at home. Commissioned a lieutenant, captain, and then major after Chateau Thierry, Cavanaugh was seriously wounded in the head and face by shrapnel during the last month of the war. The fact that he picked pieces of shrapnel from his wounds while en route to a hospital contributed to his new nickname, "The Iron Major." After the war he coached football at Boston College and Fordham, elevating both schools to national prominence. Maj. Cavanaugh died in 1933 at the age of fifty-seven. A movie about his life, suitably titled *The Iron Major*, starred the actor Pat O'Brien when it was released in 1943. *Bridgeport Telegram*, November 30, 1918, 23; *Salt Lake Tribune*, August 30, 1933, 15; *Harrisburg Telegraph*, August 30, 1933, 2; *Washington Evening Star*, December 17, 1943, II, 18.

44. An All-American fullback with the Harvard football team in 1909, Wayland M. Minot graduated in 1911 and entered the investment business. During the war he served as a captain in the 102nd Field Artillery, coming home as a major and adjutant of the 51st Artillery Brigade. He resumed his career as a Boston investment banker but remained in the Army Reserve and retired as a lieutenant colonel in 1932. Wayland Minot died in 1957 at the age of sixty-seven. Harry A. Benwell, *History of the Yankee Division* (Boston: Cornhill, 1919), 237, 267; *Boston Herald*, November 21, 1957, 43; *Boston Traveler*, November 21, 1957, 47.

45. Thomas Woodrow Wilson graduated from Princeton in 1879, attempted a career in law, but returned to Johns Hopkins University to study history and political science. He received a doctorate degree in 1886 and taught at Wesleyan University and Princeton prior to becoming president of the latter institution. Wilson campaigned as a reformer and was elected governor of New Jersey in 1910 on the Democratic ticket, using that office as a springboard to the presidency of the United States in 1912. He patiently kept the United States out of the European war and was reelected in 1916 but was forced to enter the war a year later in response to German unrestricted submarine attacks on merchant shipping. As Germany began to lose the war in 1918, its government sought to negotiate a peace on the basis of Wilson's Fourteen Points speech. President Wilson personally participated in the peace conference of 1919, where he led the push to create a League of Nations. Although he had compromised during peace talks in Paris, he refused to compromise with politicians at home, leading to defeat of the League of Nations in the US Senate. President Wilson suffered a stroke in September 1919 and never fully recovered prior to his death in 1924 at the age of sixty-seven. *Dictionary of American Biography* (New York: Charles Scribner's Sons, 1936), 20:352–67; *Washington Evening Star*, February 4, 1924, 1–2, 4.

46. While speculating that the origin of the term "doughboy" probably was post–Civil War, Runyon admitted, "I like the tribute to the American infantryman from General Douglas MacArthur, a great soldier who is fond of the sound of words and knows how to marshal them more impressively than any of our fighting chiefs since Ulysses S. Grant." MacArthur said of the World War I soldiers: "From time immemorial the victor in war has been symbolized by the foot soldier, he, who with a steel weapon in his hand, challenges his enemy to have and to hold a square yard of mud-covered ground. He is affectionately called in our army the 'doughboy.' He passed on in anonymity, except for his loved ones, but for those of us who know, we revere and bless the name of 'doughboy.'" *Canton Repository*, October 31, 1942, 6.

47. Chaplain M. A. Bennett, from Philadelphia, had a unique perspective of the Argonne fighting that he shared with the readers in Pennsylvania: "If the people at home could only see what I have seen; if they could only see

the pluck and patience of the patriotism of these boys, wet and cold, they would never complain of hardships. They fight and die like Americans and always will. It made me so proud just to see them that I had no thought of discomforts or danger. It was great to be with them." *East Liverpool Evening Review*, October 24, 1918, 7.

48. Correspondent Edwin James also complained about the "mud and rain—everlasting rain" in the Argonne Forest. He offered a few details: "I spent four hours today in that big woods and saw some things our boys are facing. Caked with mud, wet to the skin and cold they had dispositions which were a little ragged in places, but generally they bore up well. One big lad said: 'Well, I guess he (the enemy) is as wet as I am, and that helps some.'" *New York Times*, October 2, 1918, 2.

49. Correspondent Bert Ford put French mud into perspective for the civilians: "It was worse than the rats. It was worse than the itch. It was hell—that battle mud of Europe—and every man who crawled through it and fought, ate and slept in it and who drove a courier's cycle or a motor car or truck, every runner and mule-skinner will bear out what I say." Ford concluded, "It was the curse of the war—MUD, MUD, MUD." Bert Ford, *The Fighting Yankees Overseas* (Boston: Norman E. McPhail, 1919), 58.

50. A native of Franklin, Massachusetts, Edward Grant graduated from Harvard in 1905. Among his pals at Harvard was a then-unknown law student named Charles Whittlesey. The future commander of "the Lost Battalion" remembered that "when I graduated at Williams College in 1905 and matriculated at the Harvard Law School, one of the first boys I met there was this same Eddie Grant. How many times have Eddie and I sat on the law school steps or walked about Cambridge Common or taken a little trip into Boston. We went to Plattsburg together and were then transferred to Camp Upton, from which place we came to France." A popular third baseman, "Harvard Eddie" was known more for his speed and fielding ability than his hitting in the National League. He played for Philadelphia from 1907 to 1910 and for Cincinnati from 1911 through half of the 1913 season, when he was traded to the New York Giants, completing his major-league career there at the end of the 1915 season. Lt. Lloyd Nease wrote to Eddie's father: "I saw him only five minutes before the attack, and insisted that he go to hospital, as he was suffering from bronchitis and was very hoarse, but he refused, saying, 'When we get relieved, we'll go.'" Nease explained how "a shell came over and the shrapnel hit him in both lungs, and he lived but 15 minutes." *Philadelphia Inquirer*, October 22, 1918, 10; *Seattle Daily Times*, January 19, 1919, 26; *Pawtucket Times*, November 19, 1918, 8.

51. Prominent baseball reporters and star athletes launched a movement just a month after Eddie Grant's death to have the Boston Braves ballpark renamed "Grant Field" in his memory. Although Grant had played third base for the New York Giants prior to his retirement, his association with Harvard sparked the Boston connection. Among those advocating the new name were such sportswriters as Bozeman Bulger and Grantland Rice, along with baseball stars such as Hank Gowdy, Christy Mathewson, and Ty Cobb. Although their effort proved unsuccessful, a memorial to Grant was unveiled in center field at the Polo Grounds on Memorial Day, 1921. *Oregon Journal*, November 8, 1918, 11; *New York Evening World*, May 30, 1921, 1.

52. Twenty years later, Damon Runyon would admit that he had misjudged his two stories: "Anyway, we were not so much excited about the story of 'the lost battalion' at that particular time, not knowing of course that it was to take its place in history with the Alamo, Custer's Last Stand, and Beecher's Island, and all the other epic defenses by our soldiers. We thought the killing of 'Harvard Eddie' Grant, an old third baseman of the New York Giants, and a captain of the 77th, while marching to the relief of 'the lost battalion' a bigger story for New York." *Delaware County Daily Times*, September 27, 1938, 10.

53. Harry "Moose" McCormick was a National League outfielder who played off and on for the Giants, Pirates, and Phillies during the years 1904 to 1913. He was acknowledged as one of the best pinch hitters ever but admitted to at least one lapse of judgment while playing for the legendary John McGraw. He confessed in 1930, "I remember the time Mac couldn't find me to pinch hit. I was under the grand stand reading a novel and nibbling an ice cream cone." A lieutenant and later captain in the Rainbow Division, McCormick was an outspoken critic of those athletes who remained at home, often seeking shelter from the draft in essential industries such as steel mills and shipyards, and playing for company teams. Prior to the Argonne campaign, Capt. McCormick confessed to a correspondent, "A soldier in a trench cannot be expected to feel very kindly toward a man who is playing ball, while he is risking his life for a real cause." After the war he coached at Bucknell University from 1922 to 1925, and at West Point from 1926 to 1937. Moose McCormick died in 1962 at the age of eighty-one. *Boston Traveler*, July 10, 1962, 42; *Brooklyn Daily Eagle*, May 24, 1930, 12; *Harrisburg Patriot*, August 15, 1918, 7.

54. Joseph Daniel Jenkins played for the World Champion Chicago White Sox in 1917 but spent the following year in the army after attending officers' training school. He was mistakenly reported to have been wounded prior to the armistice but emerged unscathed after several close calls at the front. As a lieutenant in the 132nd Infantry, Jenkins wrote to his boss, Charles Comiskey: "To be honest with you, this is some league that I am in, and it is a lot faster than the old American, for you know that when you boot one in this league you are through and can't come back." When he returned to the White Sox in 1919, he bragged: "When I came up to hit in a pinch over there, the Kaiser lit out for Holland and he's been there ever since." Despite this bravado, his baseball career never took off and he died, forgotten by Chicago fans, in 1974. *Kansas City Star*, November 22, 1918, 25; *Baltimore American*, December 29, 1918, II, 20; *Chicago Tribune*, January 12, 1919, II, 4; *Washington Evening Star*, May 14, 1919, 24.

55. One observer offered an account of German "scientifically designed" defenses: "This would be no trench of mud-covered walls and duck boards yielding into slimy mud under the step. These trenches were lined with cement, have cement floors, along each side of which ran a little drainage ditch. Each watching soldier had a steel and concrete post with steps leading to it. Nothing could be more complete." A mile back of what had been the original front line, he inspected a cave occupied by a general and his staff: "In this club there was a large dining

hall and, perhaps, 10 rooms. The inside was lined with concrete and wooden floors had been laid. At the dining table were mahogany chairs filched from some nearby French chateau. Over the general's place hung an electric call bell and electric lights strung down the middle of the table. This was luxury of war." *Pittsburgh Post-Gazette*, September 30, 1918, 2.

56. Robert Alexander, son of a judge, always said, "My mother wanted me to study law." Admitted to the bar in 1884, two years later he chose a different career and enlisted in the 4th Infantry as a private. Prior to the war he received a commission and served in the last Sioux campaign, Spanish-American War, Philippine Insurrection, and the Mexican expedition, where he was assigned to Pershing's staff. Alexander led the 63rd Brigade of Infantry in the Second Battle of the Marne and commanded the 77th Division from August 1918 until its demobilization in 1919. Gen. Alexander was awarded a Distinguished Service Cross while with the latter unit. He remained in the army and received the permanent rank of major general shortly before his retirement, after which he became an officer in the American Legion and general chairman of the National Rifle Association. Robert Alexander died in 1941 at the age of seventy-seven. *Washington Evening Star*, August 27, 1941, 13.

57. Born in 1862, Edmund Wittenmyer graduated from West Point in 1887 and served as an infantry officer in Cuba and during the Boxer Rebellion in China. Promoted to brigadier general in 1917, he commanded the 153rd Brigade in the 77th Division until late October of the following year, when he was promoted major general and given command of the 7th Division. In 1923, after forty years of military service, Gen. Wittenmyer was placed on the retired list at his own request. He died at Walter Reed Hospital in 1937 at the age of seventy-five. Francis B. Heitman, *Historical Register and Dictionary of the United States Army* (Washington, DC: Government Printing Office, 1903), 1:1058; *Washington Evening Star*, July 6, 1937, 2; Joseph C. Chase, *Soldiers All* (New York: George H. Doran, 1920), 201.

58. The German Fokker aircraft had ruled the skies in 1916 and 1917. Fast and a quick climber, the Fokker planes could fly at a high ceiling and dive without overstraining their framework, with the additional benefit of being more maneuverable than opposing French and British airplanes. The British produced an S.E. 5 model that could outdive and was more maneuverable than the German craft but was slower and could not fly as high. The Fokker did not meet its match in the sky until the later models of the French Spad that appeared in 1918. Edward V. Rickenbacker, *Fighting the Flying Circus* (New York: Frederick A. Stokes, 1919), 147–48.

59. Hunter Liggett's lifetime of military service stretched from fighting Indians to commanding the Army of Occupation after the war. Graduated from West Point in 1879, he led troops against the Sioux, the Spanish in Cuba, and the Filipinos during the insurrection in those islands. Prior to the war, Liggett was on the general staff, president of the War College, and commander of the Western Department. After mobilizing the 40th and 41st Divisions on the West Coast, Liggett led the latter to France in 1918. Elevated to lieutenant general, he led the 1st Army and Army of Occupation until returning home. Liggett retired in 1921 as a major general, but his wartime rank was reinstated by Congress in 1930. He died in 1935, aged seventy-eight. *Washington Evening Star*, December 30, 1935, 1–2; *San Francisco Chronicle*, December 31, 1935, 1, 4.

60. Like his colleagues Joffre, Gallieni, and Mangin, Henri Gouraud had climbed through the officer ranks in the French colonies. After service in Sudan, Niger, and Chad, Gouraud was a general in Morocco when war came. Wounded early in 1914, he was given command over French troops in the Dardanelles campaign of 1915, but a Turkish shell soon broke his legs and led to the amputation of his right arm. After commanding the 4th Army in Champagne and assuming a political appointment in Morocco, Gouraud resumed command of the 4th Army, blunting the last German offensive and pushing the enemy back toward the Rhine. He served on occupation duty before leaving for Syria in 1919, and he returned in 1923 to join the Supreme War Council. This was followed by an appointment as governor of Paris, which he held until his retirement in 1938. Gen. Gouraud died in 1946. *London Times*, September 18, 1946, 6.

61. Runyon did recall one rumor about an attempted escape. It seems that the story involved an unnamed cook from the 2nd Division: "This unit often rushed out before breakfast and gained miles of territory on the enemy rather than drink its cook's breakfast coffee, it was so superbly bad. A squad of the enemy surrendered to the unit one day and was given the cook's coffee for refreshment, and that night they all tried to escape, stating that they felt it better to risk getting killed than endure more of the coffee." *Canton Repository*, December 1, 1942, 6.

62. A graduate from West Point in 1909, Thomas South Bowen became one of the American army's pioneer aviators. While serving with Pershing's punitive expedition in early 1916, Bowen made a forced landing in front of a crowd of angry Mexicans. He held them at bay with his pistol until he could repair his machine and fly off. Late in March of that year, his aircraft lost power while attempting to land at Casas Grandes and fell from a height of 100 feet, breaking Bowen's nose and bruising him badly. After studying a flock of sparrows, Bowen originated the idea of planes flying in a "V" formation. After commanding the United States Bombing Squadron during the war, he retired to Florida. Thomas Bowen died in 1927, at the age of forty-two, his death being attributed to long-term injuries resulting from his 1916 crash in Mexico. *Washington Evening Star*, July 18, 1927, 9; *Washington Post*, March 26, 1916, 3; *Brownsville Herald*, March 27, 1916, 1.

63. Colonia Dublán was a Mormon colony located along the Casas Grandes River in Chihuahua, Mexico. Gen. Pershing chose this town as the headquarters for his pursuit of Pancho Villa due to the close proximity of a railroad. Prior to Pershing's arrival the region had been extensively looted by bandits. This location proved to be surprisingly healthy after soldiers were forbidden to drink untreated water and instructed to stay out of native huts to avoid contracting typhus. *El Paso Herald*, March 24, 1916, 4.

64. Damon Runyon had known Edward Vernon Rickenbacker before the war, when he was racing automobiles. Although he would become widely known as Eddie, Runyon and his other close friends called

him Rick. Rickenbacker went to France as a member of Pershing's motor pool, occasionally driving the commanding general. He soon requested a transfer to the air service and became commander of the 94th Pursuit Squadron, personally shooting down twenty-six German aircraft although he admitted to Runyon that his weakness was in gunnery. He was awarded lots of medals, including the Medal of Honor, and became a hero to the American public. Following the war he tried to market a Rickenbacker car but eventually returned to the field of aviation and became president of Eastern Air Lines. Rickenbacker died in 1973. *Greensboro Daily News*, March 14, 1942, 7; *Boston Herald*, July 24, 1973, 2.

65. While in his sophomore year, Lansing Colton Holden Jr. entered the Princeton Aviation School, and he graduated in 1917. Commissioned a lieutenant in March 1918, Holden served with the *Lafayette Escadrille* for four months before joining the 95th Pursuit Squadron. He was credited with seven aerial victories and won a Distinguished Service Cross. An architect by training, Lt. Holden never lost his love of adventure. In 1925, he joined French forces in their campaign against native tribesmen in Morocco. Holden joined a French relief column that was ambushed, but he escaped unscathed only to be reprimanded for his risky behavior. Settling down to a career as an artist, Holden eventually became an art director in Hollywood movies and became widely noticed while working on *The Garden of Allah*, starring Marlene Dietrich and Charles Boyer. On November 13, 1938, Lansing Holden died with a fellow officer from the New York National Guard when their airplane crashed near Sparta, Tennessee, while en route to a duck-hunting vacation. *Kingsport Times*, November 14, 1938, 1; *San Francisco Chronicle*, September 30, 1925, 4; January 12, 1937, 10.

66. In February 1919, word reached the Army of Occupation that a congressional committee had voted to dispense with service stripes for overseas service. Cyril Brown, correspondent for the *New York World* and *Winston-Salem Journal*, described how this news was received: "It is safe to assert that at no time during the war have congressmen been so wholeheartedly abused and denounced by the AEF. The mildest of the doughboys' comment on congress contains allusions to hell." Brown then offered one example of the outrage felt by all: "They are a lot of damned [deleted]. Now that we've won the war they think to hell with the soldiers. They think they can do anything they want to us. First, they sprang prohibition on us while we were away. Now they want to rob us of our service stripes. They will be legislating us out of our pants next." Calmer heads finally prevailed, and the service stripes were retained. *Winston-Salem Journal*, February 14, 1919, 8.

67. 5th Division.

68. 81st Division.

69. There were three types of divisions in the American army: Regular divisions, composed of regiments of the prewar United States Army; National Guard divisions, made up of National Guard units generally descended from older militia organizations; and National Army divisions, brand-new units formed from drafted men and generally led by officers from the Regulars or National Guard.

70. Runyon would later tell of one doughboy who escorted about fifty German prisoners to the rear when he met up with another soldier with a pair of dice. The two Americans began shooting craps while the Germans crowded around to watch the action. The man with the prisoners quickly lost all his money, so the pair agreed he would wager his Germans, each being the equivalent of ten dollars. Soon he lost the prisoners as well. Runyon furnished the end of the tale: "The loser yawned and went his way along, rather pleased to be relieved of his charges while the winner escorted the prisoners into camp and was subsequently awarded a medal for capturing them." *Canton Repository*, December 27, 1943, 6.

71. News came from Cologne that a statue of the Kaiser had been decorated with a suitcase, cane, and dunce cap. Some disillusioned German had hung a sign from the Kaiser's neck that read "Here goes the greatest scoundrel of all." *Dallas Morning News*, November 30, 1918, 2.

72. Educated at Hampden-Sydney College and Richmond Presbyterian Seminary, Capt. Thomas Williamson Hooper was one of several "fighting parsons" in the AEF. Small and wiry, the Presbyterian minister chose to serve as a line officer in the 319th Infantry rather than as a chaplain or war worker. According to Reverend Hooper, "I don't see why a preacher should not go out and fight for his country the same as the laymen do." One of his men offered nothing but compliments for his commander: "Gee, how he can fight. He doesn't curse and swear like some of us guys do, by jiminy whizzigers, he is a bear cat when it comes to fighting. He was in the thick of it all. And do you know that some of our men stopped cursing too?" Following the war, Reverend Hooper returned to his pulpit in Culpeper, Virginia, until his death in 1954. *Pittsburgh Post-Gazette*, February 3, 1919, 3; *Pittsburgh Daily Post*, June 3, 1919, 8; *Richmond Times-Dispatch*, October 16, 1954, 17.

73. The son of a minister, William W. Dawson graduated from Ohio Wesleyan University in 1914 and began a law career. He enlisted in the Ohio National Guard in 1917 and went to France with the 166th Infantry. Promoted to lieutenant, Dawson was detached as an observer at an infantry school when he volunteered to advance with a body of troops under heavy machine gun fire. Armed only with an automatic pistol, Lt. Dawson suddenly confronted five Germans. Correspondent Bert Ford explained the result: "Leveling his pistol at them Dawson commanded the Germans to surrender. All of them threw up their hands." Dawson received a law degree from Western Reserve University in 1921 and, following a few years in private practice, taught law at that school. Dawson acted as a colonel in the army's civil affairs division during World War II and was military governor of Wurttemberg-Baden when he died in 1947 at the age of fifty-four. William R. Coates, *History of Cuyahoga County and the City of Cleveland* (Chicago: American Historical Society, 1924), 3:57, 59; *Warren Times Mirror*, November 7, 1918, 1; *Cleveland Plain Dealer*, February 12, 1947, 6.

74. Capt. Edwin C. Woodward, 22nd Engineers, sent home an example of German body armor, said to have been used by a machine gunner, which became a curiosity at the Fort Worth library: "The armor has hooks, which, slipping back over the shoulders, hold the breast plate in position. Swung from the bottom of the breast plate,

several smaller plates hang down and protect the abdomen. The armor is padded on the inside. The arms and legs are left free, permitting the gunner free use of his limbs." *Fort Worth Star-Telegram*, July 31, 1919, 9.

75. The famous Woolworth Building, located on Lower Broadway, was the culmination of Frank W. Woolworth's successful chain of eponymous five-and-dime stores. Begun in 1911 and eventually costing $13,000,000, Woolworth's dream became the tallest building in the world upon its completion. *New York Evening World*, April 8, 1919, 10.

76. Not only was Hill 360, lying east of the Meuse River and southeast of Damvillers, heavily fortified and desperately defended, the terrain was littered with French and German skeletons that had lain unburied for several years. Sgt. John Brace described the situation: "We went through what is known as 'Death's Valley,' facing the famous Hill 360. The Germans were on this hill and they could see everyone and everything that came over the road leading to it. At night when they could not see I believe I am safe when I say they could hear or possibly smell [us], because they sure could hit any part of this road." Despite a preliminary announcement that Hill 360 had fallen on the night of October 25, units of the 26th Division did not take that position until two days later, after five days of intense fighting. Benwell, *Yankee Division*, 188–90; *Boston Herald*, October 26, 1918, 2; *Wilkes-Barre Record*, December 25, 1918, 14.

77. Jerkins, or vests, made from sheepskin with the wool still on, were issued to combat cold weather in the trenches. *Washington Evening Star*, July 21, 1918, IV, 6.

78. John Archer Le Jeune graduated from the Naval Academy in 1888, served two years on sea duty, and was commissioned lieutenant in the Marine Corps. Le Jeune was in the Spanish-American War and commanded the Marine base at Quantico, Virginia, prior to the war. He led the famous 2nd Division in the AEF, the only Marine officer to lead an army division. Appointed commandant of the Marine Corps in 1920, he served in that capacity until 1929, when he resigned to become superintendent of the Virginia Military Institute, remaining there until 1937. In February 1942, Le Jeune was promoted to lieutenant general on the retired list and died later that year. *Brooklyn Daily Eagle*, November 20, 1942, 15; *Washington Evening Star*, November 21, 1942, 13; *Dallas Morning News*, November 21, 1942, I, 8.

79. A graduate of the Virginia Military Institute, George Catlett Marshall Jr. received a lieutenant's commission in 1901. He rose through the ranks slowly until the war brought out his real talents: organization and staff work. A protégé of Pershing, Marshall's planning in France produced great rewards on the battlefield, but his greatest contribution would come twenty-five years later, when the American army went back to fight Germany again. As army chief of staff in World War II, he again fashioned a winning strategy. Following this second war, he created an economic plan to avoid the calamitous issues that had plagued Europe after the first war. His concept of the so-called Marshall Plan won him a Nobel Peace Prize in 1953. After his service as secretary of state, George C. Marshall died in 1959. *Washington Evening Star*, October 17, 1959, 1, 4; October 18, 1951, 1, 23.

80. Alexander Woollcott wrote that "there was but one law of the highway, 'Make way for the guns—make way for the guns.' It was at once a war cry, a traffic regulation and a gospel." Woollcott, *Command Is Forward*, 173.

81. Gen. John J. Pershing had been given the nickname "Black Jack" after his service in the 10th Cavalry, a segregated unit of Negro troops. Personal tragedy struck in 1915 when a fire in his quarters at the Presidio killed his wife and three daughters, only a son escaping the flames. Despite his sorrow, Pershing continued to devote his life to the army. One retrospective said of the general: "There were, in reality, two Pershings: one a cold, hard tactician who demanded implicit obedience, the other an emotional, considerate man of quiet, personal charm." He was also described as "a curious mixture of stern disciplinarian and man-of-the-ranks." Both Pershings were evident during the war. In the first instance, doughboys swore that he "could spot an upside-down button or an unpolished rifle at 100 paces." At the conclusion of the war, Pershing confessed his love for the officers and men he had commanded: "When I think of their heroism, their patience under hardships, their unflinching spirit of offensive action, I am filled with emotions which I am unable to express. Their deeds are immortal and they have earned the eternal gratitude of our country." Gen. Pershing died in 1948 at the age of eighty-seven. *Brooklyn Daily Eagle*, July 15, 1948, 1; July 16, 1918, 7; July 18, 1948, 7; July 19, 1948, 10.

82. Francisco "Pancho" Villa was either a modern-day Robin Hood or murderous thug, depending upon which side of the Mexican political divide a person should identify. Villa's demonstrated ability to "ride, shoot and swear" won him many followers in his struggles against the established Mexican governments, but his uncontrollable temper won him just as many enemies. Villa turned against the United States when he exacted revenge on the town of Columbus, New Mexico, after the Wilson government had allowed his pursuers to cross American soil. Ambushed and killed in 1923 by a band of assassins, he supposedly left a hidden treasure of seven million pesos, a sum greater than that buried by pirates Captain Kidd and Blackbeard. For the treasure immediately available, some five widows and "a small army of children," along with two siblings, claimed a share. *Washington Evening Star*, July 21, 1923, 1–2; July 30, 1923, 6.

83. Joseph S. Gallieni graduated from the French Military Academy at Saint Cyr and began a military career that lasted forty-five years. He was responsible for establishing a protectorate over the region of Niger, pacified Indo-China, and conquered the colony of Madagascar. Explorations in Niger led the Geographical Society to award him a gold medal. Appointed to the Supreme War Council in 1908, Gen. Gallieni became military governor of Paris shortly after the advent of war in 1914. As the initial German advance neared Paris, he commandeered all the city's taxicabs and shuttled tens of thousands of soldiers to reinforce the French field army, ensuring a victory in the Battle of the Marne. Subsequently appointed minister of war in the French cabinet, Gen. Gallieni died in 1916, aged sixty-seven. *Washington Evening Star*, May 27, 1916, 8.

84. Erich Weiss (Harry Houdini his adopted stage name) began performing publicly as a trapeze artist at the age of eight, but his real talent came from learning how to pick various kinds of locks as an apprenticed

locksmith. He parlayed this knowledge into an international career as an illusionist and escape artist, escaping from handcuffs, chains, coffins, and straitjackets while buried underground, submerged under water, or suspended in midair. Houdini amassed a book collection on theater, magic, and black arts that was worth upward of $500,000. He died in 1926 of peritonitis after having been struck unexpectedly in the abdomen by a fan. *Washington Evening Star*, November 1, 1926, 1–2; *Brooklyn Daily Eagle*, November 1, 1926, 1, 14.

85. This high-octane advance by the doughboys on Sedan had embarrassed the French army. To avoid an international incident and restore some semblance of French honor, the American 1st and 42nd Divisions were withdrawn from the heights overlooking the city on the night of November 7–8. To show their gratitude, French generals invited a token force to accompany them, so Capt. Russell Baker's company turned around and headed back to Sedan. On the night of November 8–9, two of Baker's platoons, led by Lieutenants Colvin Todd and George E. Crotinger, advanced with elements of the French 252nd Infantry to within sight of the strategic railroad that ran through the city. These few squads were the closest that doughboys got to the vital city of Sedan, although the Germans did not evacuate the area until November 14. *Washington Evening Star*, November 2, 1930, VII, 24; Alison Reppy, *Rainbow Memories* (New York: Carey, 1919), 19.

86. Runyon's colleague Burr Price wrote of the French mud at this time: "Sometimes the mud was only several inches thick, politely soft, nice to look at as to color; sometimes not so thick, but slippery. But more often it was deep and thick and sticky, slippery and ugly." *Philadelphia Inquirer*, November 10, 1918, 2.

87. The American fireworks industry was working day and night to turn out huge quantities of flares and rockets to be used to illuminate No Man's Land at night. Among those produced was the Very Light, originally the Very Night Signal, invented by Edward W. Very. The Very Light was employed "for getting quick sight of objects, ascends some 300 feet and burns twenty seconds, leaving a brilliant trail that reveals all objects on the ground." *Brooklyn Daily Eagle*, September 1, 1918, II, 7; *Washington Evening Star*, March 2, 1910, 9.

88. John "Jack" Dunston (also spelled Dunstan in the press) was the owner and proprietor of Jack's Restaurant at 761 6th Avenue. Dubbed the "Handsomest Man in Manhattan" by the *New York Sun*, Dunston responded to rumors of impending Prohibition: "If it is a necessity I'm willing to make the sacrifice. Other people are making greater ones and why shouldn't I be willing to do my part? No, it won't put me out of business. I'm a restaurant man first and my receipts from food alone last year were more than half a million dollars. It will decrease profits, of course, but that can't be helped." *New York Sun*, April 21, 1917, 2; May 30, 1917, 5; *New York Evening World*, January 22, 1918, 2.

89. One early American visitor to the city of Nancy recorded his impressions: "It is a city of magnificent squares and broad parks, with beautiful monuments and arcades, a city that has the real flavor of a capital, not merely the rather dull life of a provincial city. Living on the edge of an open frontier has served to give a peculiar vitality to the population, which today lives and works within hearing of the German guns and is subject to frequent air raids." *Atlanta Constitution*, February 17, 1918, 5.

90. A wartime tourist in Nancy wrote of the imposing statue of Stanislas: "On the base of his statue in the center of Place Stanislas is inscribed the record of his good works, which reads like a Red Cross press agent booklet of today." *Brooklyn Daily Eagle*, March 24, 1918, III, 2.

91. John and Peter Delmonico opened a restaurant at 23 William Street in New York City in 1827, but that building burned in the great fire of 1835. Over the decades the main restaurant and other similarly named restaurants occupied several locations. "Old Del's" survived at Beaver and William Streets until December 1917, when high prices during wartime led to a decline in luxurious dining. Unable to make money, the owners closed their business only to open a new downtown restaurant at the original 1827 address the following month. It was asserted that dining at Delmonico's was "a fine art." *Brooklyn Daily Eagle*, October 5, 1918, 6; *New York Times*, January 31, 1918, 15; *New York Sun*, December 9, 1917, V, 7; *New York Tribune*, January 31, 1918, 14.

92. An American gastronome fondly remembered an evening in Nancy: "The exquisite Stanislas square is yet untouched and Stanislas, whose ancestors were Austrians, still stands just as he did a year ago looking over toward the front door of Waltier's restaurant—still one of the best in France." *Wichita Beacon*, October 22, 1918, 6.

93. John Davison Rockefeller, who had already proved adept at business ventures, became involved in the oil-refining business by the age of twenty-one. By the end of the Civil War, Rockefeller's firm was shipping more refined oil than any other American competitor. Headquartered in Cleveland, he set out in the 1870s to monopolize the oil market under his new corporation, Standard Oil Company. In the opinion of the infamous Jay Gould, Rockefeller had "the finest organizing brain of this generation." After gaining control of the oil industry, he invested in iron, copper, gas, and railroads, with allegations that he also controlled the meat-packing industry. When he retired in 1911, his worth was estimated at more than $1,000,000,000, with a yearly income greater than the crowned heads of Europe. His philanthropic donations were legendary, estimated to be over one-quarter of a billion dollars by 1911. After turning his empire over to his son, John D. Rockefeller lived the life of leisure until his death in 1937. *Brooklyn Daily Eagle*, May 24, 1937, 9, 13.

94. Edwin James described a meal and its cost: "Three days ago I ate this luncheon in Nancy at the Café Liegeoise: Fish, beefsteak, potatoes, and salad, paying for it the equivalent of $3.25." Two days later James had a similar meal in Trier: "Yesterday, at the Hotel Porta Nigra here, I ate fish, beefsteak, potatoes, and salad, and paid an equivalent of $2.50." *New York Times*, December 4, 1918, 1.

95. Archbishop Charles-François Turinaz died October 19, 1918.

96. Burr Price saw these same graves, writing of them: "Lying side by side along the road, as though they had been dominoes bowled over, were three graves and on freshly built crosses were the steel hats of three American doughboys. Nowhere was there any mark of a big shell explosion and what caused the deaths is a mystery." *Philadelphia Inquirer*, November 10, 1918, 2.

97. This march is currently known as "Hail to the Chief."

98. Correspondent Alexander Woollcott conducted an exhaustive investigation of campfire rumors and humorously concluded: "From a hasty compilation of the statistics there furnished, an investigator could easily establish the fact that the last shot of the war was fired 78,926 times. At least that many shells have already been sold to YMCA men and other Americans in France as certified souvenirs of the last moment of the war." Woollcott, *Command Is Forward*, 225–26.

99. Despite the impending armistice, men were still being killed and wounded, but Junius Wood captured the American mood when he exclaimed, "A fine time to be bumped off, just before the last curtain, but I wouldn't miss it for a farm Down East!" Ford, *Fighting Yankees Overseas*, 206.

100. Born within sight of the Marine Corps Barracks in Washington, DC, John Philip Sousa followed in his father's footsteps and joined the Marine Corps Band. After several years as a theatrical conductor, he rejoined the Marine Corps Band in 1880 as its new conductor. Known universally as "the March King" for the success of such compositions as "The Washington Post March," "Semper Fidelis," and "The Stars and Stripes Forever," Sousa left his position after twelve years with the Marines and became a conductor of civilian bands. During the war Sousa became a lieutenant in the Naval Reserve and led bands based at Great Lakes Naval Station. He also composed military tunes, such as "Liberty Loan March," "US Field Artillery March," "Sabre and Spurs," and "Solid Men to the Front," all available on Victor Records. Sousa even composed music to accompany John McCrae's popular poem "In Flanders Fields." To honor the young naval officers, he cut off his trademark beard, which he had worn for over thirty years. Sousa died in 1932. *Washington Post*, March 1, 1918, 7; *Chicago Tribune*, November 1, 1918, 15; *Fort Wayne Sentinel*, August 1, 1918, 9; *Washington Times*, January 24, 1918, 12; *Brooklyn Daily Eagle*, March 7, 1932, 27.

101. Alexander Woollcott observed the same phenomenon and offered this odd observation: "The man from Mars, coming to earth on the morning of November 11, 1918, would have been hard put to it to say which army had won, for, if anything, the greater celebration, the more startling outburst, came not from the American but from the German side." Woollcott, *Command Is Forward*, 213.

102. On the morning of October 23, 1917, Battery C, 6th Artillery, was in position about 400 meters east of Bathelemont. At precisely 6:05 a.m. the first American artillery round fired in the war roared through the fog over No Man's Land. According to a War Department investigation, "the gun crew of the first action was: Sergt. Alexander Arch, chief of section; Corporal Robert E. Braley, gunner; Sergts. Edward Warthan, Lonnie Dominick and Frank Grabowski and Privates Louis Varady and John Wadersak, cannoneers." The gun was a French 75 mm cannon, number 13,769, and it fired nineteen rounds that first day, fourteen high explosive and five shrapnel. After firing over 20,000 rounds, the cannon was withdrawn from service and sent to West Point as a trophy. According to Junius Wood, Sgt. Arch gave his commands "in broken Czecho-Slovak English." Arch's captain memorialized this historic moment with this laconic comment: "Well, I reckon we have done it." *Fort Wayne Sentinel*, August 20, 1919, 16; *Oregon Journal*, December 9, 1918, 2; *Macon Telegraph*, December 26, 1917, 1.

103. It seems that Stenay had actually been "captured" by four correspondents—Burr Price, Bennie O'Donnell, O. P. Higgins, and William McNutt—who had driven ahead of the advancing doughboys. Burr Price explained: "Indeed, Stenay was in reality captured by correspondents of the Associated Press, who had hastened forward into it, knowing that it would be the last Meuse stronghold to be evacuated by the Germans." Finding the town deserted, the four bold reporters walked back and found a patrol led by a sergeant, which rushed in to take possession. The only casualty occurred while crossing the Meuse on rubble from bridges destroyed by the Germans. McNutt slipped on a rock in midstream and lost his hat. *Philadelphia Inquirer*, November 14, 1918, 1; *Albuquerque Journal*, April 22, 1919, 2.

104. Friedrich Wilhelm Victor August Ernst, Crown Prince of Prussia and the German Empire.

105. More than twenty years later, Runyon had a different opinion of those hours prior to the armistice: "One of the worst crimes in military history was when the Armistice was arrived at and they permitted gunfire that cost the lives of many soldiers to continue. The time for 'cease firing' was fixed for 11 o'clock, Nov. 11, 1918, but for hours up to that time, with peace in all intents and purposes concluded, the guns kept blazing away. That was just murder." *East Liverpool Evening Review*, October 17, 1939, 4.

106. Correspondent Burr Price recalled a similar low-key acceptance of the armistice news. He received the official announcement at 9:30 on the morning of November 11 and "got in a car and started playing the reverse of Paul Revere's role, instead of announcing of a coming battle announcing the end of the fighting and of the great world war." He was surprised at the reaction displayed by America's fighting men: "Some of the boys yelled, some didn't comment at all. Others smiled and others said 'Thank you,' as though it was a personal favor I had done them." All along the lines, Price noticed, "A great silence settled over the hills and valleys." Mainly the doughboys were simply exhausted. Bert Ford told how "the big idea at first was to sleep—to sleep in comfort without fear of gas or bombs or shells—to sleep as they hadn't been able to in months and months—to sleep the sleep so well earned." *Dallas Morning News*, November 14, 1918, 2; Ford, *Fighting Yankees Overseas*, 217.

107. Born in Pennsylvania during the Civil War, Peyton March graduated from Lafayette College in 1884, and again from West Point in 1888. Assigned to the artillery, 1st Lt. March was given a commission in the US Volunteers, where he personally commanded the famous Astor Battery in the Philippines, winning the Distinguished Service Medal for his actions under fire at Manila in 1898. After the battery went home, March became an aide to Gen. Arthur MacArthur during the Insurrection. His prewar career included duty on the general staff, as the military attaché in Tokyo, and as an observer in the Russo-Japanese War. He also found time to obtain a master's degree and law degree from Lafayette College. In 1918, March was recalled from Europe to become army chief of staff and advisor to the president and secretary of war. His most important contribution to the war effort was

the mobilization, equipping, and transportation of two million American troops in time to blunt the last German offensive in 1918. Gen. March retired in 1921 and died at Walter Reed Hospital in 1955 at the age of ninety. *Washington Evening Star*, April 14, 1955, II, 17.

108. Runyon had good reason to mention the Astor Battery and Capt. Peyton March. On August 13, 1898, the Astor Battery, the 23rd US Infantry, and the 13th Minnesota Infantry broke through the earthworks on the main approach to Manila and fought their way into the city, followed by the main army. The battery, named for its donor John Jacob Astor, was lightweight and small of bore, making it more maneuverable on the battlefield than full-size guns. One member of the battery gave Capt. March credit for all that the battery accomplished: "The strictest disciplinarian we knew was our own captain. He surely was a rigid drillmaster. But I guess we needed it. Our battery was made up of lawyers and doctors and Wall Street workers and adventure seekers of all sorts, and discipline was new to them. Lots of entertainment was offered us and in San Francisco they went quite wild over the boys. But March was inflexible. 'There will be no banquets and no bouquets on this trip,' he said. 'Your loving friends can save them until you get back.'" *Cleveland Plain Dealer*, June 11, 1918, 6; August 14, 1918, 10.

109. Adm. George Dewey, commander of the American fleet in the Battle of Manila Bay.

110. This is Runyon's attempt to give a Maine accent to the well-known Luger pistol.

111. Bull Durham Tobacco.

112. Bozeman Bulger graduated from the University of Alabama with a law degree and worked in the office of his father, a prominent Birmingham attorney. After a stint working for Senator Oscar Underwood, Bulger began a newspaper career on the *Birmingham Age-Herald*. In 1905, he headed north and landed a job with the *New York Evening World*, where he wrote primarily baseball columns. With the outbreak of war, Bulger graduated from the Plattsburg Training School, went to France with the 77th Division, and attained the rank of major. Cited for bravery in the Argonne fighting, he was promoted to lieutenant colonel and given the post of chief press representative of the American Expeditionary Force. After the war he resumed writing for the *World*, remaining with that newspaper until its sale in 1931. Bulger then worked as a sports writer for the *Saturday Evening Post* until his death in 1932. Damon Runyon attended his funeral in Arlington National Cemetery. *Brooklyn Daily Eagle*, May 23, 1932, 15; *Nassau Daily Review*, May 25, 1932, 3.

113. Born in Hyde Park, New York, William Gerald Dare Morgan graduated from Yale in 1901 and spent several years with the American legation in Tokyo. Gerald, as he was commonly known, went off to France to cover the European war for the *New Republic* in 1915 but returned to be married the following year. After another overseas tour as a correspondent, he came home, attended the officers' training camp at Plattsburg in 1917, and was commissioned first lieutenant in the field artillery. Morgan was originally attached to the intelligence section of General Headquarters in France but was appointed chief field censor of the AEF on November 1, 1917. He continued in that capacity throughout the war, being promoted to captain on June 15, 1918, and major on May 1, 1919. Gerald Morgan died in 1948. US NARA, Record Group 59, US Passport Applications, 1795–1925; *New York Times*, June 4, 1916, 21; Francis R. Appleton, *War Records of the Knickerbocker Club, 1914–1918* (New York: Knickerbocker Club, 1922), 234.

114. Born in 1891, Arthur E. Hartzell became a London correspondent of the Hearst newspaper conglomerate, served as Paris correspondent for the *New York Herald*, was cable editor of the *New York Sun* from 1912 to 1916, and worked on the War Desk of the *New York Times*. After graduating from the Plattsburg training school, Hartzell went to France in January 1918 as a lieutenant in the 23rd Infantry. When correspondent Floyd Gibbons was seriously wounded at Belleau Wood, Lt. Hartzell stayed with him on the battlefield and was credited with saving his life. Shortly afterward, the lieutenant was transferred to the press section, where he acted as information officer for the American press. Following the armistice, Hartzell was assigned to the general staff and tasked with writing a monograph on the Meuse-Argonne fighting. The result was *Meuse-Argonne Battle (Sept. 26–Nov. 11, 1918)*, which was "for the confidential use of press correspondents and magazine writers as a basis for articles." After returning to civilian life, Hartzell represented the J. Walter Thompson Advertising Agency in Europe. He died in 1940. *Fourth Estate*, July 5, 1919, 19; *Washington Evening Star*, December 4, 1940, 7; *Monongahela Daily Republican*, December 5, 1940, 3; Arthur E. Hartzell, *Meuse-Argonne Battle (Sept. 26–Nov. 11, 1918)* (Chaumont, France: American Headquarters, American Expeditionary Forces, 1919), 3.

115. Floyd Gibbons studied for a year at Georgetown University but left to start a newspaper career at the *Minneapolis Daily News* in 1907. He moved to the *Chicago Tribune* in 1912 and covered major wars for over twenty-five years. Gibbons was aboard the SS *Laconia* when it was sunk by a German U-boat less than two months before the United States entered the war. At Belleau Wood he lost his left eye to a machine gun bullet that passed through his steel helmet. Gibbons was described as "a swashbuckling figure in the Richard Harding Davis tradition, 6 feet tall, weighing 200 pounds and wearing a white patch over his wounded eye." In the course of his lifetime, Gibbons traveled around the world three times and visited every continent except for Antarctica. Never married, he once bought a home in Florida but lived in it for only ten minutes. Floyd Gibbons was preparing to return to Europe to cover his second world war when he died in 1939 at the age of fifty-two. *Washington Evening Star*, September 25, 1939, 2; *Brooklyn Daily Eagle*, September 25, 1939, 9.

116. A native of England, Arthur John Delaney came to New York, by way of Bermuda, in 1906 aboard the steamer *Pretoria*. He moved to Boston and was working as a waiter when he became an American citizen in 1912. Coincidentally, his birthday was July 4. Although he served with the provost marshal's department, a colleague said of Delaney, "Humor rose from him like ripples on a spring." He always referred to himself as a "memorandum-receipt husband because he had been married just six days when he had to go overseas." Lt. Delaney died in 1960 and is buried in Arlington National Cemetery. US NARA, Record Group 21, Petitions and Records of Naturalizations

of the US District Court and Circuit Courts of the District of Massachusetts, 1906–1929; Maude R. Warren, "Living the Life of Reilly," *Saturday Evening Post*, June 21, 1919, 149.

117. Born in 1891, Conger Reynolds grew up in the small Iowa town of Dexter. He attended Drake University for a year but transferred to the University of Iowa, where he graduated Phi Beta Kappa in 1912. He began work as a reporter for the *Des Moines Register and Leader* but returned to the university in 1915 to teach and establish a school of journalism. After serving as a lieutenant and press officer during the war, Reynolds remained in France and became an editor for the Paris edition of the *Chicago Tribune*. From 1922 to 1929 he served in the consular service in Nova Scotia and Germany. In the latter year he became director of public relations for Standard Oil of Indiana. Following his retirement in 1955, he joined the US Information Agency and was a founder of the People-to-People Program during the Eisenhower administration. Conger Reynolds died in La Jolla, California, in 1971. *Chicago Tribune*, February 20, 1971, 9; *San Diego Union*, February 19, 1971, II, 5; *Fourth Estate*, September 6, 1919, 12.

118. Dennis Edward Nolan graduated from West Point in 1896, was cited for gallantry in the Spanish-American War, and served through the Philippine Insurrection. He served as an instructor at his alma mater prior to the war, when he rose to become the chief intelligence officer of the AEF. During the Meuse-Argonne Campaign he commanded a brigade in the 28th Division near Apremont, where he was awarded the Distinguished Service Cross. After the armistice Nolan served on a committee that hammered out details of the German disarmament. He remained in the army and retired as a major general in 1936 but served in prominent civilian advisory positions prior to his death in 1956 at the age of eighty-three. For his wartime service, Gen. Nolan had received decorations from the United States, Britain, France, Italy, Belgium, and Panama. *Washington Evening Star*, March 7, 1926, 22; February 25, 1956, 10.

119. James Patrick Wilson, a War Department telegrapher, was attached to Gen. Pershing's staff and was one of the first to transmit news of the armistice to the world. After the war he worked for the Associated Press and Consolidated Press before settling in St. Louis as an employee of the Postal Telegraph Company. He died there in 1938 at the age of fifty-two. *Washington Evening Star*, April 20, 1938, 12.

120. Glen Darrel Merriman, although officially a resident of Pennsylvania, had moved to Chicago, where he worked as a telegraph operator for Western Union before the war. Although suffering from a heart complaint, he entered the army on June 23, 1917, and served with the 12th Service Company as a sergeant. While stationed at Nancy, Merriman met and successfully wooed Albertine Dor, a local girl, taking her for his bride on May 31, 1919. Returning home to Pittsburgh, he again found work as a telegrapher before his death in 1944. US NARA, Record Group 163, World War I Draft Registration Cards; *Pittsburgh Daily Post*, October 27, 1918, 11; US NARA, Record Group 59, US Passport Applications; US NARA, Record Group 29, Records of the Bureau of the Census, 1790–1996: 1920 US Census, Ward 22, Pittsburgh, Pennsylvania; Pennsylvania Veteran Burial Cards, 1777–2012.

121. James Gillespie Blaine Lampert attended the University of Wisconsin until he received an appointment to West Point in the Class of 1910. Following a posting at the Panama Canal, Lampert was sent to Cornell University, where he received an ME degree in 1913. Lampert's assignment to the Army Engineer School ended with a transfer to the 1st Engineers and duty in France as a captain. An acknowledged expert in bridge building, a colleague described his inspiration: "The engineers of other armies had been trying various types of foot bridges, all of which were more or less complicated and impracticable. Lampert went back to the old military principle that a floating bridge is the quickest and most dependable bridge for military purposes and worked out a foot bridge with collapsible pontons which proved to be a marvel in its simplicity, lightness and the speed with which it could be thrown across a stream." He was awarded a Distinguished Service Medal for his innovation. Lt. Col. J. G. B. Lampert died of pneumonia in 1919 at the age of thirty-two. His father was Congressman Florian Lampert of Wisconsin. *Fiftieth Annual Report of the Association of Graduates of the United States Military Academy* (Saginaw, MI: Seemann & Peters, 1919), 159–62; *Oshkosh Daily Northwestern*, January 14, 1919, 2.

122. Ferdinand Foch served without distinction as a soldier during the Franco-Prussian War, which ended in France's ignominious defeat. Commissioned in the artillery, Foch attended, taught, and commanded at the Superior School of War in Paris, where he was remembered for his "tremendous energy, application and thoroughness." Officers who knew him said that he was the incarnation of the French military spirit. By 1914, Foch had risen to corps command, followed quickly by elevation to army command, although the latter promotion was tempered by the death of his only son in combat. Despite being due for retirement in 1916, Foch was retained on the general staff until promoted to Allied Supreme Commander and Marshal of France in 1918. Marshal Ferdinand Foch died in 1929 of complications from bronchitis contracted during the preceding Armistice Day celebrations. *Washington Evening Star*, January 14, 1929, 1; March 21, 1929, 1,4; Stephen Pope and Elizabeth-Anne Wheal, *Dictionary of the First World War* (Barnsley, UK: Pen & Sword Books, 2003), 164–65.

123. Although descended from prominent New England ancestors, Forsyth Wickes had lived in France as a youth. He graduated from Yale in 1898 and Columbia Law School in 1900, where he was a founder of the *Law Review*. During the war he reached the rank of major, and his knowledge of the French language resulted in a liaison position with the French army. In civilian life, he became senior partner in the law firm of Wickes, Ridell, Bloomer, Jacobi & McGuire in New York City. Pursuing his interest in French art, Wickes assembled a world-famous collection of French porcelain. He died at the age of eighty-eight in 1964. *Newport Daily News*, December 21, 1964, 2.

124. Burr Price described the road from the Verdun to Etain: "Along the road that I traveled the greater portion of the advancing host was composed of supply and ammunition trains and artillery units. On leaving Verdun, the city of heroic memory, I came across the tail end of a line of huge trucks that rolled onward heavily laden with the supplies of the quartermaster's corps. Next in the front line came a long string of old-time prairie

schooners, each of which was drawn by six great Missouri mules and all of them loaded with supplies. And then came the artillery—howitzers and cannon still wearing the camouflage of battle. Beside them walked or ran the cannoneers." *Philadelphia Inquirer*, November 19, 1918, 2.

125. Born in Wilkes-Barre, Pennsylvania, Cameron MacKenzie graduated from Yale Law School and the New York Law School. In 1907, he married Elizabeth McClure, daughter of the noted publisher S. S. McClure. After a career on the staff of the *New York Sun*, MacKenzie became general manager and publisher of *McClure's Magazine*. He served as a war correspondent for the *New York World* and *Saturday Evening Post* and was later attached to General Pershing's headquarters as correspondent for the *London Daily Chronicle* and the *London Post*. Following the armistice, MacKenzie acted as correspondent for the *New York Herald* in Poland. He died in 1921 while aboard the SS *Acquitania* off Newfoundland while en route from England to America. *Wilkes-Barre Times-Leader*, March 18, 1921, 3; *Washington Evening Star*, March 18, 1921, 7.

126. Everyone commented on the new army chow wagons, including one writer who said that "It was a common sight to see the old rolling kitchen lumbering toward the front, trying to get near enough to feed the company, and the cook keeping hot food steaming away as the horses dragged the 'goulash wagon' over the torn-up shell-swept roads." He explained that while cooks concentrated on feeding their own companies, they "fed anyone who was hungry, no matter what his company." One cook told of his secret to success: "Camouflage for ordinary grub, studying what the boys want, using a little diplomacy and giving them plenty—that's all there is to getting by with this cook's job." *Charlotte News*, October 19, 1918, 11.

127. Long before the United States entered the war, dispatches from Gaston Des Champs had appeared in American newspapers, such as the following description of the Verdun cathedral: "Even the huge mosaic paving stones are wrenched into masses of debris. Columns and pillars are broken into fragments, rich caulenabras and ilustres are reduced to bits and the carved pulpit and sculptured railing around the chancel are lying in shapeless piles. Near the cathedral is the monastery, whose sculptured walls were famous as a fifteenth century masterpiece. All these now have been reduced to masses of rubbish." Des Champs wrote that it appeared "as if some burlesque-hercules had used a giant hammer to crush these exquisitely delicate bits of sculpture." *Omaha World Herald*, April 28, 1916, 3.

128. Son of a Civil War veteran, Burr Price received his early newspaper training on the *St. Louis Republic*. He left for France in April 1917 aboard the *Rochambeau*, and his first dispatch to the *New York Herald* described in detail an encounter between his ship and a German submarine. After reporting war stories for the *Herald* and sharing several of Damon Runyon's adventures, he covered President Wilson and the 1919 Peace Conference. Price later worked for the Belgian government and was in charge of publicity for several organizations that emerged from the peace talks. He joined the Schnell Publishing Company in 1930 and died twenty-two years later at the age of sixty-three. *Kansas City Star*, January 9, 1919, 5; *Washington Post*, May 5, 1917, 1; *Washington Evening Star*, March 19, 1952, 26.

129. Following his graduation from West Point in 1881, Joseph T. Dickman was a cavalryman at heart until the day he died in 1927 at the age of seventy. He pursued Geronimo, fought at Santiago in Cuba, chased rebels in the Philippines, and was chief of staff of the American contingent in the Boxer Rebellion. He commanded the 2nd Cavalry when the world war broke out. After commanding Camp Greene in Charlotte, North Carolina, Dickman led the 3rd Division on the Marne River in 1918, when it earned the new designation "the Rock of the Marne." Elevated to corps command, Gen. Dickman was tapped by Pershing to command the 3rd Army during the occupation of Germany. Doughboys became used to seeing their commander walking about under desultory shelling, always wanting to be in the thick of things. His men gave him the highest tribute they could bestow, bragging that "the Old Man would have made a 'damned good buck private.'" Dickman retired in 1921 after forty-five years in military service. *Greensboro Daily News*, October 24, 1927, 1; October 25, 1927, 8; *Omaha World Herald*, October 25, 1927, 12.

130. Some twenty years later, Damon Runyon offered some observations on the raspberry: "The bird, or raspberry, as we all know, is strictly of English origin, and has no place in polite circles in this country. It is employed in the United States chiefly by movie directors as a comic touch in pictures." Apparently one George Perry, a vaudevillian straight man, popularized the distinctive act in America, where it is now generally called the "Bronx cheer." *Reading Times*, February 3, 1937, 13.

131. Born in Indiana in 1896, Dan Patch was the world champion pacing stallion. At the age of ten, Dan Patch paced a mile to set a world sulky record of one minute and fifty-five seconds. Unbeaten in a sixteen-year career, the famous stallion performed stud service until his death in 1916 at the age of twenty. His millionaire owner, Marion W. Savage, died the following day. *Kansas City Star*, July 17, 1916, 9.

132. After a visit to Chicago's Columbian Exposition in 1893, John R. Thompson and his wife stopped in a State Street restaurant for a meal. Their meal was fine, but the coffee was abysmal. Thompson declared, "I can make a better cup of coffee than that myself," and bought the restaurant. Presaging the career of Ray Kroc of McDonald's fame, Thompson opened a chain of restaurants that eventually numbered over one hundred, supplemented by some seventy grocery stores. His cafés were advertised as "one arm lunch rooms," the forerunner of today's fast-food restaurants, where the main menu consisted of sandwiches that could be eaten with one hand by busy workers. *Brooklyn Daily Eagle*, June 18, 1927, 22; *Illinois State Journal*, June 18, 1927, 2.

133. Capt. J. L. Terry, 61st Engineers, wrote about the helmets and other military equipment discarded by the retreating Germans: "I am sending you through the French post office tomorrow a box containing three German helmets, four empty shells of different sizes, one German gas mask of latest type, one German belt with buckle, and some of the cute little articles the Germans used to scatter in the road covering their retreat to injure and cripple horses, mules, perforate auto tires and cripple men. You will observe that no matter how they fall

they always have a sharp point up. The helmets are not in good shape; they are just as I found them in the Argonne Forest alongside their former owners." *Parsons Daily Sun*, December 23, 1918, 9.

134. John A. Kick enlisted in the US Army in 1899 as a telegrapher with the Signal Corps. He became wire chief and chief operator at the main telegraph hub in Manila, responsible for over 300 telegraph stations in the Philippines before his discharge in 1901. A captain in the Signal Officers' Reserve Corps, Kick was called to active duty in 1917 and assigned to the 405th Telegraph Battalion in the 91st Division. After acting as commander of the 1st Army Telegraph Battalion, Maj. Kick was assigned as signal officer of the 29th Division in 1918. Employed in management positions with the *Saturday Evening Post*, Edison Appliance, and Western Electric, Kick became advertising manager for General Tire & Rubber in 1931. He died in 1943. US NARA, Record Group 94, Records of the Adjutant General's Office, *Register of Enlistments in the United States Army, 1798–1914*; *Railroad Telegrapher* 18, no. 1 (January 1901): 48; *Baltimore American*, May 9, 1917, 3; *Journal of Electricity* 40, no. 7 (April 1, 1918): 462; *Cleveland Plain Dealer*, January 4, 1931, 12; Oregon Death Index, 1903–1998.

135. Edison gas was supposed to be a secret weapon employed by American troops, but it was only a rumor. German spies may have confused the fictitious Edison gas with the very real Lewisite, which was in production at a secret Cleveland facility when the armistice was signed. News reports claimed that "Ten airplanes carrying 'Lewisite' would have wiped out every vestige of life—human, animal and vegetable—in Berlin. A single day's output would snuff out the four million lives on Manhattan Island. A single drop poured in the palm of the hand would penetrate to the blood, reach the heart and kill the victim in great agony." Willis R. Skillman, *The AEF: Who They Were, What They Did, How They Did It* (Philadelphia: G. W. Jacobs, 1920), 172; *Washington Evening Star*, May 25, 1919, 16.

136. Elihu Howard Kelton left his civil engineering courses at Harvard to become a lieutenant in what would become known as the 185th Aero Squadron. Shot down in a dogfight with German ace Beppo Grassman on October 30, 1918, Kelton would later write that "Aside from a few scratches, bruises, the excitement of the fall and then the crash, I was alright. My opponent had landed a few hundred yards from me because my last shots had knocked out two of his cylinders." After his capture, Kelton's mail was returned with the mark "Decease Verified." A French girl, Jeannette Ramazeille, who had corresponded with Kelton since his arrival in France, was crushed to hear of his death. The pair finally reunited fifty-four years later when former lieutenant Kelton went to Paris with a group of aviators to visit scenes from their youth. He died in 1975. *Fitchburg Sentinel*, December 18, 1918, 2; *Panama City News-Herald*, October 12, 1972, III, 10.

137. Bar-le-duc, described as a "quaint little wine market city," lay some forty-five miles south of the Argonne Forest and operated as the American supply base for the offensive in that sector. It also served briefly as headquarters for the American correspondents, one of whom wrote that the city "had perhaps not had a building erected within its borders since the middle ages." In addition to being a supply depot, Bar-le-duc boasted a huge YMCA complex that drew both doughboys and aviators in need of baths, meals, tobacco, and clean beds. After the German lines had been driven out of artillery range, enemy aircraft conducted regular bombing raids, although with little effect. *Atlanta Constitution*, November 14, 1918, 8; November 26, 1918, 8.

138. En route to Germany the American correspondents continually ran into what was described as "a motley throng" of Allied prisoners released from German prison camps. One reporter wrote: "Some of them had commandeered abandoned German wagons which were heaped with baggage. In the absence of horses the men pulled the wagons themselves. Others of the prisoners carried all of their belongings in grain bags or on wheelbarrows. One group of more than 100 Scotchmen in kilts wore green German trousers underneath to keep their legs warm." *East Liverpool Evening Review*, November 20, 1918, 1.

139. Following the occupation of Germany, correspondent Parke Brown reported: "The 'Order of the Cootie" was recently organized among American forces on the Rhine. Beneath the crest showing a cootie rampant are the words 'Coot Mit Uns.' Only veterans of three months' scratching experience are eligible." *Chicago Tribune*, February 18, 1919, 1.

140. A veteran of the Spanish-American War, Leo Donnelly was over the draft age and decided not to volunteer and endure another training camp. A monologist and character actor, Donnelly was a newspaperman but switched to the stage "when he heard that a notoriously stupid actor was receiving $400 a week." Writing from his vaudeville unit in France, Donnelly said: "The boys sure do need entertainment, and just go wild over anything that smells like America. The other night we played in a town that was founded in the sixth century and just to show you what environment will do I told some gags of that period and they went just as well as new ones. The boys will laugh at a red hat." He died in Atlantic City in 1935 at the age of fifty-seven. *Baltimore Sun*, January 10, 1918, 9; *Trenton Evening Times*, August 21, 1935, 4; *Chicago Tribune*, September 29, 1918, VII, 1.

141. A famous actress and playwright, Dorothy Donnelly was an organizer of the State Women's War Relief organization but did not actually arrive in France until September 1918. Her activities were primarily centered on American headquarters at Chaumont, where she, in collaboration with Patsy Henshaw, produced one of the best soldier shows, titled "Ah, Qui, or Y Not?" Following this success, Donnelly and Henshaw presented a series of shows to soldiers during the last days of the war. After a brief rest in Paris, Donnelly traveled to Coblenz, where she produced theatrical performances for the Army of Occupation. After returning to America, Donnelly spent her last years writing and producing in the theater. She died in 1928 at the age of forty-eight. *Brooklyn Daily Eagle*, January 4, 1928, 7; James W. Evans and Gardner L. Harding, *Entertaining the American Army: The American Stage and Lyceum in the World War* (New York: Association Press, 1921), 150–54.

142. Listing herself as a musician on her passport application, Patricia Irene O'Connor Henshaw planned to serve the YMCA in Italy but ended up in France—just one of life's fateful changes. Perhaps her mission to France was inspired by a brother who was then serving in the 145th Machine Gun Battalion. Shortly after graduating from the University of California in 1912, she had married Tyler T. Henshaw, an attorney and son of

a California Supreme Court judge, but he died of disease just after the couple returned from their honeymoon. Patsy was one of those rare entertainers who had memorized the words to hundreds of popular songs. She was always able to take requests and "would sit down at the piano and play and sing the song you asked for just as the person you had in mind used to sing it on that romantic occasion you never could forget." She remarried but died on New Year's Day 1937 from injuries received in an auto accident. US NARA, Record Group 59, US Passport Applications; *Oakland Tribune*, September 26, 1913, 3; January 2, 1937, 2; Evans and Harding, *Entertaining the American Army*, 152.

143. Samuel Brinckerhoff "Brink" Thorne was one of the greatest halfbacks in Yale football. He was fondly remembered for a game against Princeton on November 23, 1895, when he scored two touchdowns in a 20–10 win before 40,000 spectators. Thorne was twenty-two at the time, stood 6 feet, 1½ inches tall, and weighed 168 pounds when he captained the Yale team to victory that day. After graduation in 1896, Thorne became controller of the Pennsylvania Coal Company and later founded the firm of Thorne, Neal & Company, prominent in the coal industry, which he headed until his death in 1930 at the age of fifty-six. He died after receiving an injury to his hip on a fishing trip, which resulted in a blood clot and subsequent infection. Thorne served on a commission sent to Europe in 1918 to report on conditions in the coal industry there. *Chicago Inter Ocean*, November 24, 1895, 2; *Washington Evening Star*, June 4, 1930, III, 2; *Bulletin of Yale University, Obituary Record of Graduates Deceased during the Year Ending July 1, 1930* (New Haven, CT: Yale University, 1930), 149–51.

144. This cordiality between American doughboys and Luxembourg young ladies did not go unnoticed by their former suitors. In order to emulate the newcomers and not lose ground in the romance field, young male Luxembourgers earnestly began shaving their prized mustaches in order to look like the clean-shaven soldiers. Burr Price explained this phenomenon and then mused on the irony, "If only they knew how these American youths had tried and failed to raise mustaches in imitation of the French allies, I wonder what they would think and do." *Dallas Morning News*, November 30, 1918, 2.

145. When one Keystone State lieutenant could not make himself understood in Luxembourg, he was surprised to discover that Pennsylvania Dutch did the trick. *Seattle Daily Times*, November 24, 1918, 10.

146. Grand Duchess Marie of Luxembourg refused when the Germans demanded passage through her country during their invasion of France. In protest she ordered her personal automobile to block the street in front of the German columns, although there was no forcible resistance. After the Germans had been driven out, she abdicated in favor of her sister Charlotte in January 1919. She became a Carmelite nun the following year and died in Bavaria in 1924. *Washington Evening Star*, January 25, 1924, 20.

147. John L. Hines was the best-known general to emerge from West Virginia since Stonewall Jackson. A graduate of West Point in 1891, he won a Silver Star for gallantry in Cuba, fought in the Philippines, and participated in the pursuit of Pancho Villa in 1916. During the world war he rose from lieutenant colonel to major general in quick succession, winning a Distinguished Service Cross on July 21, 1918, near Soissons. In 1924, Hines succeeded Gen. Pershing as army chief of staff, and in 1930 he succeeded Gen. Douglas MacArthur in command of the Department of the Philippines, retiring two years later at the age of sixty-four. Gen. Hines celebrated his one hundredth birthday at Walter Reed Hospital in May 1968 and died the following October. In addition to his distinguished military career, Lady Astor "proclaimed him the best dancer to come out of West Virginia." *Charleston Daily Mail*, October 14, 1968, 9; *Salt Lake Tribune*, May 31, 1968, 10.

148. Gen. Preston Brown, a Kentucky native, graduated from Yale in 1892 and joined the US Army as a private in 1894. Promoted to second lieutenant in 1897, he began a distinguished career that included service in the Spanish-American War, in the Philippine Insurrection, at the Army School of the Line in 1913, and at the Army Staff College in 1914. During the war Brown acted as chief of staff of the 2nd Division, commander of the 3rd Division, and commander of the 4th Army Corps, winning the Distinguished Service Medal and several European decorations. Gen. Brown became assistant chief of staff of the AEF after the armistice, prior to acting as commandant of the general staff college from 1919 to 1921. His later assignments included deputy chief of staff of the US Army and commander of the Panama Canal Zone. Brown retired in 1934 and died in 1948 at the age of seventy-six. Heitman, *Historical Register and Dictionary of the United States Army*, 1:253; *Catalogue of Yale University, 1920–1921* (New Haven, CT: Yale University, 1921), 503; *Washington Evening Star*, July 1, 1948, 22.

149. Carl Boyd graduated from West Point in 1903 and was commissioned second lieutenant in the 3rd Cavalry. During the fall of 1913 he was attached to a French dragoon regiment as a military observer, but the outbreak of war found him acting as an attaché to the American Legation in Paris. At his own request Boyd was transferred to the staff of Gen. Pershing after his arrival in Europe, where he became the commander's principal aide-de-camp. He died of pneumonia in 1919 at the age of forty. Gen. Pershing sent a personal cable to Boyd's mother that read: "We at general headquarters lose a tried and trusted friend. We all join you in sympathy at the great loss you have sustained." *New York Tribune*, February 16, 1919, 8; *Atlanta Constitution*, February 14, 1919, 7.

150. Junius Brown paid closer attention to the festivities and interviewed a woman in the crowd to obtain a detailed description of the lady's dress for his women readers. His account confirmed some of Runyon's description but added a few more details: "The young lady was dressed in a black velvet suit, a Russian squirrel fur collar, with a muff of the same trimmed with ermine, white gloves and a broad-brimmed black hat with white feathers in the low crown. She wore no jewels. Her sister, Antonia, was also dressed in black with a long, white fox fur boa and a black hat with white aigrettes." *Fort Worth Star-Telegram*, November 29, 1918, 13.

151. It was now time for the doughboys to clean up as they approached the city of Trier: "Packs and rifles had to be cleaned, and it soon became a high crime and misdemeanor, punishable as the court-martial may direct, to appear with an overcoat minus a button. For the 3rd American Army is now all dressed up in its Sunday-go-to-Germany clothes." Woollcott, *Command Is Forward*, 239.

152. Following the armistice and abdication of the Kaiser, socialist councils began to replace long-established German governments from Berlin to the smallest village. As enlisted men and groups of workers began to take over the country, they would fly red flags to denote their success in overthrowing the established order. *Augusta Chronicle*, November 25, 1918, 1.

153. Cameron MacKenzie saw one proprietor adapting to the new economic reality in Germany: "From the roof of a small hotel a scaffold had been let down and a man was at work painting out a name. The name that he was painting out was 'Kaiserhof.' A few days later in passing through the same village I observed in fresh lettering the words 'Hotel Central.' Anything, everything, you observe, goes by the board in Germany for the sake of the main chance—pride, self-respect, truth, all natural human feeling, loyalty, old-time regard—for such is the German code which has so strikingly survived the war." *Oshkosh Daily Northwestern*, July 23, 1919, 10.

154. These signs were quickly replaced by ones that read "American spoken here." *New York Evening World*, January 9, 1919, 3.

155. Max von Gallwitz proved to be an excellent field commander after being assigned to the Russian front under Gen. Hindenburg. His troops repulsed the Russian advance against Prussia and forced the enemy to retreat well beyond Warsaw, Poland. He followed this success by leading the German invasion of Serbia. In 1916, Gallwitz was posted to the western front, where he led armies at Verdun, the Somme, and Ypres before heading an army group that faced the Americans in 1918. He resigned his commission a month after the armistice and served as a conservative deputy in the Reichstag prior to his death in 1937. Pope and Wheal, *Dictionary of the First World War*, 186; *Brooklyn Daily Eagle*, April 19, 1937, 15.

156. Georg von der Marwitz's cavalry corps covered the invasion of Belgium in 1914 and operated in Flanders until the start of trench warfare. Marwitz was the only high-ranking German officer to see the Eiffel Tower, having ridden with a cavalry patrol to within twenty miles of Paris. He commanded a corps on the Russian front in 1915 and 1916 but returned to the western front to counter the British attack at Cambrai in 1917. Marwitz commanded an army against the Americans in the Argonne campaign and resigned shortly after the armistice. He died in 1929, aged seventy-three. Pope and Wheal, *Dictionary of the First World War*, 306–307; *Cleveland Plain Dealer*, December 1, 1929, 17.

157. After graduating from the New Hampshire College of Agriculture in 1901, Charles Almon Hunt received a lieutenant's commission the following year. In 1912, he was assigned to teach military science and tactics at his alma mater. A captain in the 18th Infantry when the regiment reached France, Hunt was slightly wounded in the last campaign. While on occupation duty in May 1919, Col. Hunt was selected to lead a select organization from six regiments that were to represent the American army in Britain's annual Empire Day celebration. When the 18th Infantry came home the following September, it was the only regiment authorized to wear the French *fourragere*, a braided green-and-red cord worn on the shoulder. Charles Hunt remained in the military until his death in 1963. Heitman, *Historical Register and Dictionary of the United States Army*, 1:555; *Washington Evening Star*, August 28, 1912, 12; May 9, 1919, 3; *Boston Herald*, June 12, 1919, 10; *San Francisco Chronicle*, August 17, 1919, 1; *US Army Register, 1 January 1964* (Washington, DC: Government Printing Office, 1964), 1:760.

158. Thomas Marvin Johnson, correspondent for the *New York Sun*, got his initial wartime scoop when he broke the news about the first American soldier to win the French Croix de Guerre. John McClain supposedly had run out after a German raid, picked up an unexploded bomb, and tossed it into a nearby river, thereby saving the lives of several French citizens. Johnson discovered that McClain had actually purchased the medal for eight francs, about $1.50, from a small boy who had found the medal. In 1928, he wrote his memoir of the war, titled *Without Censor*, which contained new versions of old stories. As Johnson put it, "The war-time version of the war was so often not the true version." A prolific author and reporter, Johnson continued to write well beyond World War II and died in 1970. *Peekskill Highland Democrat*, October 6, 1917, 7, 12; Johnson, *Without Censor*, 3; Minnesota Death Index, 1908–2002 (Minneapolis: Minnesota Department of Health).

159. In Burr Price's account of this adventure, he wrote: "I stopped my automobile to find out where I was. Not ten feet away from my radiator was a sign post that indicated the border between France and Belgium." *Dallas Morning News*, November 20, 1918, 1.

160. Burr Price referred to the German officer as Capt. *Rittmeister* Ihssen. Although the German soldiers appeared to be a "scraggy bunch," Ihssen "was well dressed and wore a great coat and a jaunty cap and he carried a swagger stick." He had served in the German army from 1893 to 1901 but retired to enter the lumber business. Ihssen was fluent in English, Spanish, and French. When Price inquired what he thought of the armistice, Capt. Ihssen replied, "We have been fighting the whole world for four years, and naturally I am glad that it is all over." *Dallas Morning News*, November 20, 1918, 1.

161. The third line of reservists consisted of old men and young boys.

162. Burr Price also noticed that Monsieur des Champs had no respect for the German officer: "Mr. Dechamps left our automobile when we were some distance from the German command and never once did he come near it or look toward it. Instead, he passed the time among the civilians of the near-by village, telling them that the Americans were coming in force and that it was the American soldiers who had greatly helped in ridding France of the Hun invaders." *Dallas Morning News*, November 20, 1918, 1.

163. Runyon's encounter with the rearguard of the German army was not out of the ordinary following the armistice. Raymond Carroll, Junius Wood, Bert Ford, and their driver had a similar experience after leaving Esch-sur-Alzette. Motoring along a beautiful highway, the trio came upon the rear of a German column heading to the Fatherland. Several noncommissioned officers jumped down from a supply wagon, with the following result: "Correspondent Wood, who was upon the front seat of the automobile, leaned over and politely in German

informed them we had missed our right road. He showed them our map and one of the Germans, who spoke English, indicated that we were within a few miles of the city of Luxemburg. He told us the right direction to Longwy, where were we sure that we could find the American troops." Before the correspondents could link up with any doughboys, they ran into a column of German artillery, but according to Carroll, "we slipped through without asking any questions." *Baltimore Sun*, November 22, 1918, 7.

164. Born in Newfoundland, Donald Brian's family moved to South Boston, where the youngster began singing in public, at one time appearing on the same program with the Four Cohans, whose youngest member was George M. Cohan. After a few years, Brian began acting in the theater. His big role came in 1907, when he appeared as Prince Danilo in *The Merry Widow*. A matinee idol of the first class, in 1910 over 10,000 women entered a raffle to win a kiss from the famous Donald Brian. In 1918, he starred in a production of *Her Regiment*, a musical comedy in which Brian portrayed a French officer who wooed a countess posing as a country maid. One review mentioned the highlights of Brian's performance before concluding, "Also he tried to sing. But why mention the things that were not enjoyable?" Donald Brian continued his theater work, appearing for the last time in 1943, and died five years later at the age of seventy-one. *Boston Traveler*, December 22, 1948, 9; *Brooklyn Daily Eagle*, January 29, 1918, 8.

165. After graduation from high school in 1889, Russell Baker became a hardware salesman. In 1906, he enlisted in the 4th Infantry, Ohio National Guard, and ten years later went with that regiment to the Mexican border. Called up to active duty in 1917 as a first lieutenant in the newly redesignated 166th Infantry, Baker was promoted to captain in May 1918 and served in that capacity for a year. After recounting the affair at Sedan in his book *Rainbow Memories*, Alison Reppy observed "that Capt. Baker had a propensity for having his picture taken." Not only was he photographed in a variety of poses, but the captain was filmed with French officers and dignitaries in moving pictures. Reppy thought that Capt. Russell had been photographed and filmed so often that "his stately form and handsome face" would rival that of the actor Douglas Fairbanks. In May 1919, he was transferred to the 40th Infantry until September 1920, when he was discharged to accept an appointment in the Regular Army. Russell Baker remained in the army until his death in 1963 at age seventy-four. Reppy, *Rainbow Memories*, 77; *The Official Roster of Ohio Soldiers, Sailors and Marines in the World War, 1917–1918* (Columbus, OH: F. J. Heer, 1926), 1:639; *San Antonio Express*, March 18, 1963, III, 2.

166. Alison Reppy was a star athlete and orator at the Missouri State Normal School and the University of Missouri, where he received a PhD in 1916. Reppy was described as "a short, red-haired eager youth who had the day before almost single-handed captured the town of Chevenges." At the time of this celebrated dinner, Lt. Reppy was the intelligence officer of the 1st Battalion, 166th Infantry. While serving with the Army of Occupation, he wrote *Rainbow Memories*. Following the war, Reppy received a doctorate in jurisprudence from the University of Chicago in 1922. That same year he became a member of the New York Law School, serving as dean from 1950 until his death in 1958. Prior to his death, Reppy wrote numerous judicial texts and essays on the law. *Springfield Republican*, December 15, 1918, I, 12; *Kansas City Star*, December 20, 1918, 13; *Omaha World Herald*, June 28, 1919, 3; *Bridgeport Post*, August 21, 1958, 33.

167. Noting the significance of this Allied get-together put on by the colonel of the 252nd Infantry, Thomas Johnson commented, "Only a Frenchman would have thought of giving the dinner in the circumstances, only a Frenchman could have expressed so touchingly his gratitude for the gift." *Washington Evening Star*, November 2, 1930, VII, 24; Reppy, *Rainbow Memories*, 19.

168. Bert Ford began his lifelong career as a reporter with the *Boston Herald* in 1909 but would also write for that city's *American*, *Record*, and *Sunday Advertiser*. After covering Pershing's Mexican incursion, in 1917 he went to France as correspondent for the International News Service, being assigned specifically to report on the 26th (Yankee) Division, which had been formed from New England National Guard units. He covered the US Marines in the Second Battle of the Marne and later became an honorary member of the Marine Corps League. Back in Boston, Ford reported on at least fifty of New England's most notorious murder cases and became active in various campaigns against juvenile delinquency. During World War II, Bert Ford contributed columns on military affairs in New England. He died in 1949 at the age of seventy-one. *Boston Herald*, February 4, 1949, 35; *Springfield Union*, February 4, 1949, 10.

169. Graustark was a mythical eastern European country that was the setting for a series of novels by George B. McCutcheon, which were similar to Anthony Hope's *The Prisoner of Zenda* and its sequels.

170. Quetsch is a dry, white brandy distilled from quetsch plums grown in the Alsace region of France.

171. *Rupert of Hentzau* was one of the sequels to Anthony Hope's popular novel *The Prisoner of Zenda*.

172. James Buchanan Brady was the epitome of ambition. Starting out as an errand boy, he transformed himself into one of America's premier salesmen: "Then he got into business for himself, and sold anything to railroads that they might need—from an oil can or a broom or a bunch of cotton waste up to a car, or a hundred or a thousand. He didn't wait for orders to come in; he went out and convinced railroads that they needed certain things, and then sold them to the roads—ties, rails, wheels, locomotives—there wasn't anything that he wouldn't guarantee to deliver." Brady's outsized personality matched his 6-foot, 200-pound frame. Although he neither smoked nor drank, his appetite for jewelry and pretty women was legendary. Brady delighted in adorning himself with large diamonds, emeralds, and rubies—even his dog wore diamond-rimmed sunglasses in public! A heavy eater (Lynnhaven oysters, terrapin, and canvasback duck was his favorite meal), heart disease eventually caught up with Diamond Jim and he died in 1917 at the age of sixty-two. *New York Tribune*, August 14, 1917, 11; April 22, 1917, V, 4.

173. Educated to be an attorney, Alexis "Lexi" Brasseur soon lost interest in the law and invested in the iron and steel industry in Luxembourg. He also became a popular writer, pillorying Luxembourg politicians and often

using a unique mix of vaudeville and cabaret in his stories. Brasseur also became a modest playwright and patron of the Luxembourg Conservatory. He died in 1924. www.autorenlexikon.lu.

174. Lt. William J. Penn offered his assessment of the Hotel Brasseur: "The hotel I stopped at was a very fine hotel, one of the nicest I have seen in France, or Europe rather. It is also very expensive. I believe these people think every American officer is a millionaire." *Reidsville Review*, December 31, 1918, 2.

175. American correspondents enjoyed a sumptuous Thanksgiving dinner in the barracks usually occupied by the Luxembourg army. Although the meal was a combination of army chow and local foodstuffs, it was nothing like the American version of the holiday. Soup, chicory salad, "refrigerated beef," applesauce, and apple tarts were eaten from tin plates, and German champagne was drunk from tin cups, but one homesick newsman moaned that it was "a turkeyless, celeryless, cranberryless, pumpkin pieless Thanksgiving dinner." *New York Tribune*, December 27, 1918, 10.

176. One dispatch from Luxembourg described how men of both armies reacted to the second week of peace: "Along the Moselle lagging German soldiers washed their clothing today on their side of the river. The Americans on the opposite bank did likewise. There was little conversing across the river, owing to the strict American order against fraternization." *New Orleans Times-Picayune*, November 24, 1918, 1.

177. Located on the right bank of the Moselle River, Trier was one of the oldest German cities and contained many Roman relics. An archbishop in the city in the ninth century, and his successors served both as churchmen and secular princes in the Holy Roman Empire. Recognized as a free city in the sixteenth century, Trier's ecclesiastical ties were severed during the French Revolution. Following the fall of Napoleon, Trier and the surrounding country were assigned to Prussia by diplomats at the Congress of Vienna. *New York Times*, December 2, 1918, 1.

178. Bert Ford was one correspondent who noticed the evolution of a new language in Europe, "a sort of war lingo—a shuffle of catch phrases from the allied tongues, spiced with robust American slang and army chatter." Allied soldiers began to use terms such as "have a heart," "beat it," "sit down, you're rocking the boat," and "stop your kidding." Americans interspersed their speech with *merci beaucoup*, *combien*, *c'est comme il faut*, *additione*, and *finis*. Pocket dictionaries sold briskly, and one enlisted man confessed to Ford, "Sometimes I think I'll forget how to talk my own language." *El Paso Herald*, August 31, 1918, 15.

179. Junius Wood explained the composition of the soldiers' and workmen's council at Trier: "There is a local revolutionary committee of five members. A German sailor who came from Kiel at the time of the navy mutiny and a discharged soldier who was a parlor Socialist before the war, the secretary of the local Social Democratic party, a farmer and a streetcar conductor were elected to constitute this committee. They were chosen by neighborhood organizations." *Oregon Journal*, December 9, 1918, 1.

180. Edwin James also noted the muted reception given the doughboys: "It was Sunday, but no church bells rang. There were no flags, no cheering, no smiles, few tears. It was just such a reception as only the Boche could give." *Houston Post*, December 3, 1918, 1.

181. If these officers had listened closely, they could have heard what Burr Price heard en route to Trier: "Then I saw American soldiers stepping quickly along the muddy roads. Their tread in this mud made a sound I have never heard before from marching men. It was not the sound of feet striking the earth. It was the sound of thousands of feet sinking into and being pulled out of mud like glue." *Philadelphia Inquirer*, December 3, 1918, 4.

182. Edwin James witnessed the arrival of the 6th Infantry: "It was just at 1 o'clock, German time, that Colonel [Henry J.] Hunt appeared, leading the 6th infantry of the 5th division, which is to be the permanent garrison of the city during our occupation. Behind him came a brass band, followed by doughboys, who were a full regiment strong, and a company of machine guns. They were neat and nifty, these victorious young Americans, as they marched so solemnly into this Hun city." James continued his description: "The crowd grew denser and denser as we reached the square. Here a band broke into 'Suwanee River,' and just then the standard bearer gave the *Stars and Stripes* an extra whirl and the column passed on by the ancient Porta Nigra to their barracks." *Houston Post*, December 3, 1918, 1.

183. One correspondent explained why Gen. Brown selected this particular building: "In the leading hotel, the Porta Nigra, in Treves, the suave, smiling proprietor in excellent English assured everybody that there was abundant hot water for baths and electric light at all hours of the day and night—luxuries not experienced elsewhere in this part of Europe." *Oregon Journal*, December 9, 1918, 2.

184. Harry Alexander Smith graduated from West Point in 1891 and was commissioned in the 1st Infantry. Promoted to first lieutenant in 1898, he served as major of the 21st Kansas Infantry in the Spanish-American War before reverting to his regular rank. Maj. Smith headed the department of public safety during the occupation of Vera Cruz and served on the Mexican border. After a stint in China he became a member of the general staff and was made a general in 1918. Smith was in charge of civil affairs in the occupied zone after the armistice until July 1919. He held a series of important appointments prior to his death in 1929 while commanding the 7th Army Corps. Gen. Smith died at the age of sixty-two. Heitman, *Historical Register and Dictionary of the United States Army*, 1:898; *Omaha World Herald*, May 27, 1929, 1, 4.

185. Prices current in Trier at the better restaurants were soup, one mark; trout, four marks; rump steak with potatoes and cabbage, eight marks; an "applesauce" concoction made from apples, turnips, and sugar, two marks; and Moselle wine, twenty-two marks per quart. Diners at cheaper restaurants could get a meal of soup, meat, and potatoes for about six marks. Coffee was available everywhere but cost three marks a cup. White bread, butter, and sweets were unavailable. *Washington Post*, December 3, 1918, 1.

186. Junius B. Wood began his newspaper career with the Chicago City Press Association in 1900, following his graduation from the University of Michigan. In 1907, he became a reporter and correspondent for the *Chicago*

Daily News, reporting on the occupation of Vera Cruz in 1914 and the Cuban revolt in 1917. Wood covered the American Expeditionary Force in England, France, Belgium, Luxembourg, and Germany, becoming a particular friend of Generals John J. Pershing and George C. Marshall Jr. Still with the *Daily News*, he spent the 1920s and early 1930s reporting from Russia, the Middle East, and the Far East. After covering the Japanese invasion of Manchuria, Wood was dispatched to Berlin, where he filed a "cautiously worded story" regarding a planned coup against Adolf Hitler by *General* Kurt von Schleicher. The foreign desk failed to read between the lines and chastised Wood for exhausting his monthly quota of words on a worthless "philosophical study" of German politics. When Schleicher and his wife were subsequently murdered, the *Daily News* frantically wired for details. Irritated by the obtuseness back in Chicago, Wood responded, "My quota is exhausted. Shall resume cabling next month." Wood became a contributing editor to *Nation's Business* in 1943 and moved to Silver Spring, Maryland, after his second world war but died of heart disease at the Washington Sanitarium on April 2, 1957. "Necrology," *Michigan Alumnus* 63, no. 17 (May 11, 1957): 339; *Washington Evening Star*, April 3, 1957, 40.

187. Junius B. Wood and Raymond G. Carroll had parked their automobile while they covered the fighting near Fismes along the Vesle River in August 1918. Upon returning, Wood tripped over what he thought was a wet fur coat lying in the bottom of the auto. The "coat" proved to be a stray mongrel puppy having the curly coat of a Newfoundland and the size of a spaniel, with a black coat and white feet, nose, and chest. Won over by the cold and shivering ball of fur, the two correspondents then and there adopted the animal and christened him "Vesle." Not knowing whether Vesle was friend or foe, Cameron MacKenzie dressed in a German uniform and paraded past the puppy. When Vesle tried to chew his leg off, the dog was pronounced a French refugee. Thereafter Vesle went everywhere with his two owners, eating in the trenches, at Maxim's in Paris, and everywhere in between. Vesle became world famous when he was included in a painting of an Allied War Council by the artist Dana Pond. When last heard from, his co-owners were trying to work out custody arrangements after the war. *Pittsburgh Daily Post*, February 28, 1919, 3; *Logansport Pharos-Tribune*, March 26, 1919, 7.

188. George Pattullo, of the *Saturday Evening Post*, noticed that doughboys always wanted something they did not have: "You could serve them with 10-course dinners, from hors d'oeuvres to nuts, and they'd go out to listen enviously to a guy who had had a plate of beans." This desire carried over to bread as well. Soldiers received white bread, a delicacy that German civilians had not seen for many months, but acquired a taste for the black bread available locally. Pattullo explained somewhat incredulously: "In almost every town and village where American troops are quartered, soldiers buy the heavy, dark war bread, made from the whole wheat. A steady diet of that bread would put a Mexican burro out of business, but the boys buy it and trade for it." *Colorado Springs Gazette*, February 24, 1918, 24.

189. A native of Ontario, George Robson Pattullo attended Woodstock Collegiate Institute before starting a newspaper career in Montreal, London, and Boston. Eager to report on America's involvement in the war, Pattullo sailed for France in June 1917 and, with one short return home, reported on the doughboys for the *Saturday Evening Post* for over two years. He spent most of his time with the 1st and 2nd Divisions, even acting as editor of the former's divisional newspaper after the armistice. Embarrassment came in the spring of 1918 in the form of a case of mumps. Despite his protests, Pattullo was shipped off to a field hospital: "I had expected that my service at the front would at least command respect and my present affliction gain me sympathy. Instead I got nothing but jeers. From the commanding officer, who tittered when he looked at me, to Old Man Junius Wood, who brought me a teething ring for a gift, my predicament extracted nothing but levity." After the war Pattullo became a writer of western fiction for popular magazines and the author of several novels. He died in 1967 at the age of eighty-seven. *Kansas City Star*, June 24, 1918, 14; *Dallas Morning News*, November 15, 1919, 6; July 30, 1967, 17.

190. A West Point graduate in the Class of 1889, Edward F. McGlachlin Jr. was a recognized authority on artillery. He became chief of artillery for the 1st Army as a major general and headed the 1st Division in the Army of Occupation. A visitor to the latter headquarters wrote: "The people look healthy and clean. Children everywhere. Gen. McGlachlin is living in this German home. His staff of five men, three colonels and one major and one captain, have their meals here. The general and his aide, Capt. Booth, are the only ones who sleep here." A son, Lt. Fenton H. McGlachlin, died in 1917 of injuries received when he fell from an airplane while in training at Fort Sam Houston. A recipient of the Distinguished Service Medal, the general became commandant of the Army War College and was appointed to command the Department of Panama but retired in 1923 before assuming the position. Edward F. McGlachlin Jr. died in 1946 at the age of seventy-six. *Stevens Point Gazette*, October 17, 1917, 5; January 22, 1919, 1; *Seattle Daily Times*, June 29, 1919, II, 2; *Manitowoc Herald-Times*, February 2, 1923, 3; *Eau Claire Leader*, July 18, 1923, 9; *Washington Evening Star*, November 11, 1946, 10.

191. One of the four sons of former president Theodore Roosevelt, "Young Teddy" won distinction at Cantigny, the citation reading "On the day of our attack upon Cantigny, although gassed in the eyes to blindness, Maj. Roosevelt refused to be removed, and retained the command of his battalion under a heavy bombardment throughout the engagement." A few months later, Maj. Roosevelt, while leading an advance of his battalion without his helmet, was hit by a machine gun bullet behind his left knee. He finished the war as a colonel. During World War II, Gen. Roosevelt participated in the invasions of North Africa, Sicily, and Normandy. He died of a heart attack in Normandy, on July 12, 1944. *Brooklyn Daily Eagle*, June 24, 1918, 1; July 14, 1944, 2; *New York World*, July 23, 1918, 3.

192. "Riding shanks' mare" refers to using your own legs as a means of transportation.

193. Edward Payson Weston liked to take long walks. He first walked from Boston to Washington to witness the inauguration of Abraham Lincoln. Reportedly a scout and spy during the Civil War, Weston's real walking career began in 1867, when he walked from Portland, Maine, to Chicago. Billed as "the greatest pedestrian that

ever walked," his greatest fame came late in life. In 1909, at the age of seventy, he walked from New York to San Francisco in 104 days and seven hours, despite being held up by severe storms. The following year he walked from Los Angeles to New York in ninety days. A one-time reporter for the *New York Herald*, Weston, the world's preeminent pedestrian, died in 1929 at the age of ninety. *Brooklyn Daily Eagle*, May 2, 1910, 1; May 14, 1929, 8; *Philadelphia Inquirer*, November 3, 1907, 15; *San Jose Evening News*, March 15, 1911, 1.

194. The phrase "runs for Sweeney" is racing slang for a horse that is not trying to win or has no chance of winning, while "with the Johns" refers to John Soldiers. *San Francisco Chronicle*, April 25, 1921, 10.

195. Some Coblenz café proprietors were not as law abiding as Carla. At least two owners could not resist the temptation to sell alcohol to thirsty American soldiers. Wilhelm Kalbitzer was sentenced to sixty days for selling wine after curfew, and Jacob Gerardtz spent ninety days in the lockup for watering down bottles of cognac. *Chicago Tribune*, January 28, 1919, 2.

196. In a dispatch filed on December 12, Junius Wood reported: "Almost the first man I met in Coblenz was the German officer who penned the now famous dispatch inviting Whittlesey to surrender. He is Lieut. Fritz Prinz, a tall, dark man with a stubby mustache, a member of the staff of the German 76th Division, which surrounded the battalion of the 77th American Division." Wood ascertained that Prinz, who wore an Iron Cross and spoke fluent English, previously had spent six years working for a tungsten firm in Washington State. The German officer had hoped to pay his respects to Whittlesey and was disappointed to learn that he had already returned to the States. *Washington Evening Star*, December 15, 1918, 23.

197. Coblenz was located about sixty miles southeast of Cologne and had a prewar population of about 50,000. The city was described in the following manner: "Coblenz derived its name from its location, on the triangle formed by the confluence of the Rhine and the Moselle, a location similar to that of Pittsburgh, Pa., on the Ohio and the Allegheny. A promenade along the Rhine was bordered by a bevy of hotels, restaurants, and cafés. The Romans called it 'Confluentes.'" Coblenz was the birthplace of Prince Klemens von Metternich, the famous Austrian ambassador and diplomat. *Oakland Tribune*, March 3, 1919, 8; *Gastonia Gazette*, December 23, 1918, 4.

198. These horse-drawn kitchens were built similarly to the limber and gun carriage of the artillery, with a cook stove and oven combination replacing the gun carriage and a cook chest in place of the limber. The two-shelf oven was supplemented by four 12-gallon cylindrical containers capable of holding soup, stew, meat, coffee, or tea. Two additional cylinders were carried in the cook chest. A rolling kitchen was designed to feed 200 doughboys, each one to receive a pint of stew or soup, a pint of coffee or tea, and a "liberal helping" of cooked meat. The cook's chest, which contained canisters for spices and condiments and an assortment of utensils, was proclaimed to be "comparable to the famous and inexhaustible bag of Mrs. Swiss Family Robinson." *Oakland Tribune*, June 6, 1918, 3.

199. One correspondent would later explain: "For chocolate, the enemy infants—or Hunlets, as the doughboys call them—bring helmets and lugers as bribes." Woollcott, *Command Is Forward*, 245.

200. One reporter agreed with Runyon's observation: "The comparatively light yoke the Americans have laid on the Germans appears to have influenced them in their attitude toward the Americans. When the American troops went to the barracks just evacuated by the Germans, they found they had been scrubbed to a state of spotlessness, and that the mattress coverings had been washed and refilled with fresh hay." Another correspondent stated, "Coblenz at the height of its tourist season could not have done better than this." *Charlotte News*, December 11, 1918, 1; *Gastonia Gazette*, December 23, 1918, 4.

201. Junius Wood reported on how Americans returned the Coblenz region to normalcy: "Telephone and telegraph lines are working and trains are running regularly on the opposite bank of the Rhine, bringing Berlin newspapers, which print the latest quotations from the New York Stock Exchange, the Chicago Board of Trade and the New Orleans cotton market. There is almost an unending procession of sidewheel river steamers towing long strings of barges flying German flags, up and down the river. The commercial life of the nation is continuing and even improving. The supply of sugar already has increased, since the sugar beets are no longer needed for the manufacture of high explosives." *Washington Evening Star*, December 15, 1918, 4.

202. Coblenz was of great military importance because of shipping on the Rhine and the Moselle Rivers, in addition to being an important railroad center. The extensive network of fortifications around the city was anchored by Ehrenbreitstein, a huge fort across the Moselle from Coblenz. It occupied a commanding position some 400 feet above the river. *Oakland Tribune*, March 3, 1919, 8.

203. In December 1917, Fred J. Riler left his job as a florist in Connecticut to perform relief work for the Knights of Columbus in Europe. While stationed in Paris after the armistice, he met the French lady who would become Clotilde Geffrotin Riler, their marriage certificate being issued on September 30, 1919. A son, Albert Frederic Henri, was born less than two months later to the Knights of Columbus volunteer and his war bride. Upon returning to the United States in 1920, the Riler family settled in Oregon, where the father worked for the St. Vincent de Paul Society. Fred Riler died in 1939, aged fifty-seven. NARA, Record Group 59, US Passport Applications; *Portland Oregonian*, July 12, 1934, 6; March 24, 1939, 12.

204. John J. Donovan, Boston attorney and occasional contributor to the *Boston Globe*, was a field secretary for the Knights of Columbus. Despite muddy roads and constant congestion, Donovan's truck convoy was first to reach the Rhine, beating out the Salvation Army and YMCA. In recognition of this achievement, grateful doughboys christened him "Santa Claus Jack." He would later coordinate all Knights of Columbus activities on behalf of the Army of Occupation. After returning to Boston, Donovan would return to the *Globe*, where he worked as a member of the editorial staff prior to his death in 1950. NARA, Record Group 59, US Passport Applications; Ford, *Fighting Yankees Overseas*, 200; *Boston Traveler*, November 27, 1950, 7.

205. The Knights of Columbus truck train brought a wide variety of supplies: "They opened a depot near the bank of the Rhine and began distributing their huge Christmas stock of pies, cigarets, tobacco, stationery, and gum drops. The gifts were of course free." *East Liverpool Evening Review*, December 14, 1918, 8.

206. Eddie Hodges was an actress playing in a Chicago theater when she volunteered to sell bonds for a Liberty Loan drive. A Salvation Army officer offered to get her to France, so she falsified her birth certificate and went. Miss Hodges, only twenty years old at the time, soon learned there was much for Salvation Army women to do: "[T]hey were everything, bakers, canteen workers, nurses, menders, charwomen, confidants, preachers." "Little Sister," as she was called by the doughboys, gained fame as a baker, as she later confessed: "We baked doughnuts one day and apple pies the next. But let me tell you right here that the doughnuts have had more than their share of publicity. Pie was what the American boy liked best—good old apple pie—like his father before him. Apple pie was what mother used to bake when she wanted to give him a special treat, and it seemed more like home than doughnuts." *New York Times*, October 5, 1919, VIII, 3.

207. Florence Turkington went to France with her sister Myrtle as Salvation Army officers. Myrtle described part of their transformation: "I don't know whether I can ever again get accustomed to a hat with trimmings after sporting a helmet so long. The chin strap reminds me of the elastic we wore when little girls. The gas masks and helmets are the first things we look for in the morning and the last things we note the location of late at night before retiring." Florence, "Little Turk," explained why Salvation Army huts were so popular: "Ordinarily we don't think of doughnuts as a feast, but if you were living in muddy trenches, being shot at, eating hardtack, and came out of the lines dead tired, needing sleep and a bath and a shave, and if you suddenly hit a spot where someone offered you steaming hot coffee and doughnuts, it would seem like heaven." *El Paso Herald*, May 24, 1918, 1; Harry E. Neal, *The Hallelujah Army* (Philadelphia: Chilton, 1961), 84.

208. Fred Anderson was famous throughout France by the time he crossed the German border. A Salvation Army veteran of twenty-six years when he shipped out in 1918, he quickly became known as the world champion maker of flapjacks (also called hotcakes and pancakes by the doughboys). During the St. Mihiel Offensive of that year, he, assisted by ladies of the Salvation Army, stood over a hot griddle for twenty hours and served 8,000 flapjacks (using his wife's recipe) and hundreds of gallons of coffee and chocolate to soldiers marching to the front. Ashamed to disappoint the last soldiers in line after he expended his half ton of flour, Anderson resolved to take the flapjacks to them. He started off carting eggs and flour to soldiers in a French baby buggy but improvised a traveling griddle on a wheelbarrow. With this new device, dubbed "the wheelbarrow field kitchen," Anderson could cook 3,000 flapjacks and still have time to conduct two religious services in a day that lasted from 5 a.m. to 10 p.m. *Tacoma Times*, March 14, 1918, 5; *Baltimore American*, May 13, 1919, 9; *Seattle Daily Times*, September 21, 1919, 26; *Idaho Statesman*, September 2, 1919, 5.

209. James McDonald Lockett had received an appointment as a cadet at West Point in 1902 but declined the honor and enlisted as a private because he thought advancement would be quicker in that manner. Following service in the Philippines, Lockett returned in 1907 and received a second lieutenant's commission. While a major in the 39th Infantry, Lockett was wounded in the leg by a bursting shell on the Vesle River. He remained in the army and became commander of the Military District of Washington during World War II prior to his retirement in 1944. Col. Lockett died at the age of seventy-nine in 1964. *Augusta Chronicle*, January 5, 1903, 8; *Washington Post*, February 10, 1907, II, 2; *Wilkes-Barre Times*, October 8, 1918, 16; *Washington Evening Star*, January 5, 1964, VI, 7.

210. Upon his death in 1942, George M. Cohan was described as a "dancer, actor, dramatist, producer, manager, composer and lyricist, motion picture and talkie star in a career that extended over more than 50 years." A prodigy violinist at the age of five and member of the stage family billed as the Four Cohans, George became "the man who owns Broadway." Among his greatest contributions to American song were "Yankee Doodle Boy" and "Over There." The last tune became immensely popular, a note from the Wilson administration calling it "a genuine inspiration to all American manhood." In 1940, Congress would authorize a gold medal for Cohan's part in the war effort. *Washington Evening Star*, November 5, 1942, 7.

211. One wire service dispatch described the German withdrawal from Coblenz: "While the Americans were marching into the city today the last division of the German army was only a few kilometers beyond the Rhine, moving in orderly fashion, with the spirit of a holiday rather than that of a defeated army. Almost every man had a rosette or a sprig of green in his cap. Many of the trucks and wagons were decorated with quantities of Christmas greetings." *Charlotte News*, December 11, 1918, 1.

212. Webb Miller covered the war for the United Press and became one of the greatest reporters of his generation. When he died, Miller was "at the very height of a long and consistently brilliant career which had carried him to most of the countries of the world and had brought him some of the finest beats and scoops in modern newspaper history." After the peace conference, Miller covered the Sinn Fein Troubles, the French occupation of the Ruhr, and wars in Morocco, Abyssinia, Spain, and Finland. His autobiography, published in 1936, was appropriately titled *I Found No Peace*. The *London Times* noted that sending news by cable had "taught him a rare economy in the use of language." Webb Miller died in London in 1940, when he stepped from a train during a blackout. Nazi propagandists unsuccessfully attempted to blame the British Secret Service for murdering him. *London Times*, May 9, 1940, 9; *Washington Evening Star*, May 8, 1940, 1; *Brooklyn Daily Eagle*, May 12, 1940, V, 2.

213. Frank Parker graduated from West Point in 1894 and served his country in Puerto Rico, South America, Cuba, the Philippines, China, and France prior to his retirement at age sixty-four. A major when he reached France, Parker was promoted to colonel and given command of the 18th Infantry. In October 1918, he was elevated to command the famous 1st Division, where Gen. Pershing lauded him as a man having "rare leadership and superb courage." Parker became a major general in 1929 and retired in 1936. During World

War II he was appointed director of the Illinois State Council of Defense. Gen. Parker died in 1947, aged seventy-four. *Washington Evening Star*, March 14, 1947, 10; *Illinois State Journal*, March 14, 1947, 1, 5; *Rockford Register-Republic*, March 14, 1947, 1.

214. Alexander Woollcott recalled that despite the celebratory occasion, Vesle "waddled across the Rhine ahead of the troops, wearing an intent look and bent, as it afterwards developed, on searching for the first lamp-post on the left bank." Woollcott, *Command Is Forward*, 252.

215. The Karl Baedeker firm published a series of European travel guides that were popular with tourists.

216. Maria Laach was a Benedictine abbey founded in 1093 by Count Heinrich II. *Pittsburgh Daily Post*, November 7, 1912, 6.

217. One writer said of the region: "The good wine of these valleys flows in ceaseless streams into Coblenz to be bottled, doctored and sparkled. A good share of it is sent out to the world; there is too much of it even for Coblenz, its tourists, its visitors and its great companies of officers to consume." *Gastonia Gazette*, December 23, 1918, 4.

218. Educated at Ottawa University, St. Charles College in Maryland, and St. Bernard's Seminary in Syracuse, New York, Francis P. Joyce became a chaplain in the US Army in 1905. His prewar service included assignments in the Philippines, recovery work following the San Francisco earthquake, and participation in Pershing's pursuit of Pancho Villa. A confidant of Victoriano Huerta, former head of the Mexican government, Joyce was named as an heir, his share of the estate estimated to be as much as $3,000,000. As chaplain of the 7th Field Artillery, he noted that 1st Division doughboys, both Protestant and Catholic, on one occasion had been presented miraculous medals by nuns along their march to the front, observing with pride, "These the boys guarded as they would their lives and despite the differences of religious views each trusted the articles would protect him." Wounded several times during his service, Father Joyce was assigned to Pershing's staff in 1917. He resigned in 1922 and returned to the ministry in Syracuse, New York, where he died in 1952, aged seventy-seven. *Tulsa World*, November 30, 1916, 2; *Fayetteville Bulletin*, November 16, 1917, 1; *Syracuse Post-Standard*, June 23, 1919, 2; June 28, 1952, 15.

219. Alfred von Tirpitz began his German naval career in 1865 and became an invaluable officer and bureaucrat. Promoted to rear admiral in 1895, by 1911 Tirpitz had become the first grand admiral of the German navy. In honor of his dedicated service, the Kaiser elevated him to the nobility. His goal prior to the war was to build a battle fleet capable of challenging its British counterpart on the high seas. Although Tirpitz had always championed battleships, by 1915 he supported the policy of unrestricted submarine warfare. *Adm.* Tirpitz retired in 1916 and became involved in right-wing politics until his death in 1930. Zabecki, *Germany at War*, 4:1297–98.

220. As *Gen.* Paul Hindenburg's chief of staff and quartermaster general, *Gen.* Erich Ludendorff played a major role in the outcome of the war. He was acknowledged as the tactical and strategic genius behind Hindenburg and the German war effort, and one military writer would say, "He must go down not merely as the man who lost the war for the Central powers, but the soldier who came within a hair's breadth of winning it." His later years were filled with bitterness toward Jews and Christians, making him an ideal figurehead as Adolf Hitler and the Nazi Party emerged from the chaos of postwar Germany. Ludendorff died in 1937. *Washington Evening Star*, December 20, 1937, 1; December 21, 1937, 6; December 27, 1937, 10.

221. Runyon wrote an entire column on the evolution of the popular use of the word "buddie." He concluded his analysis with this observation: "The barracks of peace time, and the camps of war, have always been productive of new additions to the language, and generally they are pretty descriptive and pretty pat. As used by the American soldier, the term 'buddie' is something more than slang because it is a term of endearment." Despite its widespread use, Runyon admitted that "it is hardly likely that the American soldiers will ever be called 'Buddies' in the same respect that the Scotch Highlanders are called 'Jocks' or the English soldiers 'Tommies.'" *Denver Post*, May 28, 1918, 10.

222. George Nicholas Ifft II was the son of a newspaperman and consular officer. Young George followed his father to stations in Canada, Germany, Switzerland, Poland, and Norway prior to being accepted at Princeton, where he graduated in 1915. He was commissioned a second lieutenant in the 361st Infantry but served in the intelligence corps, where one of his duties was to launch propaganda-laden balloons into German territory. After serving in the Army of Occupation, Ifft returned to Pocatello and entered the newspaper business, eventually becoming editor of the influential *Idaho State Journal*. A prominent historian, environmentalist, and business leader, George Ifft died in 1974 at the age of eighty-two. *Idaho State Journal*, October 30, 1974, 1.

223. Henri Francois Muller graduated from the University of Paris in 1897 and joined the staff at Columbia University in 1903 as assistant professor of Romance languages. Upon the outbreak of war, Muller requested a leave of absence to join the French colors. Despite his background, he served as a humble private in the 5th Company, 33rd Territorial Regiment. Writing in June 1916, Cpl. Muller confessed: "The war drags on and, as you say, there is no prospect of it ending soon. We have settled down to a routine and days pass quickly enough, and so do the weeks and months, and it seems that we will never go back to civil life and resume out former occupations." In his spare time, Muller reread *The Aeneid* and noted: "The battle scenes, the different kinds of courage shown by the various fighters, the reasonings of those that are weary, are strikingly true according to my small experience." *Salt Lake City Telegram*, June 25, 1916, 9.

224. Clarence O. Sherrill, after preparatory work at Trinity College, graduated second in his class at West Point in 1901 and entered the Corps of Engineers. After service on the Gulf Coast and in the Philippines and Canal Zone, Sherrill was commissioned colonel and assigned to command the 302nd Engineers in 1917. He was awarded the Croix de Guerre for action under fire on the Vesle River in 1918. After the war he was director of public parks and buildings in the District of Columbia, where he oversaw the erection of numerous monuments and began construction on the Memorial Bridge across the Potomac. At various times he acted as aide to Presidents Theodore Roosevelt, Warren G. Harding, and Calvin Coolidge. Sherrill served as city manager for Cincinnati, Ohio, from

1926 to 1930, and again from 1937 to 1943. Between these terms he was a vice president of the Kroger Company and president of the American Retail Federation. He died in his adopted home of Cincinnati at the age of eighty-three. George W. Cullum, *Biographical Register of the Officers and Graduates of the US Military Academy at West Point, New York* (Saginaw, MI: Seemann & Peters, 1920), 6A:956; *Cleveland Plain Dealer*, February 7, 1959, 5.

225. Frank C. Bolles graduated from West Point in 1896 and was severely wounded in the leg near Jaro in the Philippines while serving as a lieutenant in the 18th Infantry. Appointed colonel in 1917 shortly after America entered the war, Bolles became commander of the 39th Infantry on April 9, 1918. He led his regiment through the remainder of the war, winning a Distinguished Service Cross and Distinguished Service Medal. His division commander cited his conduct in the following manner: "Several times while under heavy machine gun and shell fire he superintended the formation and rectification of the advanced lines of his regiment and attached troops until he was wounded Sept. 28, exhibiting great coolness and indifference to danger." Maj. Gen. Bolles retired in 1936 and died in 1955 at the age of eighty-two. G. E. Ebmeyer, *School of Mines and Metallurgy, War Records* (Rolla, MO: Missouri School of Mines, 1920), 13–15; *Topeka Daily Capital*, February 18, 1899, 3; *Omaha World Herald*, October 11, 1936, 5; *Dallas Morning News*, July 16, 1955, II, 4.

226. Frederick W. Hackett graduated from the University of Vermont in 1917, joined an officer class at Plattsburg, and by the following year had become one of the two youngest majors in the American army. He was appointed educational officer for the Army of Occupation. Following the war he began an academic career as a teacher and administrator. Hackett served in three prestigious private schools: assistant headmaster at St. Marks School and headmaster at Montclair Academy and the Bolles School (no relation to his former commander). He retired from the latter school in 1964 and died in 1978. *St. Johnsbury Caledonian*, June 27, 1917, 8; *Vermont Alumni Weekly* 4, no. 29 (May 20, 1925): 464; George H. English, *History of the Eighty-Ninth Division, USA* (Kansas City, MO: War Society of the 89th Division, 1920), 279; *The Handbook of Private Schools* (Boston: Porter Sargent, 1958), 253, 390–91.

227. A synopsis of a baseball game played by the Lexington Thoroughbreds against the Lawrenceburg Distillers in 1908 pretty much summed up George Hannigan's career: "Hannigan scored twice and made two hits for the Distillers, beside taking a difficult foul. In an attempt to get another he collided with Searcy, a Distiller on the bench, and was temporarily laid out. The two errors against him were gotten by his ambition to cover the entire infield, something he is almost capable of doing." Following a couple of seasons of semipro ball, Hannigan was "a good sticker and reliable fielder" with hopes of the major leagues. A right-handed batter, he preferred to play third base but could fill in at second and shortstop. After a lackluster 1913 season at Decatur, Illinois, and with the Kansas City Packers, his baseball career was over. *Lexington Herald*, May 29, 1908, 3; *Decatur Herald*, March 23, 1913, 7.

228. Webb Miller, correspondent for United Press, noted the incongruity of this rail movement: "The special train bringing the Americans to Coblenz was composed of German cars and a German locomotive, and was operated by a German crew. German switchmen threw the switches over when the train entered the city." *Riverside Daily Press*, December 10, 1918, 3.

229. A native of London, Herbert Reginald Bailey gained an international reputation while reporting on Russian affairs in 1917. During 1918–1919, Bailey wrote war dispatches for the *London Daily Mail*. He later became a correspondent for the *Philadelphia Public Ledger* and *New York Sun* before assuming the title of managing editor of the British United Press. Bailey delighted his friends and acquaintances with anecdotes of his wartime adventures and contacts with famous personalities. One man said of him: "Like all great journalists, he had the eye of a true reporter, always seeking and finding a story wherever he might go." He died in 1939 at the age of forty-four in Brighton, England. *London Times*, March 20, 1939, 1, 16.

230. If a game of poker commenced, you can bet that Damon Runyon was among the players. Although he loved the game, Runyon was never very successful, as he readily admitted: "We learned to play stud poker practically in infancy, but we were no good at it, or at draw, either. In fact, it was often claimed for us by our admiring friends that we were undoubtedly the worst stud player in the world. We were known among stud players as Col. Doolove, because of our besetting weakness of curiosity. We just had to see what the other fellow had. One night a veteran player gave us our title when he remarked: 'He sure do love to look at 'em.'" *East Liverpool Evening Review*, December 6, 1938, 4.

231. "African golf balls" was a slang term for dice.

232. A committee composed of the burgomaster, city officials, and German officers conferred with Col. Lockett and handed over maps containing the locations of stores and munitions. One source estimated their value at $10,000,000, including railroad locomotives and cars, artillery pieces, rifles, and huge stores of ammunition. *Riverside Daily Press*, December 10, 1918, 3.

233. The regimental historian of the 39th Infantry laconically noted: "A number of newspaper men who accompanied the 2nd Battalion from Trier, ready to give wide publicity to the important event, found it less sensational than they had expected." Robert B. Cole and Barnard Eberlin, *History of the 39th US Infantry in the World War* (New York: Press of J. D. McGuire, 1919), 122.

234. Years later, Damon Runyon wrote of another incident when Grantland Rice was a bit too gullible: "Mr. Rice was always getting caught in the rain in France. He recalls the darksome night when the rain was falling fast, that he volunteered to guide none other than General Pershing himself to a remote and sequestered spot on the terrain, quite a piece from where they started. The journey was by auto, and on arriving at the spot, the general left Mr. Rice without as much as an aye, yes or no, to find his way back afoot the best he could." Obviously enjoying the story, Runyon continued: "In later years, in some bitterness of spirit, Mr. Rice recalled the incident to General Pershing as an example of the inconsiderateness of generals in general, but of course General Pershing did not remember it. He had probably left too many looeys out in the rain to remember individual cases, and most likely

he would have been surprised had he known how sternly the normally gentle Mr. Rice felt about the matter after all those years." *Canton Repository*, September 23, 1937, 4.

235. Lincoln J. Beachey began his flying career in Toledo at the age of eighteen, when he would surreptitiously make unauthorized dawn flights near the aircraft factory where he worked. By 1915, he was a first lieutenant in the United States Volunteer Aviation Reserve and was one of the most famous fliers in the country, his motto being "Rain, shine or cyclone." Early in 1915 he told an audience that he felt "safer in my own aeroplane any time than in an automobile." On March 14 of that year, while performing stunts over San Francisco Bay, he plunged to his death when his monoplane crumpled from excessive pressure. His body was recovered by sailors from the battleship *Oregon*. An autopsy revealed some lacerations, bruises, and a broken leg, but his death had been due to "asphyxiation by immersion (drowning)" when he could not extricate himself from his pilot's seat. *San Francisco Chronicle*, March 14, 1915, 1, 3.

236. A mysterious German aviator named "Fantomas," or "the Ghost," had become one of the most feared fliers on the French front. "Fantomas," based on a villainous antihero by that name in a series of French novels adapted for American theaters, would enjoy strafing the French, whether a solitary sentinel or bustling supply depots. For months he bore a charmed life but finally was shot down in late 1917. He was erroneously identified as Walter Rutt, a famous German bicyclist. The real Walter Rutt had been a world-class cyclist before the war and was employed as a dispatch rider by the German army. In his heyday he and his teammates won three six-day races at Madison Square Garden and placed second twice. Walter Rutt died in Germany in 1964 at the age of eighty-one. *Kansas City Star*, December 3, 1917, 7; *New York Sun*, November 8, 1917, 15; *Newark Star-Ledger*, June 30, 1964, 22.

237. Over 200,000 American soldiers would spend Christmas in Germany, and herculean efforts were made to create a holiday environment. Literally tons of letters were en route. Although many packages of goodies from home would not arrive due to an overloaded mail system, the YMCA and Red Cross hurried several trainloads of boxes to the Rhine. Coordination between local burgomasters and occupying troops sought to place a Christmas tree in every company. Decorations were either donated by German residents or improvised with American ingenuity. Red cloth was at a premium as soldiers created Santa Claus costumes. Donations were taken up to buy toys and candy for the German children. Despite these outward holiday trappings, all the soldiers really wanted for Christmas was to go home. *Lincoln Evening Journal*, December 24, 1918, 1.

238. Churchill's billed itself as "More Than a Restaurant—a Broadway Institution" and was located at the corner of Broadway and 49th Street in New York City. *New York Sun*, February 18, 1917, 2.

239. Café Savarin was located in the basement of the Equitable Building at 120 Broadway in New York City. One of its advertisements read, "The truly superior cuisine and the atmosphere of comfort and caste in the Café Savarin make it the desirable place to lunch or dine in downtown New York." This was a new Café Savarin, the original one having burned along with the old Equitable Building. *New York Sun*, October 12, 1915, 10; *New York Times*, July 5, 1920, 6.

240. Shanley's, which advertised itself as "A restaurant that interests clever people of discriminating taste," was located on Broadway between 43rd and 44th Streets in New York City. *New York Times*, January 7, 1918, 11.

241. Damon Runyon, himself an inveterate gambler, had a unique take on the games of craps that sprang like mushrooms after the paymaster's visit to an army camp: "Of course shooting craps is a seasonal diversion among the soldiers, usually coming on around pay day, as there has to be some excuse, such as money, to make the shooting interesting. We imagine it could be quite boring with nothing at stake. On pay days in any of the front-line divisions of Pershing's troops in France where the soldiers could not spend the dough, probably 100 thousand dollars would be in action in craps." The popularity of craps was due primarily to the portability of dice over such YMCA-approved activities as backgammon or Parcheesi. Poker was favored more by sailors because there was no level place to throw dice. *Omaha World Herald*, January 11, 1942, III, 9.

242. A *seidel* is a large beer mug.

243. The mythological woman "as old as the hills" who is the keeper of the ancient, practical ways of living.

244. Jacquelin Crosswell, a North Carolina boy serving in the Rainbow Division, spoke for the enlisted men when he complained, "There are lots of pretty girls in Coblenz, but we can't even look at them. The military police see that there is no fraternization between the Americans and Germans." *Fayetteville Weekly Observer*, March 19, 1919, 3.

245. Many doughboys chose to selectively obey the antifraternization rules, as evidenced by the following report: "Most of the doughboys have become fast friends with the German children. In the hilly section beyond the Rhine where there is well packed snow they go coasting together. The soldiers guide the bobsleds which rush merrily down the hillside with the cargo of youngsters yelling with glee. Then the doughboys haul the sleds back to the top, giving the children a second ride. The anti-frat law has not been placed on this sled-riding question so far, but in all other respects it is being rigidly enforced." *Oregon Journal*, December 30, 1918, 6.

246. The following local regulations were soon promulgated by the burgomaster. Everyone over the age of twelve was to register his or her signature and carry an identification card at all times. Inside the front door of each residence must be posted a list of each occupant, listing name, sex, age, and nationality with the occupation of the head of household. Changes of address were to be reported. All firearms and ammunition were to be turned over to the American authorities. All travel would be regulated by the burgomaster. Newspapers, periodicals, telegraph, telephone, and wireless communications would all be censored. No photographs could be taken in public without prior permission. With the exception of courts, councils, schools, and churches, public meetings were restricted. Hard liquor was banned, while sales of wine and beer would be allowed only during specified hours. *Logansport Pharos-Tribune*, December 28, 1918, 9.

247. A true soldier of fortune, Sam Dreben served in the 10th Infantry during the Spanish-American War and transferred to the 14th Infantry when he learned it would go to China to put down the Boxer Rebellion. After his discharge he fought with rebels in insurrections in Honduras and Nicaragua prior to joining the forces of Pancho Villa in Mexico. Dreben switched sides to accompany Pershing's pursuit of Villa as a sort of unofficial intelligence officer. Runyon first met Dreben during his Mexican days and would describe him in the following manner: "Sam was a short, chunky, swarthy, bandy-legged fellow with a big nose and a beautiful smile. . . . He was a lusty, gutsy chap when we first met him. He loved to laugh, sing, eat, drink and gamble. He loved to spend his money entertaining his friends. He liked expensive clothes and jewelry." Dreben enlisted in the 141st Infantry and won a Distinguished Service Cross for actions near Etienne in October 1918. Sgt. Dreben led a small group of volunteers against a German strongpoint and killed fifty-eight and captured two of the enemy, along with four machine guns. Not one of his men was wounded. Gen. Pershing said that Dreben was "the finest soldier and one of the bravest men I ever knew." Sam Dreben died in 1925, after being mistakenly injected with arsenic during an operation. Darryl F. Zanuck bought the rights to Dreben's story, but the proposed film was never made. *Jewish Daily News*, August 23, 1918, 8; *East Liverpool Evening Review*, April 11, 1940, 4; *Washington Evening Star*, March 16, 1925, 5; *Oakland Tribune*, Marsh 18, 1925, 1.

248. The fire had started backstage among scenery. One observer "could not help thinking of home when all but one nozzle in the local fire apparatus failed to work. It seems that the receding German Army had carried off all the good ones, to the considerable annoyance of the local population." Woollcott, *Command Is Forward*, 262.

249. Cpl. Harrison McMillen, of a signal platoon in the Rainbow Division, was billeted in Rolandseck and sent home a description of the region: "The place is on the Rhine river between Bonn and Coblence [*sic*] about 10 miles from Bonn. Towns are thick along the river, as soon as you pass out of one you are at the edge of another. This region is famous as a summer resort. The houses are mostly large and costly, with fine grounds about them. During the war times and at this season of the year most of the places are vacant so we have some excellent places to stay." *Arkansas Daily City Traveler*, February 3, 1919, 5.

250. William A. Clark was the son of Irish immigrants but paid for his own education at Iowa Wesleyan University. Clark first worked in the Colorado gold rush but moved on to the copper mines in Montana. After studying mineralogy at Columbia University for a year, he returned to the Montana copper mines, where he began to build his fortune. Although elected to the US Senate from Montana in 1899, the election was nullified on corruption charges. Clark was elected to the Senate again in 1901 and served his entire term. One obituary recounted the results of his business career: "At his death he was a director of 27 corporations, of 24 of which he was also president and in nearly every case he owned the majority of the stock. His wealth has been estimated at anywhere between $50,000,000 and $150,000,000." Senator Clark lived in a three-million-dollar mansion at 962 5th Avenue, where he died in 1925 at the age of eighty-six. *Brooklyn Daily Eagle*, March 3, 1925, 6, 22.

251. Bill Klem, Hall of Fame umpire from the National League, "did more umpiring and more for umpiring than any man who ever lived." Of unquestioned integrity, Klem instituted several changes to the game of baseball that are still in effect today, including a jerking thumb to indicate when a player was out, the palms-down signal that a player was safe (instituted on the fly during a bout of laryngitis), and taking position at home plate to the left of the catcher instead of directly behind him. After one bitter shouting match with legendary New York Giants manager John McGraw, the manager screamed, "I'll have your job for this!" Klem yelled back, "If you can get my job, then I don't want it!" While umpiring a game in St. Louis, Klem called three close plays against the home team. When the press found out that a fan had died of a heart attack during the game, one newspaper headline blared, "Umpire Klem Kills Innocent Fan." He died in 1951 at the age of seventy-seven. *Brooklyn Daily Eagle*, September 17, 1951, 17; July 6, 1953, 13; *Washington Evening Star*, September 19, 1951, III, 2.

252. It was about this time that a friend said of him, "Sergeant Gowdy, by the way, took two baths last week, which doubled his bathing average for the year." Woollcott, *Command Is Forward*, 260.

253. As American troops fought in the Argonne, the Anheuser-Busch Brewing Corporation had to fight a publicity war. Somehow the press had learned that Mrs. Adolphus Busch, wife of the leading stockholder, had purchased a million dollars in German bonds. The corporation spokesman tried to point out that the purchase had occurred eighteen months before the United States declared war on Germany. This was a true statement, but a disastrous public-relations mistake. By admitting the bonds were purchased in October 1915, the corporation had also admitted that they were purchased five months after the sinking of the *Lusitania*, in which American lives were lost. Editors howled that Busch money had been used to build more of those evil submarines to sink more ships to kill more Americans. One newspaper published the observation that Mrs. Busch "loves Germany so much that she spent most of her time in her beer-bought castle in Germany." *Canton Repository*, October 29, 1918, 8.

254. The Hotel Deshler opened for business on August 24, 1916, in Columbus, Ohio. An advertisement for the hotel proclaimed, "Built to meet the needs of an exacting and discriminating public, it has realized the highest ideals." The hotel boasted four hundred rooms, all with private baths. *Cleveland Plain Dealer*, August 25, 1916, 4.

255. Although there was some complaint that there were not enough castles to go around, not all doughboys were as upset as Sgt. Gowdy. One man joked that he awoke with a headache after sleeping in a bed for the first time since leaving home. As he sprawled across his bunk in the fortress of Ehrenbreitstein, Cpl. Ned Simpson, 1st Pioneer Regiment, opined on his current condition: "Well, here we are. It's from cooties to castles and from cannon balls to Christmas carols." The transformation was not lost on Pvt. Seth Ingalls, who confessed: "You know when we were trimming that Christmas tree and stringing wires for the electric lights I had to pinch myself to make sure I was not dreaming. Here we are tenants of one of the strongest forts in the world and it was occupied without even firing a cap pistol." *Washington Evening Star*, December 15, 1918, 4; *Logansport Pharos-Tribune*, December 28, 1918, 9.

256. When Runyon and Grantland Rice learned that Gowdy was stationed only ninety miles away from press headquarters, they arranged for the sergeant to join them. In addition to introducing Gowdy to Capt. Rickenbacker, Runyon and Rice "wined and dined him for the next five days as he had never been feted before, and in fact did their utmost to persuade him to stay another day or so. But Gowdy insisted on rejoining his regiment so, after a champagne breakfast, they let him go." Loading their friend into the back of an army limousine, they gave the driver detailed instructions on how to carefully transport the baseball star. As Gowdy curled up in the back seat, the driver sped off. No one knew if Gowdy ever learned that his chauffeur was actually Alexander Woollcott, drama critic for the *New York Times* and star reporter for *Stars and Stripes*. *Pottstown Mercury*, May 26, 1942, 4.

257. James A. Meissner, a native of Nova Scotia, was indeed the youngest major in the American Aviation Service during the war. He commanded the 147th Pursuit Squadron and organized the 167th Observation Squadron. A daring pilot, Meissner was officially credited with shooting down eight German planes. When asked if he intended to enter the mail service after the war, Maj. Meissner replied: "There are only two kinds of flying worth while—either war or pleasure. Aerial mail service flying will be merely high class chauffeuring. It will be a monotonous life to fly back and forth between two points." He obtained a degree in civil engineering from Cornell University and became an important official in the Alabama steel industry prior to his death in 1936 at the age of thirty-eight. *Washington Evening Star*, May 3, 1936, 19; *Santa Ana Register*, December 26, 1918, 1.

258. Capt. Douglas Campbell left Harvard to join the American flying school in France. On March 6, 1918, he and Eddie Rickenbacker flew the first American combat mission of the war. Rickenbacker would later say of his friend: "I candidly believe that had he not been wounded, Doug would have outrivaled my record. I have often thought that a great number of German airmen came to an untimely end simply because Douglas and I were striving to outdo each other, and not so much because the greatest war in history was in progress." Campbell became America's first ace on May 31, 1918, when he shot down his fifth German aircraft. He would later modestly admit, "Because I was the first American to shoot down some planes, they gave me more medals than they should have." He died in 1990 at the age of ninety-four. *San Francisco Chronicle*, June 9, 1918, 1; *San Jose Evening News*, January 12, 1921, 1; *European Stars and Stripes*, October 18, 1990, II, 4.

259. In a move that almost mimicked Johnny Cash's 1969 song "A Boy Named Sue," Mrs. William Fauntleroy named her son Cedric Errol after the hero of the book titled *Little Lord Fauntleroy*. His mother curled his long yellow hair and dressed the boy in velvet suits and lace collars, leading to a decade of fisticuffs. Cedric would later recall, "Curls and velvet pants made a man of me." With an aviation and automobile background, Fauntleroy paid his own way to France, joined the Lafayette Flying Corps, and was soon accepted into its American counterpart, where he became a test pilot. After the armistice, Maj. Fauntleroy helped to form the *Kosciuszko Escadrille* and flew for Poland against Russia from 1919 to 1920. He became a successful investment banker and horse breeder and died in 1973. Ironically, both his wife and daughter died in airplane crashes. US NARA, Record Group 59, US Passport Applications; *Baton Rouge Advocate*, June 7, 1936, 12; *Dallas Morning News*, March 17, 1936, II, 6; *Lima News*, November 17, 1946, 16.

260. Correspondent Percy Hammond, of the *Chicago Tribune*, wrote that "the happy American military police rule the city as complacently as if it were Wapakoneta in Ohio." *Lincoln Evening Journal*, January 9, 1919, 12.

261. Wilbur Forrest, correspondent for the *New York Tribune*, gave additional details on "the tars of the river navy": "A regular marine officer is in command of the river fleet of thirteen ships now patrolling the Rhine. Regular Rhine navigators do the steering and stoking, and the marines do 'theirs' in the most un-nautical language. But the navy is on the job, as these dry land marines might show if the occasion arose to work the machine guns mounted fore and aft. The 'admiral' of the navy is General Dickman." *New York Tribune*, February 6, 1919, 10.

262. When Alfred Dyreff, a Coblenz jeweler, attempted to sell watch fobs bearing an Iron Cross and crossed American flags, he was hustled off to jail by the army's intelligence service. Dyreff was eventually fined 500 marks for misconduct and misuse of the American flag. While the Iron Cross business had been brisk among the doughboys, the American motif proved too offensive to the military. *Chicago Tribune*, January 28, 1919, 2; *Winston-Salem Journal*, February 7, 1919, 2.

263. A wire service report mentioned how the Americans helped the German celebrate the coming holiday: "On the day before Christmas the Americans erected a pine tree eight meters high on the Esplanade overlooking the Rhine. After darkness had fallen the tree suddenly blazed into life. Countless electric lights were turned on and the celebration began. A band played Sousa's 'Stars and Stripes Forever' while a large crowd gathered. Paper trumpets and other articles were distributed among the children." Edwin James told of the topsy-turvy world where foreign invaders celebrated the holiday with the conquered foe: "The Christmas tree in the doughboys' barracks and the Christmas tree in the parlor of the German home grew on the same hillside, were bargained for in the same market place, and in some cases of which I know were trimmed from the same box of tinseled trappings." *Oregon Journal*, December 30, 1918, 6; *The State*, December 29, 1918, 4.

264. Paul Ludwig Hans Anton von Benekendorff und von Hindenburg came from a military family and experienced his first fighting in the Austrian-Prussian and Franco-Prussian wars of the nineteenth century. Retired by 1914, Hindenburg was recalled to service and sent to Germany's eastern front, where victories over the Russians at Tannenberg, Masurian Lakes, and Lodz won him the title of "Savior of the Fatherland." Elevated to supreme command of the Germany army in 1916, he retired again in June 1919. A force of stability in the chaos of postwar Germany, Hindenburg was elected president in 1925 and served in that capacity until his death in 1934. On the day of his death, Adolf Hitler stepped forward and took control of the German state. *Washington Evening Star*, August 2, 1934, 1, 3.

265. A doughboy named "Skinny" Jones elaborated on this new army that invaded Coblenz on the morning of December 26th: "A band of German youngsters with Christmas guns, drums and bugles tried to pass one of

the sentries. The leader was ten years old and was togged out in toy armor with a sword. He said Santa Claus gave them to him. If they had not had mostly candy guns we would all be dead ones. The rear guard was brought up by four little girls all carrying dolls." *Logansport Pharos-Tribune*, December 28, 1918, 9.

266. *The Baby Flier*.

267. Christian Donhauser was one of five German pilots selected to test-fly the aircraft that were to be turned over to the Americans at Coblenz. He claimed to have shot down some thirty Allied airplanes, including Lt. Quentin Roosevelt. Officers challenged Donhauser's assertion that he was sorry to have killed the president's son, one saying: "He lied. The Germans took pictures of Quentin's body, held between two German soldiers and sold the pictures throughout Germany. We saw the pictures." Donhauser, recently elevated to the rank of lieutenant, was seriously injured on New Year's Day 1919, when his plane crashed and he became pinned under the engine. He died less than two weeks later, when his aircraft suddenly plunged to the ground, ending his dream of becoming a flying instructor in the United States. *San Francisco Chronicle*, January 5, 1919, 1; *Oakland Tribune*, January 2, 1919, 1; *Harrisburg Evening News*, May 29, 1919, 2; *Washington Post*, February 7, 1919, 1; *Seattle Daily Times*, June 29, 1919, 24.

268. Sixty Fokker airplanes arrived by railcar in Coblenz on December 27, the first shipment of 200 German planes to be turned over to the Americans according to the armistice. One out of twenty aircraft was to be selected by American officers and then flown by German pilots to show they were airworthy. *Colorado Springs Gazette*, December 29, 1918, 1.

269. One of the youngest captains in the French air service, Georges Guynemer had been credited with shooting down fifty-three enemy airplanes in addition to another two dozen not on the official tally. He became so famous that French cafés began offering "*oeuf-a-la-coque Guynemer*," an egg dish that took exactly three minutes to prepare, supposedly the same amount of time necessary for the pilot to shoot down three enemy planes. On September 11, 1917, while patrolling northeast of Ypres in Flanders, Guynemer became separated from his patrol and was last seen pursuing a German two-seater. An investigation into his disappearance failed to discover Guynemer's fate until September 29, when a captured enemy pilot disclosed that the French airman had been killed and buried behind the German lines. *Washington Evening Star*, September 23, 1917, IV, 6; September 27, 1917, 23; September 29, 1917, 2; *Brooklyn Daily Eagle*, September 26, 1917, 1.

270. Sublieutenant Jean Navarre was one of the first French aviators to become an ace in the war, officially downing twelve enemy aircraft, although newspaper accounts listed a total of nineteen. The French ace was removed from the air service "because of his eccentric escapades" and in 1917 was imprisoned after running down several Paris policemen in his automobile. After his release, Navarre negotiated a movie contract to fly an airplane under the Arc de Triomphe during the Allied victory march, a confined space that left only five feet on each end of the wings. The stunt never came off, since Navarre crashed his civilian aircraft while avoiding another machine at the Villacoublay airfield a few days before the big event. He died shortly thereafter in a military hospital. *Washington Times*, July 11, 1919, 5; *Washington Post*, July 12, 1919, 2; *New York Times*, July 15, 1919, 3.

271. A favorite of his father, President Theodore Roosevelt, Quentin always kept the White House staff on their toes. On one occasion he smuggled a pony upstairs to his brother's sick room. On another, the youngster was found carrying an active hive of honey bees. Immediately following America's declaration of war in 1917, Quentin joined the Canadian Aviation Corps to get a jump on getting to France. On July 10, 1918, reports from France credited young Roosevelt with shooting down his first German aircraft. Four days later he failed to return from an encounter with the enemy. His father released the following statement: "Quentin's mother and I are very glad that he got to the front and had the chance to render some service to his country, and to show the stuff there was in him before his fate befell him." Following an American advance, his grave was discovered near the village of Chamery, with a wooden cross that read, "Lieut. Quentin Roosevelt, buried by the Germans." *Washington Evening Star*, April 14, 1917, 11; July 11, 1918, 11; July 17, 1918, 1; August 8, 1918, 1.

272. The most important "filbert" to arrive in Coblenz was the Prince of Wales, who arrived late in December. Two notable events occurred during his visit. Herbert Bailey, of the *London Daily Mail*, "wearing the regalia of a British war correspondent," arrived early for the prince's reception at an area castle with a retinue of American reporters. Sentries, supposing that Bailey was the anticipated royalty, saluted him. Word sped to the castle, where the garrison turned out to present arms. Snappy salutes were exchanged all around while movie cameras recorded the momentous arrival. Embarrassed officers soon learned of their mistake, and the arrival of Herbert Bailey never got into theaters. When the real prince arrived, he insisted on a visit to the war correspondents' Raspberry Club. Damon Runyon, Bozeman Bulger, and two other correspondents were playing stud poker when the prince was introduced, but quickly resumed their game. Somewhat rebuffed, the prince sauntered over to where another group of correspondents were engaged in a heated game of craps. Otto Higgins watched incredulously as the prince "pulled a roll of German marks out of his pocket and got down on his hands and knees and joined the boys in the crap game." When the prince tried to buy a round of drinks, the reporters politely told him that all drinks were free. Higgins concluded his story: "After that we took the Prince to our bosoms and took him to the New Year's Eve ball at Coblenz where we had him pose with an American telephone operator and an American nurse for his picture." *Winston-Salem Journal*, January 17, 1919, 4; *Amarillo Globe-Times*, December 8, 1936, 2.

273. Doughboys could purchase ducks and geese for from ten to fifteen dollars each. Officers and enlisted men generally chipped in to buy these supplements to army rations. *Lincoln Evening Journal*, December 24, 1918, 1.

274. James Forman Sloan would later change his name to James Todhunter Sloan to give credence to his nickname of "Tod." Called by some the greatest jockey in the world, Sloan rose from obscurity to riding horses for the Prince of Wales, for whom he perfected a crouching style of riding to lessen wind resistance. Estimated to have won more than a million dollars, Sloan slid from fame and affluence to poverty, alcoholism, divorce,

and scandal. Standing but 5 feet, 1 inch, "Little Toddy" at the age of fifty-nine admitted, "I haven't got a dime. I'm a pauper. Kicked all my money away. But if I had my life to live over again I'd do the same thing." From hobnobbing with royalty, actresses, and sporting gentlemen, Sloan ended up penniless, a charity case in the county hospital, when he died in 1933. US NARA, Record Group 59, US Passport Applications; *Washington Evening Star*, November 29, 1933, 19; *San Francisco Chronicle*, December 22, 1933, 1; *San Bernardino County Sun*, December 22, 1933, 18.

275. Maximilian Müller had been an army mechanic and driver but transferred to the air service as a pilot on the eve of the war. A bad crash resulted in two broken legs, which postponed Müller's aerial career. By the time of his death in January 1918, he claimed to have thirty-eight victories over Allied aircraft, although there seems to be some dispute over the total. Müller fell to his death after being shot down. Norman L. R. Franks, *Albatros Aces of World War I* (Oxford: Osprey, 2000), 56; *New York Sun*, January 16, 1918, 2.

276. Just days after this, Theodore Roosevelt Jr. would receive word of the death of his father, the former president. He would relay the doleful news to his brother Kermit, who was a captain in the 7th Field Artillery, and the pair would stay up all night talking in the hamlet of Holler. News dispatches the next morning confirmed the former president's death, and the brothers relayed the reports to their brother-in-law, Lt. Col. Richard Derby, a surgeon in the 2nd Division. *Chicago Tribune*, January 9, 1919, 3.

277. According to correspondent Herbert Bailey, who got his information from the disbursing officer at Coblenz, by the last week in February 1919, the German government had sent payments to cover American occupation duty that totaled 109,000,000 marks ($27,250,000). *Greensboro Daily News*, February 25, 1919, 1.

278. In order to finance the war effort, the US government began to issue Liberty Loan Bonds that paid 3.5 percent interest and were exempt from all tax. These bonds were advertised as a wise investment since the rate of return was generous and the security was better than money in a bank. One provision of the authorizing legislation stated that should future loans be authorized at a higher rate, these bonds would automatically share in that increase. *New York Times*, May 27, 1917, 1.

279. By the time War Savings Stamps were offered to patriotic investors who could not afford the higher-priced bonds, the investment rate had risen to 4 percent. For example, if an investor lent the government $4.12 and kept the stamp until its maturity date in 1923, the principal plus interest would equal $5.00. Stamps were affixed to certificates that contained an investors name and address, so that no one but the original owner could cash them. *New York Sun*, December 3, 1917, 6.

280. A leader in finance, commerce, and industry, George Walbridge Perkins started from humble origins but became personal friends with Theodore Roosevelt and J. P. Morgan. When the New York Senate refused to confirm his appointment as president of the State Food Control Commission, Perkins threw himself into patriotic endeavors with the Red Cross, Liberty Loan, and YMCA. After the armistice he went to Europe to investigate claims of waste and inefficiency against the latter organization. He published his report in 1919, explaining that "what it tried to do was to respond to every call the Army made on it." Mistakes had been made, but overall the YMCA had generally responded with speed and efficiency, despite overwhelming obstacles. George Perkins died, aged fifty-eight, in 1920, his doctors agreeing that his death had been hastened by an attack of influenza suffered in 1919. *New York Sun*, June 19, 1920, 1, 6; George W. Perkins, *Report on Activities of the YMCA with the AEF* (New York: War Work Council of the YMCA, 1919), 19–20.

281. Edwin James summed up the YMCA shortcomings as "first, the management of the canteens; second, unfortunate selection of much of its personnel; and third, too much care for the moral welfare of the American doughboy." On the first complaint James noted that the doughboys had read that folks at home had donated millions to the organization and balked at paying high prices, summing up the attitude as "why the hell should we have to pay big prices for these things when the money was given to the YMCA?" As for the second complaint, he had seen firsthand that many of the representatives were "best described in American slang as 'lemons,'" some of whom "should have stayed at home and conducted pink teas and made chatauqua speeches, or, in some instances, kept on driving trucks." As for the doughboys' moral welfare, James pointed out that "the army is no reformatory and war is no Sunday school picnic" and "American soldiers came to France to whip the Germans and not to get holy." Despite good intentions, the YMCA directors had violated common sense, which was to "go out among soldiers and talk to them to find out what they are thinking." *Houston Post*, January 7, 1919, 1, 7.

282. Edwin James offered additional comments that too much time and effort had been made in attempting to protect the doughboys "from evils which beset young men in 'leave areas.'" James continued: "The American soldier is well behaved, can take care of himself and does not look kindly upon being 'wet-nursed' when he gets leave." He also contended that the employment of female secretaries would have brought more sympathy and understanding than the "religious zeal and fervor" of the men. Cyril Brown noted that despite a smaller organization and budget, the Salvation Army "has won the respect and affection of the doughboys." Admitting that the YMCA had serious personnel and distribution problems, Brown did see one bright spot in its efforts: "The most successful phase of the YMCA's work here has been the providing of entertainment for the troops, which was badly needed, and papers to the doughboys marooned in obscure Rhine villages." *Seattle Daily Times*, January 28, 1919, 4; *Winston-Salem Journal*, January 10, 1919, 3.

283. Born just before the outbreak of the Civil War, Leonard Wood graduated from the medical school at Harvard University in 1884 and began a general practice. Adventure beckoned, and in 1886 he joined the army as a contract surgeon, serving until 1891 with such noted Indian fighters as Nelson Miles and Henry Lawton. He was awarded the Medal of Honor while acting as medical officer with Lawton's command. Selected as physician at the White House in 1892, his political connections led in 1898 to command of the "Rough Riders," of which Theodore Roosevelt became his lieutenant colonel. He rose to the rank of major general of volunteers and later

to the same rank in the US Army prior to the war. His theories on preparedness led to the Plattsburg Plan of civilian military training. Gen. Wood raised and trained the 89th Division at Camp Funston but was denied a command in France because Gen. Pershing did not want him. He ran for president in the 1920 election but was beaten by Warren G. Harding, who appointed him governor general of the Philippines. Gen. Wood returned from that post shortly before his death in 1927 at the age of sixty-six. *Washington Evening Star*, August 7, 1927, 1, 5.

284. After losing his left arm in the Sepoy Rebellion, British general Samuel Joseph Browne devised a unique belt-and-shoulder-strap arrangement that would allow an effective use of the saber or sword. First employed in Afghanistan in 1879, Sam Browne's belt was soon adopted for use by all officers in the British army. Gen. Pershing made it standard equipment for American officers to wear overseas, although the belt was not authorized for wear in the States. *Washington Evening Star*, July 24, 1921, II, 3; *Springfield Republican*, August 26, 1937, 10.

285. Runyon may have voiced this uniform complaint upon an officer's comment that had recently appeared in *Stars and Stripes*: "I will be obliged to buy a new uniform as my Sam Browne belt has worn a strip across my shoulder. If we were allowed to wear our belts I could get along with the old uniform until I am mustered out of the service. I have no overcoat. I cannot wear my trench coat, therefore I will have to spend some more of my hard earned money for a coat, which I will throw away or give to the janitor after I am mustered out." *Stars and Stripes*, January 3, 1919, 5.

286. "Omar" was the brand name for cigarettes popular during the war. *Washington Evening Star*, September 11, 1918, 10.

287. While doughboys could cuss the ubiquitous Ford trucks when they broke down or obstructed traffic, a few had a different opinion. After learning that his lieutenant colonel had found a way to ship his horse back to Massachusetts, Maj. Henry W. Wheelock, 101st Supply Train, sought to do the same with his war-worn Ford truck. The vehicle had been donated to his National Guard unit by Fitchburg Paper Company employees, and Wheelock had used it constantly in France, Luxembourg, and Germany. At last report, the major was searching for a way to smuggle his now-surplus vehicle back to America. *Fitchburg Sentinel*, March 1, 1919, 8.

288. Truck driver Fred Varner explained the perils of driving in France and Germany: "We surely have some time when we move on the road with the trucks. The road is covered with mud and when you get to the side of the road the least bit she goes into the axle, some of the boys run off the road into trees, some into curb stones, into ditches, fences, so you know what kind of a time we have over here." *Shippensburg Chronicle*, January 9, 1919, 2.

289. The entire Roosevelt family seemed to be "born of battle." In addition to President Theodore Roosevelt's service as lieutenant colonel of the 1st US Volunteer Cavalry in the Spanish-American War, all four sons went off to war. Lt. Quentin was killed when his airplane was shot down in 1918. Both Maj. Theodore Jr. and Capt. Archie were wounded that same year. Capt. Kermit served as an officer both in the British army and the AEF but emerged unscathed. During the Second World War, Theodore Jr. died in Normandy in 1944, Kermit died in Alaska in 1943, and Archie was again wounded in the South Pacific during 1944. *Brooklyn Daily Eagle*, July 22, 1918, 20; *Washington Evening Star*, July 14, 1944, 2.

290. Runyon's opinion of Pershing jumped a notch after the war, when William Randolph Hearst sent him to sound out the famous general on writing a series of war articles for the huge sum of $125,000. Pershing responded: "No, I can't accept. I don't mind telling you I could use the money, but it would be unethical for me to take it while I am in office." *Idaho Statesman*, December 11, 1941, 4.

291. In 1943, relying on his observations in two world wars, Runyon claimed that "the fact that a man is a general does not argue military genius. He may merely have lived long enough to automatically move up in the line of Army promotion." He continued: "Among our generals, in about the same proportion to numbers as among civilians, we have chowderheads and nincompoops. We have comic supplement generals with fat stomachs who have come up out of the huffle-scuffle of war from years of obscurity to great responsibilities in the military establishment and toward the civilian population and who huff and puff at the latter in a most alarming fashion." While he argued that some generals could not be "entrusted with the business details of a peanut stand," the majority were "brilliant men under any and all circumstances." The bottom line was that competent men always outnumbered the incompetent. *Macon Telegraph*, March 30, 1943, 4.

292. Douglas MacArthur conceived and organized the famous Rainbow (42nd) Division of National Guard units at the start of the war. He finished it as the youngest American general in France, with a chest full of medals. Popular with the press, he was called the D'Artagnan of the AEF. During one of the last nights of the war, MacArthur was actually arrested by his own men when they found him wandering outside the lines with his rank concealed under an overcoat. He quickly proved his identity. One little-known incident regarding MacArthur was shared by correspondent Will Irwin. On the night of November 10, 1918, MacArthur and Gen. Edward F. McGlachlin were ordered by army headquarters to take Sedan if it cost every man in their divisions. MacArthur refused to waste lives with the armistice looming next day. McGlachlin agreed that the order was foolish, but felt compelled to obey. MacArthur, who was the senior officer, thereupon placed McGlachlin under arrest until noon on November 11, one hour after the armistice had taken effect. Upon his death in 1964, Gen. Douglas MacArthur was arguably the most famous military officer in the world. *Washington Evening Star*, April 6, 1964, 8; *Philadelphia Inquirer*, November 15, 1918, 1; *East Liverpool Evening Review*, January 26, 1929, 3.

293. François de l'Espigarie de Tessan was descended from one of the old aristocratic French families. An enthusiastic traveler, Tessan became enthralled with America and wrote two books about his time there before the war, *Trans-Atlantic Sketches* and *Promenades to the Far West*. Wounded in battle with the Germans at Arras in 1915, he toured America with Marshal Joffre in 1917. While still convalescent, Lt. Tessan, who spoke perfect English, served as a press liaison officer before returning to the 237th Regiment. A prominent journalist and

politician after the war, he became an undersecretary of state and a French deputy. During World War II his friendship with President Franklin Roosevelt and affiliation with American interests led to his arrest and confinement in a German prison camp. Tessan's death was officially confirmed on April 19, 1945. *Washington Times*, April 25, 1917, 1; *San Francisco Chronicle*, April 22, 1933, 3; April 23, 1945, 14; *Cleveland Plain Dealer*, June 28, 1936, 7.

294. Felix Verdier came to San Francisco in 1849 and later founded the City of Paris Dry Goods Company. His granddaughter Suzanne went off to visit Paris in 1913, when she met François de Tessan, then a rising political figure. The couple married that year after a whirlwind courtship. *San Francisco Chronicle*, December 21, 1932, 19.

295. Joseph Jacques Cesaire Joffre served in the Franco-Prussian War as a lieutenant of artillery. As his career advanced, Joffre, noted as a mathematician and engineer, served in numerous French colonies, including Formosa, Indo-China, Sudan, and Madagascar. The outbreak of war found Joffre in command of the French army and tasked with halting the seemingly irresistible German advance on Paris. He successfully held off the Germans, but he was unprepared for the trench warfare that followed. Gen. Joffre failed to understand the political climate and was replaced at the end of 1916, although he received the promotion to Marshal of France as a reward for the Marne victory. Marshal Joffre died in 1931 at the age of seventy-nine. *Washington Evening Star*, January 3, 1931, 1, 2.

296. Edward N. Hurley, president of a machine company bearing his name, served during the war as chairman of the United States Shipping Board. Tasked first with assembling workers and building new merchant ships, then later with the shipment of men and supplies to France, Hurley would later claim that American shipping had turned the tide in the war. His efforts were rewarded with a Distinguished Service Medal. After the armistice he served on several international commissions and was a Goodwill Ambassador to the 1928 World's Fair. In his later years "he held directorships in several automobile companies, utilities, railroads, traction companies, steamship lines and banks." Edward Hurley died in 1933 at the age of sixty-nine. *Washington Evening Star*, November 15, 1933, 9.

297. Born in 1855, William S. Benson graduated from the Naval Academy in 1877. By 1907, he had risen through the ranks to become commandant at Annapolis and later of the Philadelphia Navy Yard. Appointed chief of naval operations, Benson sailed to Europe in 1917 to coordinate naval strategy with the Allies. Working primarily in London and Paris, Benson was the American naval representative at the armistice talks. He returned to the United States in 1919 to be retired after more than forty-five years of service. He served a year as the fourth chairman of the Shipping Board and remained another seven years as a commissioner of that organization. By Act of Congress, Benson was promoted to full admiral on the retired list in 1930. The admiral died two years later at the age of seventy-six. *Washington Evening Star*, May 20, 1932, 1.

298. Charles Marie Emmanuel Mangin was a lifelong soldier, his early days spent across the globe in Senegal, French Sudan, China, West Africa, and Morocco. He commanded a division, corps, and army and became famous for his recapture of Fort Douaumont in 1916. He was unjustly deprived of command in 1917 but was exonerated and reinstated in time to lead a counteroffensive that helped end the war. Afterward, Mangin was one of the French leaders who advocated the creation of a buffer state along the Rhine that would separate France from Germany. He died in 1925 at the age of fifty-eight. *Washington Evening Star*, May 12, 1925, 1; Pope and Wheal, *Dictionary of the First World War*, 302.

299. Benjamin M. Kauff played outfield for several years in the minor leagues until he became a star hitter in the short-lived Federal League in 1914 and 1915. Standing 5 feet, 6 inches, and weighing 170 pounds, Kauff joined the New York Giants in 1916, and his agent promoted him as "greater than Ty Cobb." A wartime poll of doughboys revealed that replicas of his bat were third in popularity only to Cobb and Walter Johnson. Although he was found innocent on a charge of auto theft, the baseball commissioner gave Kauff a lifetime suspension in 1921. Some complained that the punishment resulted from anti-Semitism. From 1926 to 1931, Benny faced three charges of bootlegging and one of robbery. Despite his legal troubles, he spent twenty-two years as a Giants scout and worked as a salesman prior to his death in 1961 at the age of seventy-four. *Winston-Salem Journal*, September 30, 1917, 15; *Colorado Springs Gazette*, April 18, 1920, 19; *Atlanta Constitution*, January 18, 1922, 11; *Lima News*, September 26, 1918, 8; *Wisconsin Jewish Chronicle*, August 20, 1934, 5; *Portsmouth Daily Times*, July 27, 1926, 9; *Coshocton Tribune*, April 27, 1929, 5; November 20, 1961, 13; *Sandusky Register*, March 22, 1931, 1; *New Philadelphia Daily Times*, September 9, 1926, 7.

300. In a startling premonition, Gen. Foch warned the American correspondents that within a few years Germany might again initiate another world war. According to one who was there, Foch declared: "We must make peace absolute. Our success must guard us against future aggressions. France has the right to take effective measures of protection, after her formidable efforts to save civilization. Her natural frontier, which will protect civilization, is the Rhine. It is on the Rhine we must halt the Germans. It is by using the Rhine that we must make it impossible for Germany to repeat her coup of 1914." *San Antonio Evening News*, January 18, 1919, 1.

301. Spanish fever was one of numerous synonyms for the influenza pandemic that devastated the world in the years 1918 and 1919.

302. Influenza and its variety of synonyms were not to be taken lightly. Thousands would die in the epidemic that swept the AEF in 1918–1919. One of the earliest victims had been Don Martin, correspondent of the *New York Herald*, who had died of pneumonia on October 6, 1918, after covering the Argonne battle in its cold and rainy weather. *Boston Herald*, October 8, 1918, 13.

303. Born in England and educated in France, Henry Noble Hall began his press career for a variety of European newspapers, which sent him to cover affairs in Central and South America. After coming to the United

States in 1892, Hall worked for several American papers. He reported for the *London Daily Mail* and *Times* during the war, following which he became a diplomat, internationally known writer, and lecturer. In 1921, he coauthored a history of the 4th Division in the war. When he came down with cancer in the late 1940s, Hall allowed his doctors to treat him with radioactive iodine from Oak Ridge, Tennessee. At one point he joked with his doctors, "imagine me drinking a Hiroshima cocktail," as he downed the largest dose ever voluntarily taken by a human. His first treatment proved successful, but a second led to debility from which he could not rally. Henry Nobel Hall died in 1949 at the age of seventy-six. *Trenton Evening Times*, April 28, 1915, 6; *Washington Times*, January 28, 1921, 15; *Salt Lake Tribune*, March 27, 1949, 4.

304. Thomas Aloysius "Tad" Dorgan was one of America's best-known newspaper cartoonists. After his right hand was crippled as a youth, Dorgan learned to draw with his left hand and eventually joined the staff of the *San Francisco Bulletin*. In 1902, he headed east to work for the Hearst newspapers. Dorgan was credited with being one of the most influential contributors to the jargon of Americana. Some of his most popular sayings included "23, skidoo," "drugstore cowboy," "indoor sports," "for crying out loud," "the cat's meow," and "yes, we have no bananas." When Dorgan died in 1929 at the age of fifty-two, Damon Runyon summed up the secret of his success: "He was more than a cartoonist. He was a reporter in pictures of human life. He was the modern Hogarth. He made millions laugh out loud, but under the skin of his humor was a remarkable insight into the human soul—into people as we are and as we always will be." *Brooklyn Daily Eagle*, May 2, 1929, 1; May 5, 1929, 12.

305. African golf was a synonym for craps. One columnist explained the game for those unfamiliar with this widespread form of gambling: "You get as many as you want to play into a room. You produce a pair of dice. . . . Well, you start the game of 'African golf.' Seven or eleven wins. But you must talk to 'em. The favorite expression usually is: 'Come on, dice, baby needs a pair of shoes.'" He then added: "You continue the game until several of your guests have said their bit and donated to 'baby's shoes.' When the game is over the losers usually go out talking to themselves. Contrary to American golf, the African game has no 'nineteenth hole.' When you go in the 'hole' in the African game you stay there. The object is stay out of the 'hole.'" *Duluth News-Tribune*, December 22, 1919, 8.

306. Mayence was generally known as Mainz.

307. Joe Gans, standing 5 feet, 6½ inches, and weighing 133 pounds, was the lightweight champion boxer from 1902 to 1908. The son of a poverty-stricken and illiterate family, Gans began to box while employed as a delivery boy at the Baltimore fish market. When he proved too good against single fighters, Gans fought two men at a time. The boxer admitted modestly that "I was awfully fast and I could jab with my left hand." He captured the championship in 1902, when he beat Frank Erne in just 100 seconds. In a match against "Battling Nelson" in 1906, the champion retained his title after a bout lasting forty-two rounds. Nelson took the title from him in 1908, and his career virtually ended as symptoms of consumption appeared. Racism kept him from winning as much as his white opponents, but Gans estimated that he had earned over $300,000 from boxing and theatrical appearances in his short career, more than any other Negro boxer for decades to come. A stint in Arizona failed to cure his disease, and Gans returned to Baltimore to die in 1910. *Washington Bee*, August 13, 1910, 4.

308. William Dayton Perritt was a right-handed pitcher who was best known for his years with manager John McGraw and the New York Giants. Originally with the St. Louis Cardinals, Perritt became embroiled in the dispute between the National League and the upstart Federal League. He became a Giant. With a last name like Perritt, he quickly became known as Polly, shortened to Poll or Pol. His arm gave out in 1918, and he began dabbling in the oil business in Louisiana. An attempted comeback fizzled and he remained an oil man. During his tenure with the Giants, an inventor showed up with a pitching machine for the team to use in batting practice. Feeling like a baseball version of the legendary John Henry, Poll manipulated the machine so that it fired a volley of balls at the first batter, thereby assuring that real pitchers would pitch batting practice. Perritt died in 1947 at the age of fifty-five. *Pittsburgh Daily Post*, June 30, 1914, 13; *Houston Post*, March 4, 1915, 3; *Winnipeg Tribune*, November 7, 1918, 15; *Washington Times*, August 20, 1920, 16; *Corsicana Daily Sun*, August 21, 1928, 9; *San Diego Union*, October 17, 1947, II, 3.

309. Tyrus Raymond Cobb, "the Georgia Peach," arguably the greatest baseball player ever, played to win and did not care who got in his way. One eulogist described him as "mean as a wildcat, cagey as a fox, daring as a riverboat gambler." When Cobb claimed in a luncheon speech that "I never spiked anybody deliberately in my life," Bucky Harris, who had played against him, blurted out, "He'd cut your heart out!" By the time he retired after the 1928 season, Cobb held or had tied ninety-three major-league records. He led the American League in batting twelve times and led the league in stolen bases six times. At the age of thirty-nine he got six hits in six at bats. After playing his entire career with the Detroit Tigers, Cobb signed with the Philadelphia Athletics and hit .357 at the age of forty. When the first group of players was enshrined in the Baseball Hall of Fame, Ty Cobb received more votes than anyone else, including inductees such as Babe Ruth, Honus Wagner, Walter Johnson, and Christy Mathewson. Investment in Coca-Cola allowed Cobb to retire as a millionaire until his death in 1961 at age seventy-four. *Washington Evening Star*, July 18, 1961, 21.

310. Joe Weber (Joseph Maurice Weber) and Lew Fields (Lewis Maurice Schanfeld) were sons of Jewish immigrants who rose from the Bowery to become nationally renowned comedians. From dancing and singing in black face at local taverns for two dollars a day plus five beers, Weber and Fields ended up making $4,000 a week. They became a fixture on the vaudeville circuit in 1875 and by 1885 had opened their own music hall. Performances emphasized the use of exaggerated dialects to provoke laughter, poking fun at Italians, Frenchmen, Germans, Irish, and Jews, but Fields always said "a first-class German dialect is a great deal funnier." Performances such as "Fiddle De-Dee," "Hoity Toity," "Hurly Burly," "Pousse Café," and "Twirly Whirley" made them rich. The pair split in 1904 but reunited in 1912, and they worked off and on together until Fields's death in 1941. Weber

died the following year. *New York Times*, September 11, 1904, IV, 2; February 25, 1918, 10; *Sacramento Bee*, July 21, 1941, 2; *San Luis Obispo Telegram-Tribune*, July 21, 1941, 8; *San Diego Union*, May 11, 1942, 4.

311. Tiffany & Co., located at 5th Avenue and 37th Street in New York City, specialized in the sale of pearls, diamonds, jewelry, silver, clocks, watches, china, stationery, and, during the war, Liberty Bonds. *New York Times*, December 23, 1918, 5; *New York Evening World*, May 8, 1919, 5; *Brooklyn Daily Eagle*, October 7, 1918, 11.

312. Dreicer & Co. was located at 5th Avenue and 46th Street, just a few blocks down the street from Tiffany. Dreicer boasted of having jewels "of unsurpassed design and fabrication" and engagement rings containing "diamonds of supreme quality in Dreicer settings." *New York Tribune*, March 27, 1919, 13; May 13, 1919, 13.

313. Sgt. Maj. Howard McLellan, of the 27th Division, explained how the purchase of mementos in Coblenz was conducted by the doughboys: "For a '*Gott Mitt Uns*' belt, a patent leather helmet, trench knife or any souvenir that has German written on it, they part with their luxuries, blessed, as it were, by the German's remark, "*Gott Not Mitt Uns, Gott Mitt Amerikanische*." *New York Evening World*, January 9, 1919, 3.

314. Correspondent George Pattullo wrote that the sale of Iron Crosses "has been prodigious," but he could not understand how shopkeepers could offer such symbols of courage: "Imagine an American merchant peddling the Distinguished Service Cross to a conquering enemy. He would be hanged by the neck until he was very dead, indeed. Yet these boche tradesmen make no bones about selling the decorations for which hundreds of thousands of their bravest shed their blood. Worse still, they do not appear to lose standing by it in their communities." *Baltimore American*, July 6, 1919, II, 8.

315. When the *Leviathan* left port on February 26, one of those onboard wrote, "Last sight of France about 3 o'clock. Nobody cares." *New York Evening World*, March 6, 1919, 6.

316. The *Leviathan* was commissioned in the US Navy in July 1917. It was 954 feet in length, fifty feet longer than the height of the Woolworth Building, and weighed 69,000 tons. At top speed the *Leviathan* would consume almost 1,000 tons of coal a day. When approaching Hoboken, the mammoth ship required eighteen tug boats to guide it to its dock. On ten trips to Europe prior to the armistice, it carried well over 100,000 soldiers, almost one-twentieth of the AEF. Over 10,000 wounded and sick men went home on these return voyages. *History of the USS* Leviathan (Brooklyn, NY: *Brooklyn Eagle* Job Department, 1919), 218–19.

317. John Francis O'Ryan received his education at City College of New York and New York University, being admitted to the bar in 1898. He joined the New York National Guard in 1897 and, by 1912, commanded the New York division. After attending the Army War College, O'Ryan led his New York troops on the Mexican border and after their mobilization in 1917. Newly designated the 27th Division, O'Ryan's division of New Yorkers fought on the British front in the campaigns of 1918. The general resumed his law practice, interrupting it only to act as New York City police commissioner in the 1930s and the state civilian defense director in World War II. He died in 1961. Venzon, *The United States in the First World War*, 424–25.

318. Upon the outbreak of war in 1914, the *Vaterland*, pride of the Hamburg-American Line, was interned in port at Hoboken, New Jersey. After the United States entered the war in April 1917, the ship was commissioned in the US Navy for use as a troop transport. Although there had been some malicious damage by the German crewmen, the greatest problem was that the ship's engineers had removed every blueprint, plan, and drawing. But those were not the only problems. According to Capt. Phelps, "Deterioration due to idleness, neglect and absence of upkeep was serious and widespread. The two gigantic low pressure ahead turbine rotors were found to require entire re-blading. Every length of piping, every piece of machinery had to be disassembled, inspected and then assembled and tested." It took until November before the newly christened *Leviathan* was ready for sea. *Kansas City Star*, June 22, 1919, III, 2.

319. George W. Peppard served in the Spanish-American War and on the Mexican border prior to being commissioned a lieutenant in the quartermaster department of the 27th Division. While in France, Peppard was seriously wounded in the forehead, the officer next to him being killed by the same artillery round. Commissioned captain in September 1918, he settled in Scarsdale, New York, where he died in 1941. *New York Sun*, July 15, 1917, 5; *Brooklyn Daily Eagle*, January 26, 1919, V, 6; July 26, 1941, 5.

320. Udo J. Keppler first received recognition when he was selected to the second team, New York City scholastic football team. He played multiple sports at the University of Pennsylvania. During one lacrosse contest with a bitter rival, Keppler was disqualified "for pummeling one of the Lehigh forwards," costing his team the win. He was also a star on the wrestling mats. A classmate humorously observed of Keppler and a fellow wrestler: "After the coach had taught these boys not to bite ears and pull hair they became very valuable to our wresting team. Many of us wonder what pleasure is found in sitting, for hours, half clad upon the mats. But since they win the meets we can forgive their long periods of rest." *New York Tribune*, December 7, 1913, II, 3; *Philadelphia Inquirer*, May 10, 1917, 12; *The Record of the* [University of Pennsylvania] *Class of 1918* (Philadelphia: University of Pennsylvania, 1918), 201.

321. Units from the 27th Division that did not sail on the *Leviathan* would be transported to New York aboard the *Mauretania*, *Nieuw Amsterdam*, *Agamemnon*, *Mount Vernon*, *Hollandia*, *America*, and *Missouri*. *New York Tribune*, March 4, 1919, 9; *New York Evening World*, March 8, 1919, 3.

322. The *Plattsburg* arrived in New York on March 8, bearing a squad of casuals from the 105th Machine Gun Battalion of the 27th Division. *New York Tribune*, March 9, 1919, 14.

323. The Cunard liner *Caronia* left Brest on February 25 and reached New York on March 5, a day before the arrival of the *Leviathan*. The *Caronia* carried about 4,000 passengers, mainly the 317th Engineers but also a handful of casuals from the 27th Division. *Brooklyn Daily Eagle*, March 6, 1919, 3.

324. Harry Montgomery, known to theater aficionados as "Scamp," began his career in a traveling tent show at the age of fifteen. After playing numerous small towns across the Midwest, Scamp learned to play the trombone

and became a talented musician. He came to New York before the turn of the century to become a Broadway actor. Montgomery was appearing in the play *Get Rich Quick Wallingford* when he died in 1911. *New York Times*, July 9, 1911, II, 9.

325. Runyon here alludes to the hotel empire built by Caesar Ritz, whose chain of Ritz hotels became the standard for elegance and service. The original Ritz Hotel opened forty years before the war, and it was followed by a chain of hotels around the world, including the Ritz-Carlton in New York City. Caesar Ritz died in 1918. *Brooklyn Daily Eagle*, November 6, 1918, 20; *New York Times*, November 6, 1918, 17.

326. Florenz Ziegfeld, originator of the Ziegfeld Follies, began his career with Buffalo Bill Cody's Wild West Show, but his parents' objections led him to quit and become manager of the Chicago Musical College. A successful Broadway producer, Ziegfeld produced his first Follies performance in 1907, and they ran annually for twenty years. Citing exorbitant costs of production, he suspended the Follies for four years but had one last run in 1931. The early Follies "led the trend toward nudity on the stage," leading to increased interest and revenues, but Ziegfeld's later shows glorified the American girl more fully clad. He married the famous actress Billie Burke, who would one day become Glinda the Good Witch of the North in the *Wizard of Oz*. Flo Ziegfeld died in 1932. *Brooklyn Daily Eagle*, July 23, 1932, 2.

327. After members of the Machine Gun Battalions of the 27th Division presented the minstrel show "Cavalry Days" during training camp, Gen. O'Ryan appointed Lt. William Alfred Halloran Jr. to be his "amusement officer." Halloran combed the division ranks for men with Broadway experience, from actors and directors to stage hands and electricians. The resulting musical comedy (no army stuff allowed), *You Know Me, Al*, was so popular that the stage troupe left training camp to present the play in New York City and Washington, DC. Proceeds went to purchase theatrical equipment to take overseas with the division. Halloran's play proved to be so popular with the doughboys that he continued to put on performances for veterans groups into the 1930s. *Brooklyn Daily Eagle*, January 11, 1918, 21; March 24, 1918, V, 6; April 11, 1918, II, 3; April 21, 1918, V, 8; May 14, 1932, 9; *Washington Herald*, April 19, 1918, 12.

328. March 4 was an especially rough day: "Soup at the midday meal was confined to soup plates only exercise of extreme finesse. Much soup transferred directly from plates to uniforms." Martin Green, correspondent of the *New York Evening World*, found a Brooklyn boy who, despite being the color of "weak pea soup" from sea sickness, perfectly encapsulated the feeling aboard the *Leviathan*. The young doughboy said: "I'm sick, but I'm happy. I don't care anything about the bunks and I don't care if the ship loops the loop all the way across the Atlantic. I haven't eaten anything since I came aboard and I don't care whether I eat anything or not before we land. I'M GOING HOME!" *New York Evening World*, March 6, 1919, 6.

329. Martin Green, one of Runyon's cabinmates, gave one example of the entertainment aboard: "'Broadway Boys' vaudeville show given for sailors of *Leviathan* in soldiers' mess hall. Four husky youths, dressed as soubrettes, almost cause a riot. Hundreds of sailors refuse to believe Walter Roberts, former athlete Syracuse University, is a male. Firmly believe he is one of the nurses or welfare workers. Several fights over the question." *New York Evening World*, March 6, 1919, 6.

330. Howard H. McLellan left his job on the *New York World* to enlist in the New York National Guard in 1917 and began his climb through the enlisted ranks until he finally reached the rank of sergeant major in the Headquarters Detachment, 27th Division. In the words of McLellan, who always seemed to have "a wicked little gleam in his eyes," this detachment was "mostly a clerical force," working behind the lines and trailing the division across France. At least they were safe there. McLellan wrote that after that first day attacking the Hindenburg Line, his original company in the 107th Infantry "went into the show 212 strong and is advancing now with 12 well men." *New York Evening World*, August 20, 1917, 3; February 4, 1919, 20; March 7, 1919, 20; *Gas Attack of the New York Division, 27th Div. U.S.A.*, last edition (March 1919): 43.

331. A machine gunner in the 27th Division, Russell J. Brown had teamed with James Fallon for a vaudeville act named "Me and Mickey," the former a dancer and the latter a funny man. The pair served together in France. Prior to the fighting at St. Souplet in October 1918, Brown and Fallon asked Lt. Halloran, director of the division theater group, if they could volunteer as stretcher bearers. One soldier who encountered the team at an aid station after their fifth trip carrying wounded comrades wrote that Brown was not the "dapper dancer" of old, and Fallon was no longer "the funniest man in the 27th Division." He noted the changes: "Nearly exhausted with parched throats and empty stomachs, smeared with blood and grime, helmets at jaunty angles on their tired heads, that's a sketch of those boys that night." When referencing the wounded they had to tote back, Brown remarked: "These poor devils are out of this hell, anyhow." *New York Tribune*, January 3, 1919, 11.

332. G. William Breck was the illustrator for Edward Streeter's letters that eventually appeared in *Dere Mable*. He had studied under the acclaimed art teacher Robert Henri and worked as an illustrator for the *New York Press* prior to his enlistment in the 107th Infantry. Breck explained that the former newsmen and artists of the division managed to build a room under a mess shack in South Carolina, giving some interesting details: "We accumulated a collection of pictures for the board walls, odd dishes and pots and cups, strangely military in contour were collected. We wrote and drew and lied and every night drank quarts of Sawtie's cocoa and ate pounds of cake and chocolate." In civilian life Breck became an editor for Brandt and Brandt literary agents and painted several murals at Colgate University prior to his death in 1936. *Gas Attack of the New York Division* 1, no. 24 (May 4, 1918): 8; *New York Evening World*, March 7, 1919, 20; *Pottstown Mercury*, November 17, 1936, 3.

333. *Dere Mable* was a collection of letters that had originally appeared in *Gas Attack of the New York Division* and appeared in book form in 1918. Its immense popularity can be divined from the following notice: "'*Dere Mable*,' Lt. Edward Streeter's joyous book about the life and love of a rookie, is now in its fourteenth printing, with a total output of 500,000 copies. It is selling at the rate of 5,000 copies per day, while a Special Overseas

Edition, printed on thin paper, lately brought out, was exhausted before the books were ready for shipment." *New York Times Book Review*, October 27, 1918, 464.

334. Edward Streeter graduated from Harvard in 1914, his college experience having included a stint as editor of the *Harvard Lampoon*. He was a reporter for the *Buffalo Express* when he joined the artillery in the 27th Division. While in training camp in South Carolina, Lt. Streeter contributed humorous letters from a fictitious soldier, challenged both by the grammar and spelling of the English language, to his best girl back home. A banker and bestselling author, Streeter wrote the popular novel *Father of the Bride*, which was made into an equally successful motion picture starring Spencer Tracy. He retired from the banking business in 1960 and died in 1976. *Boston Herald American*, April 3, 1976, 21.

335. An artist on the staffs of the *Kansas City Star*, *Chicago Tribune*, and *Judge Magazine*, Lauren Stout was a freelance artist when he enlisted in the 107th Infantry. "Stoutie" also had a way with words, as a fellow soldier noted: "His profanity is marvelous for its effective originality." Another comrade recalled that Stout "mixed with his paints a little of the something that lies at the bottom of the fleshpots of the world." He also had an interesting sense of humor. One of his sketches, titled "Camouflage," supposedly portrayed the 27th Division marching to billets as a group of soldiers are sitting around a table filled with wines and delicacies. The panel was, of course, completely blank. Echoing his comrades in 1919, Stout admitted, "Our return home was, of course, the happiest experience of all our happy army experiences." He died in 1942. *Seventh Regiment Gazette* 32, no. 8 (May 1918): 420; *Gas Attack of the New York Division* 1, no. 14 (February 23, 1918): 9; *New York Evening World*, March 7, 1919, 20; *History of the 107th Infantry, U.S.A.* (New York: Seventh Regiment Armory, 1920), 344; US NARA, Record Group 92, Records of the Office of the Quartermaster General, Interment Control Forms.

336. Hugh Stanislaus Stange's prewar credentials had included the dramatization of Booth Tarkington's play *Seventeen*, which was still running on Broadway when he went off to war. Part of the quartermaster department in the 27th Division's Headquarters Train, he and a coauthor wrote the script for *You Know Me, Al*. Stange became a prominent playwright after the war, a string of hits in the 1920s leading to an autobiographical portrayal of his wartime service, *The Long Road*, whose "scenes, its atmosphere, and its detail is pictured by one who went through the war in its most dramatic form." New York Adjutant General's Office, Abstracts of World War I Military Service, 1917–1919; *Washington Evening Star*, April 18, 1918, 5; *Boston Herald*, July 6, 1930, III, 8.

337. A well-known producer in New York with a long string of hit shows, David Belasco had been sent off to be educated at a monastery in Vancouver, where his father was mayor. After listening to a circus calliope for several nights, Belasco ran off and began a short-lived career as "Davido, the Boy Bareback Rider." Rescued from poverty in South America, Belasco acquired his own theater in 1902. Said to have amassed the largest dramatic library in the world, he also collected artifacts relating to Napoleon. Belasco was a firm believer in reincarnation and, upon the death of his beloved daughter, placed a guard and eternal flame outside her mausoleum to welcome her back. She did not reappear, nor did David Belasco after his death in 1931. *Brooklyn Daily Eagle*, May 15, 1931, 17.

338. Like many boxing promoters, Dick Curley had dealings with the shady side of the business. He was arrested in 1911 for "aiding and abetting a prize fight" when such bouts were illegal. The following year he was shot at from a moving car while walking innocently on the sidewalk at 3 a.m. By the time the United States entered the war, Curley had become a "special representative" of John Torrio, head of organized crime in Chicago and mentor to Al Capone. Following a brawl after a bout in 1924 in which he kicked a referee in the head, Curley was given a lifetime suspension by the New York Boxing Commission. Without access to the large venues in New York, Curley gradually disappeared from the boxing scene. *Brooklyn Daily Eagle*, April 28, 1919, II, 1; November 22, 1924, 15; *New York Evening World*, June 5, 1911, 2; *New York Tribune*, October 26, 1917, 17.

339. Cornelius Vanderbilt Jr. (actually Cornelius Vanderbilt IV) was the great-great-grandson of the builder of the New York Central Railroad. Embarrassed by his family's wealth, Cornelius enlisted as a private and spent most of his military career as a driver. He drove for Douglas Haig, commander of British forces in the war, and recalled one wartime experience during a gas attack: "There were five officers with me and they adjusted their masks but by the time I got the car to safety and began placing my mask in position the gas had taken effect on me. When I came to this country I lost fourteen of my teeth." After the war, Vanderbilt became a newspaperman and author. Before his death in 1974, he had married seven times and once quipped to a friend about his alimony payments: "It's expensive. None of them seem to remarry or die." *Brooklyn Daily Eagle*, January 21, 1919, 3; *Dallas Morning News*, July 8, 1974, 3; *New Orleans States-Item*, July 29, 1974, II, 2.

340. Raeburn Van Buren began his career as a cartoonist with the *Kansas City Star* but moved to New York in 1913, where he continued to draw until he went to France as a private in the 107th infantry. His illustrations would later appear in *Life Magazine*, *Saturday Evening Post*, *Collier's*, *Redbook*, and other magazines. In 1937, Van Buren created "Abbie an' Slats," a comic strip about life in small-town America that eventually appeared in 400 newspapers. Raeburn Van Buren died in 1987 after a fall at the age of ninety-six. *New York Times*, January 1, 1988, II, 4; *Cleveland Plain Dealer*, January 1, 1988, III, 12.

341. A private in the 107th Infantry, Cecil Calvert Beall had previously worked as an art director for a large film company in New York. When the division produced *You Know Me, Al*, Beall was placed in charge of scenery, costumes, and lighting. He received a week's leave to head for New York, where he gathered "materials for settings, costumes, and all the details that make a Broadway production just that." Between actions in Europe, Beall would practice his artwork by painting on the walls of broken-down buildings and "before very long a goodly sized chorus girl would appear." Upon reaching America, the success of *You Know Me, Al* led to a sequel of sorts, called *Let's Beat It*. Beall was again to supervise the scenery and costumes. During World War II he reproduced on canvas the famous photograph of the Marines raising the American flag on Mount Suribachi, Beall's newly created

image being used to advertise war bonds. *Duluth News-Tribune*, April 21, 1918, V, 8; *New York Times*, March 14, 1919, 11; March 23, 1919, IV, 7; *Omaha World Herald*, March 25, 1945, 11.

342. After attending Brooklyn College, John Phineas Deery enlisted in the New York National Guard a month after the declaration of war. He served as a private in the 107th Infantry until his discharge but reenlisted in the National Guard in 1921. He worked as an insurance adjuster and investment broker prior to his death in 1945. *Brooklyn Daily Eagle*, March 16, 1907, 6; New York Adjutant General's Office, Abstracts of World War I Military Service, 1917–1919; *Seventh Regiment Gazette* 36, no. 3 (December 1921): 29; US NARA, Record Group 29, US Census, 1920 and 1930, Brooklyn, New York; *New York Times*, November 13, 1945, II, 8.

343. Robert H. Deery was superintendent of the composing room for the *Morning* and *Evening World* when he died in 1920. After becoming a compositor on various New York newspapers, Deery came to the *Evening World* in 1888 and remained there until his death. A proud member of the *Evening World* Quarter Century Club, Deery was known universally as Bob. In a notice of his death, his employer noted that "the world at large suffers loss in his passing away." *New York Evening World*, April 16, 1920, 30; *Brooklyn Daily Eagle*, April 15, 1920, 2.

344. A graduate of Brooklyn College, Sgt. Robert J. Deery had served for three years in the old New York 7th Regiment. While in action with the 107th Infantry on September 28, 1918, Sgt. Deery was gassed and was hit in the leg by a bullet. *Brooklyn Daily Eagle*, December 20, 1918, 4.

345. Robert Winsor McCay, later known professionally as R. Winsor McCay Jr., was the model for the cartoon strip *Little Nemo*, which was created by his father. While a corporal with the Headquarters Troop, 27th Division, he won the British Military Medal. Following the war, Bob followed in the footsteps of his father and became a popular editorial cartoonist and illustrator. His work appeared in the Hearst publications, through the King Features Syndicate, and in the *Los Angeles Examiner*. After retiring from the newspaper business, Bob spent his last years producing artwork for the US Army at Fort Ord. He died in 1962. John F. O'Ryan, *The Story of the 27th Division* (New York: Wynkoop Hallenbeck Crawford, 1921), 921; *Boston Record American*, April 22, 1962, 12; *Santa Cruz Sentinel*, April 22, 1962, 1.

346. Winsor McCay began his artistic career painting street signs and theater posters. He worked for several Cincinnati newspapers, reporting the news and illustrating his own stories. McCay went to New York in 1902, and worked successively on the *Telegram*, *Evening Journal*, *Herald*, and *American*. He created several early comic strips, including the immensely popular *Little Nemo*, based on the antics of his son. McCay created the first animated cartoon, a short film based on 4,000 individual drawings, that laid the groundwork for Mickey Mouse and other Disney characters. Having enjoyed a life of wealth and fame, Winsor McCay died in 1934. *Washington Evening Star*, July 27, 1934, 9; *Dallas Morning News*, August 20, 1934, 4.

347. Raymond Thomas Moniz was famous throughout Brooklyn for "one of the most romantic marriages growing out of the mobilization of the Brooklyn National Guard." Then Capt. Moniz, after one day's engagement to Marian Elizabeth McCay, arrived early on Tuesday, October 2, 1917, and announced to Marian's parents: "I don't care whether you object or not. I am going to marry your daughter." The parents, who had known Moniz for a number of years, agreed. The captain and his bride-to-be drove to Manhattan to purchase an engagement ring and wedding ring. The couple was married on Wednesday and held a wedding dinner at the Hotel Knickerbocker before Moniz headed for training camp on Saturday. After serving as a major in the Quartermaster Department, Moniz sold real estate and worked as a county investigator until his death in 1961. *Brooklyn Daily Eagle*, October 4, 1917, 3; US NARA, Record Group 29, US Census, 1930 and 1940, Peekskill, New York; Record Group 92, Applications for Headstones, 1925–1970.

348. Martin Green left school at the age of fifteen to begin a newspaper career that took him from Iowa to Missouri to New York. He worked at the *Evening World* from 1901 until its suspension in 1931, then worked as a rewrite man at the *Sun* until his retirement in 1938. One of his editors at the *Evening World* called him "a shining star," boasting that Green's war reporting "made the other war correspondents look like a bunch of cubs." Before leaving his desk for the last time, Green wrote out the material for his own obituary and filed it for use when he died the following year. Stanley Walker, *City Editor* (Baltimore: Johns Hopkins University Press, 1934), 317; Charles E. Chapin, *Charles Chapin's Story* (New York: G. P. Putnam's Sons, 1920), 191; *Daily Illinois State Journal*, December 9, 1939, 2.

349. Lucius Horatio Bigelow Jr. was an acknowledged sports star at Yale. Recognized as an All-American in football, he also participated in rowing, shot putting, and hammer throwing and skated for the hockey team. His classmates voted him "the man most to be admired at Yale, the best athlete, and the man who has done the most for Yale." After graduating from Yale in 1908, Bigelow graduated from Columbia Law School in 1911. He served with the 105th Machine Gun Battalion in France, returned, and began a law practice in Connecticut, where he died in 1961. *Brooklyn Daily Eagle*, June 7, 1908, II, 1; O'Ryan, *Story of the 27th Division*, 1109; *Bridgeport Post*, July 10, 1961, 27.

350. Following his graduation from Princeton in 1914, Alwyn Ball III went to Europe, where he drove an ambulance for the American Field Service until February 1915. He was cited for gallantry twice while with the 105th Machine Gun Battalion, first "for determined courage and qualities of skilled leadership frequently demonstrated under fire" and a second time "for courage and determination in making personal reconnaissance under heavy enemy shell and machine gun fire." Ball entered the real-estate business after the war but reentered the army as a major in 1942. He served at the Army War College until his death in 1944. John B. Edmonds, ed., *St. Paul's School in the Second World War* (Concord, NH: Alumni Association, St. Paul's School, 1950), not paginated.

351. Walter G. Andrews, known as "Ham" to his friends, was a grandson of Gen. Walter Q. Gresham, who had served as President Cleveland's secretary of state. A Princeton graduate in 1913, Andrews was working in a paint factory when he enlisted and joined the New York National Guard on the Mexican border in 1916. He

ended the world war as a major and was awarded the Distinguished Service Cross after being wounded while assaulting the Hindenburg Line while with the Machine Gun Battalion of the 107th Infantry. Turning to politics after coming home, Andrews served as a New York congressman from 1931 to 1949. Upon advice of his doctors, he declined to run for reelection in 1948 and died the following March. O'Ryan, *Story of the 27th Division*, 897; *Washington Evening Star*, March 6, 1949, II, 2.

352. George Reynolds graduated from Harvard in 1907 and got a masters degree in 1908 and a law degree in 1910. Reynolds was manager of the Harvard football team in 1906. Commissioned a second lieutenant in the National Guard in 1917, he was given the same rank in the 105th Machine Gun Battalion. Promoted to first lieutenant and captain, Reynolds was cited in division orders for conducting a "courageous reconnaissance of enemy lines along the Selle River, October 16, 1918." *Boston Journal*, January 16, 1907, 9; Frederick S. Mead, *Harvard's Military Record in the World War* (Boston: Harvard Alumni Association, 1921), 797.

353. A graduate of Princeton in 1905, Robert Highet Leake became an investment banker prior to the war and served on the Mexican border with the National Guard. Described as "unassuming" and having a "likeable personality," Leake also became an outstanding combat officer. As a lieutenant in the 105th Machine Gun Battalion, he was cited for the Silver Star: "For courage and qualities of leadership demonstrated while in command of his company at a time when the company had sustained heavy casualties from enemy shell fire at Le Selle River, Oct. 17, 1918." Capt. Robert Leake died in 1941. *Princeton Alumni Weekly*, August 2, 1919, 517; February 10, 1941, 26; *New York Times*, January 19, 1941, 17.

354. Charles I. DeBevoise graduated from Yale in 1894 and became a stockbroker. He joined the New York National Guard in 1895 as a private and served in the New York Volunteer Cavalry in Puerto Rico as a sergeant. DeBevoise rose through the ranks to become colonel of his regiment in 1912 and led it along the Mexican border in 1916–1917. Assigned to other duties at the war's outbreak, the colonel became commander of the 107th Infantry in the summer of 1918. Elevated to general rank in October, he commanded the 53rd Brigade until its demobilization in 1919. DeBevoise returned to his business and the National Guard until his retirement, dying in 1958. Frederick Dwight, ed., *Quarter Century Record Class of 1894 Yale College* (New Haven, CT: Class of 1894, Yale University, 1922), 132–35; Davis, *Generals in Khaki*, 106.

355. Harry T. Blythe's military career began with his enlistment in 1893, and by the Spanish-American War he had achieved the elevated rank of corporal. He was promoted in the National Guard to second lieutenant in 1905, first lieutenant in 1911, and captain in 1916. He served in the latter rank in the 107th Infantry and was wounded in action on August 23, 1918. Blythe worked as an electrician prior to his death in 1928. *History of the 107th Infantry, U.S.A.*, 452; New York Adjutant General's Office, Abstracts of National Guard Service in World War I; *Newburgh Beacon Directory 1929* (New Haven, CT: Price & Lee, 1929), 142.

356. Major (his name, not his rank) A. Hart had enlisted in the army at the age of seventeen and served in the Philippines, on the Mexican border, and in France, the latter tour as orderly to Gen. O'Ryan. In 1923, Hart joined the Prohibition Bureau and quickly became known for his sensational raids on lawbreakers. In one raid near Buffalo he followed a truck for three miles, broke down a barricaded door, and, armed only with a baseball bat, confronted four bootleggers. They submitted and Hart seized 2,500 gallons of alcohol, two stills, and a complete whiskey-manufacturing plant. Major Hart was killed in an auto accident in 1927, ending the career of an agent who had "raided more wildcat breweries and stills than any other man in the service." *Brooklyn Daily Eagle*, June 17, 1927, 2; *Washington Evening Star*, July 17, 1927, 2.

357. Gen. O'Ryan's Belgian police dog was named "Flique." *New York Times*, VI, 1.

358. This truck was the one German war relic in the grand parade for the 27th Division down 5th Avenue in New York. The truck bore a sign painted on its sides that said it had been captured on October 17, 1918, at the battle on Le Selle River. *New York Times*, March 26, 1919, 4.

359. A native of Wyoming, Thomas Harry Shanton was seemingly born in the saddle and quickly won the sobriquet "the Laramie Kid." His excellence as a horseman caught the attention of Buffalo Bill Cody, who hired him to work in his famous Wild West Show. Cody would later remark: "I have seen great horsemen all over the world, but T. Harry Shanton is in a class by himself." After five years with Buffalo Bill, Shanton worked for the New York Street Department before assuming control of the police department's transportation division. Shanton had enlisted in the 69th Regiment as a private in 1907 and came up through the ranks to become a captain. He was a perfect fit to act as major of the 102nd Military Police. Maj. Shanton died in 1942. *Gas Attack of the New York Division* 1, no. 24 (May 4, 1918): 10; *Brooklyn Daily Eagle*, September 27, 1908, 11; *Rochester Democrat and Chronicle*, February 6, 1942, 36.

360. The son of James S. Sherman, long-time congressman and vice president in the Taft administration, Thomas M. Sherman graduated from Clinton College in 1906. An exceptional athlete in tennis, basketball, and golf, Thomas competed in numerous national golf tournaments and nearly won the national amateur championship in that sport in 1909. He went with the National Guard to the Mexican border and became a lieutenant colonel in the world war. Sherman resumed his banking career and served as assistant director of New York Civilian Defense in World War II until his death in 1944. *Washington Evening Star*, March 1, 1944, 8; *Brooklyn Daily Eagle*, March 1, 1944, 15.

361. Jay L. Rogers was an up-and-coming catcher in the Virginia League but was stricken with appendicitis in 1912. The following year he hit .286 and threw out sixty-five runners in sixty-four games. Several major-league baseball clubs sought to sign Rogers, but the newly named Yankees signed him to a $5,000 contract. His hitting was atrocious, exemplified by a game in late June 1914 when he was sent in to pinch-hit in the tenth inning and "he watched Dutch Leonard bend three strikes across the plate and never even took his bat off his shoulder." His big-league dreams having been crushed, Rogers became a lieutenant in the 107th Infantry. He coached semipro

baseball and died in 1964. *New York Times*, June 22, 1913, IV, 2; *New York Evening World*, February 6, 1914, 16; *History of the 107th Infantry, U.S.A.*, 462; *Hornell Evening Tribune*, April 26, 1923, 10; *Carlisle Evening Sentinel*, July 2, 1964, 6.

362. Carroll Judson House, a tenor, was a prominent Brooklyn soloist prior to his enlistment, his last position being at the Montclair Congregational Church in New Jersey. A veteran of the Mexican expedition, House wrote from France: "I wanted excitement, and, believe, me, I am getting it." In the same letter he admitted that "conditions here are rather noisy." After his discharge from the 102nd Military Police, House sang in Chicago and San Francisco opera companies and became widely known as "the Silver Voice of Radio," predating the successful career of singing sensation John Gary. House was a civilian flying instructor for the army at Yale University until his death in 1945. *Brooklyn Daily Eagle*, September 23, 1917, 5; *Spartanburg Herald*, September 26, 1918, 8; *Trenton Evening Times*, January 7, 1945, II, 5.

363. George Anderson was an actor/manager in New York when he saw a performance of *You Know Me, Al*. Impressed, Anderson volunteered the next day. He had previously been a confidential advisor and business manager for Fritzi Scheff, whom he married in 1915. This marriage had brought him wealth and status far above some of his previous employment, such as one job as a "tailor's manikin." Wounded while in France with the 105th Machine Gun Battalion, Anderson summed up his unit's wartime service: "From the satiated lap of ease in beloved Manhattan to the deprivations of the blood-stained, muddy battlefields of Flanders and Central France is a long cry to test one's courage, fortitude, stamina and tenacity of purpose. Yet, without undue praise, it may be said that such was the accomplishment of the 105th Machine Gun Battalion." In 1919, Anderson turned to writing and was credited with *There and Back*, a postwar comedy that was first among the flood of soldier stories brought to the stage. *El Paso Herald*, November 2, 1918, II, 3; *Gas Attack of the New York Division*, March 1919, 48; *Winnipeg Tribune*, January 22, 1921, 30.

364. A native of Vienna, Fritzi Scheff appeared in opera houses throughout Europe, once performing for Queen Victoria, until her arrival in America in 1900. Described as "a saucy, piquant star," Scheff originally starred in New York but toured the country from 1913 to 1918 in vaudeville shows. She made as much as $4,000 a week and had her own private railway car, but her earnings declined with vaudeville. Relegated to nightclubs and cabarets, Fritzi Scheff appeared on the television program *This Is Your Life* just one month before her death in 1954. She had been married three times. *Brooklyn Daily Eagle*, April 9, 1954, 11.

365. "Young Mike" Donovan, actually Arthur B. Donovan, wanted to be like his father and began boxing at the age of eleven. The war interrupted a promising career in the ring, although he did pass on one promoter's scheme while in training camp. Young Mike was offered $10,000 to fight Mike O'Dowd, then the reigning middleweight champ, but responded: "I haven't fought in a year. I could not get into shape to give O'Dowd a fair and square fight. The people paying to see a fight would be bunked. I don't need the money bad enough to be a party to trickery. Anyhow, I'm a soldier. Get someone else." After his service in the 102nd Military Police, Donovan became best known as a boxing referee, the classic "third man in the ring." *Gas Attack of the New York Division* 1, no. 20 (April 6, 1918): 22; New York Adjutant General's Office, Abstracts of World War I Military Service, 1917–1919; *Bluefield Daily Telegraph*, January 18, 1936, 8.

366. A Civil War veteran, Mike Donovan learned to box in the army and eventually became the world's undefeated middleweight boxer. His victims included John L. Sullivan and Jack Dempsey. Donovan served as boxing instructor for the New York Athletic Club in 1884 and remained in that position until his death in 1918. One of his students was President Theodore Roosevelt, whom he would occasionally box in the White House. Although he raised a hospital unit, "Old Mike" was deemed too old to accompany it to France and contented himself with recruiting efforts in his last days. *New York Evening World*, March 25, 1918, 12.

367. Richard Raphael Cotter, a right-handed catcher from Brooklyn, was a minor-league and, briefly, major-league baseball player. He left Brooklyn College to begin his professional career in the Tri-State League in 1911. The next year he played in the National League for the Phillies and Cubs, in 1913 was sent down to the American Association, but came back to catch for the New York Giants in 1914. Cotter's arm "went back on him" and he never appeared in another major-league game, although he knocked around in the minors into the 1920s. Despite Runyon's assertion that Cotter played for the Yankees, there is no indication that Cotter was ever on that team's roster. *Brooklyn Daily Eagle*, February 4, 1915, 2; *Reading Times*, April 11, 1921, 10.

368. John and Charles Arbuckle founded the firm of Arbuckle Brothers in 1871. Up to this time, coffee had been sold only in bean form. The brothers originated the sale of roasted coffee in sealed packages, guaranteeing the quality of the contents. *Brooklyn Daily Eagle*, March 27, 1912, 1.

369. A merchant explained the difference in the three basic types of tea: "There are three kinds of tea—the fermented, the semifermented and the unfermented. Black teas belong to the first class. Oolong teas belong to the second and green teas to the third class." *Houston Post*, March 16, 1916, 10.

370. Nicholas Giannakopolus (one of many spellings of his name) was a native of Greece and served as a cook in the 106th Infantry. A distance runner, "Nick the Greek" was noted "not so much in the matter of speed and records as for his bulldog tenacity and capacity for work." His greatest feat occurred in 1914 in a National Guard competition, where eight-man squads ran nine miles in heavy marching order. Nick finished the race in first place, carrying not only his own rifle and equipment but seven rifles and two packs belonging to his squad. New York State Adjutant General's Office, Abstracts of World War I Military Service, 1917–1919; *Springfield Union*, February 16, 1915, 15; *New York National Guardsman* 8, no. 6 (September 1931): 44.

371. In 1916, Walter L. Glass graduated from Syracuse University, where he starred as a halfback on the football team and captain of the rowing crew. Lt. Glass was wounded in the fighting around LaRoux Farm on October 18, 1918. Unable to walk, Glass "impressed a German prisoner to carry him to the rear where he acted

as guard for 20 prisoners who had been captured by his platoon during the advance until such time as the prisoners could be turned over to the military police." He would receive a Silver Star for his actions. After the war Glass became a manager for B. F. Goodrich. *Duluth News-Tribune*, November 26, 1918, 8; *Boston Herald*, September 5, 1928, 15.

372. Chaplain Francis A. Kelly, 104th Machine Gun Battalion, was a graduate of Niagara University. Nicknamed one of the army's "fighting chaplains," the citation for his Distinguished Service Cross read: "For repeated acts of extraordinary heroism in action near Ronssoy, France, Sept. 26–30, 1918. And east of the Le Selle River, France, Oct. 13–20, 1918. During the operations of his regiment against the Hindenburg line and later east of the Le Selle River, Chaplain Kelly was constantly at the front, caring for the wounded and supervising the burial of the dead, often under heavy shell and machine gun fire. His fearless conduct afforded an inspiring example to the combat troops." Kelly's lungs had been weakened in three gas attacks, and he developed tuberculosis, dying of that disease in 1931. *New York Evening World*, December 20, 1918, 4; *Brooklyn Daily Eagle*, October 16, 1931, 14.

373. A native of Canada, Francis P. Duffy served as a chaplain in the Spanish-American War, in Pershing's Mexican expedition, and with the 42nd (Rainbow) Division in France. A parish priest in the Bronx before the war, Duffy, another one of America's "fighting chaplains," was awarded the Distinguished Service Cross and French Croix de Guerre. At one point, Gen. Douglas MacArthur recommended that Father Duffy be given command of the 165th Infantry, writing later: "This is one of the few occasions in the history of the American army when the suggestion was made that a minister of the gospel be converted into the commander of a fighting unit." Upon his death in 1932, MacArthur added: "His death will be mourned by thousands of his comrades in the Old Rainbow." *Brooklyn Daily Eagle*, June 27, 1932, 15.

374. William S. McLaughlin was New York's most famous deep-sea pilot. When his father would take Bill to Staten Island to watch ships arrive, he remembered, "I thought that if I could ever get on the bridge of one of those ships and steer it, I'd be the happiest person in the world." He eventually became an apprentice and obtained a pilot's license but discovered that repetition dulled his dreams: "Hell, there's nothing interesting about chasing up and down the bay all day." A distinguished member of the Sandy Hook Pilots' Association, McLaughlin specialized in taking the *Leviathan* into and out of her berth at Hoboken. He did this so often that the ship took on its own persona, remarking that the ship "behaves or misbehaves like a stubborn, moody human." After shuttling big liners in and out of port since 1892, McLaughlin retired in 1939 and died twenty years later. *New York Evening World*, October 4, 1919, II, 1; *Yonkers Herald Statesman*, February 11, 1959, 31.

375. The Ambrose Light marked the entrance to the Ambrose Channel, named for John W. Ambrose, who planned to dredge a channel that would allow the largest ocean liners to dock on the Brooklyn waterfront. *New York Tribune*, April 15, 1904, 3.

376. There was a special delegation arranged to welcome back to Brooklyn Sgt. Frank A. Conklin, Machine Gun Company of the 106th Infantry, who was a cousin of County Clerk William E. Kelly. This group included a judge, the chief clerk of the county court, and members of the clerk's office and judicial staff. *Brooklyn Daily Eagle*, March 5, 1919, 1.

377. Lt. Cmdr. Vaughn Veazey Woodward had graduated from the Naval Academy in 1907 and was chief engineer on the SS *Leviathan*. He would recount what the Germans had done when they abandoned the ship: "They did all sorts of tricky things with those engines, and it was necessary to ferret them all out before we threw the steam into her. If we had overlooked anything there might have been an accident that would have done more damage than the Germans did. Maybe that's what they were figuring on. They'd stuff up a pipe somewhere about forty feet below the waterline, and it would take us a week to locate it. Most of the trouble took a week to locate and a few hours to fix." Woodward received a Navy Cross for refurbishing the *Leviathan* and died in 1951. *New York Evening World*, December 19, 1918, 20; *Charleston Gazette*, June 21, 1951, 18.

378. After graduating from the Naval Academy in 1889, William Woodward Phelps served in the Spanish-American War. A captain commanding a battleship when America entered the war, Phelps switched roles to oversee the transports *Great Northern* and *Leviathan*, duties for which he was awarded the Navy Cross. He spent tenures at the Naval War College, the Asiatic Station, and the naval yards at Portsmouth and Brooklyn. RAdm. Phelps retired in 1933 and became a governor of the Army and Navy Club. When he died in 1938, the *Leviathan* was in a Scottish boneyard, her great hulk being cut apart to repurpose steel for Britain's modern military. *Brooklyn Daily Eagle*, January 30, 1938, III, 1; May 12, 1938, 19; *Washington Evening Star*, May 13, 1938, 28.

379. The two casuals were Anderson Kimble, 309th Infantry, of Queen City, Texas, and Allen Stokes, 302nd Infantry, of Wadesboro, North Carolina. *Harrisburg Telegraph*, March 8, 1919, 13.

380. Even though officially a casual, Runyon shared a stateroom with correspondent Martin Green, of the *New York World*, Capt. G. W. Peppard, Quartermaster Corps, from Brooklyn, and Capt. Harry T. Blythe, Adjutant General's Office, from Newburgh, New York. *New York Evening World*, March 6, 1919, 6.

381. Good rumors could always be traced back to what appeared to be a reliable source aboard ship: "People can be found who know the officer who was told by the officer who got it from another officer who saw the wireless message to Gen. O'Ryan." *New York Evening World*, March 6, 1919, 6.

382. "Buster," a dog who had been found in France by the 102nd Engineers, was one dog who wore a wound stripe and an overseas stripe denoting six months with his unit in France. *New York Evening World*, March 25, 1919, 4.

383. Georges Carpentier began boxing in France at the age of fourteen in the flyweight category, but as he grew and added muscle the youngster eventually fought in every classification through heavyweight. His early wins included victories over such notable fighters as "Bombardier" Wells, "Kid" Jackson, and "Gunboat" Wells. Within hours of his last fight in 1914, Carpentier boarded a boat for France and enlisted, serving in his

country's aviation service for five years. His personal investments of half a million dollars evaporated with the Germany invasion. The pinnacle of Carpentier's career came in 1921, when he fought Jack Dempsey for the heavyweight championship of the world, the first to be broadcast on radio. In the second round, Georges hit Dempsey so hard that he broke his hand, which led to his defeat. He eventually retired in 1927 and toured Europe and America in vaudeville shows. He lost a second fortune in the Stock Market Crash of 1929 and relied on his celebrity status for income until his death in 1975. *Washington Post*, December 5, 1919, 10; *Hartford Courant*, October 29, 1975, 60.

384. Maxim's Café was located just around the corner from the Hotel Crillon, which the American peace commissioners used as their headquarters. Always popular with US troops, Maxim's became the first French establishment to introduce American dancing after the armistice. From four o'clock until seven in the evening, a jazz band belted out popular music as patrons guzzled martinis, champagne, and tea "without cream, milk or sugar." The cheapest drink was a glass of beer that cost sixty cents. Affairs got out of hand at Christmas, when the proprietor violated the 9:30 p.m. curfew. One diner noticed that "the revolving doors at Maxim's are always revolving," since the café seemed to be "basking in the same brilliant sunshine of prosperity as a 'Last Chance' bar on the edge of the Sahara desert." *Salt Lake Herald-Republican*, February 16, 1919, 20; *Oregon Daily Journal*, December 27, 1918, 10; December 29, 1918, 14.

385. Twice light-heavyweight champion of England, in 1914 and 1918, Dick Smith became famous for his bouts against soldiers and discharged veterans after the war. Despite being knocked out in a fight three weeks previously, Smith fought Mike O'Dowd of the US Engineers, whom Americans recognized as the world middleweight champion. Obviously outclassed by O'Dowd, Smith, with one eye swollen shut, lost the fight in December 1918 but won enough press coverage to arrange a bout with Georges Carpentier the following July for a purse of $20,000. The Frenchman won by a knockout in the eighth round. His career began to wane, and he fought boxers such as former sergeant Harry Reeve, whose shrapnel wounds broke open during the contest. Dick Smith gradually faded from memory and died in 1950 at Dartford, England. *Brooklyn Daily Eagle*, December 13, 1918, 18; January 29, 1920, 45; *London Times*, December 13, 1918, 12; *New York Herald*, January 1, 1919, 15; *New York Times*, July 20, 1919, 20; *Dundee Courier*, January 9, 1950, 71.

386. As a promoter, Jack Curley made P. T. Barnum look like a novice. Born Jacques Armand Schuel, his curly hair led to the nickname Curley, which he eventually had legalized. Curley would promote anything that could make him a dollar, including such events as "flea circuses, dance marathons, wrestling matches to bull fights." Not all went as planned at one bull fight, when the matador readied himself only to have the bulls sit down and look at the crowd, which responded by trying to tear down the stadium. While promoting the tour of Annette Kellerman, he invented the one-piece bathing suit to highlight her figure. Curley's most successful tour was that of Rudolph Valentino, the Italian heartthrob. As a boxing promoter, his greatest match was the Havana slugfest between Jack Johnson and Jess Willard. On the other side of the coin, Frank James, brother of outlaw Jesse, had to protect Curley from the citizens of Springfield, Illinois, when they suspected a fight had been rigged and came after the man to whom they had given their money. Jack Curley died in 1937 after a lifetime of adventures. *Cincinnati Enquirer*, July 13, 1937, 12.

387. William J. "Billy" Gibson, a prominent boxing manager, spent his money as fast as he made it. Manager for world champion boxers Benny Leonard and Gene Tunney, Gibson admitted he knew nothing about boxing and simply let his fighters take care of themselves in the ring. His biggest payday came in 1927, when he received over $300,000 after Tunney defended his crown against Jack Dempsey in the famous "long count" bout. Gibson was the favorite of New York bookies. Attired in his trademark camel hair polo coat, Gibson belonged to that elite crowd that "even when they did back the right horse it never did them any good for they spent it as fast as they got it." Another member of that exclusive club of losers, "Dumb Dan" Morgan, said, "If Billy had $100,000,000 he'd have died broke." Judged incompetent to manage his personal affairs in the early 1930s, he was declared competent in 1947 but died later that year. *St. Louis Star and Times*, July 22, 1947, 17; *Chicago Tribune*, July 22, 1947, 27; *Cincinnati Enquirer*, July 24, 1947, 17.

388. Willie Lewis burst onto the New York boxing scene in 1900, a handsome sixteen-year-old kid from the Gashouse District. Although he never weighed more than 150 pounds, Lewis fought virtually anyone he could get into a ring—lightweights, welterweights, and middleweights—size or ability made no difference. In a match with Stanley Ketchel, Willie staggered his opponent with a punch on the chin, prompting Tad Dorgan to yell from ringside, "Don't get him mad, Willie." Next round Ketchel knocked Lewis out, but the following day the pair went out on the town and drank together for a solid week. When his manager, Dan McKetrick, took Willie to Paris in 1908, he became the rage of France's sports world, probably because he beat a series of English boxers. While there he introduced the heretofore unknown one-two combination—"a left jab followed by a lightning right hand smash." Lewis remained in Paris until 1914 but returned to New York, where he worked as a bartender in a series of saloons as he battled cancer until his death in 1949. *Ottawa Journal*, May 25, 1949, 23.

389. Daniel "Dapper Dan" McKetrik was described variously as an "energetic bundle of nerves" and "one of the many New York city slickers who manages boxing persons for plenty of cakes." A stockbroker during the war, he was also a partner in the Washington Park Sports and Amusement Club of Brooklyn. After the war he became a charter member of the National Sports Alliance, an organization "composed of managers and promoters of professional boxing and other athletic sports." In 1946, Damon Runyon would describe his friend as one of the old-school managers who were "wine drinkers, first nighters, top-hat-and-tails fellows and that was the life he loved." Always smiling and never without a cane that he didn't need, McKetrick went through money like water, Runyon summing up his turbulent financial life: "Chicken today and feathers tomorrow." From an apartment on Central Park West, dubbed the Salon of Fistiana, "Dapper Dan," at least according to Runyon, could be found

"giving a party every time he got hold of $8 in one bundle." He never changed his lifestyle and died in 1948. *El Paso Herald*, August 17, 1912, 23; *Philadelphia Inquirer*, January 27, 1922, 16; US NARA, Record Group 163, World War I Draft Registration Cards; *Brooklyn Daily Eagle*, April 18, 1916, II, 2; *Buffalo Enquirer*, November 11, 1924, 8; *Detroit Times*, October 8, 1948, 13.

390. Joe Jennette, Jeannette being his professional name, was one of a quartet of famous black boxers in the early twentieth century, the others being Jack Johnson, Sam McVey, and Sam Langford. It was estimated that Jeannette fought as many as 400 bouts in his career, twenty-eight of them against the other three members of the so-called "Ebony Big Four." Perhaps his most memorable fight occurred in Paris against McVey in 1909, a grueling match that lasted forty-nine rounds and 210 minutes. Officials scored thirty-nine knockdowns before McVey gave up, the win being officially a knockout. At six o'clock the next morning, Jeannette, saying he was "a little stiff and sore," restarted his training routine. After retiring in 1918, Joe ran a gym in New Jersey, but during World War II he built up a fleet of limousines that he rented for weddings and funerals, keeping a gym on the second floor to develop young boxers. Jeannette died in 1958. *Trenton Evening Times*, July 3, 1958, 4; *Omaha World Herald*, August 31, 1958, 15.

391. Charles Ladoux.

392. Ercole Balzac.

393. Eugène Criqui.

394. A newsboy in Findlay, Ohio, when he became a boxer, Frank Mackey "was the busiest newsy you ever set your lamps on"; hence his nickname "Biz." He fought hundreds of bouts throughout the Midwest in every sort of venue, one night defeating a black boxer called the "Yellow Kid" in some woods outside Cleveland illuminated by gasoline lamps. On another occasion "Biz" and his opponent fought so dirty that police stopped their fight. After a so-so career, Mackey retired to Cleveland to run "a thirst parlor." Relaunching his career in 1913, "Biz" became a popular athlete in Europe. While fighting in England in 1914, his manager told fans back home: "Biz broke his arm again in the first round of his fight at the National Sporting Club. The referee wanted him to give up the fight, but he refused and went on until he was knocked out in the fourth round." When asked why he refused to quit, Mackey responded, "Because I'm a Yankee." His career effectively over, and rejected by the army because of his accumulated injuries, "Biz" joined the Knights of Columbus in 1918, went to France, and taught boxing to the troops. He would die almost unnoticed in 1962. *Cincinnati Enquirer*, December 18, 1910, III, 4; *Indianapolis News*, April 29, 1907, 13; *Akron Beacon*, March 24, 1910, 10; *Lima News*, July 26, 1915, 6; *Akron Evening Times*, March 16, 1914, 9; *Fort Wayne Sentinel*, October 3, 1918, 4; *Jersey City Journal*, June 23, 1962, 7.

395. A descendant of the famous Fish family of New York, Hamilton Fish III was an All-American tackle on the Harvard football team, generally recognized as the national champions in 1908. He served in the New York legislature from 1913 to 1915. A captain in the New York National Guard, Fish served through the war in the 169th Infantry, known as the Harlem Hellfighters. He won the French Croix de Guerre for returning from a furlough when he heard his regiment had become engaged in battle. He would later claim, "I fought for civil rights before there were any such things." Elected to Congress in 1919, Fish served for twenty-six years and became an outspoken critic of everything that President Franklin Roosevelt stood for. After leaving Congress in 1945, Fish devoted his time to a law practice and writing before dying at the age of 102 in 1991. *Los Angeles Times*, January 20, 1991, I, 42; *Baltimore Sun*, February 1, 1919, 7.

396. Harry W. LeGore had worked in his father's lime-and-stone business prior to attending Yale, where he played fullback on the football team and shortstop on the baseball team. In 1915, he and four teammates admitted to accepting room and board while playing in a summer league, thus disqualifying them from collegiate athletics until their later reinstatement. The well-respected sportswriter Walter Camp said that LeGore was the best college fullback in the country prior to his misstep. At the outbreak of war, Harry was one of ten Yale students recommended by the university president for commissions in the Marine Corps. Rising to captain, LeGore coached the 2nd Division football squad in the AEF championship tournament, losing to the 1st Division 6–0 in a game called "but little better in ferocity" than the battle of Chateau Thierry. After the war, Capt. LeGore was elected to several statewide offices in Maryland before resuming management of the family business until his death in 1956. *Frederick News*, June 9, 1956, 4; *The Outlook*, October 27, 1915, 456–457; *Minneapolis Star Tribune*, October 26, 1919, 32.

397. William F. McKenna had joined the old 69th Regiment of New York's National Guard in 1917, where he served as a lieutenant and battalion adjutant. Lt. McKenna went overseas with the 165th Infantry and served in the same battalion with his older brother James. Writing from France in the spring of 1918, James explained to the family: "Have no fear, dad, for if my turn or Billy's comes to take the trip you need not apologize for the manner of our going. We will give our best, and the count will not be against us. If the Germans get us they must pay the bill in men either to us or our pals." When James was killed at the crossing of the Ourcq River, now Capt. McKenna remarked: "Well, Jim went the way he wished to go. I've lost not only my brother but the best friend I had in the world." Capt. William McKenna received a mention in army orders for his organizational skill prior to returning to America. New York Adjutant General's Office, Abstracts of National Guard Service in World War I, 1917–1919; *Ogden Standard*, September 14, 1918, 5; *Newport News Daily Press*, May 2, 1919, 11; "Letters from the Front to the Folks at Home," *Journal of the American Irish Historical Society* 17 (1918): 233.

398. Born in 1871, George Albert Wingate enlisted in the New York National Guard when he turned eighteen. After serving in every enlisted rank, Wingate joined the officer corps and received successive promotions to colonel, at which rank he retired in 1912. Recalled to duty, he was commissioned brigadier general on May 1, 1918. Gen. Wingate was cited twice, the first time for "great gallantry and determination in riding forward over a shell-swept road under direct enemy observation for the purpose of supervising the forward batteries of his brigade" on October 5, 1918. His second citation acknowledged "exceptional qualities of leadership, great energy

and industry and a thorough knowledge of the field artillery arm." Wingate's brigade was officially commended by commanders of the 33rd and 79th Divisions for its efficiency during the Meuse-Argonne Campaign. New York Adjutant General's Office, Abstracts of National Guard Service in World War I, 1917–1919.

399. Col. Merritt Haviland Smith balanced his National Guard duties with a series of civilian appointments as an engineer to various New York departments. In 1914, he was appointed to oversee the city's water supply. In May 1917, city newspapers announced the death of his son, Merritt Haviland Smith Jr., after he had accidentally stabbed himself at the Plattsburg Training Camp. It soon came out, however, that the young Smith had mental issues. An inquisitive reporter discovered that Smith had stabbed himself with a bayonet "when temporarily deranged by the nervous reaction induced by the realistic bayonet exercises of the day before." Officers "suppressed the news" and "all who knew of the incident were pledged to secrecy," but the military did not understand the zeal of New York newsmen. Col. Smith made arrangements to remove his son to New York City, but he worsened and could not be saved. *New York Evening World*, July 1, 1914, 13; May 28, 1917, 1; *New York Tribune*, May 29, 1917, 14.

400. Col. Dewitt Clinton Weld Jr. began his National Guard service in 1887 as a private and steadily advanced through the ranks. By the time he reached the rank of first lieutenant in 1896, one local newspaper observed: "If every regiment could have six or seven such officers as Lieutenant Weld scattered throughout its ranks, its professional tone would be higher." While in France, Col. Weld depended on his government-issued Dodge sedan, which carried him more than 7,500 miles without breaking down. When the windshield was shattered by shrapnel, Weld admitted, "In keeping with the occasion, I had a wound stripe painted on the right side and a service stripe on the left side." He rejoined the firm of Weld & Suydam but remained in the National Guard, reaching the rank of brigadier general prior to his death in 1937. *Brooklyn Life*, October 4, 1902, 24; *New York Tribune*, March 30, 1919, 21; *Brooklyn Daily Eagle*, September 13, 1937, 13.

401. Emery Taylor Smith enlisted in the Fourteenth Infantry as a private in 1898 and served in the Philippines. Appointed lieutenant in the 9th Infantry, he led troops in Peking during the Boxer Rebellion. After acting as an aide to Gen. J. Franklin Bell and serving on the Mexican border, Smith became an instructor to National Guard units on the Pacific coast prior to the war. After his wartime stint with the 106th Field Artillery, Smith had a series of assignments in New England prior to his appointment to the Command and General Staff School at Fort Leavenworth. While at this post in 1924, then Lt. Col. Smith committed suicide by hanging himself from a pipe in his bathroom. *Boston Herald*, December 5, 1924, 1; *Oakland Tribune*, December 8, 1924, 4.

402. Lansford F. Sherry started his National Guard service as a private in 1883 and served in every rank through captain when he commanded a battery in the Spanish-American War. He retired at his own request in 1912 but accepted a commission as major to command the 102nd Ammunition Train. He died at the age of seventy-two in 1940. New York Adjutant General's Office, Military Service Records, 1816–1979; *New York Sun*, March 22, 1912, 7; *Canton Repository*, January 15, 1940, 6.

403. Charles Pearson Jr. had belonged to the 1st Cavalry in the New York National Guard and served on the Mexican border. He was a partner in a Buffalo company that specialized in manufacturing and sales of firearm attachments. As captain of the 102nd Trench Mortar, he and his unit had little to do in the final push against the Hindenburg Line. Proving to be a resourceful commander, Pearson noted the difficulty of hauling heavy mortars, ammunition, and supplies over rugged terrain in government-issued Nash trucks. He commandeered machine gun carts and mules, thereby proving his ability to keep pace with the advancing infantrymen. Capt. Pearson's unit, at least part of it, was the first of the 27th Division to return home, reaching New York on January 24, 1919. New York Adjutant General's Office, Abstracts of World War I Military Service, 1917–1919; *Iron Age* 91, no. 15 (April 10, 1913): 922; Francis L. Huidekoper, *The History of the 33rd Division AEF* (Springfield: Illinois State Historical Library, 1921), 289–90; *New York Times*, January 25, 1919, 11.

404. Isaac J. Lovell was an acclaimed athlete at Pittston High School in Pennsylvania. He joined the Irish-American Athletic Club after moving to New York and in 1910 broke the world record for running the 75-yard hurdles. A veteran of the National Guard, Maj. Lovell became Gen. Wingate's chief of staff, was eventually promoted to lieutenant colonel, and received the following citation: "For exceptional administrative ability and rare military attainments displayed as chief of staff and operations officer of the 52nd Field Artillery Brigade in performing his tasks with unremitting zeal, rendering services that were a most important factor in the success of the brigade operations in the Meuse-Argonne Offensive, September 9 to November 11, 1918." *Pittston Gazette*, February 8, 1910, 6; New York Adjutant General's Office, Abstracts of World War I Military Service, 1917–1919.

405. Walter Horton Schoellkopf was an experienced National Guard officer when he took command of a company in the 108th Field Artillery. Promoted to major in 1919, this Buffalo native was cited in division orders: "For his energy and zealous efforts as Artillery Information Officer of the 52nd Field Artillery Brigade, which were of conspicuous worth, and were a deciding factor in the effective direction of artillery fire in the Meuse-Argonne offensive, from September 9 to November 11, 1918." New York Adjutant General's Office, Abstracts of World War I Military Service, 1917–1919; O'Ryan, *Story of the 27th Division*, 941.

406. A Stanford graduate, Maximilian Langdon Van Norden was a lieutenant in the 105th Field Artillery. He was cited in division orders twice for gallantry in action, the first occasion for "promptly extending the telephonic communications between supporting artillery stations and advancing positions of infantry commands" on September 26 and 27, 1918. The second citation was for "reconnoitering and establishing forward telephone central stations under fire to connect the artillery not with forward infantry positions" on November 8 and 9, 1918. A third citation mentioned "his energy and zealous efforts" in establishing and maintaining telephone service "when all other communication failed," leading to the 33rd Division's successful operations from September 9 to November 11, 1918. New York Adjutant General's Office, Abstracts of World War I Military Service, 1917–1919.

407. A veteran of the New York National Guard and the Mexican border service, Harold Hill Jones had graduated from Cornell with an engineering degree in 1910 and worked in the Canadian forestry industry prior to the war. Originally a second lieutenant, Jones was promoted to first lieutenant and captain before he came home. His division citation read: "For his rare ability, initiative and untiring energy and great resourcefulness as Brigade Supply Officer and as Munitions Officer of the 52nd Field Artillery from September 9 to November 11, 1918 during the Meuse-Argonne Offensive, in which he rendered services of conspicuous worth during the entire service of the Brigade." *San Rafael Daily Independent Journal*, April 6, 1972, 4; New York Adjutant General's Office, Abstracts of World War I Military Service, 1917–1919.

408. Hector Turnbull, a veteran of the Regular Army and formerly a drama critic with the *New York Tribune*, left for Plattsburg Training Camp in June 1917. His most recent employment had been in the scenario department of the Famous Players–Lasky Corporation, a leader in production and distribution of silent films. Turnbull was engaged to a sister of the producer Jesse Lasky when he left for France and married her five days after his return home. The happy couple set off for California, where Turnbull planned a writing career. He eventually became a director as well, one of his most successful films being the original version of *Gentlemen Prefer Blondes*. *New York Tribune*, June 29, 1917, 4; March 27, 1919, 13; *Brooklyn Daily Eagle*, June 1, 1927, 36.

409. A Cornell graduate in 1910, Thomas H. S. Andrews was a veteran of the New York National Guard when he was assigned to the 105th Field Artillery in 1917. Andrews was assigned to brigade headquarters and received a citation that read: "For his exceptional services in making artillery reconnaissance during advances, as Assistant Artillery Information Officer of the 52nd Field Artillery Brigade, in the Meuse-Argonne Offensive from September 26 to November 11, 1918." New York Adjutant General's Office, Abstracts of World War I Military Service, 1917–1919; O'Ryan, *Story of the 27th Division*, 943.

410. Charles Effingham Burnett attended school in Buffalo before entering Princeton. He joined the New York Telephone Company in 1914 and returned to that company following the war. He became successive a unit manager, a commercial representative, district manager, and commercial supervisor of field operations. *Kingston Daily Freeman*, October 21, 1953, 13.

411. These officers were second lieutenants William C. North and Francis B. Lloyd.

412. A graduate of Yale in 1903, Chauncey Jerome Hamlin was a well-known lawyer, clubman, and National Guard officer prior to receiving his commission in the 106th Field Artillery. Hamlin ran unsuccessfully for the office of lieutenant governor of New York on the Bull Moose ticket in 1914. He was cited in division orders in the following manner: "For his untiring energy and exceptional resourcefulness in the face of great obstacles, as munitions officer of the 52nd Field Artillery Brig. in delivering adequate supplies of ammunition at battery positions to meet all requests for fire, during the Meuse-Argonne offensive, Nov. 8 and 9, 1918." *New York Times*, June 24, 1914, 1; Daniel J. Sweeney, ed., *History of Buffalo and Erie County, 1914–1919* (Buffalo, NY: Committee of One Hundred, 1919), 253; New York Adjutant General's Office, Abstracts of World War I Military Service, 1917–1919.

413. During the 52nd Field Artillery Brigade's service, the individual batteries fired the following number of rounds: 104th Field Artillery, 66,782; 105th Field Artillery, 81,096; and 106th Field Artillery, 33,036. The combined weight of these shells was 5,290,518 pounds. *New York Evening World*, March 12, 1919, 3.

414. This horse, Red Check, had been newly purchased and was esteemed for its beauty and breeding, but the throngs of people bewildered the animal. Just as Gen. O'Ryan reached 8th Street, the horse either threw or almost threw its rider (witness accounts varied). The general remounted or regained control of his horse (again depending upon varying witness testimony), but Red Check refused to budge. Rather than hold up the entire parade and prolong the wait of several million New Yorkers, O'Ryan swapped animals with a private in the Headquarters Detachment and continued on. *Brooklyn Daily Eagle*, March 25, 1919, 1; *New York Evening World*, March 25, 1919, 4.

415. Field Marshal Douglas Haig, senior officer in the British Army.

416. This massive flag held 1,980 stars, one for every member of the division who had died in service overseas. *New York Times*, March 25, 1919, 4.

417. Eager spectators were determined to have an unobstructed view of the parade. Women came with soap boxes and stepladders, while boys showed up with stilts, figuring they could lean against poles or the sides of businesses. One of the youngsters said, "If we are not allowed to do that, we'll just let the crowd hold us up." *New York Evening World*, March 25, 1919, 4.

418. The insignia of the 27th Division was a black circle with a red circle around the perimeter. In the center was a stylized "NYD," also in red, which stood for the New York Division. Scattered around the black field were red stars that formed the constellation Orion, a pun on the surname of John F. O'Ryan, the division commander.

419. Wounded soldiers pinned these flowers to their tunics, bringing back "memories of a few months ago when the men marched into action with poppies in the straps of their steel helmets." *New York Evening World*, March 25, 1919, 2.

420. The "Hall Room Boys" was the name of a comic strip created by Harold A MacGill that poked fun at ordinary people who pretended to be more than they were. MacGill would explain his inspiration for his comics: "One evening on the gay white way of the Broadway theatrical district, I saw an elegantly dressed man, in a top hat and all the accessories, with a young lady whom I knew. I was curious as to who he was, and found out that he lived in a boarding house, kept his shiny hat under the bed, timed his rising in the morning by an alarm clock, punched the time clock at a department store, and there juggled rugs in the rug department for the balance of the day." *Rockford Republic*, April 22, 1922, 5.

421. A native of Scotland, Andrew Carnegie resided in a palatial residence at the corner of 5th Avenue and 91st Street. From his first job as a bobbin boy in a mill that paid $1.20 a week, Carnegie had amassed a fortune

estimated to be $500,000,000 prior to his death in 1919. Although he was the acknowledged captain of the iron-and-steel industry, perhaps his greatest contribution lay elsewhere. He remembered: "When I began getting ahead in the world, I was always able to trace back each advance to the reading that I did in those mill days. That's why I have always wanted to make it easy for young people to read good books." He did so by donating millions of dollars to build public library buildings across the country, in addition to financing numerous charitable, literary, and scientific foundations. *New York Evening World*, August 11, 1919, 3.

422. Jacob Ruppert's home was located at 1120 5th Avenue. A lifelong bachelor, he served in Congress from 1899 to 1907 and amassed real-estate holdings in New York second only to the Astor family. Owner of the world's largest brewery, Ruppert and his partner, Thomas L. Huston, bought the New York Yankees in 1915. Never a fan of baseball, he gloried in owning the team more than he enjoyed watching them play. His personal tastes ran more to yachts and thoroughbred horses, although his last visitor before he died in 1939 was Babe Ruth. *Brooklyn Daily Eagle*, January 13, 1939, 1, 18.

423. Among the many recorded incidents was one involving a kind-hearted New York police officer:

> "A little woman with tear-stained face and a black band on her arm with two gold stars tried to get a better view of her son's company as it filed by.
>
> 'Room there!' shouted Patrolman Kelly as he swept the crowd apart. 'This woman's got more right than any to see these men.'
>
> He made way for her and she gratefully accepted his escort to the front line.
>
> 'Anything else I can do for you?' he asked. 'I lost a brother myself, over there.'
>
> 'No,' said she gently, 'I just want to see the men who were with my two sons when they fell. Later they'll tell me all about it.' She smiled bravely and waved her regimental flag." *Brooklyn Daily Eagle*, March 25, 1919, II, 1.

424. Martin Green described the scene for the *Evening World*: "Together, in perfect symmetry, came the crash of heavy Army boots as they struck the pavements together—one, two, three, four—like the rumble and grumble and the thunder of the guns, as the troops, never losing step, went forward—always forward—while New York went mad." *New York Evening World*, March 25, 1919, 1.

Poetry

1. Thomas L. Huston, a co-owner of the New York Yankees, had been a captain of engineers in the Spanish-American War. He gathered together a group of engineers who had been with him in Cuba, and took them to France, where he served as a lieutenant colonel in the 16th Engineers. A few years after the war, Huston sold his interest in the Yankees to Col. Jacob Ruppert and retired to a plantation in Georgia. Col. Huston devoted his time to raising purebred livestock until his death in 1938. He was buried in the same cemetery as William O. McGeehan, a close friend who had worked as sports editor for the *New York Herald*. *Brooklyn Daily Eagle*, March 30, 1938, 18; *Macon Telegraph*, March 31 1938, 14.

2. A graduate of West Point in 1883, Omar Bundy fought in the Cuba campaign of 1898 and in the Philippine Insurrection. After graduating from the Army War College in 1913, he led an infantry regiment on the Mexican border. Bundy went to France as a brigade commander in the 1st Division in 1917 but was later promoted to command the 2nd Division. After assisting in the defeat of the German offensive at Chateau Thierry in 1918, Gen. Bundy was briefly elevated to corps command but was soon sent back to America to oversee training of new troops. He retired from the army in 1925 and died in 1940 at the age of seventy-eight. *Washington Evening Star*, January 22, 1940, 13.

Bibliography

Government Documents

Minnesota Death Index, 1908–2002. Minneapolis: Minnesota Department of Health.

New York, Adjutant General's Office. Abstracts of National Guard Service in World War I, 1917–1919. Albany: New York State Archives.

New York, Adjutant General's Office. Abstracts of World War I Military Service, 1917–1919. Albany: New York State Archives.

New York, Adjutant General's Office. Military Service Records, 1816–1979. Albany: New York State Archives.

Oregon Death Index, 1903–1998. Salem: Oregon State Archives and Record Center.

Pennsylvania Veteran Burial Cards, 1777–2012. Harrisburg: Pennsylvania Historical and Museum Commission, Bureau of Archives and History.

US National Archives and Records Administration (NARA), Record Group 21. Petitions and Records of Naturalizations of the US District and Circuit Courts of the District of Massachusetts, 1906–1929.

US NARA, Record Group 29. Records of the Bureau of the Census, 1790–1996.

US NARA, Record Group 59. US Passport Applications, 1795–1925.

US NARA, Record Group 92. Records of the Office of the Quartermaster General, Applications for Headstones, 1925–1970.

US NARA, Record Group 92. Records of the Office of the Quartermaster General, 1774–1985, Interment Control Forms, 1928–1962.

US NARA, Record Group 94. Records of the Adjutant General's Office, Registers of Enlistments in the United States Army, 1798–1914.

US NARA, Record Group 163. World War I Draft Registrations Cards.

Books and Articles

Appleton, Francis R. *War Records of the Knickerbocker Club, 1914–1918*. New York: Knickerbocker Club, 1922.

Bacon, William J., ed. *History of the Fifty-Fifth Field Artillery Brigade*. Nashville: Benson, 1920.

Benwell, Harry A. *History of the Yankee Division*. Boston: Cornhill, 1919.

Breslin, Jimmy. *Damon Runyon*. New York: Ticknor & Fields, 1991.

Bulletin of Yale University, Obituary Record of Graduates Deceased during the Year Ending July 1, 1930. New Haven, CT: Yale University, 1930.

Catalogue of Yale University, 1920–1921. New Haven, CT: Yale University, 1921.

Chapin, Charles E. *Charles Chapin's Story*. New York: G. P. Putnam's Sons, 1920.

Chase, Joseph C. *Soldiers All*. New York: George H. Doran, 1920.

Clark, Tom. *The World of Damon Runyon*. New York: Harper & Row, 1978.

Coates, William R. *History of Cuyahoga County and the City of Cleveland*. 3 vols. Chicago: American Historical Society, 1924.

Cole, Robert B., and Barnard Eberlin. *History of the 39th US Infantry in the World War*. New York: Press of J. D. McGuire, 1919.

Cullum, George W. *Biographical Register of the Officers and Graduates of the US Military Academy at West Point, New York*. 6 vols. Saginaw, MI: Seemann & Peters, 1920.

Dictionary of American Biography. 20 vols. New York: Charles Scribner's Sons, 1928–1936.

D'Itri, Patricia W. *Damon Runyon*. Boston: Twayne, 1982.

Dwight, Frederick, ed. *Quarter Century Record Class of 1894 Yale College*. New Haven, CT: Class of 1894, Yale University, 1922.

Ebmeyer, G. E., comp. *School of Mines and Metallurgy, War Records*. Rolla, MO: Missouri School of Mines, 1920.

Edmonds, John B., ed. *St. Paul's School in the Second World War*. Concord, NH: Alumni Association, St. Paul's School, 1950.

English, George H. *History of the Eighty-Ninth Division, USA*. Kansas City, MO: War Society of the 89th Division, 1920.

Evans, James W., and Gardner L. Harding. *Entertaining the American Army: The American Stage and Lyceum in the World War*. New York: Association Press, 1921.

Fiftieth Annual Report of the Association of Graduates of the United States Military Academy. Saginaw, MI: Seemann & Peters, 1919.

Foote, Lisle. *Buster Keaton's Crew: The Team behind His Silent Films*. Jefferson, NC: McFarland, 2014.

Ford, Bert. *The Fighting Yankees Overseas*. Boston: Norman E. McPhail, 1919.

Franks, Norman L. R. *Albatros Aces of World War I*. Oxford: Osprey, 2000.

Gaff, Alan D. *Blood in the Argonne: The "Lost Battalion" of World War I*. Norman: University of Oklahoma Press, 2005.

The Handbook of Private Schools. Boston: Porter Sargent, 1958.

Hartzell, Arthur E. *Meuse-Argonne Battle (Sept. 26–Nov. 11, 1918)*. Chaumont, France: American Headquarters, American Expeditionary Forces, 1919.

Heitman, Francis B. *Historical Register and Dictionary of the United States Army*. 2 vols. Washington, DC: Government Printing Office, 1903.

History of the 107th Infantry, U.S.A. New York: Seventh Regiment Armory, 1920.

History of the USS Leviathan. Brooklyn, NY: *Brooklyn Eagle* Job Department, 1919.

Hoyt, Edwin P. *A Gentleman of Broadway*. Boston: Little, Brown, 1964.

Huidekoper, Francis L. *The History of the 33rd Division AEF*. Springfield: Illinois State Historical Library, 1921.

Johnson, Thomas M. *Without Censor*. Indianapolis, IN: Bobbs-Merrill, 1928.

Kinnaird, Clark. *A Treasury of Damon Runyon*. New York: Modern Library, 1958.

Knightley, Phillip. *The First Casualty: The War Correspondent as Hero and Myth-Maker from Crimea to Iraq*. Baltimore: Johns Hopkins University Press, 2004.

McNeil, W. K. *Encyclopedia of American Gospel Music*. New York: Routledge, 2005.

Mead, Frederick S. *Harvard's Military Record in the World War*. Boston: Harvard Alumni Association, 1921.

Mencken, H. L. *A Mencken Chrestomathy*. New York: Vintage Books, 1982.

Mencken, H. L. *Newspaper Days, 1899–1906*. New York: A. A. Knopf, 1941.

Miles, L. Wardlaw. *History of the 308th Infantry, 1917–1919*. New York: G. P. Putnam's Sons, 1927.

Miller, Webb. *I Found No Peace*. New York: Simon & Schuster, 1936.

Neal, Harry E. *The Hallelujah Army*. Philadelphia: Chilton, 1961.

Newburgh Beacon Directory 1929. New Haven, CT: Price & Lee, 1929.

The Official Roster of Ohio Soldiers, Sailors and Marines in the World War, 1917–1918. 23 vols. Columbus, OH: F. J. Heer, 1926–1929.

O'Ryan, John F. *The Story of the 27th Division*. New York: Wynkoop Hallenbeck Crawford, 1921.

Perkins, George W. *Report on Activities of the YMCA with the AEF*. New York: War Work Council of the YMCA, 1919.

Pope, Stephen, and Elizabeth-Anne Wheal. *Dictionary of the First World War*. Barnsley, UK: Pen & Sword Books, 2003.

The Record of the [University of Pennsylvania] *Class of 1918*. Philadelphia: University of Pennsylvania, 1918.

Reppy, Alison. *Rainbow Memories*. New York: Carey, 1919.

Richardson, Antona H., ed. *Minnesotans in the Spanish-American War and the Philippine Insurrection, April 21, 1898–July 4, 1902*. St. Paul, MN: Paduan, 1998.

Rickenbacker, Edward V. *Fighting the Flying Circus*. New York: Frederick A. Stokes, 1919.

Schwarz, Daniel R. *Broadway Boogie Woogie: Damon Runyon and the Making of New York City Culture*. New York: Palgrave Macmillan, 2003.

Skillman, Willis R. *The AEF: Who They Were, What They Did, How They Did It*. Philadelphia: G. W. Jacobs, 1920.

Sweeney, Daniel J., ed. *History of Buffalo and Erie County, 1914–1919*. Buffalo, NY: Committee of One Hundred, 1919.

Sweeney, Michael S. *The Military and the Press: An Uneasy Truce*. Evanston, IL: Northwestern University Press, 2006.

US Army Register, 1 January 1964. 2 vols. Washington, DC: Government Printing Office, 1964.

Venzon, Anne C., ed. *The United States in the First World War*. New York: Garland, 1995.

Wagner, Jean. *Runyonese: The Mind and Craft of Damon Runyon*. Paris: Stechert Hafner, 1965.

Walker, Stanley. *City Editor*. Baltimore: Johns Hopkins University Press, 1934.
Ward, Kyle R. *In the Shadow of Glory: The Thirteenth Minnesota in the Spanish-American and Philippine-American Wars, 1898 to 1899*. St. Cloud, MN: North Star, 2000.
Warren, Maude R. "Living the Life of Reilly." *Saturday Evening Post*, June 21, 1919: 32, 34, 36, 149–50.
Woollcott, Alexander. *The Command Is Forward: Tales of the AEF Battlefields as They Appeared in the* Stars and Stripes. New York: Century, 1919.
Zabecki, David T. *Germany at War: 400 Years of Military History*. 4 vols. Santa Barbara, CA: ABC-CLIO, 2014.

Periodicals

Abilene Reporter-News
Akron Beacon
Akron Evening Times
Albuquerque Journal
Amarillo Globe-Times
Arkansas City [Kansas] *Daily Traveler*
Atlanta Constitution
Augusta Chronicle
Bakersfield Californian
Baltimore American
Baltimore Sun
Baton Rouge Advocate
Berkshire Eagle [Pittsfield, Massachusetts]
Bluefield [West Virginia] *Daily Telegraph*
Boston Herald
Boston Herald American
Boston Record American
Boston Traveler
Bridgeport [Connecticut] *Post*
Bridgeport [Connecticut] *Telegram*
Brooklyn Daily Eagle
Brooklyn Daily Life
Brownsville [Texas] *Herald*
Canton Repository
Charleston [West Virginia] *Daily Mail*
Charleston [South Carolina] *Evening Post*
Charleston [West Virginia] *Gazette*
Charlotte News
Chicago Tribune
Cleveland Plain Dealer
Colorado Springs Gazette
Columbus [Georgia] *Ledger*
Corsicana [Texas] *Daily Sun*
Coshocton [Ohio] *Tribune*
Dallas Morning News
Decatur [Illinois] *Herald*
Delaware County [Pennsylvania] *Daily Times*
Denver Post
Denver Rocky Mountain News
Detroit Times
Duluth News-Tribune
Dundee [Scotland] *Courier*
East Liverpool [Ohio] *Evening Review*
Eau Claire Leader
El Paso Herald
European Stars and Stripes
Fayetteville [New York] *Bulletin*
Fayetteville [North Carolina] *Weekly Observer*
Fitchburg [Massachusetts] *Sentinel*
Fort Wayne Sentinel
Fort Worth Star-Telegram
The Fourth Estate
Franklin [Pennsylvania] *News-Herald*
Frederick [Maryland] *News*
Gas Attack of the New York Division, 27th Div. U.S.A.
Gastonia [North Carolina] *Gazette*
Greensboro [North Carolina] *Daily News*
Harrisburg Evening News
Harrisburg Patriot
Harrisburg Telegraph
Hornell [New York] *Evening Tribune*
Houston Post
Idaho State Journal
Idaho Statesman
Illinois State Journal
Indiana [Pennsylvania] *Gazette*
Indianapolis News
Iron Age
Jersey City Journal
Jewish Daily News
Journal of the American Irish Historical Society
Journal of Electricity
Kansas City Star
Kansas City Times
Kingsport [Tennessee] *Times*
Kingston [New York] *Daily Freeman*
Lexington Herald
Lima News
Lincoln Evening Mail
Logansport [Indiana] *Pharos-Tribune*

London Times
Long Beach Independent
Lubbock Evening Journal
Macon Telegraph
Manitowoc Herald-Times
Michigan Alumnus
Minneapolis Star Tribune
Monongahela [Pennsylvania] *Daily Republican*
Nassau Daily Review [Freeport, New York]
New Orleans States-Item
New Orleans Times-Picayune
New Philadelphia [Ohio] *Daily Times*
New York Evening World
New York National Guardsman
New York Sun
New York Times
New York Times Book Review
New York Tribune
Newark Star-Ledger
Oakland Tribune
Ogden [Utah] *Standard*
Olean [New York] *Times Herald*
Oregon Daily Journal
Oshkosh Daily Northwestern
Ottawa [Canada] *Journal*
The Outlook
Panama City [Florida] *News-Herald*
Parsons [Kansas] *Daily Sun*
Pawtucket Times
Peekskill Highland Democrat
Philadelphia Inquirer
Pittsburgh Daily Post
Pittsburgh Post
Pittsburgh Post-Gazette
Pittston [Pennsylvania] *Gazette*
Portland Oregonian
Portsmouth [Ohio] *Daily Times*
Pottstown [Pennsylvania] *Mercury*
Princeton Alumni Weekly
Railroad Telegrapher
Reading [Pennsylvania] *Times*
Reidsville [North Carolina] *Review*
Richmond Times-Dispatch
Riverside [California] *Daily Press*
Rockford [Illinois] *Register-Republic*
Rockford [Illinois] *Republic*
Salt Lake City Telegram
Salt Lake Herald-Republican
Salt Lake Tribune
San Antonio Evening News
San Bernardino County Sun
San Diego Evening Tribune
San Diego Union
San Francisco Chronicle
San Jose Evening News
San Luis Obispo Telegram-Tribune
San Rafael Daily Independent Journal
Sandusky Register
Santa Ana Register
Santa Cruz Sentinel
Seattle Daily Times
The Seventh Regiment Gazette
Shamokin [Pennsylvania] *News-Dispatch*
Shippensburg Chronicle
Spartanburg Herald
Springfield [Massachusetts] *Daily News*
Springfield [Massachusetts] *Republican*
Springfield [Massachusetts] *Union*
St. Johnsbury Caledonian
St. Louis Star and Times
Stars and Stripes
The State [Columbia, South Carolina]
Stevens Point [Wisconsin] *Gazette*
Syracuse Post-Standard
Tacoma Times
Topeka Daily Capital
Trenton Evening Times
Tulsa World
Variety
Vermont Alumni Weekly
Warren [Pennsylvania] *Times Mirror*
Washington Evening Star
Washington Herald
Washington Post
Washington Times
Wichita Beacon
Wilkes-Barre Record
Wilkes-Barre Times
Wilkes-Barre Times Leader
Winnipeg Tribune
Winston-Salem Journal
Yonkers Herald Statesman

Index